THE
THIRTY-SIXTH YEARBOOK

OF THE

NATIONAL SOCIETY FOR THE STUDY OF EDUCATION

$2.50

PART I
THE TEACHING OF READING: A SECOND REPORT

Prepared by the Society's Committee on Reading
WILLIAM S. GRAY (Chairman), JEAN BETZNER, DONALD DURRELL, ARTHUR I. GATES,
BESS GOODYKOONTZ, ERNEST HORN, B. LAMAR JOHNSON, ROLLO L. LYMAN,
PAUL McKEE, VERA A. PAUL, MABEL SNEDAKER, WILLIS L. UHL,
and GERALD A. YOAKAM
Assisted by Members of the Society and Others

Edited by
GUY MONTROSE WHIPPLE

THIS PART OF THE YEARBOOK WILL BE DISCUSSED AT THE NEW ORLEANS MEETING
OF THE NATIONAL SOCIETY, SATURDAY, FEBRUARY 20, 1937, 2:00 P.M.

PUBLIC SCHOOL PUBLISHING COMPANY
BLOOMINGTON, ILLINOIS
1937

OFFICERS OF THE SOCIETY

FOR 1936–1937

Board of Directors
(Term of office expires March 1 of the year indicated)

GEORGE S. COUNTS (1938)
Teachers College, Columbia University, New York City

FRANK N. FREEMAN (1939)
University of Chicago, Chicago, Illinois

M. E. HAGGERTY, *Chairman* (1937)
University of Minnesota, Minneapolis, Minnesota

ERNEST HORN (1940) *
State University of Iowa, Iowa City, Iowa

M. R. TRABUE (1939)
University of North Carolina, Chapel Hill, North Carolina

RALPH W. TYLER (1940) †
Ohio State University, Columbus, Ohio

WILLIS L. UHL (1938)
University of Washington, Seattle, Washington

GUY MONTROSE WHIPPLE (*Ex-officio*)
Clifton, Massachusetts

Secretary-Treasurer
GUY MONTROSE WHIPPLE (1938)
Clifton, Massachusetts

* Reëlected for three years beginning March, 1937.
† Elected for three years beginning March, 1937.

iii

THE SOCIETY'S COMMITTEE ON READING

WILLIAM S. GRAY (*Chairman*), Professor of Education, University of Chicago, Chicago, Illinois

JEAN BETZNER, Assistant Professor of Education, Teachers College, Columbia University, New York City

DONALD DURRELL, Professor of Education, Boston University, Boston, Massachusetts

ARTHUR I. GATES, Professor of Education, Teachers College, Columbia University, New York City

BESS GOODYKOONTZ, Assistant Commissioner of Education, Office of Education, Washington, D. C.

ERNEST HORN, Professor of Education and Director of University Elementary School, State University of Iowa, Iowa City, Iowa

B. LAMAR JOHNSON, Librarian and Dean of Instruction, Stephens College, Columbia, Missouri

ROLLO L. LYMAN, Professor in the Teaching of English, University of Chicago, Chicago, Illinois

PAUL MCKEE, Professor of Education and Director, College Elementary School, State College of Education, Greeley, Colorado

VERA A. PAUL, Associate Professor of Speech, Whitworth College, Spokane, Washington

MABEL SNEDAKER, Supervisor of Social Studies, University Elementary School, University of Iowa, Iowa City, Iowa

WILLIS L. UHL, Dean, College of Education, University of Washington, Seattle, Washington

GERALD A. YOAKAM, Professor of Education and Director of Courses in Elementary Education, University of Pittsburgh, Pittsburgh, Pennsylvania

Lot No: CRM

Write or type title, volume, months, page nos., year, call nos, imprint in the exact order to be stamped on the spine.

Name of Library: W. R. Banks

☐ Repeat   Color No.   Number of Bindings of Same Title
☑ New   240   1

Stamping   ☑ Standard   ☐ Custom

Lettering
☐ Gold   ☑ Black   ☐ White

Library Imprint   Yes ☑   No ☐

Decorative Lines   Yes☐   No ☑

Call Numbers
☐ No   ☑ Block Form
☑ Yes   ☐ Centered

Covers
☐ Bind In Place   ☑ Remove All Covers
☐ Bind All Front Covers In Place
☐ Bind In First Cover Only For Title Page

Table of Contents
☑ Bind In Place
☐ Bind In Front
☐ Gather Individual T. of C. & Bind In Front

Ads
☐ Bind In Place
☐ Remove Full Page Ad Only When NOT Texted In
☐ Remove Full Page Ads Even When Texted In ★

Index
☑ Bind In Place   ☐ Not Published
☐ Bind In Back

Special Instructions
☐ Do Not Trim Outside Margin
   Bind Regardless of Missing Issues:
☐ Yes   ☐ No

Other Instructions:

The Teaching of Reading: A Second Report

Ref
LB
5
N25
361ᵗ
Pt. 1

2¹

Bindery Use Only

Trim	Pica	Cover	No.
6½	3		

TABLE OF CONTENTS

For Constitution of the Society, Minutes of the St. Louis Meeting,
Synopsis of the Proceedings of the Board of Directors, Report of
the Treasurer, and List of Members, see Part II of this Yearbook.

EDITOR'S PREFACE

About three years ago, in the course of some correspondence with Dr. Gray, I inquired whether he thought that any significant facts had been unearthed or new trends established that would appreciably change the principles and recommendations set forth in the *Report of the National Committee on Reading* comprising Part I of the Twenty-Fourth Yearbook. Dr. Gray replied unhesitatingly in the affirmative and enumerated offhand a half-dozen or more changes that he would recommend if the 1925 Yearbook on reading were to be revised.

This correspondence was one of several reasons that led to the suggestion made to the Board of Directors at their Chicago meeting in December, 1935, that it would be worth while in the near future to arrange for a new yearbook on reading. The " near future " turned out, after brief discussion, to be " right away." The subsequent rapid formulation and development of plans is described by Dr. Gray, himself, in his " Introduction " immediately following.

It ought to be clear to members of the Society that a remarkably fine piece of work has been done for their benefit by dint of conscientious industry, well-planned distribution of responsibility, and painstaking provision for coöperation. The Board of Directors, at least, is satisfied that the sum appropriated for the use of the Committee on Reading ($1800) has been a very wise investment.

The critical reader may detect some overlapping of treatment, some inconsistencies of statement, and some unevenness of presentation. When many hands combine to push through at high speed a comprehensive exposition of so complex a topic as the teaching of reading, these minor inadequacies become excusable, if they are not, indeed, inevitable.

It will interest members of the Society to learn that the earlier *Report on Reading* is far and away the Society's ' best seller '; more than 30,000 copies had been distributed when it celebrated its tenth birthday. It must have been a most potent influence in American educational thinking. The Directors of the Society firmly believe that this *Second Report* will become equally influential and will reflect equal credit upon both the Society and its Committee on Reading.

G. M. W.

INTRODUCTION: THE ORGANIZATION AND PURPOSES
OF THE YEARBOOK COMMITTEE

In its report in 1925, the National Committee on Reading recommended that subsequent yearbooks on reading should be published at more or less frequent intervals. This suggestion was based on the conviction that problems relating to instruction in any subject should be reviewed deliberately from time to time and recommendations prepared in harmony with changing needs and the results of experimentation.

For several years following the 1925 report many notable changes in teaching occurred that were based directly upon the Committee's recommendations. In the course of time, however, an increasing number of other reforms in the teaching of reading were introduced that were based upon new social demands, upon important changes in educational theory and practice, and upon the findings of hundreds of scientific studies. As a result of such developments the recommendations of a decade ago no longer provide adequately for current educational and social needs.

Accordingly, the Board of Directors of the National Society appointed an advisory committee in December, 1935, to consider the need for a new yearbook on reading and to make recommendations concerning its purpose and scope. This committee, which included Prudence Cutright, Arthur I. Gates, Bess Goodykoontz, William S. Gray, and Ernest Horn, met in St. Louis in December, 1935. As a result of this conference tentative recommendations were submitted to the Board of Directors, which authorized a second meeting of the advisory committee. This meeting was held on February 21 and 22, 1936, to which three additional persons were invited; namely, Emmett A. Betts, Paul McKee, and Willis L. Uhl. As a result of the second conference, which was attended by seven persons, recommendations concerning the purpose, scope, and organization of the *Yearbook* were prepared. These were approved by the Directors who shortly after appointed members of the Yearbook Committee.

As defined by the Advisory Committee, the purpose of the new *Yearbook* was threefold: (a) to trace briefly the developments in the field of reading during the last decade and to identify the major problems that schools face today; (b) to provide in specific and non-technical terms the information needed by teachers and school officers in

1

reorganizing and improving instruction, especially by making specific constructive recommendations that are supported both by experience and by the results of experiments reported during the last decade; and (c) to provide, as a guide in the case of debatable issues, tentative suggestions to be formulated after careful and deliberate study by a group of qualified experts.

As an aid in achieving the foregoing purposes groups of specialists were associated with members of the Yearbook Committee in the preparation of the several chapters. The function of each such group was to advise its chairman concerning the scope and organization of the chapter for which he was responsible, to offer vigorous but constructive criticisms of the content of the chapter at various stages in its development, and to aid in formulating valid recommendations in the case of debatable issues. In view of the fact that the judgments of the members of a group often differed widely, the chairman was authorized to formulate final recommendations after considering carefully all the arguments and evidence presented. Consequently, the reader will understand, some pronouncements are made in the *Yearbook* that do not represent the specific views of all who coöperated in the preparation of the chapters in which the pronouncements appear. The general plan followed, however, has had the unique advantage of providing the writers of the respective chapters with critical judgments and constructive suggestions on which recommendations could be based.

The schedule followed by the Yearbook Committee in preparing its report may be summarized briefly. During the Spring of 1936 each member of the Committee and his associates prepared a preliminary outline of the chapter assigned to him. Copies of these outlines were exchanged in mimeographed form and made the basis of a three-day conference during the latter part of June. The chief purposes of the conference were to review critically the aims and scope of the *Yearbook*, to study intensively the outline of each chapter, and to offer constructive suggestions for improving the organization, validity, and practical value of the various sections of the report. Copies of most of the chapters were prepared during the two months that followed and were submitted to an editorial committee of three, which met for two days during the latter part of August. Final revisions were made during September and October.

As the work of the Committee progressed, the need for limiting the scope of the *Yearbook* as originally planned became obvious. For example, the Committee found it impossible within the space allotted to include detailed suggestions concerning many phases of reading on which teachers need help today. As a result the Committee was forced to adopt the policy of dealing primarily with basic facts and principles and with general policies underlying a comprehensive reading program. However, generous reference has been made in many sections to specific methods of teaching; furthermore, frequent reference has been made to sources where helpful suggestions may be secured. It was necessary also to omit certain problems that are in urgent need of careful consideration — a striking example relates to the training of teachers of reading. If the program recommended in this *Yearbook* is to be adopted widely in the near future, the types of preservice and inservice training provided for teachers must be radically modified. This problem is of such large significance that it should be made the basis of intensive study by some qualified agency in the near future.

A review of the conditions under which the 1925 report and the present *Yearbook* were prepared reveals two significant differences. In the first place much more time was allowed for the preparation of the former report, thus permitting many more joint conferences and far more deliberate consideration of recommendations. As a result, the present *Yearbook* does not represent so finished a product as the 1925 report and is open to criticism with respect to various features that could have been improved or corrected had time permitted. In the second place, several members of the earlier committee were released for a period of time from their regular duties in order to devote themselves fully to the report. No such provision was made in the case of the present report. The various chapters had to be prepared as spare time could be found in the already overcrowded programs of most members of the Committee.

Although this 1937 report on reading is thus subject to many limitations, the Committee believes that it represents a significant step forward. We say " a step," because we understand clearly that many of the recommendations we have made cannot be carried out effectively without additional study and experiment. It is hoped, therefore, that the present report will be as successful as the *Twenty-Fourth Yearbook* in stimulating productive research as well as constructive effort in classrooms to improve the teaching of reading. As a result of vigorous effort in both directions, instruction in reading should increase steadily during the next decade in both scope and quality.

WILLIAM S. GRAY, *Chairman.*

SUB–COMMITTEE ON CHAPTER I

Chairman

WILLIAM S. GRAY, Professor of Education, University of Chicago, Chicago, Illinois

Associates

WILLARD V. BEATTY, Director of Education, Office of Indian Affairs, Department of the Interior, Washington, D. C.

C. L. CUSHMAN, Director, Department of Research and Curriculum, Denver Public Schools, Denver, Colorado

ROBERT S. LANE, Assistant Superintendent of Schools, Los Angeles, California

LOIS HAYDEN MEEK, Teachers College, Columbia University, New York City

NILA B. SMITH, School of Education, Indiana University, Bloomington, Indiana

LOUIS R. WILSON, Dean, Graduate Library School, University of Chicago, Chicago, Illinois

CHAPTER I

A DECADE OF PROGRESS

WILLIAM S. GRAY
FOR
THE YEARBOOK COMMITTEE

The last ten years form a notable period in the history of reading. As a result of the stimulus provided by such publications as the *Report of the National Committee on Reading*,[1] the place of reading in the curriculum has greatly expanded and the content and methods of teaching pupils to read have improved rapidly. Of even greater importance is the fact that reading has acquired broader relationships than formerly in both child and adult life. With increasing frequency the fact has been emphasized that reading must provide more largely in the future than in the past for promoting clear understanding, developing habits of good thinking, stimulating broad interests, cultivating appreciations, and establishing stable personalities. Furthermore, the results of scientific studies have given us a clearer understanding of the nature of reading and of the basic processes involved.

With each step forward have come new problems and challenging issues. For example, newer types of teaching units make much more varied demands on the reader than was true formerly; furthermore, a large percentage of the slow pupils who dropped out of school in the past now remain throughout the secondary-school period. As a result, the reading program of a decade ago no longer provides adequately for current educational and social needs. We face the responsibilities, therefore, of a deliberate review of recent developments, of a rigorous appraisal of current reading programs, and of making necessary changes to meet contemporary needs. If these ends can be achieved, instruction should continue to improve during the next decade even more rapidly than during the last ten years.

[1] *Report of the National Committee on Reading.* The Twenty-Fourth Yearbook of this Society, Part I. (Public School Publishing Company: Bloomington, Illinois, 1925)

I. DESIRABLE TRENDS

Various sources of information were used in determining the nature of the progress made and in identifying trends. The literature relating to reading, such as professional books, bulletins, courses of study, and magazine articles, was examined for evidence of significant developments. The recent survey of " best classroom practices "[1] and of " research problems in reading "[2] were especially illuminating and suggestive. In addition, the judgments of specialists in the field were solicited widely. The statements that follow provide a reasonable picture of desirable developments and trends during the past decade.

1. Interest in reading problems has increased with gratifying rapidity among both educators and laymen, as shown by numerous local, state, regional, and national conferences devoted to the subject, frequent revisions of courses of study, the publication of a large number of professional books on reading, and more than a thousand scientific studies relating to reading.

2. The fact has gained wide recognition that every teacher should be, to a significant extent, a teacher of reading. This implies that why, when, and how children read, the interest and tastes they develop, and the sources of reading material available to them are concerns of all teachers at every level. Although the view that reading is a universal subject has been accepted in theory, much remains to be achieved in actual practice.

3. The relative importance attached to the reading period and to reading in other curriculum fields in developing desirable attitudes and habits has been greatly modified. The fact is now clearly recognized that guidance provided in the reading period promotes growth primarily in basic reading attitudes, habits, and skills, and that training in the various uses of reading in study situations can be provided best in the different curriculum fields. The acceptance of this view has resulted in a reduction in many schools of the time allotted to the reading period and an increase in the amount of guidance in reading

---

[1] *Better Reading Instruction: A Survey of Research and Successful Practice.* Research Bulletin of the National Education Association, Vol. XIII, No. 5. (National Education Association: Washington, D. C., November, 1935)

[2] D. D. Durrell. *Research Problems in Reading in the Elementary School.* Fourth Annual Research Bulletin of the National Conference on Research in Elementary-School English. (C. C. Certain: Box 67, North End Station; Detroit, 1936)

provided elsewhere. However, much remains to be done in the development of appropriate reading habits and study techniques in the various curricular fields.

4. Distinct progress has been made in both the theory and practice of ' reading readiness.' Many studies have considered the relation of physical, mental, social, and emotional characteristics of children to progress in learning to read. As a result, the attainments and needs of children who enter many school systems are examined far more carefully than formerly and the instruction provided is better adapted to their needs. Unfortunately, not all of the conditions that make for reading readiness and the methods that promote desirable types of growth have been recognized in the past.

5. The various activities of the reading period have been notably enriched. This enrichment includes provision of reading materials that relate to the interests of pupils, that stimulate inquiring attitudes, that have real worth in terms of the values contributed, and that are closely related to their experiences. The statement should be added that uninteresting and purposeless types of teaching still prevail all too widely in many sections of the country.

6. Increased provision has been made, in practically all curricular fields, of reading material that is more interesting and challenging, that can be read with greater ease and understanding, and that is far better graded and organized than formerly. School books reveal the progress that has been made during the last decade in the art of bookmaking, including a clearer knowledge of what makes books both attractive and readable. The need is urgent, however, for additional improvement in reading materials for use in the content fields with special reference to the interests and needs of poor readers.

7. The amount of reading material provided has increased during recent years wherever the necessary funds could be secured. As a result, classroom procedures have been modified in many schools to promote library methods as contrasted with textbook methods of study. Unfortunately, this trend has found expression in far too few centers, either because of failure to recognize its value or because of desire for economy.

8. The materials read have been organized increasingly in terms of thought-provoking units, problems, or areas of interests, as contrasted with a series of unrelated passages or selections. This plan insures challenging trains of thought that promote good interpretation and more thorough organization and use of the ideas gained through

reading. It also aids in providing the variety of activities and the wide range of content and levels of difficulty essential in adapting instruction to individual differences.

9. Great improvement has been made in methods of teaching reading, resulting in increased emphasis upon the meaning or content of what is read and in the elimination of much of the formal drill required in the past. Particularly noteworthy is the fact that teachers in the upper grades and the high school have become increasingly conscious of the need of pupils for frequent guidance in reading activities and are seeking for effective methods of promoting satisfactory growth.

10. Effort has been made to stimulate motives for reading on the part of an increasing percentage of pupils and to provide an adequate number of attractive books for use in satisfying the reading interests of children. Unfortunately, the quality of much that is selected and read by children is disappointing and the quantity is often far below the minimum necessary for promoting efficient reading habits.

11. The importance of adequate library facilities has been widely recognized. As a result of studies of book selection, experiments in integrating library and classroom activities, and instruction in the use of books, the service rendered by libraries has increased rapidly. But the number of schools that provide satisfactory library facilities is as yet far too limited.

12. Commendable progress has been made in the description and interpretation of individual differences and in the development of forms of class organization that aid in adapting instruction to group and individual needs. Of special importance are the results of studies that show the relation of reading difficulties to emotional adjustment and personality development. The non-reading child, for example, makes certain adjustments when assigned to a group of young children who can read that usually are expressed in undesirable changes in personal and social behavior. Likewise the older child who is retarded in reading adopts defenses that affect his personality and keep him from making normal social contacts and from benefiting largely from school experiences.

13. The number of reading tests has increased rapidly during recent years; furthermore, significant progress has been made in improving their validity, reliability, and usefulness. Unfortunately, few of the tests developed thus far measure progress in certain highly important phases of reading, such as interpretation, appreciation, and ability to apply what is read in the solution of challenging problems.

14. Distinctive progress has been made in the development of diagnostic and of corrective and remedial procedures as aids in identifying and eliminating deficiencies. The amount of attention given to diagnosis and remedial instruction at the secondary school and college levels has increased with great rapidity.

II. UNDESIRABLE TRENDS

Paralleling the commendable elements of progress just named, a number of questionable trends and practices have developed, of which the following are examples.

1. Extreme positions have been assumed in many schools concerning the value of reading as an aid to learning. On the one hand, many schools have attached so much importance to reading that other forms of experience have often been neglected. This trend is associated with a narrow view of the educational value of some types of experiences. On the other hand, vigorous opposition to reading as an aid in learning has developed in certain centers, with the result that oral and visual instruction are used almost exclusively, particularly in the lower and middle grades. Advocates of this view apparently fail to recognize clearly both the advantages and limitations of reading as a form of experience and as an aid to learning.

2. The large importance attached to silent reading has resulted unfortunately in several related practices and trends that cannot be defended. Among them are the almost exclusive emphasis on silent reading in many schools and a corresponding neglect of oral reading, the adoption of methods of teaching beginning reading that result in memorizing the statements presented rather than in developing independence in recognizing words and meanings, the preparation of elaborate and detailed comprehension exercises that have little or no relation to vital situations or needs, and the production of a large amount of poorly prepared and often inaccurate informational reading material. The criticism has rightly been made that methods of teaching silent reading have become as formal and limited in value in some schools as was true in the case of oral reading in the past. Furthermore, the routine level at which reading has been taught in many schools has resulted in failure to stir the interest and promote the maximal development of bright pupils.

3. Closely associated with the foregoing criticisms is the fact that current reading programs often give unwarranted emphasis to particular types of training, such as those relating to recreational reading,

to work-type reading, or to remedial treatment. This error frequently occurs during a period of transition in the teaching of any subject and is due in part to poor judgment or inaccurate information concerning the relative importance of different types of training. For example, the recognition of the value of recreational reading has often resulted in almost complete reliance on related types of guidance in promoting efficient reading habits in study situations; on the other hand, the emphasis given to work-type reading in some schools has sometimes resulted in the neglect of reading for recreation and appreciation. Furthermore, legitimate enthusiasm for corrective and remedial training has frequently resulted in undue reduction in the amount of time devoted to instruction of a developmental type. One of the urgent needs today is a well-balanced reading program that gives adequate emphasis to the various types of reading in which children should engage.

In planning for the future, clear recognition should be given to current trends of established worth and an effort made to eliminate undesirable practices. A reading program that is both adequate and valid should take account also of recent social changes, significant developments in educational theory and practice, and the results of scientific studies relating to reading. In the sections of the chapter that follow, an effort will be made to point out important implications of developments in these three fields.

III. READING IN CONTEMPORARY LIFE

During the decade since 1925, social changes have occurred with unusual rapidity. New issues and problems have presented themselves on every hand. The need for clear understanding and discriminating insight has never been greater. Young people and adults have drawn heavily upon every available source of information — the forum, the press, the radio — in facing emergencies as well as in meeting the normal demands made upon them. Furthermore, individuals, agencies, and ' pressure groups ' have used these means in developing attitudes and sentiments. As a result, the social significance of reading, as well as that of other means of informing or influencing the public, has greatly increased during recent years. A few striking examples of developments follow:

1. The amount of reading has increased very rapidly among the great mass of our adult population. This is due in part to the publication of relatively simple tabloid newspapers, the expanded programs of adult elementary education since 1926, the successive drives

to eliminate illiteracy, and numerous efforts to discover and prepare simple readable books relating to adult interests.

2. A new vigor in systematic reading has developed among those who read well. This is due in part to the desire for economic security, cultural advancement, better social adjustment, and clear understanding of local, state, national, and international problems. Evidence of increased interest in reading is found in the increasing demand made upon librarians [1] for guides to purposeful and sequential reading and upon adult education leaders for materials to accompany forum discussions and radio programs.

Two views prevail concerning the value of the reading in which the great mass of our population engages. A national committee [2] affirms that " it is reasonable to suppose that a community or social group benefits in proportion to the amount it reads of literature adapted to its social, intellectual, emotional, esthetic, and other needs." This assumption is based on the fact that " the amount and quality of reading by population groups in society at large has been found an excellent index of social competence." Other educational leaders recognize that, although reading may serve as an aid to social progress, the results achieved to date are far from satisfactory. They believe that if reading is to serve as an effective aid in the lives of children and adults in their search for truth and beauty, and if their minds are to be increasingly free rather than more enslaved, radical improvements must be made in the development of reading attitudes and habits in the near future. While this Yearbook Committee is in hearty agreement with the general point of view expressed, it believes that many of the problems involved have wide implications and cannot be solved merely by the adoption of improved techniques in reading.

3. The need for information concerning the sources of material relating to specific interests and needs, and for greater ability to understand and interpret printed materials has been emphasized vigorously of late, as adults have faced perplexing personal and social problems. For example, numerous requests have been made recently for guidance that will enable the reader to make needed vocational and professional adjustments, to determine the validity of statements by

---

[1] Jennie M. Flexner and Sigrid A. Edge. *A Readers' Advisory Service.* (American Association for Adult Education: New York, 1934. 60 pp.)

[2] *Evaluation of Reading.* Progressive Education Association, Evaluation in the Eight-Year Study; Bulletin No. 4, January, 1936. (Ohio State University: Columbus, Ohio)

commercial agencies and pressure groups, and to evaluate critically
the various proposals appearing in print for changing and redirecting
social life.

4. Reading for recreation and enlightenment has also assumed
added significance as a result of increased leisure and the large emphasis attached to the values inherent in it by specialists in this field.
And what an array of possibilities they present: ' information,' ' enjoyment,' ' understanding,' ' stimulation,' ' inspiration,' [1] a necessary
' outlook,' a ' vision of the ideal,' ' a better knowledge of human nature,' ' the glory of the commonplace,' [2] and catholicity of mind with its
time, space, and thought dimensions! [3] These are resources on which
we may draw heavily during leisure hours. Of special significance are
those that contribute to social understanding,[4] that stimulate and inspire the reader to creative effort, that provide a common culture so
much needed in American life, and that promote the development of enriched and stable personalities.

5. Striking evidence of the increasing importance of reading in
social life is also found in numerous recent studies of the nature of the
reading interests and habits of young people and adults,[5] the characteristics of material that can be read with ease and understanding by
adults of limited education,[6] and the place of books in a democracy.[7]

The evidence that has been presented leads to the conclusion that
reading must contribute in the future, more largely than in the past,
to the understandings and appreciations on which personal welfare and
social progress depend. In making this statement, the Yearbook Com-

[1] Leal A. Headley. *Making the Most of Books.* Pp. 3–10. (American Library Association: Chicago, 1932)

[2] C. Alphonso Smith. *What Can Literature Do for Me?* (Doubleday, Page,
and Company: New York, 1925)

[3] Frank Luther Mott. *Rewards of Reading.* P. 7. (Henry Holt and Company: New York, 1926)

[4] George B. Zehmer. " What ought we to do when at leisure? " *The University of Virginia News Letter,* 9: April 1, 1934.

[5] William S. Gray and Ruth Munroe. *The Reading Interests and Habits of
Adults.* (The Macmillan Company: New York, 1929. 305 pp.)

Douglas Waples and Ralph W. Tyler. *What People Want to Read About.*
(The American Library Association and the University of Chicago Press: Chicago,
1931. 312 pp.)

[6] William S. Gray and Bernice E. Leary. *What Makes a Book Readable.*
(University of Chicago Press: Chicago, 1935. 358 pp.)

[7] R. L. Duffus. *Books: Their Place in a Democracy.* (Houghton Mifflin
Company: Boston, 1930. 225 pp.)

mittee recognizes clearly that many other agencies share this responsibility, such as the radio, the public forum, and the motion picture. As the demand for social enlightenment increases, every means of providing individuals with needed information and stimulation should be used.

If reading is to serve its largest function in social life, teachers face real problems and responsibilities: they must promote clear understanding and discriminating insight in each of the broader phases of contemporary life; familiarize young people with persistent social issues and current problems; introduce themes and issues at appropriate levels of school progress; develop habits of accurate, precise comprehension and interpretation, including critical evaluation; promote greater power in applying the content of what is read, thus contributing to intelligent self-direction and social reconstruction; stimulate interests that will contribute both to the wholesome use of leisure time and to the solution of personal and social problems; and provide a broad common culture to insure an appreciation of the finer elements in contemporary life. As indicated in the next section, all these results must be secured in harmony with the normal development of children, their ability to understand, and their ability to make the necessary intellectual and emotional adjustments.

IV. Developments in Educational Theory and Practice

Paralleling recent social changes, notable developments have occurred in educational theory and practice. These developments have already affected the content and methods of reading in various ways and should exert even greater influence during the next decade. Some are the results of efforts to meet effectively the various needs that the New Age imposes. Others are concerned specifically with the place and function of education in child life and represent the result of constructive thinking and effort during several decades. The general nature and direction of these developments may be reviewed briefly:

1. Education is conceived primarily as a process of growth toward desirable goals, rather than as a series of lessons that aim merely to promote the memorization of facts. This view implies a clear understanding of the processes of child development (mental, social, physical, and emotional), including growth toward understanding, independence, and maturity, and an appreciation of the effect of growth on child interests, abilities, responses, and needs.

2. The process and direction of growth are determined by all the

experiences that children encounter, both in school and out of school. Accordingly, good teaching utilizes, and in no small measure directs, the latter as well as the former and helps the child to associate them appropriately and to see their significance.

3. In organizing school activities persistent attention is given to the interests, needs, and capacities of the learners, with the view to promoting types of growth that harmonize with the learner's level of development and that are most helpful in meeting vital situations.

4. Many of the problems studied are organized around basic functions and major interests of society. Of special significance are the experiences that promote social understanding, develop power to solve personal and social problems intelligently, and build up appreciations that are directly valuable in promoting the best in contemporary civilization. A danger obviously inherent in this trend is that pupils may be asked too early to study problems that have little significance to them or that are too difficult for them to consider effectively.

5. Improved plans of classifying and promoting pupils are being developed in order to adapt instruction more effectively to varying capacities and needs of children and to provide longer periods of successful progress.

6. The fact that education is a continuous process that extends throughout life is now widely recognized. Accordingly, schools are attempting to equip individuals with the understandings, interests, and controls essential for continuous growth and efficient living in a changing civilization.

In keeping with the trends described above, instruction in reading should be based on a clear recognition of the needs of child life. Desirable type of growth should be achieved through activities that are purposeful, challenging, and enriching. This implies less formal practice in establishing desirable reading habits and greater reliance on activities in which reading serves other valuable purposes. The materials provided should be highly charged with interest and adapted to the level of reading achievement of the learners. The basic instruction given should be organized so as to provide more widely than in the past for continuous successful progress from one stage of development to another.

V. Results of Scientific Studies

The progress during the last decade in the scientific study of reading problems is in keeping with the social changes and educational developments to which reference has been made. The number of studies published since 1925 exceeds twelve hundred, which is more than twice the number reported during the preceding century. This increase is due primarily to a clear recognition of the need for objective evidence in solving the numerous problems that reading presents. The questions studied have by no means been restricted to the elementary-school level. With increasing frequency, significant problems have been attacked also at the secondary-school and college levels.

Furthermore, the studies reported relate to practically all phases of reading — its general nature, the fundamental processes involved, the factors that influence progress in learning to read, the relative merits of different methods of promoting growth, the characteristics of readable material, and the nature and causes of reading disabilities. As a result, a body of evidence has developed that will be invaluable in efforts to improve teaching in the future. It is impossible to detail the results of the reported studies. Fortunately, reviews of significant findings and conclusions are available elsewhere.[1] It will suffice at this time to present a few pertinent examples.

1. One of the significant facts emphasized by the results of recent investigations is that a surprisingly large percentage of pupils encounter serious difficulty in reading or are unable to engage successfully in required reading activities. The situation is particularly acute in the upper grades and in high-schools.[2] Experiments show, however, that most reading difficulties can be corrected or eliminated and the general level of achievement greatly increased through the use of instruction adapted to the interests, needs, and capacity of the pupils.

2. The advantage of carefully planned procedures in attaining specific types of progress in reading has been demonstrated. For example, investigators [3] have found that a systematic method of teaching beginning reading is more effective in promoting the development of basic reading habits than incidental or opportunistic methods. Carefully

---

[1] See, for example, reports and summaries by William S. Gray in *Review of Educational Research,* 1: 1931, 247–260, 328–336; 2: 1932, 29–34; 4: 1934, 135–138; 4: 1935, 54–69; also J. Paul Leonard, *ibid.,* 4: 1935, 453–457.

[2] James M. McCallister. *Remedial and Corrective Instruction in Reading.* (D. Appleton-Century Company: New York, 1936. 300 pp.)

[3] Arthur I. Gates, assisted by Mildred I. Batchelder and Jean Betzner. "A modern, systematic versus an opportunistic method of teaching: An experimental study." *Teachers College Record,* 27: 1926, 679–700.

planned guidance[1] relating to other phases of reading has proved equally valuable in promoting rapid progress. Such findings have wide implications in efforts to improve instruction in the future.

3. Extended studies [2] made at the adult level show that from one-third to two-fifths of the adult population of the United States are unable to read, with ease and understanding, material of sixth-grade difficulty. They also show that the great bulk of the literature for adults is above that grade level in difficulty. These facts emphasize the urgent need of simple reading material for adults of limited reading ability and the importance of increasing the achievement of pupils well above the sixth-grade level.

4. Encouraging progress has been made during the last decade in identifying the factors that influence the difficulty of reading material for both children [3] and adults.[4] Thus far attention has been directed largely to structural elements such as length of sentences, the percentage of easy or hard words, and the number of prepositional phrases or pronouns per unit of material. Very little study has been made as yet concerning the nature of the concepts involved. The available findings should not only aid in the development of more readable materials in various fields and for different types of readers, but should also stimulate further research.

5. Various experiments [5] show that wisely planned efforts to reorganize and improve the teaching of reading are usually accompanied

---

[1] George H. Hilliard. "Extensive library reading versus special drill as an aid in improving certain reading abilities." *Educational News Bulletin,* 2: 1932, 6–12. (Western State Teachers College, Kalamazoo, Michigan)

[2] William S. Gray and Bernice E. Leary. *What Makes a Book Readable.* (University of Chicago Press: Chicago, 1935. 358 pp.)

[3] Mabel Vogel and Carleton Washburne. "An objective method of determining grade placement of children's reading material." *Elementary School Journal,* 28: 1928, 373–381.

Alfred S. Lewerenz. "Measurement of the difficulty of reading materials." *Educational Research Bulletin,* 8: 1929, 11–16.

Edward L. Thorndike. "Improving the ability to read." *Teachers College Record,* 36: October, November, and December, 1934, 1–19, 123–144, 229–241.

[4] Edgar Dale and Ralph W. Tyler. "A study of the factors influencing the difficulty of reading materials for adults of limited reading ability." *Library Quarterly,* 4: 1934, 384–412.

[5] William S. Gray, with the assistance of Gertrude Whipple. *Improving Instruction in Reading: An Experimental Study.* (Supplementary Educational Monographs, No. 40. Department of Education, University of Chicago: Chicago, 1933. 226 pp.)

by evidence of distinct progress in the interests and habits of pupils and in their achievement in content fields. Such findings justify vigorous effort during the next decade to increase the breadth and excellence of instruction in reading.

The examples that have been given illustrate the nature of the findings of recent scientific studies of reading. The larger body of evidence available provides a background on which many recommendations for the future can be based with reasonable confidence.

VI. BASIC PRINCIPLES AND ASSUMPTIONS UNDERLYING THE COMMITTEE'S RECOMMENDATIONS

When the significant trends are considered critically, some of them, as we have said, appear to be valid and highly desirable, others to be questionable and in need of modification. Furthermore, the analysis we have presented of the place of reading in contemporary life and of recent developments in educational practice suggests needed expansions in current reading programs and new emphases in its teaching. The Yearbook Committee recognized in this situation the opportunity and the obligation to recommend an improved reading program that retains valid procedures in current practice and also provides for such changes as will insure more efficient instruction during the coming decade.

As an essential step in developing such a program, the Committee has attempted to identify significant facts, basic principles, and assumptions that underlie an adequate program of instruction in reading and that give due recognition to the needs of child life, to current social demands, and to valid trends in educational theory and practice. At the risk of repetition, they are summarized briefly in this section, and are discussed in detail in subsequent chapters. As presented here, they serve as a platform, on which the specific recommendations of the Committee are based.

1. As a result of recent social changes and the expansion of the curriculum, the actual and potential value of reading, both in and out of school, is far greater today than formerly. Together with the radio, motion pictures, and other aids to learning, reading serves as an indispensable means of stimulating and directing child and adult life and likewise of increasing social understanding. It follows that instruction in reading should increase in breadth and efficiency in the immediate future if reading is to serve its broadest function as an instrument of intellectual and social life.

2. The broad objectives of reading; namely, to enrich experience, to broaden interests, to develop appreciations, and to cultivate ideal and appropriate attitudes have changed but little during recent years. However, many of the specific aims of reading assume a new significance in the light of contemporary social and educational developments. Examples of such aims are to broaden the vision of readers, to make their lives richer and more meaningful, and to enable them to meet the practical needs of life more effectively; to develop social understanding and the ability to use reading in the intelligent search for truth; to promote a broad common culture and a growing appreciation of the finer elements in contemporary life; and to stimulate wholesome interests in reading.

3. If schooling is to contribute more largely in the future than in the past to intelligent self-direction and social progress, it is imperative that children and young people acquire greater independence and efficiency in reading. This implies greater accuracy in recognition and comprehension than prevails today, greater clarity of interpretation, increased efficiency in the use of the content of what is read, wider familiarity with the sources and values of reading material, and more critical attitudes and greater discrimination and skill in reading activities. The need for carefully planned guidance in attaining desired levels of efficiency is especially urgent in the middle grades and in secondary schools. In this connection, every effort should be made to eliminate formal procedures and activities that serve no vital purpose; but numerous opportunities should be provided for learners to work intelligently with books in achieving worthwhile and varied purposes.

4. Paralleling the need for greater independence and efficiency in reading is the imperative need of abundant materials that can be read with ease and understanding by those at different levels of advancement from the primary grades to adulthood. This implies noteworthy improvement in the quality and readability of materials in various curricular fields for pupils of various levels of ability; it implies also the development of much simple material that will intrigue or enlighten young people and adults of limited reading ability. The progress made in these directions during the last decade should be greatly accelerated in the immediate future. Such developments should keep pace with improvements in other aids to learning, reinforcing rather than competing with them.

5. Experience and the results of experiments show that rapid progress in learning to read and in making intelligent use of reading in study

activities presupposes careful planning and guidance on the part of teachers. In this connection reading is conceived as a component part of a unified program rather than an isolated activity; it is also recognized as a phase of child development rather than an end in itself. Accordingly, the types of growth stimulated at each level should be selected in keeping with the learner's interests, needs, and stage of development. This principle is admirably illustrated in the concept of 'reading readiness.' Instead, however, of indicating merely that a child is ready for initial guidance in learning to read, the term ' readiness ' is applied in this report to the successive stages of development through which the individual passes in acquiring mature reading habits. It implies also the need for continuous study of the learner's progress and of steps to promote readiness for greater achievement in reading at successive levels of development from the kindergarten to the university.

6. Until further evidence develops, the Yearbook Committee recommends the use of specific periods for carefully planned guidance in reading throughout the elementary-school, secondary-school, and college periods. This recommendation is based on a clear recognition of the fact that pupils encounter many difficulties in learning to read and in making efficient use of reading both in and out of school. As here conceived, the major purposes of guidance are to insure initial right learnings, to promote the sequential development of basic reading habits, to increase efficiency in applying reading to study situations that are common to various curricular fields, to prepare pupils for higher attainments at successive levels of progress, to prevent the development of wrong attitudes and inefficient habits, and to provide needed corrective and remedial training. The time allotment for such activities should vary with the needs of the learners and their general level of advancement. In making the foregoing recommendations, the Committee recognizes that satisfactory results have often been achieved under highly favorable conditions, such as small classes, unusually competent teachers, and appropriate materials, without special periods reserved for teaching pupils to read. The fact should be pointed out, however, that even in such cases specific guidance in learning to read is provided at times and in very effective ways.

7. The teacher of every curriculum field is recognized as a teacher of reading in the sense that he stimulates and directs the experiences of pupils and promotes increased efficiency in the various activities required. In the judgment of the Committee, the greatest opportunity for progress in teaching reading during the next decade lies in an

intelligent attack on reading problems that arise in the content fields. Satisfactory results can be attained only as improved reading materials are prepared for use in each curricular field and as teachers from the kindergarten to the university recognize clearly their responsibility for promoting the development of desirable reading attitudes and habits in the reading activities that they direct and greater intelligence and discrimination in the use of printed instructional materials. The statement should be added that the contribution of effective reading habits to achievement in all school subjects is no more significant than is that of enriched curriculums in the various fields to the development of proficiency in reading.

8. In planning special guidance in reading, teachers should recognize that a requisite of first importance is a stimulating purpose, a motivating drive, on the part of the learner that leads to vigorous application, along with such guidance as will insure rapid progress and optimal achievement. The materials used should be intriguing to those taught. Furthermore, they should be truthful, wholesome, and enlightening; the content should be worth while in itself in terms of the pleasure or information contributed; and the materials used should be so selected and prepared that they promote continuous growth in specific phases of reading.

9. The development of sound reading interests and the elevation of standards and tastes in reading present problems of major importance. During the last two decades, notable progress was made in increasing the percentage of pupils who engage in independent reading. An urgent need during the next decade is to elevate standards and tastes for reading. This responsibility should be shared, not only by teachers of reading and literature and by librarians, but also by teachers of the various curricular fields and by parents.

10. School and classroom libraries are of primary importance in initiating and establishing satisfactory reading attitudes and habits. A generous supply of attractive and suitable books enriches instruction, satisfies the reading interests of pupils, and modifies to a large extent the procedures adopted in teaching and study. The need for an adequate supply of available reading material cannot be over-emphasized in view of the broader purposes that the curriculum must now serve.

11. The results of studies of individual differences emphasize the importance of adapting instruction effectively to the capacities, interests, and needs of pupils. This implies improved techniques for study-

ing their needs and progress, reading materials that are adapted to a wide range of interest and reading ability, flexible plans of class organization, and standards of promotion that provide longer periods of successful application and growth. Non-promotions merely because of difficulty in reading can no longer be defended. Qualitative standards of promotion that consider the total progress of the child should be developed and applied widely.

12. The need for permanent records of attainments for continuous diagnosis and for corrective and remedial instruction is imperative at all levels. The Committee recommends that appropriate provision be made for poor readers, with but few exceptions, as a part of the regular program of reading instruction rather than in so-called ' corrective ' or ' remedial ' classes. The evidence available justifies the conclusion that the need for remedial teaching at the higher levels can be greatly reduced in the future through carefully-planned programs of developmental training in reading in which there is made adequate provision for individual needs at the elementary-school level.

The foregoing statements present major facts, principles, and assumptions on which the program outlined in the Yearbook is based. They will be supplemented in the chapters that follow by reference to other basic facts and principles that support the recommendations presented. As experimentation continues, additions and modifications will undoubtedly be necessary. They provide, however, direction and stimulus to the constructive effort necessary in developing for the future a reading program of desirable breadth and excellence.

SUB–COMMITTEE ON CHAPTER II

Chairman

WILLIAM S. GRAY, Professor of Education, University of Chicago, Chicago, Illinois

Associates

FOWLER D. BROOKS, Head, Departments of Education and Psychology, De-Pauw University, Greencastle, Indiana

EDWARD W. DOLCH, Assistant Professor of Education, University of Illinois, Urbana, Illinois

FRANK N. FREEMAN, Professor of Educational Psychology, University of Chicago, Chicago, Illinois

EDWARD L. THORNDIKE, Professor of Education, Teachers College, Columbia University, New York City

CHAPTER II

THE NATURE AND TYPES OF READING

WILLIAM S. GRAY
Professor of Education, The University of Chicago
Chicago, Illinois

The facts presented in Chapter I showed the need of improved programs of reading that will serve adequately the needs of contemporary life. The development of such programs presupposes a clear understanding of the nature of reading and of the fundamental processes involved. The latter are determined in large measure by the types and purposes of reading in which children and adults engage. It is obvious, for example, that reading to find the answer to a question of fact differs in many respects from reading that involves a critical evaluation of the views of an author. In the discussion that follows, an effort will be made to define reading in sufficiently broad terms to embrace its essential uses in contemporary life, to describe significant purposes of readers, and to suggest important problems involved in improving achievement in reading. Preliminary to these discussions, the relation of reading to learning will be considered briefly.

I. RELATION OF READING TO LEARNING

Children learn specific facts and extend their experiences in many ways. They observe what goes on about them; they listen to the conversation or reports of others; they engage in constructive activities that stimulate thinking and provide motives for learning; they listen to the radio and follow the presentation of sound-motion pictures; they experiment, explore, and investigate with or without guidance; they go to museums and art galleries, or wherever their interests direct; they read widely in school, at home, or in the library. In these and other ways they continuously gain new insights, broader understandings, and deeper interests.

As an aid to learning, reading possesses unique characteristics. Of special significance is the fact that it utilizes printed or written words as symbols of meaning. For this reason it is often called an indirect form of learning. Through the associations aroused when symbols are

23

recognized, experience is extended, new concepts developed, and thinking clarified. Thus it is possible for one to learn about or gain understanding of persons, places, or events that he has never seen or witnessed. The extent, however, to which meaningful associations are
aroused depends in large measure on the background of related experiences that the reader possesses. In this respect, the interpretation
of printed and of oral symbols is quite similar. Furthermore, the mental processes involved in interpretation are identical. In fact, the fundamental difference between reading and listening lies in the sense
avenue through which the stimuli are received.

Various advantages attach to reading as an aid to learning. Its
most obvious value arises from the fact that many of the experiences
that children should acquire cannot be gained directly. The vast majority must be learned indirectly, as children look at pictures, listen to
oral presentations, or read well-written accounts prepared by others.
In the case of those who have acquired reasonable fluency, reading is
a more rapid method of learning than is listening to an oral report of
the same content. Furthermore, reading is admirably adapted to differences in rates of learning, since each child may proceed at a rate
most suitable to himself. It also stimulates the development of habits
essential in independent learning; if the materials read are properly
prepared, they may greatly facilitate self-learning.

Reading is also subject to serious limitations as an aid to learning.
The fact is well known that both the printed and the spoken word fail
at times to convey to the learner as clear and vivid concepts as does
direct contact with reality. Far too much of the material placed in
children's hands today presupposes a broader background of related
experiences than they possess; consequently readers are often unable
to comprehend or interpret the author's meaning. Furthermore, the
printed page is often ill-adapted to the varying individual experiences
and reading abilities of the pupils and, therefore, contributes less to
some than to others. Not infrequently, the ideas that the page is intended to convey are inadequately expressed and, as a result, cannot
be readily understood. Teachers should be conscious of these limitations and take such steps as may be necessary to avoid or overcome
them.

In view of the considerations presented, reading and other aids to
learning should be used as they best serve the needs of pupils. The
basic problem we face is not to determine whether a specific method
of learning should be used to the exclusion of others, but rather the

conditions under which each may be employed to greatest advantage. The answer, as it relates to reading, depends in part on the function of reading in child life.

II. READING DEFINED BROADLY

Reading has been variously defined by different writers and at different periods in history. At one time, a narrow conception of reading prevailed. Not infrequently, it was defined as the process of recognizing printed or written symbols, involving such habits as accuracy in recognizing the words that make up a passage, span of recognition, rate at which words and phrases are recognized, rhythmical progress of perceptions along the lines, and accurate return sweep of the eyes from the end of one line to the beginning of the next. The proponents of this view maintained that the comprehension and interpretation of meaning were not a part of the reading act, but involved supplementary thought processes. No one questions today the need for accurate, fluent habits of recognition. However, programs of teaching based upon the foregoing definition would be very narrow and provide primarily for the mastery of the mechanics of reading.

A broader view of the nature of reading is that it involves the recognition of the important elements of meaning in their essential relations, including accuracy and thoroughness in comprehension. This definition, while implying a thorough mastery of word recognition, attaches major importance to thought-getting. Those who hold this view believe that reading involves both the recognition of the meaning of words and phrases, and the fusing or organization of the various elements of meaning into a chain of ideas or an integrated system of thought. The need is urgent today for greater accuracy, precision, and thoroughness in comprehension among both elementary- and secondary-school pupils. It is imperative that teachers of the content fields, as well as of reading, devote themselves with increased vigor to the exacting obligations involved in promoting efficient habits of comprehension. The fact should be pointed out, however, that comprehension, as the term is used here, provides merely for a grasp of meaning in the form in which it is presented. It does not include the reader's reaction to the facts or view apprehended nor the discovery of their value or significance. It follows that a definition of reading limited to desirable habits of recognition and comprehension is inadequate to meet current needs.

A third definition implies that reading is a much more inclusive process than either of the preceding. It assumes that the reader not only recognizes the essential facts or ideas presented, but also reflects on their significance, evaluates them critically, discovers relationships between them, and clarifies his understanding of the ideas apprehended. In reading for a particular purpose, such as to determine the relative merits of the views presented by two authors, the reader may select and organize pertinent facts as he reads and may weigh values carefully. The superior quality and unique advantage of reading of this type have been discussed pointedly by Wheat:

> The active selection, organization, and assimilation of thought from the printed page in terms of the author's purpose is coming to be recognized as a mental activity that is not only more important but also of a higher order. In the former activity, the writer controls the thinking of the reader; in the latter, the reader controls his own thinking.[1]

The Yearbook Committee believes that any conception of reading that fails to include reflection, critical evaluation, and the clarification of meaning is inadequate. It recognizes that this very broad use of the term implies that reading includes much that psychologists and educators have commonly called thinking. The Committee does not object if anyone wishes to make a distinction between securing ideas on the one hand and using them in thinking on the other. It takes the position, however, that since efficient readers do think about what they read while they are reading it, the teacher should provide needed stimulus and guidance both in securing ideas from the page and in dealing reflectively with them.

The implications of the foregoing discussion are quite clear. During the next decade, teachers should increase their efforts to guide pupils in the deliberate study of the meaning and significance of what they read. Related concepts, experiences, and principles should be recalled and the facts apprehended should be interpreted in the light of them. As Pyle [2] has aptly pointed out, it is not what is presented to the child that promotes growth but rather the reaction that he makes to what is presented. It follows that, beginning in the earliest grades, there should be much clear thinking and weighing of values during the act of reading as well as subsequent to it. This may result at times

---

[1] Harry G. Wheat. *The Psychology of the Elementary School.* P. 234. (Silver, Burdett and Company: Newark, New Jersey, 1931)

[2] William H. Pyle. *The Psychology of the Common Branches.* P. 77. (Warwick and York: Baltimore, 1930)

in reducing the speed of reading. However, the content of what is read should be more fully apprehended because its value, significance, and implications are understood. In this connection, the teachers of various other fields, as well as of reading, have heavy responsibilities. Only as adequate guidance is provided in all fields will reading serve most effectively in promoting broad understanding and social enlightenment.

But it is not sufficient that pupils merely recognize the words of a passage and comprehend and interpret their meaning. If they are aided through reading in acquiring adequate power of self-direction and ability to solve personal and social problems, they must learn to apply successfully the ideas gained from the printed page. As pointed out by Book,[1] "No one has really learned to read aright who does not apply to his own problems and work the thoughts which he has acquired from his reading." Desirable results are attained most economically when pupils make application of what they learn from the page while in the act of reading. It follows that reading, as here conceived, includes not only recognition, comprehension, and interpretation, but also the application of the facts apprehended in the study of personal and social problems.

Some of the reading activities to which reference has been made are often referred to as 'study.' According to Webster's International Dictionary, *study* is a setting of the mind with "absorbed or thoughtful attention" to some task or purpose. The source of information, or the materials studied, are not only books, but in addition, laboratories, people, nature, and things. The steps or processes involved include, in addition to reading, observation, discussion, and inquiry, the recording and interpreting of the findings, and oftentimes their organization for presentation to others. Reading becomes an essential part of a study situation when books and other printed materials form a valuable source of information and help. The purpose of reading in a study project and the steps that are involved depend upon the reader's needs. On some occasions, he may engage in general assimilative reading; on other occasions he may read rapidly to locate specific items of information or proceed very deliberately in order to apply the ideas apprehended to a problem situation. Whatever demands are made upon the pupil while engaged in the act of reading are here conceived as contributing to the total problem involved in teaching reading.

---

[1] William F. Book. "Analysis of the task of learning to read." *Journal of Educational Research,* 21: 1930, 2.

Inherent in the foregoing discussion is the conception that reading is also a form of experience that modifies personality. As pupils comprehend accurately, interpret broadly, and apply what they learn wisely, they acquire new understandings, broader interests, and deeper appreciations. Thus, personality is continually modified and enriched through reading. Furthermore, the fact is well known that reading, as well as other forms of experience, may produce various kinds of reaction — fear, ambition, appreciation, happiness, illness, action, critical thinking. Teachers should realize that such emotional responses are often aroused without adequate understanding on the part of the reader and that there may be decision and action without due consideration of all the facts involved. A properly conceived and intelligently directed reading program should reduce such responses to the minimum and should aid materially in developing a generation of citizens with social, stable, and enriched personalities. The fact is recognized that all children and young people will not rise to equal heights. It is essential, however, that everyone receive appropriate stimulus and guidance.

In adopting the broad conception of reading that has been discussed, the fact is recognized that many of the mental processes included are not confined to reading. In this report, therefore, reading is not conceived as a psychologically unique mental process but rather as a complex of mental activities having much in common with other complex operations and also some elements that are unique. The inclusion of the whole group of associated processes is justified by the fact that they make up an educationally coherent unit of organization.

The attainment of reading attitudes and habits, appropriate for contemporary needs, requires a much more comprehensive program of reading instruction than has been provided in the past. It will not be sufficient to plan merely for the development of habits that underlie accurate recognition, speed, and comprehension in silent reading, and fluent oral reading. Equally, if not more, important is the need for the development and refinement of habits of interpretation, critical evaluation, and the application of the facts apprehended. Since these processes are of primary importance in all curricular fields, appropriate guidance should be provided wherever reading aids in enriching experience, in stimulating thought, and in modifying personality.

III. Important Types and Purposes of Reading

The nature of the instruction provided in reading depends not only upon the basic conception of reading adopted, but also upon the types and purposes of reading in which children and adults engage. Experiments show clearly, for example, that the specific habits involved in reading vary with such factors as the kinds of material read, their difficulty, and the reader's purpose. Furthermore, classroom studies justify the conclusion that whereas some transfer of training occurs from one type of reading situation to another, the best guarantee of efficient reading habits lies in the provision of specific guidance in each. As an aid in identifying the major types and purposes of reading for which provision should be made in teaching, the results of a four-fold analysis will be presented.

1. Types of Reading with Respect to Its General Form

Two types of reading are easily distinguished; namely, silent reading and oral reading. Their general characteristics are so well known that they do not require a detailed description here. Both involve the recognition of symbols and the comprehension and interpretation of meaning by the reader. In addition, oral reading involves the interpretation to others of the thoughts, sentiments, and ideals expressed. Obviously, the oral interpretation of a given passage is a more complex process than the silent apprehension of its meaning. As revealed by laboratory studies, good oral reading utilizes all the basic attitudes and habits involved in efficient silent reading and, in addition, those that are essential in interpreting the content of a passage to others.

The life situations in which need arises for silent reading and oral reading are numerous and varied. Unfortunately, a scientifically derived list is not available. Use has been made, therefore, of a very suggestive list prepared recently by McKee.[1] Examples follow:

1. Situations in which one reads silently:
   a. Reading the newspaper to keep informed about current events.
   b. Reading a magazine or book of current fiction to idle away time or to relieve the strain of the day's work.
   c. Reading a book that has suddenly captured public interest.
   a. Reading excellent character portrayals to be better able to interpret human life and motives.

---

[1] Paul McKee. *Reading and Literature in the Elementary School.* Pp. 48-55. (Houghton Mifflin Company: Boston, 1934)

    e. Reading cartoons, jokes, and comical short stories for fun.

    f. Reading to understand a situation, such as why Brazil is the leading country in the production of coffee.

    g. Reading to secure information that will aid in the solution of a problem.

    h. Reading to form an opinion concerning a program or issue.

    i. Reading to guide action; for example, what to do to cure a cold in the head.

    j. Reading to become acquainted with the best work in a field, such as modern plays, or short stories.

2. Situations in which one reads orally:

    a. Reading passages to others to support a position taken in class discussion.

    b. Reading to give directions or instructions, such as the steps to be taken in reporting a fire.

    c. Reading to provide general information, such as an illuminating news item.

    d. Reading to recall past action, such as the minutes of a meeting.

    e. Reading magazines or books to or with others for pleasure and enjoyment.

    f. Reading a poem aloud to enjoy its rhythm more fully.

The foregoing list, which is far from complete, shows that both silent and oral reading meet vital needs in the lives of children and adults. *The Twenty-fourth Yearbook* rightly emphasized the importance of the former because of its greater social value, economy, and efficiency. As a result, increasingly wide provision for silent reading has been made during recent years in most school systems. The enthusiasm for it has been so great in many centers that provision for oral reading has been neglected, particularly above the primary grades. As a result, pupils have often been deprived of various values inherent in a well-conceived program including both silent and oral reading.

The great social value of silent reading has become more and more widely recognized during the last decade. Accordingly, the Yearbook Committee has endeavored in subsequent chapters to suggest ways and means of increasing the breadth and value of the guidance provided. The Committee is aware also that oral reading serves many practical needs both in and out of school and that it possesses distinct possibilities in broadening the appreciational and cultural life of a people. In order to provide teachers with specific suggestions for improving oral reading, Chapter X has been prepared. The advisability of such a chapter lies in two facts; namely, the neglect of oral reading in many centers during the last decade, and the inadequacy of traditional methods of teaching it. The need is urgent today for an enriched reading program that retains and further emphasizes all the values inherent in intelligent silent reading and in addition secures economically and effectively the unique values that oral reading may contribute.

2. Types of Reading Based on the Reader's General Attitude

Two types of reading that are determined by the reader's general attitude were identified by the National Committee on Reading [1] in 1925; namely, "work-type" and "recreational." They were emphasized vigorously in the *Twenty-Fourth Yearbook* on the assumption that they had either been neglected or sadly confused. As a result, rapid progress has been made during the last decade in providing appropriate emphasis on each. In retaining the distinction in this Yearbook no claim is made that work-type and recreational reading are mutually exclusive. As a matter of fact almost any book or selection may be read with different purposes by various readers or by the same reader on different occasions. Indeed, a reader's purpose or attitude may change during the course of the reading of a given selection or book. The distinction between "work-type" and "recreatory" reading, as presented in the 1925 report, may be reviewed here to advantage.

a. Work-Type Reading. "The work-type of reading is associated with the demands of our vocations, civic duties, and other phases of daily life. Such reading, it should be noted, is directed most often by relatively conscious and practical purposes. Thus, adults turn to professional, trade, or home-making journals to discover new and important items of information. Most people read news items, advertisements, editorials, and notices purposively, to direct action, to study current problems, and, if possible, to arrive at principles of conduct in civic and personal affairs."

Similarly, children engage in much the same sort of reading. Boys read and follow directions in the *Scout Manual* and books on radio, and girls read about campcraft, cooking, and sewing. "Children's magazines abound in puzzles, construction problems, and directions for various activities. Moreover, since schools are organized, in large part, for definite increase of knowledge, a great deal of the reading as-

[1] *Report of the National Committee on Reading.* The Twenty-Fourth Yearbook of this Society, Part I. Pp. 4–8. (Public School Publishing Company: Bloomington, Illinois, 1925)

signed there belongs primarily to the work type. Most lessons in history and civics, geography and other sciences, mathematics, and language require this kind of reading."

Typical situations that lead children and adults to reading of the work type are:

1. Crossing streets, finding stores and houses, and making longer journeys; reading signs, railroad folders, maps, road guides.

2. Understanding assignments and directions in both school and life activities.

3. Working out complicated problems or experiments: reading scout manuals, materials on radio, cookbooks, problems in arithmetic, or other textbooks and science manuals.

4. Finding or verifying spelling, pronunciation, meaning, use of words; using the dictionary, encyclopedia, and other reference books.

5. Gathering material for fuller understanding, for talking or writing on one's hobby, for assigned papers and discussions in school or club, and for experiments.

6. Informing or convincing others; reading aloud.

7. Finding out what is going on.

8. Deciding how to act in new situations.

9. Reaching conclusions as to guiding principles, relative values, or cause and effect.

b. Recreational Reading. Recreational reading " is associated with the wholesome enjoyment of leisure time." Two varieties of recreational reading are quite familiar.

One of these grows out of natural and useful curiosity about human nature and the condition of our lives. " Such curiosity begins with the child's first interest in stories and pictures, and continues increasingly through life. We want to know about the ways of animals and about strange countries and stars and times different from our own. A parallel concern is with pictures of things and happenings that are most familiar to us. Following on a quite opposite recreational track, we often seek mere enjoyment and rest through getting away from reality. Children's engrossment in fairy tales and tales of wonderland and nonsense is an example of this enjoyable kind of recreational reading. It is wholesome and harmless for all of us so long as it is not taken for reality."

Typical situations that lead children and adults to reading of the recreational type are:

1. Reliving common everyday experiences.
2. Seeking fun or sheer enjoyment during leisure time.
3. Enjoying sudden changes or sharp contrasts.
4. Getting away from real life.
5. Enjoying ready-made emotional reactions.
6. Satisfying natural and valuable curiosities about human nature and motives.
7. Giving pleasure to others.
8. Reading aloud parts of plays and dramatic dialogue.
9. Satisfying curiosity about animals, strange regions and times, and current happenings away from one's own environment.
10. Pursuing a hobby.

The importance of both work-type and recreational reading has increased conspicuously during the last decade. The enrichment of the course of study and the growing complexity of social life have greatly enlarged the demand for reading of the study type. Likewise, the need for diversion, enjoyable pastime, and the satisfaction of interests and curiosities has stimulated greater interest in recreational reading. By and large, the more versatile and broad one's interests, the more frequent the occasion for recreational reading. It is obvious that any reading program organized at this time should make adequate provision for both types of reading. In view of the fact that reading is described in this Yearbook under four classifications rather than one, the distinction between " work-type " and " recreational " reading does not receive so much emphasis in this report as in the 1925 report.

3. Types of Reading Based on Specific Purposes of the Reader

Types of reading can be classified, not only with respect to form and the reader's general attitude, but also with respect to the specific purposes that lead to reading on given occasions. For example, children read to find information relating to a problem or to follow detailed directions; adults read to understand a situation better or to determine the validity of arguments relating to a social issue. When the steps or processes involved in such reading activities are analyzed, significant differences are noted. It is obvious, for example, that the mental processes involved in reading to answer a question involving judgment are much more elaborate than in reading to answer a factual question. In the latter situation, one recognizes the various elements of meaning in a passage and identifies the particular word or phrase that answers the question. In reading to answer a question involving judgment, a greater amount of analysis, reflection, and organization of ideas is essential.

Such differences as the foregoing may be readily explained. When one reads for a given purpose, his attention is directed to certain meanings more than to others; furthermore, he is stimulated to use the facts apprehended in a particular way. On one occasion, for example, he merely remembers the facts apprehended well enough to report them in class. On another occasion, he reflects on the meaning of the statements read or applies them in the solution of problems. As revealed by laboratory studies made by Judd and Buswell,[1] changes in the purpose of reading result in differences in the mental processes involved in reading. The records they secured showed that many pupils are relatively unprepared to engage effectively in reading for various purposes. They rightly concluded that if the school is going to hold the pupil for specific responses to the printed page, it should " train him in methods of meeting its demands."

The number of specific purposes for which pupils read is surprisingly large. In perhaps the most elaborate study reported thus far, Hathaway[2] identified 1620 purposes of reading, which were classified under nine major headings; namely, " to gain meanings," " to gain information," " to guide activity," " for social motives " (that is, to influence or entertain others), " to find values," " to organize," " to solve problems," " to remember," " to enjoy."

When the specific purposes were ranked for usefulness by twenty-five judges, the following were among those ranking highest:

To satisfy an eagerness for knowledge.
To compare views on a subject.
To find illustrations of an idea.
To discover relationships.
To note the degree to which a thing is true.
To view two sides of a question.
To seek advice.
To attain an attitude of open-mindedness and ability to form a tentative judgment.

---

[1] Charles H. Judd and Guy T. Buswell. *Silent Reading: A Study of the Various Types.* Supplementary Educational Monographs, No. 23, pp. 44–45. (Department of Education, University of Chicago: Chicago, 1922)

[2] Gladys M. Hathaway. " Purposes for which people read: A technique for their discovery," *University of Pittsburgh School of Education Journal*, 4: 1929, 83–89.

To entertain children.
To learn the opinions of a district upon a political issue.

The foregoing list has value only in suggesting the wide variety of purposes that were identified.

Studies of the purposes for reading in classrooms are equally illuminating. An effort to identify those which have been emphasized repeatedly in recent reports and investigations resulted in the following interesting list:

1. To find answers to specific questions.
2. To determine the author's aim or purpose.
3. To find the central thought of a selection.
4. To follow a sequence of related events.
5. To enjoy the facts or story presented.
6. To find the most important points and supporting details.
7. To select facts which relate to a problem.
8. To judge the validity of statements.
9. To find facts supporting a point of view.
10. To draw valid conclusions from materials read.
11. To discover problems for additional study.
12. To remember what is read.
13. To determine the essential conditions of a problem.
14. To follow directions with reasonable speed and accuracy.

When the results of various studies are combined, three conclusions stand out clearly: first, reading is used for a surprisingly wide variety of purposes; second, the purposes of reading in one curricular field vary to a considerable extent from those in other fields; and third, the purposes change from one level of scholastic advancement to another. In view of the facts presented earlier, it is evident that teachers of all subjects from the primary grades to the university face a major responsibility in training pupils to engage effectively in the various types of reading activities in which they should participate.

4. Types of Reading Based on the Relation of the Ideas Involved

Types of reading may also be identified in terms of the relation of the ideas involved. For example, geography is often defined as the relation between natural environmental conditions and human activities. To read geographically, according to this definition, involves the interpretation of facts in terms of such relations. It follows that a child or an adult might read a geography merely for the facts presented; in that case he would not be interpreting its content geographically. It also follows that he might read and interpret geographically a newspaper article or a passage in a popular novel. Obviously we are thus brought to deal with types of reading that are determined by facts and by relations inherent in the materials read. Such reading can be cultivated best under the expert guidance of teachers in the various curricular fields.

In order to exemplify further important differences in the relations involved in reading material, reference will be made next to the fields of history and sociology. In discussing these two fields, Fling [1] points out that " all past social facts are not necessarily historical facts." A social fact becomes " an historical fact when it has been made a part of an historical synthesis." . . . As limited to human affairs, history concerns itself with the " unique evolution of man in his activities as a social being." It follows that one who interprets historically is concerned with specific kinds of relations between the facts presented and must carry on corresponding chains of thinking while reading. If, on the contrary, " we are interested in *what past social facts have in common,* in the way in which *social facts repeat themselves,* if our purpose is to form *generalizations,* or *laws* concerning social activities, we employ another logical method, the method of the natural sciences. . . . The result of our work is sociology, not history." Specialists in these fields may take exception to the definitions quoted. The purpose here is not to defend the validity of a specific definition. The examples quoted serve their purpose if they indicate that the two fields involve different kinds of relationships and therefore require different modes of interpretation.

Distinctions similar to those already pointed out may be made in the case of most curricular fields. Not infrequently, as in the case of English, various types of interpretation are required in the materials studied; for example, fiction, argumentation, drama. Furthermore, the material presented in one field should often be interpreted in the light of the relationships emphasized in other fields. For example, the facts presented in a history should often be interpreted geographically or mathematically, and the facts presented in a geography should be interpreted in terms of their economic or historical significance. Teachers should identify the types of relations that are involved in specific

---

[1] Fred Morrow Fling. *The Writing of History: An Introduction to Historical Method.* Chapter I. (Yale University Press: New Haven, 1920)

fields and should provide guidance in developing appropriate habits of interpretation.

We are now prepared to point out a major difference between the responsibilities of the teacher of reading and the teacher of the content fields in promoting desirable reading habits. The teacher of reading is responsible for developing the basic attitudes and habits that underlie all reading activities or are common to the various curricular fields. The teachers of the content fields are responsible not only for guidance, as needed, in applying basic reading habits to their respective fields, but, in addition, for developing and refining the various modes of thinking and interpretation involved in these fields. Only through a clear recognition of such responsibilities will adequate guidance in reading be provided during the next decade.

IV. CONCLUDING STATEMENTS

The facts presented in this chapter show clearly that reading is a varied and highly complex process. In order to provide adequately for the needs of child and adult life, the definition of reading adopted by the Committee includes not only the processes involved in recognition and comprehension, but also those involved in interpretation and application. The analysis of types of reading in which persons engage both in and out of school shows that reading assumes different forms and that it varies with the reader's general attitude, with specific purposes for reading, and with the kind of material read. Its varied nature has been described in impressive terms by Judd and Buswell,[1] as a result of a detailed laboratory analysis of silent reading. The printed page is the source, according to them

> of a mass of impressions which the active mind begins to organize and arrange with reference to some pattern which it is trained to work out. If the mind is fitting together the impressions so as to bring into high relief grammatical distinctions, the grouping of words and the distribution of emphasis will be according to one pattern. If the mind is intent on something wholly different from grammar, as, for example, the experiences which the author is trying to picture, the whole mental and physical attitude of the reader will be very different. . . . The grammatical attitude is not the same as the attitude of reading for understanding a scene; nor are the grammatical attitude and the drama atti-

---

[1] Charles H. Judd and Guy T. Buswell. *Silent Reading: A Study of Its Various Types.* Supplementary Educational Monographs, No. 23, pp. 4–5. (University of Chicago: Chicago, 1922)

tude interchangeable parts of a single mental complex. . . . Mental life is a complex of organized attitudes, not a collection of mechanical associations.

One of the important conclusions the foregoing explanation justifies is that the task of teaching reading is by no means a simple one. It involves not only vigorous effort on the part of teachers of reading but also of teachers of every curricular field. The fact is also apparent that satisfactory results cannot be attained easily or quickly. It is true that maturity in basic habits of recognition and comprehension is often acquired by the end of the sixth grade. However, the attainment of the necessary background and the mental habits involved in reading different kinds of material for different purposes comes only as a result of wide experience and carefully planned guidance extending throughout the elementary, secondary, and college periods.

The problem of helping pupils attain an adequate grasp of the meaning of given passages is complicated by a series of factors or conditions, such as: (1) the inherent nature and difficulty of the concepts with which the passage deals; (2) the adequacy with which the concepts are presented through the language of the text; and (3) the reader's ability, including his intelligence, experience, interest, and command of reading habits. Such factors merit intensive study in every classroom in order that necessary adjustments may be made and conditions favorable to rapid progress established.

In adopting the broader conception of reading that has been outlined, the Committee recognizes that it is impossible at present to provide a complete and detailed program for realizing all the values suggested. It is willing to accept the criticisms that arise from such limitations. The Committee is unanimous in its judgment, however, that a broad definition of reading should be adopted if instruction is to provide adequately for contemporary needs. In the chapters that follow, numerous constructive suggestions are offered that aim to promote the development of desirable types of reading attitudes and habits. Through creative effort in the classroom and laboratory, the program outlined should be improved and refined rapidly during the next few years.

SUB–COMMITTEE ON CHAPTER III

Chairman

BESS GOODYKOONTZ, Assistant Commissioner, Office of Education, Department of the Interior, Washington, D. C.

Associates

H. L. CASWELL, Associate Director of Division of Surveys and Field Studies, George Peabody College for Teachers, Nashville, Tennessee

C. L. CUSHMAN, Director, Department of Research and Curriculum, Denver Public Schools, Denver, Colorado

MILDRED ENGLISH, Superintendent, Peabody Training School, Georgia State College for Women, Milledgeville, Georgia

FLORENCE STRATEMEYER, Associate Professor of Education, Teachers College, Columbia University, New York City

CHAPTER III

THE PLACE OF READING IN THE CURRICULUM

Bess Goodykoontz
Assistant Commissioner, U. S. Office of Education
Washington, D. C.

One of the fundamental problems in the teaching of reading is to determine its place in the whole curriculum. Earlier chapters have defined the nature of reading and some of the problems involved in developing good reading habits. They have also shown the numerous demands the present day makes for ability to read widely, understandingly, and almost continually. This chapter will attempt to show how reading plays an increasingly heavy rôle in the developing school program, and the ways in which the curriculum affords opportunities for the growth of reading interests, habits, and skills.

I. The Evolution of Reading in the Curriculum

1. Reading in Early American Schools

The early schools of the American colonists carried a heavy responsibility to colonial society. The colonists had come to their new homes resenting and resisting any curtailment of their religious liberty. To worship as they chose was the deep purpose that had torn them from all that was familiar and safe and brought them to a strange, difficult, and even dangerous land. No sooner did they settle some of their problems of daily living than they turned their attention to making sure that their children should continue in the same religious faith and that they should be able to read the Scriptures to that end.

In the 3-R curriculum of colonial times, reading was far more than training in a particular set of skills. Together with oral instruction by the teacher, reading carried a large share of the civic-social part of the curriculum; through it literary tastes were cultivated; whatever of the meager science of the day the school's program included was more than likely to come in through reading. In other words, since courses of study were limited and textbooks few, reading as a subject in the curriculum provided whatever liberalizing content elements there were

41

in the school's program, as well as instruction in reading habits themselves.

Succeeding periods of the nation's economic and cultural development brought new demands upon reading, at one time emphasizing nationalistic ideals, at another, content values, at another, cultural values, and still later almost exclusively the 'service functions' of reading; that is, promoting the development of abilities essential to carry on reading-study obligations successfully. But different as the emphasis was in one period and another, reading always carried an important share of the responsibility put upon the schools by society.[1]

2. The Place of Reading in the Present-Day Curriculum

The present-day curriculum, equally responsive to the changing demands of society, continues emphasis upon reading. Before considering the part reading plays in the program of the modern school, it may be helpful to define some of the distinguishing characteristics of the present-day curriculum.

a. Characteristics of the Present-day Curriculum. The modern curriculum recognizes educational values, not only in the academic experiences, but also in all the experiences in which pupils engage both at school and, through school direction, at home. Since the lunchroom as well as the classroom, the safety patrol as well as the health class, the community-chest campaign as well as the arithmetic drill period, are considered means to the all-round development of pupils, critical attention is given to the selection and planning of all the activities in which children or older students engage. All activities must be valuable for pupil growth; they must be consecutive, or at least have some cumulative effect; they must provide a well-rounded experience for boys and girls at each stage of development. This involves the inclusion of many types of experiences, among them some that contribute primarily to development of social understandings, that provide for participation in significant aspects of social life, that acquaint the child with the physical environment in which he lives, that contribute to healthful living, that offer opportunity for individual and group creative activities, that provide for the development of efficient methods of work, and the like. To do this the curriculum must be thoroughly responsive to the changing demands of contemporary life.

As implied above, the present-day curriculum emphasizes learning

[1] Nila Banton Smith. *A Historical Analysis of American Reading Instruction.* (Silver, Burdett and Company: Newark, New Jersey, 1934)

through many and varied non-reading means, such as experimentation, investigation, discussion, collecting, construction, examination, listening, and many others. Verbs used to indicate learning processes have become very ' active ' indeed. New-type study assignments accompanying chapters in textbooks, workbooks in content subjects, activity programs, and large units of work all demand a wide variety of learning techniques.

This is well illustrated by a recent course of study in a section on how machine production modifies art, literature, music, and architecture. Only ten (and those somewhat abbreviated) of a list of twenty-five " Suggestive Activities " are quoted: [1]

1. Telling about and listing the different types of musical instruments found in the community.

2. Discussing and reporting on how the machine has made available in large quantities reproductions of famous buildings, pictures, and sculpture.

3. Making well-designed handmade articles for a sale or for gifts, using different mediums, such as, crayons on wood or cloth, gesso, enamel, stenciling on cloth, dyeing cloth, etc.

4. Making a collection of pictures and objects illustrating design, principles of rhythm, proportion, balance, emphasis, and harmony.

5. Discussing and demonstrating the selection and use of wall hangings and pictures in the home.

6. Discussing the work of commercial artists — the difference in the reproduction of drawings due to modern methods.

7. Selecting an appropriate picture from a group of standard reproductions for a place in the school or home.

8. Finding interesting facts about artists heard over the radio.

9. Bringing in brief reports on current happenings showing modern trends in art.

10. Making a study of factors influencing the art of any period, such as available materials, natural resources and environment, religion, encouragement given artists, leisure, etc.

Clearly, to the extent to which the activities listed above are representative of school curriculums on all levels — elementary, secondary, and college — it is evident that reading plays an all important part in the modern curriculum. Some of the activities do not require reading and may not lead to reading, but they do develop backgrounds of ex-

---

[1] *Tentative Course of Study for Virginia Elementary Schools. Grades I–VII.* P. 245. (State Board of Education: Richmond, Virginia, 1934)

perience that are invaluable in giving meaning and significance to later reading. Some of the activities that have little connection with reading nevertheless encourage the use of language, which has an indirect effect on reading ability by developing facility in sentence formation and in vocabulary. Other activities lead naturally to voluntary reading, as a means either of checking the accuracy of conclusions or of broadening experience. Still other activities can be carried on only through reading of a very demanding type.

These concepts of the curriculum hold a number of implications for reading. The position is sometimes taken that the new curriculum places less emphasis on reading than was true in the early schools. As a matter of fact the opposite is the case. As the variety of activities included in the curriculum increases, the greater the need is for reading ability, because children must read in so many different types of situations. On every hand children must read in order to accomplish the ends for which they are striving. The contrast, then, between reading in the modern school and in the early school is that the early school tended to see reading as an end in itself, whereas the modern school sees reading as an essential whereby children may realize their varied purposes. In brief, the modern school is characterized by reading for a purpose.

b. How Reading Functions throughout the Curriculum. If ability is to be developed to meet the many reading needs of children and adults, specific arrangements must be made for the inclusion of reading instruction in the school program, and for the assignment of the responsibility for such instruction at all levels of the school. This does not mean, however, that the arrangements and the assignment will be the same for all schools, for all classes within a school, for all classes of the same grade within a school system, or even for all pupils within a given class. The first responsibility in program-making as it pertains to reading instruction is to assay the reading habits and needs of a particular group. Only after this step is taken is it possible to plan the types and amounts of reading instruction required for individuals and for groups.

In general, however, instruction or guidance in the development of good reading habits has a legitimate place in three distinct phases of the school's program. Of major importance is the fact that motives and opportunities for reading arise for the most part out of the activities and experiences encountered in the various curricular fields. Furthermore, by far the most guidance and practice in reading is secured in connection with such activities. Underlying the effective use of reading in these various fields, however, is the need for the initial development of, and continuous emphasis upon, certain basic or common reading attitudes and habits essential in all reading activities. These can be developed most economically and effectively in special periods reserved for the purpose. As will be pointed out, such reading periods have specific purposes to serve. In addition, opportunity for and guidance in independent reading are found sometimes in a special period set aside for it, sometimes in connection with various aspects of the curriculum.

The Yearbook Committee advocates no single pattern of reading instruction in the school program. However, the Committee calls attention in this chapter to the opportunities afforded for reading instruction in each of the three aspects of the curriculum detailed above, and outlines the functions that each type of program is designed to serve. The discussion leaves with school officials and classroom teachers the responsibility of analyzing their needs and of planning programs designed in type and extent to meet those needs in the most effective way.

II. Reading in All Curricular Fields

Evidence is plentiful to show that at each level of the school — elementary, secondary, and college — proficiency in reading is necessary for success in practically every subject field. Reading is not, of course, the only method of study, but it is so clearly the most frequently used method in our schools that to many persons ' study ' is synonymous with ' reading,' and increased importance has been attached to discovering and remedying reading difficulties as a means of increasing efficiency in all phases of school work.

Recently a study reported the relationship of reading ability to the achievement of 204 children in Grades IV, V, and VI in reading, arithmetic, spelling, health, language, social studies, and some other fields. By comparing the pupils' actual achievements in these fields and what they were capable of doing, as indicated by an intelligence test, it was found that pupils having reading scores below fourth-grade standards are practically certain to do less well in all phases of school work that depend upon reading than their general intellectual ability would lead one to anticipate.[1]

---

[1] Dorris May Lee. *The Importance of Reading for Achieving in Grades Four, Five, and Six.* (Teachers College, Columbia University: New York City, 1933. Doctor's thesis.)

Other studies have shown the relationship of reading to various curricular fields by analyzing specific ways in which reading is needed or used in carrying on school work,[1] by showing the very close relation between reading ability and success or failure in school work,[2] and by measuring the effect of practice in reading skills upon success in other school subjects.[3] These studies support the conclusion that the greatly increased emphasis upon learning through a variety of activities does not lessen the need for efficiency in reading, but rather increases this need. Especially is this true in relation to fields that require such study skills as outlining, summarizing, briefing, memorizing; or in which specific projects require extensive reference work; or which depend for understanding and appreciation upon an enriched experience through extensive voluntary reading.[4]

[1] Cecile Flemming and Maxine Woodring. " Problems in directing study of high school pupils." *Teachers College Record,* 29: 1928, 318–333.

Ernest Horn and Maude McBroom. *A Survey of the Course of Study in Reading.* University of Iowa Extension Bulletin, No. 99, February, 1924. (State University of Iowa: Iowa City, Iowa)

W. S. Monroe. *Types of Learning Required of Pupils in the Seventh and Eighth Grades and in the High School.* University of Illinois Bulletin, Vol. 19, No. 15. (University of Illinois: Urbana, 1921)

[2] Adelaide M. Ayer. *Some Difficulties in Elementary School History.* (Teachers College, Columbia University: New York City, 1926. Doctor's thesis.)

Ivan Albert Booker. *The Measurement and Improvement of Silent Reading among College Freshmen.* (The University of Chicago: Chicago, 1934. Part of Doctor's thesis.)

F. D. Brooks. " Predicting scholarship in the junior high school." *Bulletin of the School of Education, Indiana University,* 7: May, 1931, 73–80.

Joseph C. Dewey. *A Case Study of Reading Comprehension Difficulties in American History.* (State University of Iowa: Iowa City, Iowa, 1931. Doctor's thesis.)

E. L. Thorndike. " Improving the ability to read." *Teachers College Record,* 36: October, 1934, 1–19.

[3] Edgar M. Finck. " Relation of ability in reading to success in other subjects." *Elementary School Journal,* 36: 1935, 260–267.

H. A. Greene. " Directed drill in the comprehension of verbal problems in arithmetic." *Journal of Educational Research,* 11: January, 1925, 33–40.

[4] *For elementary schools:*

W. A. Barton. *Outlining as a Study Procedure.* Contributions to Education, No. 411. (Teachers College, Columbia University: New York City, 1930)

L. J. Brueckner and Prudence Cutright. *The Technics and Evaluation of a Supervisory Program in Work Reading.* Minneapolis Board of Education, Bulletin No. 12. (Minneapolis, April, 1927)

Bessie W. Stillman. *Training Children to Study: Practical Suggestions.* (D. C. Heath and Co.: Boston, 1928)

As has been indicated, children must use a wide variety of reading habits and skills in carrying on specific projects. Frequently the same habit is used on several different levels of difficulty in the same project. Often a reader must shift quickly from one reading procedure to another. For example, in securing information on how to make costumes for a dramatization, a reader might need to use an index, look up a reference, skim a section, examine informational pictures, compare factual statements, take notes, sketch important items, read carefully material of a technical character, make a report in which he reads part and tells part. In other words, carrying on projects largely dependent upon reading is like driving a car, in that it involves some difficult and some easy activities, all going on practically at the same time. Each can be practiced alone, but each must be so well mastered as to function readily in connection with other related activities. The recent increase in the use of large units of work in the curriculum has magnified this dependence of practically all phases of the curriculum upon effective reading skills.

Reading also plays an important part in every phase of the curriculum in providing enriching experiences through extensive voluntary reading. This broadens the understanding, deepens appreciation, heightens interest, clarifies meanings, corrects misconceptions. As will be shown in Chapter IX, for many students limited experience creates serious difficulty in getting any meaning at all for some of the concepts in each field. Wide reading of carefully chosen material can aid materially in obviating this difficulty, and in making purposeful reading a thoroughly enjoyable and enriching activity.

The foregoing considerations lead to a realization of the great re-

---

For secondary schools:

J. S. Butterweck. *The Problem of Teaching High School Pupils How to Study.* Contributions to Education, No. 237. (Teachers College, Columbia University: New York City, 1926)

F. C. Touton and A. B. Struthers. *Junior High School Procedure.* (Ginn and Company: Boston, 1926)

G. M. Whipple. *How to Study Effectively.* (Public School Publishing Company: Bloomington, Illinois, Rev. Ed. 1927)

M. N. Woodring and C. W. Flemming. *Directing Study of High School Pupils.* Chapter V. (Bureau of Publications, Teachers College, Columbia University: New York, 1935)

For college students:

W. F. Book. *Learning How to Study and Work Effectively.* (Ginn and Company: Boston, 1926)

sponsibility each teacher has in his particular field for guidance in reading as it is used in that field. Every situation calling for a new or difficult reading skill or procedure affords a valuable opportunity for effective teaching. Such a situation has decided advantages over separate, isolated periods for reading. In the first place, the situation that requires reading of a specific type provides excellent motivation for learning. " This is what we need to do; how can we do it? " Furthermore, the situation itself provides the reading materials. There is no need to hunt " suitable selections." Whether or not the vocabulary is easy, whether or not the article is well organized, whatever the limitations — " these are the materials we need to use." And still further, reading lessons as part of the instruction in each phase of the curriculum provide the opportunity to secure an immediate check on the effectiveness of the learning.

" Every teacher a reading teacher " has become a widely accepted slogan, and certainly much progress has been made in its attainment. Possibly most has been done in the elementary school, where frequently the classroom teacher is responsible for most if not all of the work of a given class or group. Ideally, reading instruction can then be integrated with other phases of the curriculum — at one time with social studies, at another time with literature, and at another time with arithmetic — to the very great increase in effectiveness of learning in each. Methods of achieving this purpose are numerous, as Chapter V will show.

A similar obligation is now placed on the teachers in secondary schools, and to a lesser degree in the colleges, to provide instruction and practice in reading as needed for successful work in the fields they represent. Techniques of supervised study, workbooks (both general and in specific fields), teachers' manuals on methods of study, and the various laboratory procedures have all aided in providing students with the necessary tools of study. In spite of progress in this respect, however, it must be continually emphasized, first, that good teaching of reading is bound to improve other phases of school work, and, second, that good teaching in the content studies and literature always results in greatly improved reading ability.

A. W. Kornhauser. *How to Study.* (University of Chicago Press: Chicago, 1924)

R. L. Lyman. *The Mind at Work in Studying, Thinking, and Reading.* (Scott, Foresman & Company: Chicago, 1924)

G. M. Whipple. *Op. cit.*

III. The Reading Period in the Present-day Curriculum

1. Reading as a Subject

With such definite relationships in purpose and method as exist between reading and other phases of the curriculum, it might be assumed that special instruction in reading is unnecessary aside from the guidance needed whenever reading is required. This ideal of the complete integration of the various related phases of the curriculum is held by many as one important objective toward which all schools should strive. For example, in describing the new type of daily program Rugg says:

> The first characteristic of this new curriculum organization is the daily time allotment of long, flexible periods of three-quarters of an hour, an hour, or an hour and a half in which a teacher directs a group of children. These children are free to study problems, work out answers and questions, make excursions in the community, build things in the schoolroom, organize plays, write creatively, paint, dance, make music, read in the library, have open forum discussions.
>
> The second characteristic is that there is no reading, writing, arithmetic, geography, civics, patriotism, or physical inspection on this program. . . . There is one single reference to reading, suggesting " special help in reading." In the fourth grade these children have perfected the fundamental reading habits and most of them need no instruction in reading. They need rather to read and read and read and talk and make and play and create.
>
> So this wise school sets aside a time when the teacher can be free from other things to give the six, eight, or ten children the special help in reading which that number may require.[1]

Various arguments have been advanced in favor of eliminating special periods for teaching reading. Some maintain that such periods do not provide natural opportunities for highly motivated reading activities. For example, one writer [2] states that the best way to teach reading " is not to teach reading but to provide the occasion — normal in the lives of little children — in which certain reading functions." Closely associated with this view is the assumption that essential reading attitudes and habits can be learned best incidentally. Meriam expresses this view as follows: " Let children read to learn, incidentally they will learn to read." Those who subscribe without reservation to the fore-

---

[1] *Curriculum-Making in Current Practice.* P. 26. (School of Education, Northwestern University: Evanston, Illinois, 1932)

[2] J. L. Meriam. " Avoiding difficulties in learning to read." *Educational Method,* 9: April, 1930, 413–419.

going statements would eliminate special reading periods at all grade levels.

Others believe that special guidance in reading should be provided until pupils are able to engage in the continuous meaningful reading of simple passages. From that time on, it is assumed reading should be taught only as pupils read and study in the content fields. For example, one school officer [1] maintains that facility in rapid, exact reading of subject matter " does not result from general training in reading. Even training in reading the subject matter of one field does not provide sufficient ability to read other types of material." Such statements have often been interpreted to signify that all the guidance in reading needed by pupils above the primary grades can be provided best in content fields. As a result, some schools have discontinued a special reading period in the middle grades.

Those who differ from this point of view maintain that regular periods devoted to carefully planned guidance in learning to read on successively higher levels are essential. There are many goals to achieve in learning to read well, such as attaching meanings to written or printed words that relate to familiar experience, learning to engage in continuous meaningful reading, and acquiring the attitudes and habits essential in reading different types of material for various purposes. Many examples could be presented to indicate that there are critical stages in learning to read and internal relationships among reading habits for which appropriate instruction should be provided. Many believe that help can be given most economically and effectively during periods in which the teacher is free to adapt the content and methods to the reading needs of pupils.

Investigations have centered principally on three phases of this problem: the reading achievement of pupils in activity-type schools, which give relatively less attention to systematic guidance in reading than do other schools; the comparative effectiveness of systematic, or intensive, reading instruction as contrasted with extensive library reading; and a comparison of the progress in reading made by pupils who have systematic instruction with those whose guidance in reading is incidental, or opportunistic.

On the first aspect of the problem, numerous studies [2] are in agree-

---

[1] Olive Gray. "Teaching pupils to read arithmetic and other subject-matter." *Elementary School Journal,* 26: April, 1926, 607–618.

[2] Claude C. Crawford and Lillian Gray. "Measured results of activity teaching." *Journal of the National Education Association,* 20: October, 1931, 270.

ment concerning the value of well-selected activities that supply meaning to reading, develop accurate vocabularies, and provide worth-while purposes for reading. Most of these studies report normal or better progress in reading as measured by standardized tests for those pupils whose programs provide such meaningful activities with comparatively less formal instruction in reading.

The belief that the way to learn to read is to read extensively has led to numerous investigations of the effectiveness of wide reading upon the development of basic reading habits and skills. One such study [1] indicates that extensive reading appears to be superior for bright pupils, but that the lower part of the group profited more from intensive instruction. A recent comparison [2] of the effectiveness of extensive library reading and specific drill in silent reading with the usual classroom procedures shows larger average gains for both the extensive library group and the specific drill group. In such abilities as rate, total meaning, and following directions as measured by a standardized reading test, the extensive library reading produced larger gains, whereas in knowledge, fact material, central thought, and organization greater growth was secured by specific drill. In general the investigations in this field point to the importance of utilizing both methods rather than either one alone.

As to the relative effectiveness of the direct and the incidental meth-

---

Julia E. Dickson and Mary E. McLean. " An integrated activity program try-out in a first grade of the public schools." *Educational Method,* 9: October, 1929, 31–42.

L. Thomas Hopkins. " Learning essentials in an activity curriculum." *Journal of Experimental Education,* 1: June, 1933, 298–303.

Etta Howell, Maude Wilson Dunn, and Dora Stoker. " Measuring the skills in an integrated program." *Journal of Experimental Education,* 1: June, 1933, 316–319.

J. Murray Lee. " Reading achievement in first-grade activity programs." *Elementary School Journal,* 33: February, 1933, 447–451.

Junius L. Meriam. " An activity curriculum in a school of Mexican children." *Journal of Experimental Education,* 1: June, 1933, 304–308.

J. Wayne Wrightstone. *Appraisal of Newer Practices in Selected Public Schools.* (Bureau of Publications, Teachers College, Columbia University: New York City, 1935)

[1] Laura Zirbes, Katherine Keelor, and Pauline Miner. *Practice Exercises and Checks on Silent Reading in the Primary Grades.* (Lincoln School of Teachers College, Columbia University: New York, 1925)

[2] George H. Hilliard. " Extensive library reading versus specific drill as an aid in improving certain reading abilities." *Educational News Bulletin,* 2: June, 1932, 6–12. (Western State Teachers College: Kalamazoo, Michigan)

ods in reading, a few objective studies yield pertinent results. Thus, certain investigations have shown that a " modern systematic method " secured considerably greater average achievement in silent and oral reading among first-grade pupils than " an opportunistic method." [1] Other values, such as the development of interest in reading, were secured equally well by either method. Such findings indicate that at least for the first grade some systematic teaching of reading, supplemented by many purposeful reading activities during other periods of the day, is superior to the exclusive use of either plan. Another study,[2] though not directly in the field of reading, has a bearing on this problem inasmuch as it shows that in fourth-grade history the direct method proved superior to incidental teaching in increasing vocabulary, in improving both oral and silent reading, in improving ability to discuss what was read, and in sustaining interest in the subject considered.

In general, practice seems to justify the conclusion that in most schools there will be found a need for separate reading periods. A recent investigation [3] of current practices in 203 selected schools and school systems shows that 99 percent of the school systems reporting set aside certain definite periods for reading instruction in Grades I and II; in 97 percent, separate reading periods are provided in Grade III; in Grades IV, V, and VI the percents run 94, 93, and 90, respectively.

Available evidence from both experiments and progressive practice tends to favor specific provision for guidance in reading at times reserved for the purpose. The Committee recognizes that this evidence is not conclusive, but, until it has been established that fundamental reading habits can be developed economically for all pupils without such provision, the Committee recommends specific periods for guidance in reading throughout the elementary school, the secondary school, and the college. Since the functions are not the same, the Committee further recommends that basic instruction in reading and guidance in literature be provided during separate periods.

---

[1] Arthur I. Gates, assisted by Mildred I. Batchelder and Jean Betzner. " A modern systematic versus an opportunistic method of teaching: An experimental study." *Teachers College Record*, 27: April, 1926, 679–700.

[2] Eleanor Holmes. "Vocabulary instruction and reading." *Elementary English Review*, 11: April, 1934, 103–105, 110.

[3] "Better reading instruction." *Research Bulletin of the National Education Association*, 13: November, 1935, 320. (National Education Association, Research Division: Washington, D. C.)

2. Specific Functions Served by a Separate Reading Period

As indicated in the preceding section, the separate reading period has specific functions to perform in the development of reading ability. The fact merits vigorous emphasis that these functions, or services, make the reading period coördinate with, not a substitute for, the well-planned, continuous program of reading instruction throughout all other phases of the school's program. Specific functions of the reading period include the following:

1. The basic reading period prepares for various reading situations by initiating appropriate interests and skills. The teacher who analyzes carefully the reading demands of the curriculum, so far as they can be anticipated, often will, through well-planned activities in the reading period, forestall confusion or failure when situations requiring certain reading abilities arise, and will provide for such a degree of success in the initial application of a newly developed skill as will encourage further use and keener satisfactions.

2. The basic reading period provides supplementary instruction and practice in reading activities initially developed in other parts of the school program.

The needs for reading arising in rich, varied school programs serve as the best possible motivation for undertaking new or more difficult steps in reading skills, but they will usually need considerable additional practice, which the reading period can afford.

3. The basic reading period provides for continuity in the development of successively difficult steps in the various reading skills, habits, and attitudes.

Basic instruction in reading is responsible for the orderly development of the attitudes, habits, and skills required in all types of reading situations. Such proficiencies may be frequently and well taught in other parts of the curriculum, but in the reading periods pupils will gain an understanding of how and for what purposes each type of reading procedure is used, and will develop facility in successively difficult stages of its use.

4. The basic reading period serves as a constant reminder and provides examples of what to do in other parts of the school program in order to develop reading ability.

The activities of the reading period should be so well planned and carried out that pupils, in other parts of the school program, can and will refer constantly to the way in which specific types of reading were practiced in the reading period. This constant check should serve to correct many inefficient or incorrect individual techniques. Furthermore, during the reading period there is opportunity for teachers to study individual needs so that they may later give direct help where the need arises.

5. The basic reading period provides opportunity for continuous examination of the achievements and needs of children.

As indicated in Chapters XI and XII, the Committee recommends continuous observation and examination of the interests, abilities, and difficulties of individual children for the purpose of insuring the development of effective reading abilities and the prevention of difficulties. It further recommends prompt and effective remedial treatment of disabilities when occasions demand.

6. The basic reading period provides opportunity for promoting wide reading interests and habits of fluent, intelligent reading.

Reading for enjoyment is an acquired taste. It may be developed in such a way as to add greatly to an individual's means of enjoyment, personality development, occupational efficiency, and general ability to adapt to new situations, new demands, new persons. Through the reading period pupils may be introduced to the wealth of wholesome material available to them and be encouraged to develop fundamental attitudes, habits, and skills inherent in good recreational reading.

3. Scheduling the Reading Period

The amount of time required for the basic reading period to satisfy the purposes outlined in this and succeeding chapters depends upon many factors. If reading instruction in connection with all other phases of the school program is effective, the separate reading period has proportionately less to accomplish and may therefore be shortened or in some cases eliminated. Again, if a class has already attained a high degree of reading efficiency, less time may be needed for direct instruction. Other determining factors in this matter include such considerations as the amount of time and materials available both in and outside school hours for independent reading, the skill of the reading teacher, whether or not time is scheduled for literature, and the number of pupils who need remedial training. Consequently, recommendations concerning scheduling the reading period can be suggestive only, and must be interpreted carefully in terms of specific situations.

a. Reading Instruction in the Elementary School. Current progressive practice points toward a weekly time allotment of from 150 to 200 minutes per week in primary grades, with daily periods of 30, 40, or 50 minutes for basic reading instruction, and additional time for literature and reading activities in other parts of the program. The following schedule [1] illustrates this point. The details are quoted only for periods that involve considerable reading. Apparently they include time for both reading and literature.

---

[1] *Curriculum Records of the Children's School.* Pp. 256–259. (Bureau of Publications, National College of Education: Evanston, Illinois, 1932)

Daily Procedure in the First Grade

8:30 Health inspection, care of room, self-directed activities

9:40 Music activities

10:00 Reading activities, which may include group composition of stories about some special interest, reading of such stories from charts or booklets made by the children, or reading of interesting stories from 'real books' (The class is always divided into small groups for reading and one group is usually engaged in some sort of silent reading activity.)

10:30 Rest and play

11:15 Reading, writing, and art activities

12:15 Dismissal

12:30 Dinner

1:15 Naps

2:00 Activities adapted to group interests or needs (These may include stories, art work, more reading, or other types of experiences.)

2:30 Outdoor play

3:00 Dismissal

In some intermediate grades it will probably be found desirable to devote at least 100 minutes per week to basic reading instruction, in addition to whatever reading time is allotted in other parts of the program, including literature. Some schools recommend considerably more time, as is shown in the following recent statement:

Reading skills. Time: 45 to 60 minutes (daily). This period should be used for establishing skills in reading. . . .

Children should be grouped according to ability in reading. If more than one grade is in a classroom, grade lines should be disregarded in following such a plan. Three groups can be handled efficiently in a 45-minute period in either a graded class of fourth-, fifth-, or sixth-grade pupils, or in an ungraded room by a plan of alternation.

This can well be a period in which data are gathered for a unit of work in the social studies, or a report in the language arts, or for club work. Weaknesses of individuals or groups should be corrected, and needed techniques established during this period. Free reading and use of the library are legitimate parts of the reading period.

Reading is a part of every other subject. Some reading skill is in use every period of the day. These skills must be well established to insure efficient use of this tool of learning.

Music, art, literature. Time: 30 to 40 minutes. This should be a period in which children become acquainted with as many of the art products as can be included. . . . Appreciation lessons, poetry study, dramatics, and enjoyment of literature should be included in this period.[1]

---

[1] *Teachers' Guide to Child Development in the Intermediate Grades.* Pp.

In the upper grades of the elementary school considerably less time will be needed for a separate period for basic instruction in reading, provided that instruction in the earlier grades has been efficient and that reading instruction and independent reading are continually emphasized throughout the whole school program. In many schools, however, it will be found desirable to set aside at least one period each week for practice in reading skills on progressively higher levels.[1]

It should be added that within the recommended time allotments great flexibility should be provided for individual pupils, some needing much more and some less time. Furthermore, additional time may be required if there are a number of children in a given group who need considerable time for remedial instruction.

b. Reading Instruction in the Secondary School. Though reading problems in the secondary school are different in degree from those in the elementary school, they are not different in kind.[2] Secondary-school pupils need instruction in how to read and study in connection with practically every phase of their curriculum; they need guidance in their voluntary reading; and they frequently need direct instruction in reading skills that have proved difficult. Provided that every teacher gives careful attention to these reading needs as they arise, probably few separate periods for reading will be necessary in most secondary schools, except for pupils who have serious reading difficulties.

To meet these needs one or two separate periods for developmental and remedial instruction each week are usually desirable. This instruction should be given by teachers who understand the functions of study-reading and how correct reading habits, attitudes, and skills are developed. Sometimes teachers of English will be found particularly capable in this line; sometimes teachers of social studies or the sciences, in which reading ability plays so large a part, will be the appropriate

---

27, 29. (California State Department of Education: Sacramento, California, 1936)

[1] *Course of Study in English, Part III.* Pp. 3–4. (Board of Education of Baltimore County: Towson, Maryland, 1935)

[2] William S. Gray. "Reading and literature." *Review of Educational Research*, 2: February, 1932, 29–34. (Chapter III of report of Committee on Special Methods on High-School Level, Walter S. Monroe, Chairman)

Carol Hovious. "What should be done about reading in secondary schools." *California Journal of Secondary Education*, 11: January, 1936, 17–21.

Peter L. Spencer. "Principles of teaching reading in secondary schools." *California Journal of Secondary Education*, 11: January, 1936, 13–16.

persons for this type of instruction. Since reading instruction is as closely related to history or botany as it is to literature or composition, no hard and fast rule can be followed in its assignment to certain teachers or classes. Competence to give reading instruction is the criterion in selecting the reading teacher.

c. Reading Instruction on the College Level. As one writer [1] points out, until comparatively recently it was generally assumed that reading presented no problems at the college level. But in the last few years there has come about a widespread recognition of the fact that many students enter college so deficient in reading as to be ill prepared for college work, no matter what their other preparation has been, and that there is a very definite relation between reading efficiency and academic success in college. Consequently, in many colleges and universities,[2] classes for remedial instruction in reading have been developed, particularly for freshmen.

There is considerable agreement that an adequate program to improve the reading habits of college students should include provision for at least the following:

(1) a detailed study of the reading efficiency and study habits of all students at the time of admission; (2) information and guidance in general reading and study habits for all students in connection with some regular course, such as English, or a special ' how to study ' course which is required of everyone; (3) special sections of this course, in which additional intensive training may be provided for deficient readers who are above the twenty-fifth percentile in intelligence; (4) a special remedial group, or groups, with provision for clinical assistance, for students who rank below the twenty-fifth percentile of intelligence, and for others who are handicapped by unusual reading deficiencies; and (5) systematic guidance of a developmental type, as needed in each college course, which will enable students to acquire, as rapidly as their qualifications will permit, those habits of intelligent reading and efficient study that characterize superior students and productive workers in given fields.[3]

The last point furnishes a clue to what may possibly be the line of greatest development in the decade just ahead. College instruction in reading on successively higher levels, not merely for remedial cases,

---

[1] William S. Gray. *Provision for the Individual in College Education.* Chapter XIII. (The University of Chicago Press: Chicago, 1932)

[2] Frank W. Parr. " The extent of remedial reading work in state universities in the United States." *School and Society,* 31: April, 19, 1930, 547–548.

[3] William S. Gray. *Op. cit.* P. 158. Reprinted by permission of the University of Chicago Press.

may prove desirable and feasible. Certainly the courses in 'how-to-study' and 'research techniques for graduate students' seem to point in that direction.[1]

4. Materials and Methods for the Reading Period

Throughout this discussion the close relationship in purpose of the reading period to all other phases of the curriculum has been emphasized. Later chapters will treat in detail the problems of selecting appropriate materials and effective methods for developing reading ability. Attention is directed to the fact that since the reading period aims to make pupils more successful in all phases of the curriculum depending upon reading, so far as possible the purposes, materials, and methods of the reading period should both represent and supplement those of other phases of the program that involve reading. Furthermore, since the reading period is planned to provide for individual needs in a way frequently not possible in other parts of the program, reading materials should be varied in type and degrees of difficulty, and plentiful enough to permit the optimal development of essential skills and to encourage extensive reading in many fields.

IV. THE PLACE OF INDEPENDENT READING IN THE CURRICULUM

1. Important Purposes

Many adults must read frequently because of occupational or social demands, but except for those persons who are engaged in 'reading occupations' the reading of most adults is largely voluntary, or independent. Sometimes it appears desultory, but usually a purpose can be distinguished. Chapter II has analyzed in detail the important purposes, such as reading for enjoyment, reliving common everyday experiences through reading, satisfying natural and valuable curiosities, pursuing a hobby, keeping up in a field of some special personal interest.

These same purposes, in greater or less degree, are those that motivate children's independent reading, both in and out of school. One

---

[1] William F. Book. "Results obtained in a special 'How to study' course given to college students." *School and Society,* 26: October 22, 1927, 529–534.

Alvin C. Eurich. *The Reading Abilities of College Students: An Experimental Study.* (University of Minnesota Press: Minneapolis, 1931)

C. W. Stone and Carl Colvin. "'How to study' as a source of motive in educational psychology." *Journal of Educational Psychology,* 11: September, 1920, 348–354.

obligation of the school is to encourage independent reading for constructive purposes in every possible way, to include both time and place for such experiences in the program, and to provide acquaintance with appropriate materials for fulfilling these purposes.

2. Materials and Sources of Stimulation for Independent Reading

Other chapters, particularly Chapter VI, discuss in detail the materials and methods useful in the cultivation of desirable independent reading. Attention is here directed to the unexcelled opportunities that practically all aspects of the curriculum have for stimulating independent reading and suggesting suitable materials. Science classrooms will open many by-paths for individual exploration through reading; social sciences will introduce readers to new persons, countries, and periods of time, and will set a stage before them to be peopled by characters from the books they read; the literature period will create demands for more and more time and materials for free reading. In fact, the vitality of the students' voluntary reading activities will be largely determined by the stimulus and guidance provided through all phases of the school program, not alone through the reading, or English, or literature courses of study.

This is not the place to describe methods of guidance in voluntary reading. Situations conducive to growth in voluntary reading may, however, be listed:

1. Abundant materials of a wide variety and range in difficulty.
2. Extensive opportunity throughout the school program for pupils to report or to use the results of their individual reading encourages more reading.
3. Easy access to books, freedom to examine and choose, and time for browsing provide the stimulation necessary for some readers.
4. Frequent reference to books and recourse to books to illustrate difficult concepts, or to prove points, or to settle controversies help to develop habits of reading.
5. Opportunities to hear good reading of a wide variety of types of materials open new doors for many readers.

3. Relation of Independent Reading to the Development of Reading Skills

Independent reading in the classroom, in the library, or at home affords opportunity for the cultivation of many reading attitudes, habits, and skills under exceptionally favorable circumstances. Such opportunities help to develop habits of rapid reading, to encourage independent recognition of words, to enlarge vocabulary, and to improve language usage. Motives are present, but the strains of group competition, or necessity for speed, or annoyance at one's own ineptitude are lacking. Therein are both advantages and dangers — advantages, in that pupils are encouraged to read fluently, extensively, appreciatively, meaningfully with proper safeguards against superficiality; dangers, in that inefficient or inaccurate habits may be developed when there is no close supervision. The teacher in whatever field of work voluntary reading is encouraged must keep a close and sympathetic interest in both the difficulties readers encounter and the progress they make.

V. READING IN RELATION TO CURRENT PROBLEMS IN CURRICULAR ORGANIZATION

Curriculum-workers face many problems of major importance as they attempt to select and organize significant experiences adapted to the needs of particular groups. Many of these problems have a direct relation to reading. A few of the most pressing may be briefly described.

1. Providing Reading Curriculums for Beginners

Other sections of this Yearbook, particularly Chapters IV and XII, consider various aspects of reading readiness at all levels and call attention to serious curricular problems involved. In primary grades, for example, schools must provide suitable curriculums for all beginning children, with proper amounts and types of instruction that insure the development of an adequate background for reading. Not infrequently such guidance is necessary for a considerable period before children can undertake reading from books. During this period it is not a question of ' reading or no reading,' but rather of formulating a curriculum full of meaningful experiences, training in language, enjoyment of stories, and other activities that serve excellently as an introduction to the use of books.[1]

2. Selecting and Grading Units of Work with Relation to Reading Materials

In curriculum-planning it is continually necessary to choose from many possible experiences or units of work those which may be used

---

[1] Arthur I. Gates and Guy L. Bond. " Reading readiness. A study of factors determining success and failure in beginning reading." *Teachers College Record*, 37: May, 1936, 679–685.

to best advantage to develop certain large concepts. For some units requiring wide reading for satisfactory mastery of the subject, materials are not available, or are not available on the desired level of understanding. It therefore frequently happens that certain units of work must be delayed to await greater reading skill, or must be used on a non-reading basis. One of the most difficult tasks curriculum-makers face at each school level is the selection of units for which there is reference material satisfactory in degree of difficulty and adequate in amount. Not infrequently they must write or adapt material for some of the newer units.

3. Providing a Curriculum for Pupils of Limited Reading Ability

Throughout the school wide differences exist among pupils in the ability to read, in the capacity to improve in reading skills, in the extent of their interest in reading, in the amount and kind of voluntary reading, in the extent to which reading is used for informational purposes. Fundamental differences are heightened in secondary schools as a larger proportion of the secondary-school population attend school, and the practice spreads of sending adolescents on to upper grades or to junior high school irrespective of whether they have mastered the fundamental reading skills or not.

This situation has a very important bearing on the development of the curriculum for the secondary level. At present the secondary-school curriculum counts very heavily upon reading ability and versatility. But large numbers of students do not now, and in the future probably will not, depend extensively on reading either for their vocational advancement or for their enjoyment. Probably throughout the schools, but particularly in upper elementary grades and secondary schools, new curriculums and materials must be developed, the reading requirements for which will be more in keeping with the interests and needs of pupils of limited reading ability.

4. Modification of Systems of School and Class Organization and of Promotion to Facilitate Curricular Objectives (Including Reading)

Since school enrollments on all levels are too large for individual instruction, administrative devices of grouping, class organization, and promotion have developed to provide that each pupil shall work with others who have somewhat similar interests, abilities, and needs. But interests and needs vary greatly from person to person. For any one person they vary greatly from time to time, and reading abilities develop at widely differing rates. At their best, administrative devices must, therefore, be flexible, so that students may move easily from one group to another as need dictates. It is commonly agreed that the fixed grade organization and regular periodic promotions, especially for primary-grade children, are not conducive to the all-round development of pupils. Experimentation is greatly needed to determine types of school and class organization and bases for promotion that will permit stages of growth or levels of pupil attainment to be used more generally and adequately as the basis of grouping.

SUB–COMMITTEE ON CHAPTER IV

Chairman

WILLIAM S. GRAY, Professor of Education, The University of Chicago, Chicago, Illinois

Associates

PRUDENCE CUTRIGHT, Assistant Superintendent of Schools, Minneapolis, Minnesota

ALVIN C. EURICH, Assistant Professor of Educational Psychology, University of Minnesota, Minneapolis, Minnesota

ETHEL MABIE FALK, Supervisor, Department of Curriculum, Public Schools, Madison, Wisconsin

J. R. GERBERICH, Office of Education, Washington, D. C.

HELEN R. GUMLICK, Supervisor of Elementary Grades, Public Schools, Denver, Colorado

JULIA HAHN, Supervising Principal, Third Division, Public Schools of the District of Columbia, Washington, D. C.

MARJORIE HARDY, Germantown Friends School, Philadelphia, Pennsylvania

M. LUCILE HARRISON, Colorado State College of Education, Greeley, Colorado

ALLIE M. HINES, Director of Primary Grades, Public Schools, Cincinnati, Ohio

JOHN A. HOCKETT, School of Education, University of California, Berkeley, California

MOSSIE D. HOLMES, Director of Tests and Measurements, Public Schools, Tulsa, Oklahoma

DELIA E. KIBBE, Supervisor of Elementary Grades, Department of Public Instruction, Madison, Wisconsin

PAUL KLAPPER, Dean, School of Education, College of the City of New York, New York City

HOWARD McCLUSKY, School of Education, University of Michigan, Ann Arbor, Michigan

SAMUEL W. PATTERSON, Professor of Education, Hunter College of the City of New York, New York City

FRANCIS F. POWERS, College of Education, University of Washington, Seattle, Washington

CLARENCE R. STONE, Berkeley, California

ARTHUR TRAXLER, Educational Records Bureau, New York City

H. G. WHEAT, Professor of Education, West Virginia University, Morgantown, West Virginia

EDNA L. WIESE, Assistant Supervisor, Board of Education, Los Angeles, California

MAXIE N. WOODRING, Teachers College, Columbia University, New York City

CHAPTER IV

THE NATURE AND ORGANIZATION OF BASIC INSTRUCTION IN READING

WILLIAM S. GRAY
Professor of Education, The University of Chicago,
Chicago, Illinois

One of the major objectives of a comprehensive reading program is the development of a high level of efficiency in all reading activities. As pointed out in Chapter III, the attainment of this objective requires a broad program of guidance in reading, with special provision for the orderly development of fundamental reading attitudes, habits, and related skills. Various arguments supporting basic instruction in reading were considered at length in the preceding chapter. Attention, therefore, will be directed in this chapter to the nature and organization of instruction by means of which fundamental reading attitudes and habits may be economically and effectively developed.

Two important motives underlie the program that is recommended; namely, to provide appropriate initial teaching, thus securing the development of right attitudes and habits and the prevention of wrong ones, and to promote growth at each level of advancement sufficient to insure maximal achievement in all reading activities in which children engage both in and out of school. Although it is assumed that the guidance outlined will be provided in most cases during specific reading periods, the problems considered are pertinent also in highly integrated programs of teaching.

I. SPECIFIC AIMS OF BASIC INSTRUCTION IN READING

The broader objectives [1] of most reading activities in which pupils engage are to extend and enrich their experiences, to promote social

---

[1] A very illuminating discussion of the objectives and values of reading are found in Chapter VII of English Monograph No. 4, *An Experience Curriculum in English,* prepared by the National Council of Teachers of English, and published by D. Appleton-Century Company, 1935; see also, *Evaluation of Reading,* Evaluation in the Eight-Year Study, Bulletin No. 4, prepared by the Progressive Education Association, Ohio State University, Columbus, Ohio, 1936.

understanding and elevate tastes, to stimulate broad reading interests, to cultivate appreciations, and to develop stable and alert personalities; and, of special importance, to contribute measurably to growth in all of these directions. The reading materials provided should be highly interesting, purposeful, and challenging, and should be adapted to the reader's level of advancement. In fact, the reading period should be one of the most interesting and valuable periods of the school day. It must be, if pupils are to acquire a growing interest in worthwhile reading and are stimulated to apply themselves with sufficient vigor to learn to read with ease and understanding.

An analysis of current aims of teaching reading shows that, for the purposes of this discussion, they may be divided into two groups. The first includes those shared jointly by the reading period and the various curricular fields. Because of their very nature, they determine to a large extent the broader outcomes of instruction in reading. At least six such aims may be readily identified:

1. To arouse keen interest in learning to read.
2. To promote increased efficiency in both silent and oral reading.
3. To extend and enrich experience and to satisfy interests and needs.
4. To cultivate strong motives for and permanent interest in reading.
5. To elevate tastes in reading and to promote discrimination in selecting books, magazines, and newspapers to read.
6. To acquaint pupils with the sources and values of different kinds of reading material and to develop ability to use them intelligently and critically.

The second group includes those aims that are concerned more directly with the development of fundamental reading attitudes and habits, and that help to distinguish the functions of the reading period from those of the various curricular fields. They may be defined as follows:

1. To provide for the continuous, orderly, and economical development of the fundamental attitudes and habits involved in efficient silent reading and good oral reading. This aim includes also the systematic study of the progress of pupils in reading and the provision of corrective and remedial instruction, as needed, adapted to their individual difficulties and needs. (See Chapters XI, XII, and XIII.)

2. To aid in promoting the development of the attitudes, habits, and skills common to study situations in the various curricular fields. Frequently the motives for such training arise in connection with the study activities in which pupils engage. Not infrequently the needs of pupils in the different curricular fields are anticipated and provided for during the reading period, in order that

the pupils may participate in essential reading activities at a higher level of learning.

The preceding statements attach large importance to the development of the fundamental habits and skills involved in reading and study. It must not be concluded, however, that the reading period is devoted largely to routine or formal activities. As pointed out earlier, basic instruction in reading should be as interesting, challenging, vital, and enriching as that provided in any field of the curriculum. This is of primary importance if pupils are to acquire right attitudes toward reading and make rapid progress in learning to read efficiently.

II. Fundamental Attitudes, Habits, and Skills

Since a major responsibility of basic instruction in reading is the orderly development of fundamental attitudes and habits, these latter should be identified in somewhat specific terms before prescribing a program for their development.

1. Basic Attitudes and Habits Common to Most Reading Situations [1]

Many of the attitudes and habits involved in reading are common to practically all reading situations. For example:

1. A thoughtful reading attitude and the anticipation of the sequence of ideas in sentences and paragraphs.

2. Accuracy in recognizing words and groups of words, rapid rate and wide span of recognition, rhythmical progress of perceptions from left to right along the lines, and accurate return sweeps from the end of one line to the beginning of the next.

3. The recognition and interpretation of typographical devices, such as punctuation, paragraphing, indentation, italics, marginal or paragraph headings, references to footnotes or the appendix.

4. Conformity to hygienic requirements for reading, such as securing good lighting conditions, holding books to facilitate ease in recognition, assuming and sustaining desirable sitting or standing positions while reading.

2. Attitudes and Habits Involved in Comprehension and Interpretation

Accurate comprehension and interpretation involve the clear recognition of the meanings of words and of groups of words, and an understanding of the thought, sentiments, and ideals expressed. They

---

[1] Throughout this chapter generous use has been made of statements appearing in Chapter III of the *Report of the National Committee on Reading*, 1925.

presuppose keen interest in what is read and strong impelling motives for reading. A large number of habits and skills are involved in comprehension and interpretation, and these should be considered in connection with three types of reading situations:

a. *General Cursory Reading.* In the case of general cursory reading, the following are involved:

1. Concentrating attention on the content.
2. Associating meanings and symbols.
3. Deriving meanings for context and pictures.
4. Anticipating ideas or thought units in sequence.
5. Assigning to each word or phrase its appropriate meaning in the sentence.
6. Fusing related ideas into thought units.
7. Classifying and organizing facts.
8. Recognizing the essential or important meanings.
9. Interpreting the facts presented in the light of related experiences.
10. Forming, verifying, and revising judgments on the basis of the facts presented.
11. Remembering important items of meaning.
12. Discovering new problems or centers of interest.

b. *Study Situations.* Because of the close relation between reading and study, the various attitudes and habits involved in comprehension and interpretation in general cursory reading function also in most study situations. To these should be added still others, such as:

1. Finding likenesses and differences in the facts presented.
2. Selecting facts for a particular purpose.
3. Distinguishing between fact and opinion.
4. Determining the cause of known conditions; discovering facts resulting from certain factors.
5. Generalizing on the basis of evidence obtained.
6. Judging the worth of facts presented.
7. Classifying and organizing items of information secured through reading.

Experiments show clearly that pupils who have not acquired efficient study habits may be aided in doing so if strong incentives and purposes are aroused and appropriate guidance is provided.

c. *Reading for Appreciation.* Obviously, appreciation depends to a large extent upon accurate comprehension and interpretation of content. Furthermore, many of the habits and skills listed in connection with study situations function here also. Attitudes and appreciations result, however, from learning activities in which emotional reactions are a dominant factor. This element of feeling involves additional attitudes and habits, such as:

1. Entering into the reading in a sympathetic mood.
2. Identifying oneself imaginatively with characters and loyalties.
3. Participating emotionally in social situations, moods, or events set forth in the material read.
4. Identifying oneself with the author's techniques — word pictures, plot, cumulative effects, and so forth.

The purpose of one's reading determines to some degree the processes involved in comprehension and interpretation. For example, analysis, selection, and judgment are very prominent when one is reading to discover important points and supporting details or to find passages related to a given problem; association and organization are essential when reading to grasp the author's organization or to supplement or validate previous experience; critical evaluation is important when appraising the worth, relevancy, or consistency of statements, and when weighing the validity of the evidence presented; association, organization, and retention are prominent in reading to reproduce or to make specific use of the facts apprehended; and emotional responses to the events and situations presented are prominent when one is reading to develop appreciation or literary taste.

3. Effective Oral Reading

Effective oral reading presupposes a thorough mastery of the fundamental habits of recognition, accuracy of pronunciation and enunciation, and efficiency in comprehension and interpretation. It also includes a variety of important attitudes, habits, and skills, of which the following are typical:

1. A definite motive for reading to others.
2. A sense of the importance of the message.
3. Sympathetic regard for the listener.
4. A clear understanding of the meaning and purpose of the selection.
5. Clear oral presentation of thought relationships.
6. Adjustment to, and the expression of, changes in character and mood presented in the subject matter.
7. Vocal adjustment to the rhythm of poetry.
8. Appropriate facial expression, subordinated to the thought of the selection and indicative of the reader's understanding and appreciation.

9. Controlled bodily movement and breathing.

10. Confidence in one's own ability; freedom from tension; naturalness and sincerity; and convincing speech and manner.

The foregoing attributes of effective oral reading suggest interesting instructional problems. Each must be attacked systematically in stimulating reading situations if desirable results are to be attained. Appropriate attitudes on the part of the listening group should also be cultivated; for example, thoughtful attention to the materials presented and responsiveness.

4. Intelligent Use of Books, Libraries, and Sources of Information

One of the important obligations of the school is to provide training in the intelligent and skillful use of various types of printed material. The outline that follows suggests essential attitudes, habits, and skills that the reading period may help to develop.

1. In the use of books and sources of information
    Opening books, turning pages with care, and finding pages accurately
    Skillful use of preface, index, table of contents, pictures, chapter and
        paragraph headings, keys, tables, graphs, glossary, appendix
    Effective use of the dictionary
        in finding words
        in deriving pronunciations
        in selecting appropriate meanings for words
    Skillful use of other sources of information
        in finding references quickly
        in selecting relevant items of information
        in evaluating the material found
        in selecting parts for future use
        in organizing data secured from various sources
2. In the use of libraries
    Effective use of library privileges and aids
    Techniques of withdrawing and returning books

In addition, it is necessary to train pupils to ascertain the reliability of printed material and to prejudge and select books intelligently for specific purposes. Some of the points that must be considered in this connection are the date of publication, the position or reputation of the author, the nature of the evidence presented, and the character of the author's interpretations. Through wide contacts with reference materials, pupils should acquire an interest in such facilities and the habit of using them independently. It is obvious that little more than a beginning can be made during reading periods to develop the attitudes and habits involved in the efficient use of various types of printed material. Additional instruction in the library and in connection with the various subjects of the curriculum is essential.

The foregoing analysis of basic reading attitudes, habits, and skills is by no means complete. It is sufficiently detailed, however, to suggest the general character and the broad scope of the problems that teachers face. In providing needed guidance, an essential requisite is material highly charged with interest and of appropriate difficulty. A clear understanding of appropriate methods of promoting desirable types of growth is also needed. In this connection, teachers should know which habits and skills have been thoroughly mastered, which require additional practice and refinement, and which are new and in need of special emphasis. Of major importance is the adaptation of the guidance provided to the general stage of development of the learners and to their varying interests, abilities, achievements, and needs. Through carefully planned programs based on interesting, purposeful, and challenging reading activities, rapid progress can be made in improving the reading efficiency of most pupils.

III. FACTORS UNDERLYING THE ORGANIZATION OF BASIC INSTRUCTION IN READING

In order to insure the continuous and orderly development of essential attitudes and habits, the program of activities should be sequential and carefully organized. This requires, first, a clear recognition of the broad divisions into which a reading program may be divided, and second, a knowledge of the specific facts and relations that determine the sequence of teaching activities from day to day. At least three types of information were considered in developing the basic reading program that is outlined in subsequent sections of this chapter; namely, significant facts about child life that suggest the nature of the reading activities appropriate at different levels of development; studies of the progress of children in basic reading habits; and the levels of achievement in reading needed to meet current curricular demands.

1. Facts Relating to Child Development

During recent years curriculum-makers have given increased attention to child growth and development,[1] and to the factors that con-

---

[1] *Growth and Development: The Basis for Educational Programs.* (Progressive Education Association: 310 W. 90th Street, New York, 1936)

dition learning and insure maximal educational growth. Because the traditional types of subject matter and teaching procedures had little or no relation to child activities and needs, they have broken down under the increasing emphasis placed upon the changes involved in child development — physical, mental, emotional, and social. Facts pertaining to child growth now form the body of much of the basic literature of the modern curriculum and methods of teaching. Research in these fields reveals significant correspondence between a child's stage of development and the success with which certain types of subject matter and different kinds of method can be employed. To organize units of learning opportunely is, therefore, a challenging aim of the curriculum-maker. To fit content and method to the enlarged experiences and expanding interests of pupils means increased economy and efficiency in learning.

In the field of reading, studies of the mental, physical, and emotional aspects of child development have given rise to the concept of reading readiness,[1] including adequate preparation for increased achievement at successive stages of development. Available evidence shows that the time at which desirable attainments in reading may be secured most readily depends upon the mental, emotional, and physical maturity of the child as well as upon the methods and materials used in teaching. Too early introduction to reading or the use of over-mature reading material at any stage of progress promises failure and disappointment to the child who is mentally or experientially unprepared. Because children mature at different rates, individual differences must be recognized in initiating the child to reading, in providing later reading experiences that will be vital and significant to him, and in adapting methods and techniques of teaching.

The interests and motives of children are also of considerable importance in determining reading activities at successive levels of progress. Such trends and shifts in interest have been widely studied.[2]

---

[1] Emmett Albert Betts. *The Prevention and Correction of Reading Difficulties.* (Row, Peterson and Company: Evanston, Illinois, 1936, 402 pp.)

M. Lucile Harrison. *Reading Readiness.* (Houghton Mifflin Company: Boston, 1936, 166 pp.)

[2] Percival Symonds. "Life problems and interests of adolescents," *School Review,* 44: September, 1936, 506–518.

C. A. Pollock. "Children's interest as a basis for what to teach in general science," *Educational Research Bulletin,* Ohio State University, 3: January 9, 1924, 3–6.

(*Continued p. 73*)

Scientific studies as well as careful observation of children's self-directed activities show that certain interests are more or less common to successive age- or grade-levels. Thus, the primary child is usually interested in home, school, play, playmates, toys, and pets. During the period from seven to ten the child's interests tend to center around animals, children in other lands, travel, fairies, inventions, and hobbies. During the next two or three years his interests usually shift to adventure, mystery, exploration, heroism, mechanics, aircraft, and the like. These interests in turn give way later to those relating to history, science, biography, vocations, romance.

Although changes in patterns of interest are discernible throughout the grades, there is far less uniformity in their development than was formerly believed.[1] Differences in the interests of boys and girls at any given chronological age are frequently as marked as are differences in height or weight. Such factors as rate of physical and mental development, sex, emotional endowment and temperament, environment, and social and economic status accentuate differences in interests and influence the rate of their development. Studies of a child's interests, as revealed by conversation, questions, objects brought to school, and playground activities, should furnish the teacher of reading with a basis for motivation and for selecting content in harmony with his needs and desires. To the extent that wholesome attitudes can be maintained in reading activities, progress is more rapid and specific attainments are more permanent.

2. Growth in Basic Reading Habits

The nature of basic instruction in reading is determined not only by the general maturity and interests of children but also by the progress they have made in reading. Because the records of growth in fundamental habits of reading that are now available are based on the results of instruction as it has been given in the past, it follows that any conclusions drawn from them concerning phases of reading that

---

A. M. Jordan. *Children's Interests in Reading.* Contributions to Education, No. 107. (Teachers College, Columbia University: New York, 1921)

Arthur I. Gates. *Interest and Ability in Reading.* Chapter III. (The Macmillan Company: New York, 1930)

[1] A. T. Jersild, F. V. Markey, and C. L. Jersild. *Children's Fears, Dreams, Wishes, Daydreams, Likes, Dislikes, Pleasant and Unpleasant Memories.* (Bureau of Publications, Teachers College, Columbia University: New York, 1933)

F. V. Markey. *Imaginative Behavior of Preschool Children.* (Bureau of Publications, Teachers College, Columbia University: New York, 1935)

should be emphasized at different grade levels must be tentative and subject to revision from time to time. However, the general trends illustrated by the average achievement of large groups of children in various sections of the country merit careful consideration. Space will permit the presentation of only a few examples.

1. Ability to interpret simple passages accurately increases rapidly in the early grades and may reach a high level of efficiency by the end of the third grade.

2. Ability to interpret passages of increasing difficulty and to read for different purposes increases steadily throughout the grades, high school, and college.

3. Speed of silent reading increases rapidly throughout the first four grades and continues to improve steadily but somewhat less rapidly during the middle and upper grades.

4. Progress in speed and accuracy of oral reading is very rapid in the primary grades and gradual but far less rapid in the upper grades. By the end of the third grade good readers have acquired four-fifths of the ability of college students, as measured by the Standardized Oral Reading Paragraphs.

5. Progress in the fundamental habits of recognition, including rate, span, and the rhythmical progress of perceptions, is very rapid in the first four grades and relatively slow and somewhat irregular in the higher grades.[1]

The detailed records on which the foregoing statements are based reveal three general facts of significance: first, pupils pass through various stages of development on their way to mature reading habits; second, the rate of progress varies widely among individuals; and, third, the progress made at a given grade level varies definitely with such factors as the learner's general stage of development, his interest in reading, his attainments in reading, his ability to learn, and the amount of incentive and guidance afforded by his total environment.

3. Desirable Levels of Achievement in Reading

Since pupils advance in reading at different rates, questions arise concerning the levels of achievement that should be expected in the various grades. In this Yearbook the minimal standards set up are those that enable pupils to engage with reasonable efficiency in the reading activities required in the various curricular fields of the grades

---

[1] Guy T. Buswell. *Fundamental Reading Habits: A Study of Their Development.* Chapter II. Supplementary Educational Monographs, No. 21. (Department of Education, University of Chicago: Chicago, 1922)

in question. These, of course, should be commensurate with the general stage of development attained by the children and should, therefore, take into account individual differences. If the pupils in a given classroom do not exhibit the levels of progress in reading normally attained by pupils of their respective grades, at least two steps should be taken: first, reading materials should be selected for them that can be read with reasonable ease and understanding; and second, carefully planned guidance based upon their needs should be provided until they have made up their deficiences.

Unfortunately, the evidence on which desirable standards of achievement in reading can be based is limited. The facts available, however, justify the following tentative conclusions:

1. Readiness to engage in simple reading activities should be attained at or near the beginning of the first grade by a large majority of pupils who are six or more years old.

2. Ability to read very simple informational and story material with keen interest and understanding by the end of the first grade is very important, in view of the recent efforts to enrich and vitalize the curriculum of the early grades.

3. Studies of reading in relation to the achievement of pupils in various curricular fields indicate that a grade score in silent reading of 4.0 [1] or better by the beginning of the fourth grade is essential to satisfactory achievement during the middle grades.[2]

4. Unpublished studies made in various schools show clearly that a grade score in silent reading of 7.0 or better is essential if pupils are able to engage successfully in the reading activities normally required at the junior-high-school level.

5. Recent analyses of the difficulty of books usually read by senior-high-school and college students show that much greater maturity in reading habits than was suggested in 4 above is essential if students at this level are to comprehend and interpret successfully what they read.[3]

6. The same studies show that the general recreational reading of a large majority of adults requires a level of reading efficiency little, if any, higher than that prescribed for junior-high-school pupils.

---

[1] By grade score of 4.0 is meant the average score on a standardized silent-reading test made by pupils who are just beginning fourth-grade work.

[2] Dorris May Lee. *The Importance of Reading for Achieving in Grades Four, Five, and Six.* Contributions to Education, No. 556. (Bureau of Publications, Teachers College, Columbia University: New York, 1933. 64 pp.)

[3] William S. Gray and Bernice E. Leary. *What Makes a Book Readable.* (University of Chicago Press: Chicago, 1935. 358 pp.)

IV. The Basic Reading Program

1. Five Important Stages of Development in Reading

In harmony with the facts presented in the preceding sections, the basic reading program recommended in this Yearbook is organized in terms of five broad stages of development in reading. They will be characterized briefly at this point; detailed statements of the purpose and organization of instruction and the desirable types of achievement for each stage will be presented in later sections of the chapter.

1. *The stage at which readiness for reading is attained.* This stage usually comprises the pre-school years, the kindergarten, and often the early part of the first grade. The chief purpose of the guidance recommended is to provide the experiences and training that promote reading readiness. In addition, steps should be taken to overcome physical and emotional deficiencies that might interfere with progress.

2. *The initial stage in learning to read.* For pupils who advance normally, this stage usually occurs during the first grade. Among other attainments, pupils acquire keen interest in learning to read and a thoughtful reading attitude. They learn to engage in continuous meaningful reading, read simple interesting material with keen interest and absorption in the content, and begin to read independently.

3. *The stage of rapid progress in fundamental reading attitudes and habits.* This stage of development occurs usually during the second and third grades. It is characterized by rapid growth in reading interests and by notable progress in accuracy of comprehension, depth of interpretation, independence in word recognition, fluency in oral reading, and increased speed of silent reading. By the end of this stage of development pupils should read silently more rapidly than orally, and should be able to read with reasonable ease, understanding, and pleasure both informational and literary materials such as are usually assigned early in the fourth grade. To do this efficiently, a grade score of 4.0 in silent reading should be attained.

4. *The stage at which experience is extended rapidly and increased power, efficiency, and excellence in reading are acquired.* The fourth stage of development occurs normally during Grades IV, V, and VI and is characterized by wide reading that extends and enriches the experiences of the reader and broadens his vision. The chief purposes of the guidance provided are to promote greater power in comprehension and interpretation, greater efficiency in rate of reading and in reading for different purposes, improvement in the quality of oral reading, the extension of the pupil's interests, the elevation of reading tastes, and greater skill in the use of books and other printed sources of information. A grade score of 7.0 in silent reading is desirable by the end of this stage of development.

5. *The stage at which reading interests, habits, and tastes are refined.* The fifth stage of development occurs as a rule during the junior-high-school, senior-high-school, and junior-college periods. The chief purposes of guidance in reading during these years are to promote the further development and refinement of the attitudes and habits involved in various types of reading, to broaden interests and elevate tastes in reading, to develop increased efficiency in the use of books, libraries, and sources of information, and to secure a high level of efficiency in all study activities that involve reading.

The foregoing outline is intended as a general guide in defining important aims and attainments and in determining the sequence of activities essential in an adequate reading program. In organizing specific recommendations for each stage an effort will be made to develop a flexible program readily adaptable to widely varying conditions.

2. Adjusting the Reading Program to Individuals

Studies of the achievements of pupils in reading show that they differ widely at each grade level. A striking illustration of this fact is presented in Chapter XI, which is concerned with individual differences. In order to provide adequately for the varying needs of children it is essential that teachers study frequently the attainments and needs of their pupils and organize instruction accordingly at appropriate levels of advancement. This may mean, for example, that in a second-grade class, some pupils may require guidance of the type usually provided for those at the initial stage in learning to read; others may require guidance similar to that usually provided at the second-grade level; and still others may be so advanced that they are able to read easily and with adequate comprehension all materials used by pupils of that grade. Pupils in the latter group should be encouraged to read widely on frequent occasions without the restrictions that group instruction imposes.

Chapter XI discusses at length the methods of determining individual attainments and needs and desirable procedures in grouping pupils for purposes of instruction. In order to avoid duplication, we shall give here only a brief summary of the essential steps in providing adequately for individual differences in reading.

1. Systematic and continuous study of the attainments and needs of pupils through the use of both informal and formal methods. (See Chapters XI and XII.)

2. A flexible scheme of grouping pupils within a grade or classroom that recognizes individual differences and provides for them. (See Chapter XI.)

3. The provision of different kinds of guidance in reading in the same grade

or classroom in harmony with the varying needs of the pupils taught. (The adoption of this procedure should result in greatly reducing the need for so-called ' remedial teaching.')

4. Differentiation in the materials and methods of teaching in order to provide adequately for differences in capacity and rates of learning.

5. The provision of extended periods of work, uninterrupted by failure, whereby pupils may make satisfactory progress from one level of advancement to the next.

6. The exemption of pupils from systematic effort to improve their mastery of basic reading habits as soon as they are able to engage efficiently in all the reading activities essential in meeting the general curricular demands at their respective levels of advancement.

7. The substitution of various aspects of child growth for progress in reading as the basis of promotion from grade to grade.

Small schools, including the one-room rural type, present special problems and at the same time offer unique opportunities for adapting the reading program to individual needs. For example, pupils of similar attainments but in different grades may often engage to advantage in the same reading project. Furthermore, pupils belonging to different grades frequently need similar types of training in overcoming specific difficulties, such as those involved in word recognition. In such cases pupils from two or more different grades may be taught as a group, thus saving the time that would be required in repeating the same instruction for pupils reciting in different grade groups. Owing to the small number of pupils involved, the opportunity for individual instruction is often much greater in small schools than in larger schools.

V. Stage One: Reading Readiness

The Twenty-Fourth Yearbook emphasized the importance of carefully planned guidance that prepares for reading. The value of appropriate experience and training was discussed in the following terms:

The child who becomes interested in reading at any age does so because of previous experiences in the home or at school. For example, he may have looked at pictures in attractive books provided for him. His parents or teachers may have read or told stories to him from these books. They may have encouraged him to find out stories for himself by studying the pictures that illustrate them. He may have discussed these stories with his playmates, thereby gaining facility in the use of ideas, a relatively wide reading vocabulary, and habits of good expression. In these ways, as well as through experiences which do not include books, parents and teachers stimulate interest in reading and provide for the development of habits that are essential to rapid progress. On the other hand, many children who do not have such advantages, and some who do, spend all their time in whatever way fancy directs. Consequently, they are not attracted to reading as a form of activity. When these pupils enter the first grade their preparation for, and attitude toward, reading differ widely from those of children whose activities have been carefully directed.[1]

1. Attainment of Reading Readiness

During the last decade the factors that influence reading readiness and the types of experience and training that prepare for reading have been studied intensively. As a result, our understanding of such problems has been greatly extended and our views concerning their implications modified in several respects. It is now generally agreed that successful reading at all grade levels is conditioned in large measure by the physical, mental, emotional, and social maturity of the learners and by proper adaptation of instruction to their needs. The factors that presumably influence readiness for beginning reading have been identified and treated at length by recent writers.[2] One of them, Harrison, classifies the chief factors under three major categories: (1) intellectual development, including mental age, ability to remember word forms, ability to do abstract thinking; (2) physical development, including general health, vision, hearing; and (3) personal development, including emotional stability and the desirable attitudes and habits needed for adjustment to the school situation.

Less agreement exists as to the means of attaining reading readiness. The view is held by some that readiness for initial instruction in reading is attained best through so-called ' natural processes ' of growth and development. Undoubtedly, many characteristics or qualities develop

---

[1] *Report of the National Committee on Reading.* Twenty-Fourth Yearbook of this Society, Part I. P. 26. (Public School Publishing Company: Bloomington, Illinois, 1925)

[2] Emmett Albert Betts. *The Prevention and Correction of Reading Difficulties.* (Row, Peterson and Company: Evanston, Illinois, 1936. 402 pp.)

M. Lucile Harrison. *Reading Readiness.* (Houghton Mifflin Company: Boston, 1936. 166 pp.)

Arthur I. Gates and Guy L. Bond. "Reading readiness: A study of factors determining success and failure in beginning reading," *Teachers College Record,* 37: May, 1936, 679–685.

Clarence R. Stone. *Better Primary Reading.* (Webster Publishing Company: St. Louis, 1936. 536 pp.)

and mature largely through processes that are little influenced by school training. For example, growth in span of perception and the physical maturity of the eyes are largely matters of sheer growing up. But other functions involved in reading, such as observation, range of vocabulary, and desire to read, may, and generally do, benefit from training and guidance. It follows that a child's preparation for reading may be affected by the training and guidance provided. This view harmonizes with a basic educational principle to the effect that the activity for which a child is ready at any stage in his development depends on what has preceded that stage. Accordingly, the position taken in this Yearbook is that readiness for reading is something that can be developed to a considerable extent through intelligent direction, rather than something merely to wait for.

2. When Appropriate Training Should Be Provided

Many of the experiences that prepare for reading may be acquired by children in good homes before they enter the kindergarten or first grade. The kind of guidance that should be given in the kindergarten presupposes a program of varied activities. The chief purpose of the kindergarten, however, is not to teach children to read, for reading is rarely more than an incidental part of the school program before the first grade. Rather, a major purpose of the kindergarten is to adjust the pupil to an enlarged social environment through activities appropriate to his stage of development. But it is believed that when this purpose has been effectively accomplished, the attitudes and habits that prepare for reading will in large measure have been developed. Unfortunately, many pupils enter the first grade with inadequate preliminary experiences and training. It is necessary in such cases for teachers to determine the pupils' needs and deficiences, and to provide desirable training and necessary corrective treatment. Such procedures are especially important in the cases of children who come from poor economic and cultural environments, or from homes in which a foreign language is spoken, who enter the first grade unusually immature or with no kindergarten experience, and who suffer from poor health or physical disabilities.

3. The Relative Importance of Various Factors of Readiness

In a series of recent investigations, an attempt was made to determine the extent to which many of the factors that presumably influence reading readiness are closely related to success or failure in beginning reading.[1] Among the factors and abilities considered were mental age; brightness (I.Q.) ; naming letters; reading letters; matching or comparing words, nonsense syllables, and geometrical figures; repeating letter sounds or nonsense words; rhyming ability; phonetic aptitude; hearing (as measured by a 2A audiometer) ; various phases of vision (as measured by the Betts' telebinocular tests of vision) ; hand and eye dominance; motor coördination; speech defects; different combinations of these factors (as measured by the pencil and paper readiness tests), and various aspects of pre-school life, such as social-economic status, play and game interests, foreign language contacts. The findings showed that the relation between the factors examined and progress in learning to read differed widely. In some cases the correlations were reasonably high; in other cases they were negligible. Of special importance is the fact that some of the factors for which significant correlations were found " were by no means invariably successful in indicating either the best or the poorest readers." The lesson these facts teach is that reading readiness is not determined uniformly by the presence of certain specific attitudes or attainments; it is rather the result of combinations of factors that differ somewhat in individual cases. The evidence also shows that physiological handicaps, especially sensory, may interfere with progress in reading at any stage of development. It seems safe to conclude, therefore, that constitutional handicaps to reading will not be removed or overcome by mere lapse of time. The remedy lies, in part at least, in the " correction of the difficulties or adjustment to them rather than merely waiting for time to cure them."

4. The Essential Prerequisites to Reading

A careful survey of the results of classroom experience and experimentation justifies the conclusion that reasonable attainments of at least seven specific types are essential to rapid progress in learning to read. It will be impossible here to do more than identify these prerequisites to reading and to suggest briefly appropriate kinds of guidance.[2]

---

[1] Arthur I. Gates and Guy L. Bond. " Reading readiness: A study of factors determining success and failure in beginning reading," *Teachers College Record*, 37: May, 1936, 679–685.

[2] Detailed suggestions concerning a wide variety of desirable steps and activities appear in the following references listed on the next page:

a. Wide Experience. A wealth of vivid experiences relating to the interests of the pupils is of prime importance in preparing them to interpret intelligently what they read. The larger the number of interesting experiences, the broader their background for interpretation. One writer [1] classifies the activities of the kindergarten that provide pupils with essential experiences into five categories: (1) construction activities — making a flower garden, making valentines, making a snow man, making a bird bath; (2) excursions — trips to the creamery, bakery, grocery store; (3) social activities — giving a party, dramatizing manners; (4) other practical activities — churning butter, making jelly, setting a hen and watching the chicks hatch, becoming acquainted with the school building; and (5) games.

C. J. Anderson and I. Davidson. *Reading Objectives.* Chapter III. (Laurel Book Co.: Chicago, 1925)

Emmett Albert Betts. *The Prevention and Correction of Reading Difficulties.* (Row, Peterson and Company: Evanston, Illinois, 1936)

M. Lucile Harrison. *Reading Readiness.* (Houghton Mifflin Company: Boston, 1936)

Patty Hill, and others. *A Conduct Curriculum for the Kindergarten and First Grade.* (Charles Scribner's Sons: New York, 1923)

Paul McKee. *Reading and Literature in the Elementary School.* (Houghton Mifflin Company: Boston, 1934)

Annie E. Moore. *The Primary School.* (Houghton Mifflin Company: Boston, 1925)

Samuel Chester Parker and Alice Temple. *Unified Kindergarten-First Grade Teaching.* (Ginn and Company: Boston, 1925)

Samuel W. Patterson. *Teaching the Child to Read.* Chapter VI. (Doubleday Doran and Co.: New York, 1930)

Mary E. Pennell and Alice M. Cusack. *The Teaching of Reading.* Pp. 147–168. (Houghton Mifflin Company: Boston, 1935)

Marion Paine Stevens, *The Activities Curriculum in the Primary Grades.* (D. C. Heath and Company: Boston, 1931)

Clarence R. Stone. *Better Primary Reading.* Pp. 207–233. (Webster Publishing Company: St. Louis, 1936)

Grace E. Storm and Nila B. Smith. *Reading Activities in the Primary Grades.* Chapter VI. (Ginn and Company: Boston, 1930)

The Classroom Teacher, Volume II, Chapter II. (The Classroom Teacher, Inc.: Chicago, 1927)

The Twenty-Fourth Yearbook, Part I, of this Society. Pp. 26–30. (Public School Publishing Company: Bloomington, Illinois, 1925)

Lula S. Wright. *A First Grade at Work: A Non-Reading Curriculum.* (Bureau of Publications, Teachers College, Columbia University: New York, 1932)

[1] Paul McKee. *Reading and Literature in the Elementary School.* P. 101. (Houghton Mifflin Company: Boston, 1934)

Pupils should be encouraged to discuss such experiences freely and to add rapidly to their stock of ideas.

b. Reasonable Facility in the Use of Ideas. This includes ability in the use of experience in conversation, in solving simple problems, and in thinking clearly about the content of what is read. Opportunities for the use of ideas should grow naturally out of children's experiences. Real problems, such as how to make a rabbit pen, and actual experiences, such as visiting a florist's shop, buying and learning to care for a plant, afford opportunities for good thinking on the part of the pupil. He must recall related experiences, make relevant suggestions, organize ideas, weigh values, and make judgments. Such steps are characteristic of good thinking and promote thoughtful interpretation.

c. Reasonable Command of Simple English Sentences. This attainment not only enables pupils to speak with ease and freedom but also aids them in anticipating the meaning of passages and in reading fluently. Classroom experience shows that children who speak the English language readily and who possess a reasonably wide speaking vocabulary usually tend to read with greater ease and fluency than those who do not. Two general types of training in the use of English have been recognized.[1] Spontaneous expression is probably the most natural and therefore the most desirable medium for the free use of language. Excursions, constructive activities, projects, games and play, all furnish impetus to conversation and free discussion. More highly organized activities provide a second type of opportunity for training in oral expression but should grow from needs revealed in spontaneous conversation. Examples of worthwhile activities include composing invitations and letters, reporting individual or group experiences, planning class dramatization, and telling stories.

d. A Relatively Wide Speaking Vocabulary. This prerequisite for reading is closely related to the three already considered. Rich, varied, and meaningful experiences should increase the child's speaking vocabulary, particularly if they are made the basis of spirited discussions. Similarly, engaging in interesting activities should stimulate growth of vocabulary if the situations involved are new and interesting. A child's vocabulary is further extended through hearing stories told or read by the teacher, and through listening to her instructions and her discussion of matters of common interest. The teacher should consciously use new words within the pupil's comprehension and encourage

---

[1] Grace E. Storm and Nila B. Smith. *Reading Activities in the Primary Grades.* P. 120. (Ginn and Company: Boston, 1930)

him to use them later. Whatever efforts are taken to develop a broad speaking vocabulary must be done systematically. They should aim to acquaint the child with words that are of most value to him; namely, those that are in the speaking vocabulary of children at his stage of development, and those that occur most frequently in early reading.

e. Accuracy in Enunciation and Pronunciation. This attainment insures right habits in speaking and eliminates the need of corrective exercises later in reading. Training in enunciation and pronunciation can be given most effectively, as a rule, through example. Children who come from cultured homes generally exhibit greater precision of speech than do children from homes of limited advantages; indeed the latter often require continuous help if satisfactory progress is made. Teachers should take particular care in speaking to young children in order that imitation may promote correct habits, but artificially precise or forced enunciation should be avoided. Word games, poetry, and rhymes are devices that can be used advantageously both to enrich vocabulary and to reduce or prevent slovenliness in speech.

f. Reasonable Accuracy in Visual and Auditory Discrimination. The fact has long been recognized that ability to observe likenesses and differences in word forms is a good index of readiness for reading. Several tests of reading readiness now include measures of this ability. As a rule, a first-grade pupil has had little or no occasion before entering school to compare the general configuration or details of words. Neither has he, in most cases, been conscious of likenesses and differences in the general sound of words, or of their initial sounds or endings.

Some training in visual discrimination in preparation for reading is very valuable. It may be provided through matching of forms that have meaning to the child and in noting differences in the words used in informal reading. This training later provides a background for attacking difficulties in word recognition. Training in auditory discrimination is valuable also. Such training may include word games to which reference was made earlier; repetition of rhyming words; and the recognition of names that begin or end alike. Whatever training the teacher provides to promote visual and auditory discrimination should have some immediate value in the pupils' program of work.

g. Keen Interest in Learning to Read. Of major importance among the prerequisites of reading is keen interest in learning to read. Interest not only promotes desirable initial attitudes but also insures sustained effort, which is essential in overcoming many difficulties in learning to read. Keen interest in reading develops naturally from experiences that reveal to pupils that reading contributes to their pleasure and satisfaction. Among the devices commonly used by teachers in stimulating interest and curiosity are: (1) calling attention to signs, directions, and notices both in and out of school; (2) reading or telling interesting stories that please or entertain; (3) providing stimulating contacts with picture books; (4) arousing the child's natural curiosity concerning the content of books; (5) making books as a class project; (6) introducing informal reading activities whenever they serve a valuable purpose; (7) making little newspapers or chart references to children's experiences. By the end of the kindergarten period all children of average or superior ability should be keenly interested in learning to read.

Conscious attention at home, in the kindergarten, and often during the early part of the first grade to the types of training that have been listed here promotes growth that makes reading a natural and desirable activity. The omission of appropriate training and corrective measures may result in the undue postponement of the time when guidance in reading may be introduced to advantage.

5. Checking Attainment in Reading Readiness

Throughout the kindergarten and early part of the first grade teachers should study the attainments and needs of pupils to determine the kinds of guidance they require and their readiness to learn to read. Specific methods of measuring the progress and needs of pupils are discussed at length in Chapters XI and XII. It may be appropriate here to comment briefly upon a few related issues.

It has often been assumed that readiness to learn to read represents a highly specific point in a child's development. Consequently, attempts are often made to determine through the use of reading-readiness tests when pupils reach that particular point. The value of such tests is clearly recognized in this discussion. However, the complex nature of the condition known as reading readiness necessitates the study of many factors rather than a few. Furthermore, any effort to measure reading readiness must begin and end by inquiring " Ready to read what? " and " Ready to read how? " These questions must be answered before valid tests can be selected or valid interpretations made of the results. The fact that a pupil is not ready to learn to read one type of material by one method may not indicate the same degree of unreadiness for a different type of material. Unfortunately, available reading tests do not specify the attainments essential for different types or levels of initial instruction in reading.

Cautions are also necessary concerning the interpretations of the results of tests in reading readiness. One very valuable study [1] of the relation between mental age and progress in learning to read led to the conclusion that, " by postponing the teaching of reading until children reach a mental age of six and a half years, teachers can greatly decrease the chances of failure and discouragement and can correspondingly increase their efficiency." In interpreting the results of this study it must be remembered that in it specific standards for satisfactory progress were adopted. A mental age of six and a half may be the optimal age for beginning reading according to the standards adopted. It does not follow, however, that this age is equally valid in schools that use different materials and methods and that adopt radically different standards of achievement.

With the foregoing reservations in mind, mental tests and reading readiness tests have a very definite place in determining the extent to which children are prepared for early reading activities. The findings should be supplemented through systematic observations of attainments and needs with respect to the seven prerequisites for reading referred to above. Furthermore, health records and measurements of vision and hearing are very important. If pupils are discovered whose general health is poor or who exhibit defects in vision and hearing, they should receive attention from the home or school physician or from eye and ear specialists.

VI. Stage Two: Initial Guidance in Learning to Read

As soon as pupils are adequately prepared for reading, they should be given initial guidance in learning to read. The chief aims of the instruction provided are to stimulate keen interest in reading, to cultivate a thoughtful reading attitude, and to establish the habits involved in reading simple material, both orally and silently, with ease and understanding. Two important goals have been attained when pupils begin to read easy books independently with evident interest and absorption. Before discussing in detail appropriate methods and procedures, three controversial issues relating to this stage of development will be considered.

---

[1] Mabel V. Morphett and Carleton Washburne. " When should children begin to read?" *The Elementary School Journal*, 29: March, 1931, pp. 496–503.

1. When Initial Instruction Should Begin

As indicated earlier, the time at which basic instruction in reading should begin varies with the capacity of children to learn, with their general stage of development, and with the nature of the early reading activities that are required. Since the kindergarten contributes so much to the extension and enrichment of first-hand experience, systematic training in reading should rarely be provided before pupils enter the first grade. However, pupils of superior intelligence who have made rapid progress in practically all kindergarten activities and who express a very strong desire to learn to read may engage in informal reading activities during the last few months of the kindergarten period. These activities should grow out of, and be intimately related to, the various enterprises in which the children engage with keen interest. The foregoing statements should not be interpreted as justifying the systematic and indiscriminate teaching of reading in kindergartens in which some communities engage.

Experience teaches that a majority of pupils, particularly those who have attended good kindergartens, are reasonably well prepared for basic instruction in reading when assigned to the first grade. On the other hand, many pupils who enter school are more or less handicapped because they are mentally retarded, cannot speak the English language readily, or are seriously deficient in some of the other requisites for reading. It is essential, therefore, that each school study the needs of its pupils carefully and provide preparatory training and experience in harmony with their attainments and needs.

Some teachers and school officers, however, object for both physiological and psychological reasons to the introduction of basic instruction in reading for any pupils until they are well advanced in the first grade or have entered the second. These teachers believe that many injurious results, such as increased myopia and general impairment of vision, dislike for reading, the development of fear complexes, and the adoption of poor habits that must be corrected later follow the early introduction of reading.

In the judgment of the Yearbook Committee, reading has a legitimate place in the program of activities for first-grade pupils. The members of the Committee believe that reading is not only a very desirable activity at this level of advancement but is also an essential means of attaining the objectives of an enriched curriculum. They recognize, however, that the general mental and physical development of many children, and their specific attainments and needs, are such that additional experience and training are desirable before much systematic training in reading is desirable. In such cases a carefully planned program of activities similar to those outlined in the preceding section is recommended. In addition, informal reading activities of a very simple type may be introduced relatively early. A distinct advantage of such activities is that they stimulate favorable attitudes toward reading and enable children to enjoy early some of the pleasures that simple reading affords. Furthermore, they provide motives for many of the experiences and types of training essential in promoting greater readiness for reading.

2. Relation of Reading to Other School Activities

Experience has clearly shown that children should learn to read in an environment that stimulates interest and provides continuous opportunity to engage in thoughtful reading. Such stimulus may be provided by announcements on the bulletin board, titles of pictures on the wall, picture and story books on the reading table, and daily schedules of events that appear on the blackboard. Informal reading activities carried on in all curricular fields also motivate reading and provide valuable practice. When pupils can read simple informational material relating to the problems studied in the various fields, the opportunities for reading become greatly enlarged. The story hour and dramatization period also provide continuous opportunity for informal but carefully directed reading activities.

Wide differences exist in both theory and practice concerning the time or occasion for specific guidance in learning to read. Some teachers believe that strong purposes for reading can be provided best in connection with large units, activities, or projects that are pursued in specific fields, such as the social studies or science. Consequently they select reading materials and provide incentives for reading that enable individuals and groups to gather information and solve problems in connection with a vital unit of work. In such a procedure there is need, of course, for developing fundamental reading habits just as in any other approach. The chief issue is whether basic instruction in reading shall be given in a series of purposeful activities provided during the reading period or as a part of a more inclusive program of experiences. While the fact is recognized that progress in learning to read can be secured in either way, the Committee recommends that a reading period be provided in which the development of basic attitudes and habits in reading may be made the object of specific attention.

In the type of program recommended in this Yearbook, the reading period supplements opportunity for much reading in connection with vital units of work by providing a sequence of equally interesting, challenging, and purposeful activities designed to promote rapid growth in learning to read. By utilizing every phase of the school's program for incidental, basic, and correlated reading, children learn to engage earlier and with greater efficiency in the various opportunities for reading that the classroom provides. Such a program also reveals to pupils in convincing ways the fact that reading is a convenient, useful means of extending experience and satisfying interests both in and out of school.

3. Materials and Methods of Beginning Reading

Closely associated with the foregoing issue are questions relating to the materials and methods of beginning reading. Teachers are in general agreement that the early activities provided should introduce pupils to reading as a thought-getting process. Some believe that this end can be best achieved through the so-called ' experience-activity ' approach; others definitely prefer the use of commercially prepared materials.

The experience-activity approach relates beginning reading to the group and individual experiences of the pupils. Teacher and pupils co-operate in planning projects and in composing reading lessons for the blackboard or chart. One writer [1] emphasizes, among others, the following functions and values of this approach to reading:

> An important means of developing a correct and adequate concept of reading as a meaningful process closely related to life activities.
>
> An aid in fostering an attitude of thought-getting rather than mere word recognition and pronunciation.
>
> A means of arousing, maintaining, and increasing the child's desire to learn to read.
>
> An excellent means of integrating a project, oral and written composition, and reading.

Concerning the limitations of this approach, the same writer,[2] points out that the extensive vocabulary that is necessary permits little time

---

[1] Clarence R. Stone. *Better Primary Reading.* P. 198. (Webster Publishing Company: St. Louis, 1936)

[2] Clarence R. Stone. " The current-experience method in beginning reading," *Elementary School Journal,* 36: October, 1935, 105–109.

for needed repetition, and hence fosters memory reading. The fact is also emphasized that the content is often too difficult and the vocabulary too extensive for successful results excepting with those children who would learn to read by any method. Another limitation lies in what is frequently recognized as its chief merit; namely, the restriction of content to immediate activities and experiences. To what extent such restriction makes reading more or less enjoyable or profitable is a problem meriting further study. Some argue that the child finds greater interest in content that is outside the realm of his immediate everyday activities. Questions are raised, too, concerning the quality of the reading material that teachers prepare. It is asserted, for example, that " the average teacher does not have the technological knowledge, the resourcefulness, and the time required to produce the materials needed." It is hardly necessary to say that efficient teachers endeavor to avoid the dangers and limitations to which reference has been made.

The approach to reading through materials carefully prepared for general use also has definite limitations and advantages. One of its chief limitations lies in the fact that the activities prescribed often do not relate to the immediate interests of the children. This can be overcome in part, at least, by using only materials that are interesting or relevant. In other cases, preparatory steps may be introduced that will provide a desirable background. A second limitation emphasized by advocates of the experience-activity approach is that the use of prepared materials precludes the possibility of planning by the pupil, thus reducing the opportunity for adequate understanding and growth. A third danger lies in the fact that the teaching of reading through the use of prepared materials often becomes a routine, formal procedure. Unfortunately, teaching in far too many classrooms remains on a formal basis no matter what general type of procedure is adopted.

The following advantages of materials prepared for general use should be mentioned. When based on the *common* interests of children, the early steps in learning to read may be very interesting, purposeful, and challenging. If properly planned, they extend and enrich the experiences of pupils. If intelligently used, they provide abundant opportunity for planning on the part of pupils in connection with the interpretation and use of the ideas presented. Furthermore, prepared materials are, as a rule, more skillfully organized and are technically superior to those developed daily in the classroom. Because they follow a sequential plan, the chance for so-called ' gaps in learning ' is greatly reduced.

The Yearbook Committee recognizes that each of the foregoing approaches has its advantages and limitations. It recommends that the total program of activities provided should utilize the advantages of both procedures. At times reading materials based upon experience should be employed in order to gain as full benefit as possible from the values that attach to the use of immediate interests, pupil planning, and symbols with which vivid meanings may be associated. To an increasing extent, however, as pupils learn to read, use should be made of books the content of which is sequential, that are skillfully prepared with respect to word frequency and distribution, and that provide opportunity for varying amounts of practice in harmony with individual needs.

4. Successive Goals in Learning to Read

In former decades it was customary to define the aims and activities of early instruction in reading in terms of time units — the year or term. More recently the tendency has been to define them in terms of the periods in which certain materials are used — blackboard, chart, and preprimer materials, primers, first readers. In harmony with the recent emphasis given to child growth and development, it seems more valid to direct attention to successive goals in achieving the aims of early instruction in reading. Three such goals have been identified and are used as guides in organizing and evaluating the methods and techniques used in attaining them.

a. Ability to read with keen interest and understanding simple records of experience and simple printed booklets of the preprimer type. The time devoted to the attainment of this goal is often called the ' pre-book ' or ' preprimer ' period. Specific aims of the period are:

(1) To stimulate interest in informal reading activities and in looking at pictures in books independently.

(2) To cultivate a thoughtful reading attitude.

(3) To develop a small sight vocabulary, the number of words varying with the materials used, and the habit of recognizing them quickly and accurately in thought units.

(4) To develop good habits of recognizing and interpreting simple sentence units in both silent and oral reading.

(5) To develop ability to follow directions for seat work and to engage in

other activities that apply ideas secured through the simple reading activities provided.

(6) To cultivate social attitudes desirable in a reading group.

(7) To develop proper habits in the care and use of books.

In attaining these aims, the following suggestions merit careful consideration. First, early instruction in reading should be very informal and closely related to the immediate interests and activities of the pupils. This implies that the occasion and basis of the instruction given often differ for the various members of a group.

Second, the development of keen interest in reading and favorable attitudes toward it are quite as important at this stage of development as is the mastery of the fundamental habits involved in word recognition. Accordingly, teachers should study deliberately the varying interests and needs of their pupils and make use of materials and methods that will insure pleasurable contacts with reading and heighten interest in learning to read.

Third, in order that pupils may grow in ability to engage in reading activities independently, they should acquire a sight vocabulary of words of high frequency in simple reading material. To this end pupils should have daily contact under the direction of the teacher with carefully prepared materials based on common interests and characterized by abundant repetition of very useful words. As implied by the foregoing statement, the chief means of vocabulary development at this stage of progress is abundant contact with words in simple materials that are highly charged with interest.

Fourth, the progress of pupils in the attainment of the foregoing aims varies widely with their previous attainments and capacity. The fact cannot be overemphasized that children should not be urged forward unduly at this stage. Those who learn easily should be permitted to advance in accordance with their capacity; those who learn slowly should be allowed additional time. The interests and needs of such pupils should be studied carefully and whatever guidance and corrective measures are necessary to insure growth should be provided according to capacity and stage of development.[1]

---

[1] Because of the limitations of space it will be impossible to discuss at greater length the numerous problems encountered in promoting desirable types of growth. Attention is therefore directed to the following references for guidance:

Arthur I. Gates. *New Methods in Primary Reading*. Chapter XII. (Bureau of Publications, Teachers College, Columbia University: New York, 1928)

Desirable outcomes of instruction during the pre-book stage may be defined in terms of pupil activity as follows:

(1) Is vitally interested in posters, signs, notices, bulletins, and written instructions, and manifests curiosity about them.

(2) Has some appreciation of the value of reading for information and for fun.

(3) Shows eager interest in books, and enjoys illustrations.

(4) Assimilates the content read as indicated by reaction to such items as elements of surprise, humor, and conversation.

(5) Reads simple sentences silently before reading them aloud.

(6) Carries out unaided directions from blackboard, chart, or workbook.

(7) Reproduces in sequence main incidents of the stories that he hears.

(8) Handles books with care.

(9) Manifests good habits in reading from left to right.

(10) Coöperates with the group and contributes to the progress of its members.

The amount of time required to attain these standards varies from three to eight weeks or more, depending upon the capacity and previous attainments of the pupils, the skill of the teacher, the adequacy of the materials used, and the degree of emphasis given to reading in the various activities of the school day. Not infrequently pupils enter the first grade who are adequately prepared to read from books without preliminary training.

b. Ability to engage in continuous meaningful reading from simple books (such as those of primer difficulty). As soon as pupils have acquired interest in reading and a vocabulary adequate for the materials to be used, they should learn to read for meaning with reasonable fluency from simple books. Among the various aims that should be emphasized in attaining this goal, the following are important:

(1) To stimulate an increasing interest in reading and a desire to read well.

(2) To cultivate spontaneous interest in the content read.

Paul McKee. *Reading and Literature in the Elementary School.* Pp. 138–170. (Houghton Mifflin Company: Boston, 1934)

Samuel W. Patterson. *Teaching the Child to Read.* Chapter VII. (Doubleday, Doran and Company: Garden City, New York, 1930)

Mary E. Pennell and Alice M. Cusack. *The Teaching of Reading for Better Living.* Pp. 174–200. (Houghton Mifflin Company: Boston, 1935)

Clarence R. Stone. *Better Primary Reading.* Pp. 233–272. (Webster Publishing Company: St. Louis, 1936)

Grace E. Storm and Nila B. Smith. *Reading Activities in the Primary Grades.* Pp. 148–171. (Ginn and Company: Boston, 1930)

(3) To train in anticipating the meanings of words and in securing meaning from the context in silent reading.

(4) To increase the sight vocabulary and ability to use context clues in recognizing words.

(5) To assist pupils to observe the important or most useful characteristics of word forms.

(6) To read orally with ease.

(7) To develop care in the use of books and ability to locate pages quickly.

(8) To promote the development of left-to-right movements of the eyes in reading.

The attainment of these aims presents a variety of teaching problems of which the following are typical: creating keen interest in reading from books; training pupils to open books and to turn pages carefully; acquainting them with the parts of the book used, such as its title, content, pictures, familiar stories, if any, and page numbers; training pupils to follow lines accurately from left to right and to make the return sweep from the end of one line to the beginning of the next; teaching them to study pictures as an aid in interpreting the story; directing their attention to distinguishing features of words, to similarities and differences in familiar words, and to frequently recurring elements of words; stimulating growth in anticipating meaning and in recognizing new words from the context; aiding in the enlargement of their recognitive vocabularies; training pupils to read short units with attention centered upon the content; and promoting growth in habits of continuous, fluent, meaningful reading.[1]

---

[1] Appropriate methods and techniques in promoting desirable types of growth are discussed helpfully in the following references:

Arthur I. Gates. *Interest and Effort in Reading.* Part II. (The Macmillan Company: New York, 1931)

Arthur S. Gist and William A. King. *The Teaching and Supervision of Reading.* See Index. (Charles Scribner's Sons: New York, 1927. 337 pp.)

Julia M. Harris, H. T. Donovan, and Thomas Alexander. *Supervision and Teaching of Reading.* See Index. (Johnson Publishing Company: Richmond, Virginia, 1927)

Paul McKee. *Reading and Literature in the Elementary School.* Pp. 170–225. (Houghton Mifflin Company: Boston, 1934)

Mary E. Pennell and Alice M. Cusack. *The Teaching of Reading for Better Living.* Pp. 201–230. (Houghton Mifflin Company: Boston, 1935)

Clarence R. Stone. *Better Primary Reading.* Chapter VII. (Webster Publishing Company: St. Louis, 1936)

Grace E. Storm and Nila B. Smith. *Reading Activities in the Primary Grades.* Pp. 172–177. (Ginn and Company: Boston, 1930)

While pupils are learning to read from books a large amount of incidental reading, based upon their immediate experiences and activities, should be provided. If possible, reading material should be presented not only on the blackboard, but also in mimeographed or printed form, since such material stimulates added interest, provides highly motivated learning situations, and insures frequent opportunity to associate meanings with symbols. Furthermore, effort should be made during the story hour and dramatization period to deepen interests in reading and to broaden the child's background for interpretation and appreciation. In addition, attractive material, appropriate for each group in the room, should be placed on the reading table, which becomes a center of increasing interest during this period.

A pupil's attainments while learning to read from books of primer difficulty may be judged in terms of the following desirable standards:

(1) Reads voluntarily in various classroom activities.

(2) Gives evidence of a growing interest in books by going to the library or reading table to look at pictures or to read.

(3) Is able to read simple stories (of primer difficulty) continuously with attention directed to the content.

(4) Understands and enjoys the plots of the stories read in class.

(5) Discusses freely what is read, asks questions about the content, and shows ability in making deductions.

(6) Prefers to read rather than merely to look at pictures.

(7) Recognizes readily most of the sight words taught.

(8) Shows definite progress in recognizing new words through simple forms of analysis.

(9) Reads aloud with good phrasing, inflection, and stress.

(10) Knows how to care for books properly, opening them and turning pages carefully, and using the table of contents and page numbers in finding stories.

The time required to attain these standards varies widely. Some children make very rapid progress and require a relatively small amount of guidance and practice to attain them; others need extended practice and much help. As in the case of the previous period, pupils should not be forced to engage in more advanced types of reading until they have attained considerable fluency in reading very simple material. In general, from twelve to twenty weeks are required to make the necessary progress through this stage.

c. Ability to read books (of average first-reader difficulty) with keen interest and absorption in content, and growth of interest in read-

ing independently. As soon as pupils have learned to engage in continuous meaningful reading from books, it is possible to provide a broader and more varied reading program. Two important goals to be attained are ability on the part of pupils to read simple material with evident interest and absorption in the content, and the desire to read books independently. Supplementary aims at this stage of development are:

(1) To provide broad opportunities for reading.

(2) To introduce pupils to different kinds of reading material, such as story, informational, and study types.

(3) To provide guidance in reading for different purposes, such as to enjoy a story or to find the answers to questions.

(4) To stimulate habits of good thinking while reading.

(5) To develop increased independence in the recognition of new words.

(6) To increase fluency in both oral and silent reading.

(7) To improve the quality of oral reading.

Basic instruction in reading should be so organized as to promote rapid growth in achieving the foregoing aims. It is not sufficient at this stage of development merely to provide pupils with opportunities to read. Systematic guidance is essential to insure the development of appropriate reading attitudes and habits, to eliminate undesirable ones, and to provide for those pupils who encounter difficulties in learning to read. Pupils who advance slowly will need much attention during regular reading periods. Those who advance rapidly may often be excused from directed activities and be permitted to engage in independent reading. A list of desirable types of reading activities follow:

(1) Silent and oral reading, based on group projects, stories, and informational selections, to insure growth in recognition and intelligent interpretation.

(2) Directed silent reading for information and pleasure to establish habits of continuous, intelligent reading and study.

(3) Motivated oral reading following silent preparation to develop ability to recognize increasingly larger units at each fixation and to read effectively to others.

(4) Participation in dramatization to aid in mastering the thought of a selection and in realizing experience more fully, and to provide opportunity to give to others one's own interpretation of the meaning of a selection.

(5) Specific exercises to promote habits of accuracy and independence in word recognition, a wide span of recognition, and fluent recognition. (See Chapter IX.)

(6) Supervised seat activities to train pupils in habits of independent study and in the thoughtful interpretation of what is read.

(7) Frequent tests of the attainments and needs of pupils and such corrective and remedial steps as may be necessary. (See Chapters XI, XII, XIII.) [1]

While the foregoing types of instruction are in progress, reading should be used widely in most classroom activities. This reading should include directions for work, announcements, records of group activities, mimeographed materials prepared for specific purposes, and simple books dealing with the problems discussed in the various curricular fields (see Chapter V). As soon as pupils have learned to read with reasonable ease, a period should be reserved each day for establishing habits of reading independently for pleasure. Experience shows that pupils usually need careful guidance during these periods. In some cases, specific steps will be necessary to stimulate interest in reading. The poorer readers will need help on both meanings and pronunciations. All will profit from the teacher's suggestions and her display of interest in particular selections. As soon as pupils show evidence of keen interest in reading to themselves and ability to read thoughtfully with little or no assistance, they should be permitted to read at the library table while the teacher aids those who are less well advanced.

The following characteristics distinguish the pupil who has satisfactorily completed the requirements of the initial period in learning to read:

(1) Becomes absorbed in the content of interesting selections and books when reading independently.

(2) Reads silently with few or no lip movements.

(3) Asks questions about and discusses intelligently the content of what is read.

---

[1] For additional suggestions concerning the techniques and methods of conducting the various types of reading activities, the following references should be consulted:

Edgar William Dolch. *The Psychology and Teaching of Reading.* Chapters IV and V. (Ginn and Company: New York, 1931)

Arthur I. Gates. *The Improvement of Reading.* Part II. (The Macmillan Company: New York, 1932)

Samuel W. Patterson. *Teaching the Child to Read.* Chapters VII and VIII. (Doubleday, Doran and Company: Garden City, New York, 1930)

Mary E. Pennell and Alice M. Cusack. *The Teaching of Reading for Better Living.* Pp. 249–259. (Houghton Mifflin Company: Boston, 1935)

(4) Reads increasingly longer units for pleasure or in response to a specific purpose.

(5) Reads aloud clearly, and in thought units, rather than by individual words.

(6) Uses various aids independently in recognizing unknown words.

(7) Recognizes and interprets the significance of certain typographical devices, such as the period, question mark, and quotation marks.

(8) Handles books with care, opens and turns pages properly, knows the order of paging, and is able to find readily what he is looking for.

(9) Attains a grade score of 2.0 or above on standardized silent reading tests.

5. Duration of Initial Instruction in Reading

Experience shows that a majority of first-grade children learn to read simple books with keen interest and absorption and do some independent reading by the end of the first grade. As reading materials are improved and instruction is better adjusted to the needs of individuals, a much larger proportion of first-grade pupils should be able to attain the desired goals. Those who do not should be advanced to the next grade or retained in the first on the basis of their total progress and needs rather than their attainments in reading only. If the pupil is promoted to the second grade, guidance in reading should begin at the level exhibited when he enters that grade.

In order to insure maximal progress, teachers should make continuous studies of the achievements and needs of their pupils and appraise the efficiency of their teaching in accordance with the methods suggested in Chapter XII. Furthermore, the instruction provided should be constantly adapted to the varying needs of the pupils. This implies a flexible plan of classification that permits frequent regrouping of pupils and the use of corrective and remedial measures as a part of the regular program of teaching. It implies also that the pupils in a given classroom will receive instruction in reading at different levels of advancement according to their attainments and needs. If teaching is properly organized and administered, pupils should receive the stimulus that comes from successful effort rather than the discouragement that results from frequent failure and repetition of the work of a grade or term. In order to insure favorable conditions for progress in learning, some school systems have reorganized the primary grades into a single administrative unit without grade boundaries, and provide for continuous progress, uninterrupted by failure or repetition, from one stage of advancement to another. This type of organization is based on a clear recognition of important characteristics of child development and needs.

VII. Stage Three: Rapid Progress in Fundamental Reading Attitudes and Habits

When children are able to read simple books with ease and understanding, as prescribed in the preceding section, and when they begin to read independently with intelligent curiosity, they have reached a very important stage of development in reading. This stage is characterized by rapid progress in the fundamental attitudes, habits, and skills on which clear comprehension and interpretation, speed of silent reading, and fluent, accurate oral reading depend. In terms of school organization this stage of development normally occurs during the second and third grades, but it may be considerably advanced or delayed in the case of individual pupils. For example, some pupils may enter the second grade who have not attained the standards set for the end of the initial period of instruction in reading. Others may have acquired such attainments during the first grade and may be considerably more advanced.

By the end of the third stage of development pupils should be able to read independently and intelligently, both silently and orally, the various types of reading materials used widely at the beginning of the fourth grade. Not all pupils will attain this goal equally well. Furthermore, they will not attain it at the same time nor in the same way. Hence, adjustments must be made here, as at earlier stages, to fit the program of basic instruction in reading to the abilities and needs of each pupil. The fact cannot be overemphasized that instruction in reading must be adapted to individual differences.

1. Importance of the Period

The importance of the stage of development in reading with which we are now concerned is emphasized by a series of significant facts:

1. For pupils who have attained satisfactorily the goals set for the earlier period, the opportunities for stimulating reading are greatly extended. The reading program that is now adopted should aid pupils in acquiring experience beyond the limits of the immediate environment and of that afforded by pictures, conversation, and story telling, which were used widely during earlier stages of development. Furthermore, the reading experiences provided are no longer restricted largely to school readers. A greater amount of interesting and worth-while ma-

terial of varied types is now available for children who have reached this stage; for example, story books to suit a variety of interests, and fascinating books relating to art, travel, health, science, and other areas of useful information. A few newspapers and magazines have been adapted to the reading level of children in the second and third grades and afford additional opportunity for wide reading. Such materials have distinct values in broadening and enriching the experiences of pupils and in laying a foundation for later interpretations in reading.

2. The growing interest and pleasure that children find in independent reading serve many purposes in the classroom. Such attitudes should guide the teacher in motivating instruction, in selecting materials for reading, and in planning teaching procedures. They should be preserved and fostered to the end that they will develop later into permanent attitudes.

3. The increasing demands made upon children at successive levels of advancement emphasize the need of preparing them for the larger and more varied types of reading activities in which they should sooner or later engage. By the beginning of the fourth grade, for example, broader curricular content is introduced in textbooks and reference materials, which require varied types of reading commonly designated as ' study.' It must not be assumed that pupils should be prepared for study activities by large amounts of work-type reading. They should, rather, be introduced to different kinds of informational material in the various fields of the curriculum and should be taught to read for a variety of purposes. A foundation for habits of reading that are appropriate in study situations should also be laid at this time.

4. The importance of this stage of development is further emphasized by the fact that it represents a period of unusually rapid development in such fundamental habits as those involved in accuracy, rate, and span of recognition, the comprehension and interpretation of content, ability to read for different purposes, speed of silent reading, and fluency in oral reading. Furthermore, the attainments and needs of pupils change with surprising rapidity. As a result, constant adjustments are necessary in the grouping of pupils and daily provision for individual differences and needs is essential.

2. Specific Aims

The specific aims of instruction during the third stage of development in reading may be stated as follows:

1. To provide a rich variety of reading experiences based on the world's greatest stories for children and on informational materials that challenge interest, including topics relating to various curricular fields.

2. To stimulate keen interest in reading wholesome books and selections for pleasure and to establish the habit of reading independently.

3. To secure rapid progress in the development of habits of intelligent interpretation when reading for a variety of purposes.

4. To increase the speed with which passages are read silently within the limits of accurate comprehension. This includes rapid increase in span and rate of recognition and a corresponding decrease in number and duration of eye-fixations per line in both oral and silent reading.

5. To provide for the development of desirable standards and habits involved in good oral reading.

6. To promote continuous development in accuracy and independence in word recognition.

7. To continue training in the skillful use of books and to familiarize pupils with the privileges and opportunities of libraries.

3. Essential Activities

The attainment of these aims depends on a broad program of reading activities. In harmony with the plan adopted during the preceding stage, incidental and informal reading should be continued in all school activities in which they serve useful purposes. Since pupils are now able to read simple material with ease and understanding, a greater amount of reading should be done in the various fields of the curriculum. In fact, such reading should aid greatly in extending and enriching experience in various fields of interest and activity. Furthermore, the story hour, the dramatization period, and the school assembly may serve many valuable purposes in developing proper attitudes and habits involved in various types of reading. Free reading at the library table or at home is indispensable in enriching experience, in stimulating vital interest in reading, and in training in the use of leisure. In addition, basic instruction in reading provides systematic and orderly guidance in the fundamental reading attitudes, habits, and skills in which children at this period should progress most rapidly.

4. Provision for Individual Differences

Because of the wide range of interests, abilities, and needs of children on entering the second and third grades, a temporary classification of pupils should be made as early as possible, and instruction should be provided in keeping with their varying stages of development and needs. Specific suggestions for measuring attainments are presented in Chapter XII. A flexible plan of grouping, which permits frequent adjustments to rapid changes in progress and needs, is imperative. A rigid plan of classification tends to produce a highly artificial and uneconomical situation — artificial, because it fails to correspond with the facts relating to child development, and uneconomical, because it fails to provide reading activities in accordance with the child's needs.

The adoption of the plan of grouping pupils within a class raises the question of finding time to conduct two, three, or four recitations in the time alloted for one. Various compensating factors may be pointed out. In the first place, subdividing a class into groups reduces the number of pupils who receive attention at any one time. In the second place, a relatively homogeneous group that reads material suited to the general reading level of its members requires less time than a group not so organized. If a class is divided into three groups, probably the most satisfactory arrangement is to increase the amount of independent reading for the best group in order to permit more time for the teacher to guide the average and poorest groups. Nevertheless, the reading done by the brighter groups should be carefully planned and should challenge the interest and capacity of the pupils. Furthermore, the findings and interpretations of the pupils should be definitely checked. Otherwise, there is danger that these pupils will fail to receive adequate stimulus and guidance and will not develop to the full extent of their potentialities.

5. Materials of Instruction

The material for basic instruction used most widely at this stage of development includes readers, supplementary books, and workbooks of various types. The use of such material is desirable, if adequately supplemented by library books, because the former are usually organized to promote the orderly development of basic attitudes, habits, and skills at this level. In most school readers the vocabulary is carefully controlled so as to provide gradual increase in difficulty. Assuming that the selections included are interesting and sequential in content, they may be read in the order in which they appear in the book. This is not only a safe procedure, but also one that reduces the possibility of unexpected handicaps to progress.

Supplementary selections of the same level of difficulty and pertaining to the same content should be used widely. Indeed, many units that do not have their origin in readers may be introduced freely. If properly administered, a unit relating to a single theme and including material from several sources has much educational value. Pupils gain confidence in their own ability and receive stimulus for continued effort from a long period of successful reading about a single center of interest. Furthermore, the repetition of meanings and vocabulary is very valuable.

Materials for free reading should also be available. Through their use, teachers can broaden children's interests in reading and promote the development of habits of reading during leisure hours.

6. Means of Realizing Major Aims

The means by which the major aims of this stage of development may be attained are described under four headings; namely, developing power as a reader, making desirable habits permanent, providing corrective or remedial teaching, and promoting the establishment of permanent interests in reading.

a. Developing Power as a Reader. By this is meant securing rapid growth in ability to deal successfully with reading situations of increasing difficulty. In view of the stage of development to which pupils have attained at the beginning of this period, rapid progress in basic reading attitudes and habits is highly desirable during the second and third grades. Suggested activities of value in developing power follow:

(1) Providing Strong Motives for Reading. Since interest is closely related to success, it is important that the teacher should stimulate interest through the use of materials and motives for reading that make a strong appeal. This step has become greatly simplified because of the increasing amount of excellent material now available for use at the second- and third-grade levels. Both interest and good thinking can be promoted by providing purposes for reading that are important to the child. For example, reading to find the sequence of incidents in a story, to find a suitable story for dramatizing, to learn how to make something needed by a class, or to find something to tell the rest of the class not only furnishes a real purpose for reading but also utilizes the ideas secured through reading in later activities. Such training should result in rapid growth in both accuracy and depth of interpretation and should lay the foundation for good study habits.

(2) Stimulating Growth in Comprehension and Interpretation. As indicated earlier, one of the most successful aids to growth in comprehension and interpretation is a strong motive to read interesting, stim-

ulating material. Among the specific problems that merit special attention at this stage of development are the following: enlarging the meaning vocabulary as new meanings for words previously learned are discovered and as new words and concepts are introduced; recognizing and relating ideas in proper sequence; recognizing the relation of ideas in various types of informational and story material; identifying the major divisions or thought units into which a selection is divided; differentiating between the large ideas and supporting details; comparing the facts presented with the previous experiences of the reader; sensing the broader meaning or significance of the facts presented; differentiating between records of real and of imaginary experiences. This list may be extended almost indefinitely. Teachers should lose no opportunity to promote growth in the various phases of comprehension and interpretation that are essential in achieving the goals of purposeful reading.

(3) Reading for Specific Purposes. Closely associated with the foregoing series of problems is that of training pupils to read for specific purposes. Among the purposes that are especially appropriate at this stage are reading to answer questions; to select main ideas and supporting details; to secure information for use in class discussion; to follow directions; to draw conclusions or to verify an opinion. If the guidance provided is carefully planned, it should promote rapid growth in various kinds of reading activities. Selections from readers and informational books may be used to advantage in securing the types of progress desired.

(4) Promoting Growth in Accuracy and Independence in Word Recognition. As pointed out earlier, growth in skill and facility in attacking new words is very important at this level. The training provided centers around two major problems; one, that of increasing the sight vocabulary; and the other, continued guidance in attacking new and unfamiliar words. Appropriate methods for promoting growth in word recognition are discussed at length in Chapter IX. It will suffice here to point out the fact that the wide reading of selections highly charged with interest and within the comprehension of pupils is one of the most effective means of enlarging the pupil's sight vocabulary. Furthermore, training in independent recognition of new words involves systematic guidance in the visual and phonetic analysis of short words and in the syllabication of words of two or more syllables.

(5) Improving the Quality of Oral Interpretation. Improvement in oral interpretation should grow out of strong motives for reading in

a stimulating audience situation; that is, a situation in which the one reading presents to the listeners information or a story that they do not already know and that they do not have before them in printed form. The teacher should read aloud so that pupils may hear good reading and recognize appropriate standards. Individual assignments and group practice lessons, including some sight reading, are types of activities that may be used in promoting desirable kinds of growth. For detailed suggestions see Chapter X.

(6) *Increasing the Rate and Span of Recognition.* Much reading of simple, interesting material is without doubt the most effective method of increasing the rate and span of recognition. Only in exceptional cases are flash card exercises and timed exercises in silent reading of distinct value at this level. Related problems are considered in the latter part of Chapter IX.

b. Making Desirable Habits Permanent. Directed reading of relatively simple selections should be a frequent part of the basic reading program. One of its chief values lies in the fact that it promotes the permanent establishment of the habits and skills that have been partly developed through the types of training described above. Such reading should be carried on under conditions that insure hearty enjoyment. The use of simple materials relieves pupils from the strain of constantly attacking new meanings and pronunciations and enables them to become absorbed in the content of selections unhampered by mechanical difficulties. Valuable types of activities that contribute to the further development of desirable habits and skills include: supervised silent reading for information or pleasure; oral reading with attention directed to the content; dramatization; and audience reading by the pupil of selections of his own choice.

A large amount of reading material of various types and degrees of difficulty is essential for this phase of the reading program. All children who have made satisfactory progress in the acquisition of desirable attitudes, habits, and skills should have abundant opportunity to read simple material as an aid both in enriching experience and in making learnings permanent.

c. Correcting or Eliminating Poor Reading Habits. Of major importance is the fact that corrective measures should be adopted as soon as errors develop or difficulties arise. By identifying and treating reading defects at the outset, severe cases of reading deficiencies may be prevented. An effective corrective program should begin with careful individual diagnosis by the classroom teacher, who should have some knowledge of mental hygiene, desirable goals in reading, testing techniques, and remedial procedures.

In most cases of reading deficiencies extended diagnosis is unnecessary. Similarly, elaborate clinical methods of correction should be tried only when the ordinary types of corrective and remedial procedures have failed. As a rule, the correction of physical handicaps is a problem for the specialist; however, the establishment of right attitudes toward reading and the development of effective reading habits and skills are the tasks of the classroom teacher.

As soon as a careful diagnosis has been made, the pupil should be taken into the teacher's confidence and be shown what is causing his errors in reading. Among the types of difficulties that arise the following are very common: failure to hear or see words clearly; failure to group words in thought units; giving attention chiefly to word recognition at the sacrifice of meaning; failure to read with appropriate rhythm and expression; lack of interest in the content of what is read or in becoming a good reader; tendency to report incidents not included in the story, to read aloud indistinctly, to exhibit speech defects, to point with fingers or move lips expressively in silent reading; and inability to use as needed and in combination various cues to rapid and effective word recognition. The methods used should be adapted to individual needs and encouragement should be given to pupils as evidence of improvement is secured. Keeping an objective, graphical record of progress is an important means of motivating further effort. Fortunately, most pupils coöperate in remedial programs and make measurable gains. For detailed suggestions see Chapters XI, XII, and XIII.

d. Promoting the Establishment of Permanent Interests in Reading. Independent reading in school and at home is indispensable in enriching the experiences of pupils, in stimulating keen interest in reading, in training pupils in the wholesome use of leisure, and in making reading activities pleasurable. Inasmuch as children normally advance rapidly in ease and fluency of reading at this stage, they should be provided with a large amount of worthwhile reading suited to their interests and attainments. The reading table, the school library, and the public library should offer abundant opportunities for independent reading.

The teacher can promote the establishment of permanent interests by reading parts of stories or books to the pupils and leaving the remainder for independent reading; by permitting pupils who read well to do likewise; by keeping a record of pupils' voluntary, independent reading; by encouraging reports and discussions of outside reading; and by providing time in the daily program for independent reading for pleasure.

7. Standards of Attainments

Pupils who complete satisfactorily the third level of development in reading exhibit the following attainments:

1. They have established the habit of reading independently.
2. They interpret accurately the materials related to other curricular fields.
3. They seek reading materials that relate to activities in which they are interested.
4. They read more rapidly silently than orally.
5. They are able to read at sight materials suited to their stage of development.
6. They show increasing skill in combining contextual clues with visual and auditory elements in recognizing unfamiliar words.
7. They show increased ability to make the adjustments required when reading for different purposes.
8. They exhibit rapid progress in acquiring wholesome and diversified reading interests.

The attainments of pupils may be determined in part through the use of standardized and informal tests. A grade score of 4.0 or better in silent reading is an index of needed attainment at this stage of development. A description of available tests and a discussion of their function in the reading program are presented in Chapter XII.

VIII. Stage Four: The Extension of Experience and the Increase in Reading Efficiency

(Fourth, Fifth, and Sixth Grades)

When pupils have acquired the experiences and the reading attitudes and habits that were recommended in the preceding section, the opportunities to engage in enriching reading activities increase rapidly. This fact was recognized in the Twenty-Fourth Yearbook, which characterized the fourth, fifth, and sixth grades as a " period for wide reading to extend experience." It has been recognized also by curriculum-makers, as shown by the enriched programs of reading and study that have been provided recently in the fourth, fifth, and sixth grades.

Closely associated with the opportunity for wide reading in various fields is the demand for greater power and efficiency in all reading

activities. This includes, on the one hand, greater accuracy and independence in word recognition, rapid growth in meaning vocabulary,
increased clarity in comprehension, greater ability to interpret, increased speed of silent reading adjusted to the purpose at hand, and
improved quality of oral reading. It includes, on the other hand, wider
familiarity with the sources and values of reading material, greater
skill in the use of books and other printed sources of information, and
greater efficiency in study activities that involve reading. To these
should be added the urgent need for broader reading interests and for
improved tastes in recreational reading. Such statements suggest the
wide range of possibilities for growth in fundamental reading attitudes
and habits during the important stage of development with which we
are now concerned.

In the judgment of the Yearbook Committee schools in general are
achieving far less satisfactory results today in the fourth, fifth, and
sixth grades than in the preceding grades. It recommends vigorous
effort during the next decade to increase the efficiency of the instruction given in the middle grades and to provide corresponding improvement in the reading attitudes and attainments of pupils.

1. Need for Continued Guidance

A survey of current practice reveals three divergent views concerning the need for continued guidance in basic attitudes and habits during
the fourth stage of development in reading. One view is represented
by those who make no provision for guidance during the middle grades.
This practice is based in part on the assumption that essential reading
attitudes and habits have been reasonably well developed by the end
of the primary grades, and that further growth will result from participation in a wide range of reading activities in which guidance is
provided only incidentally. The proponents of this view point to the
fact that much of the reading instruction now provided in the middle
grades is vaguely defined and loosely organized, and secures but slight
returns for the time and energy required. The Yearbook Committee
is in hearty agreement with the assertion that, unless a reading program
can justify itself in terms of definite objectives and sound teaching
procedures, it has no excuse for continued support.

Other advocates for abolishing basic instruction in reading in the
middle grades support their claims on different grounds. In their judgment, the attitudes and habits developed in the primary grades can
best be maintained and further developed through systematic guidance

provided in various reading activities other than those normally included in a reading period. They assert, for example, that habits and skills of recognized value can be developed most economically and effectively in the various fields of the curriculum as the need for them arises; furthermore, that desirable reading attitudes and interests can be stimulated best through wide independent reading that is tactfully guided and directed. The chief value of such a program lies in its emphases on training for immediate use and in situations that insure highly motivated application.

According to a third view, desirable growth in reading can be secured most effectively when a broad program of training is provided, including both basic instruction in reading and systematic guidance in reading in the various curricular fields. The proponents of this view point to the fact that pupils who reach the fourth stage of development in reading are far from mature in basic reading attitudes and habits. They also maintain that many of the uses of reading in study activities are common to the various fields of the curriculum and can be cultivated initially to best advantage during a period reserved specially for such purposes. Through continuous basic training during a reading period, they believe that pupils can be prepared to engage with increasing efficiency in all reading activities. Through additional guidance provided in different curricular fields, rapid growth can be secured in the various uses and applications of reading that are required.

The Yearbook Committee heartily endorses the third of the views presented. It believes that a well-rounded program of basic instruction in reading, supplemented by systematic guidance in the various curricular fields, is essential for most pupils in the middle grades. The evidence available shows conclusively that rapid growth in desirable reading attitudes and habits can be secured through carefully planned guidance of both types. In view of marked deficiencies today in the reading accomplishments of pupils in the middle and upper grades, the Committee believes that reading problems during the fourth stage of development are among the most challenging that elementary schools now face. It recommends, therefore, that teachers and school officers devote themselves with renewed energy and determination to the exacting obligations involved in promoting greater power and efficiency in reading during the middle grades.

2. Major Aims and Objectives

The more or less futile types of instruction in reading that have often been provided in the middle grades may be attributed in part at least to the absence of clearly defined purposeful objectives. The major aims that follow have been determined in the light of the pupils' immediate school and personal needs and the ultimate social purposes to be served. They are presented here very briefly and will be considered in detail later.

1. To extend and enrich the experiences of pupils through wide reading in the various fields in which pupils are and should be interested at this stage of their development.

2. To broaden and elevate reading interests and tastes and to establish the habit of reading regularly for recreation and pleasure.

3. To promote the development of increased power and efficiency in various important phases of reading. This includes rapid growth in recognition and meaning vocabularies, in accurate comprehension of increasingly difficult materials, in breadth and depth of interpretation, in speed of silent reading, and in quality of oral reading.

4. To stimulate, in conjunction with work in the various subjects, the development of attitudes and habits that enable pupils to engage effectively in different study activities that require reading.

5. To make continuous studies of the attainments and needs of pupils in reading and to provide necessary corrective and remedial instruction.

Appropriate types of training should be continued until pupils have attained a grade score of 7.0 or better on a standardized silent reading test and corresponding levels of progress in other phases of reading. This level of achievement has unique educational and social significance. It marks the minimal attainments in reading essential for satisfactory scholastic progress during the junior-high-school period. It also represents the level of achievement in basic reading habits essential to read with ease and understanding adult reading materials of average difficulty.

3. Organization of Instruction in Reading

The kind of training given and the amount provided are conditioned at all levels of development by the achievements and needs of the pupils. At the beginning of the fourth grade those pupils who have attained the standards described for the third stage of development should receive systematic guidance that promotes orderly growth in reading efficiency. Other pupils who show lack of readiness for the broader reading and study activities that the curriculum now requires should receive training and guidance appropriate for those at the third stage of development. Such training should be continued until they have acquired the attainments normally expected of pupils at the beginning of the fourth grade. Until satisfactory progress has been made, it will not be possible for them to engage successfully in the reading activities usually required in other fields of the curriculum. Accordingly, teachers should provide such pupils for the time being with very simple textbooks and reference materials and make somewhat larger use than otherwise of oral and visual methods of training.

In order to maintain a high level of interest among the various groups in a classroom many teachers make use of a common core of interest. This procedure requires the use of reading materials of several levels of difficulty. Following a stimulating introduction to a given unit, the various groups begin their reading and study through the use of materials adapted to their respective levels of advancement. The systematic instruction and guidance provided by the teacher is organized in terms of the needs of the children in the different groups. Those who are greatly retarded receive basic instruction at a level that corresponds with their needs. The most advanced pupils may require very little guidance in the more rudimentary phases of reading but profit greatly from guidance in the interpretation and application of what is read. At times the different groups report as a unit, sharing experiences, insights, and conclusions. Through such means class unity is maintained while at the same time instruction is adapted to the varying needs and capacities of the pupils.

What has been said concerning the adjustment of instruction in the fourth grade to the varying needs of pupils applies likewise to the fifth and sixth grades. As pupils in the different grades reach and surpass the desired levels of achievement in basic reading habits, emphasis should be given in the units studied to such matters as the extension of experience, increase of skill in interpretation, the improvement of study habits and techniques, and the application of what is read in problem situations. In these connections, the possibility for growth is almost unlimited.

4. Specific Teaching Problems

Because of the large demand for intelligent reading made on pupils during the middle grades, the number of teaching problems is unusually large. Unfortunately space will not permit even a brief dis-

cussion of many of them. Consequently, attention will be directed only
to a few that merit special consideration. The suggestions offered have
been organized under the five general aims of basic instruction that
were emphasized earlier.

a. To Extend and Enrich Experience. Of special importance is the
fact that the materials selected for basic instruction in reading should
contribute richly to the expanding experiences of children from nine to
twelve years of age. As pointed out by Bobbitt,[1] the total reading
program should give " a balanced vision of the various things that
make up the world past and present." To achieve this end, there should
be stories of travel that " reveal nations and peoples; biographical and
historical stories of people in all land and regions; stories of persons of
all social types and classes; stories of persons of all ages from infancy
to old age; in sum, stories, descriptions, and expositions, which reveal
the world in all its varied aspects, moods, and changes." From these
and other fields of interest, challenging units should be selected to extend and enrich the experiences of pupils, broaden their vision and insights, and provide the motive and opportunity for developing increased
power and efficiency in purposeful reading and study activities. Other
units should be used from time to time that acquaint the pupils with
the world's best stories for children, that promote keen interest in reading, and that stimulate a growing preference for the better forms of
literature.

b. To Stimulate Interest in Reading. The stimulation of broad
interests in reading is of special importance during the fourth, fifth, and
sixth grades. The fact is widely recognized that the interests developed at this time determine to a large extent the nature and variety
of the pupil's subsequent reading activities. The steps taken, therefore, should lay a broad foundation for permanent interest in the reading of books and magazines appropriate to the level of advancement
of the child. Keen interest in reading is also a means to an end. It
stimulates pupils to engage in wide reading, which is essential if fluent
habits are acquired. Every opportunity should be utilized, therefore,
to broaden and deepen the reading interests of children. In harmony
with good teaching procedure, each unit taught should be closely related to the present interests of the children. Through discussion,
explanation, carefully directed questioning, the use of pictures, and the
provision of attractive readable material present interests should be

[1] Franklin Bobbitt. " The Wider Vision," *The New Wonder World: A Library of Knowledge.* Pp. 52–54. (George L. Shuman & Co.: Chicago, 1932)

strengthened and new interests developed. As an essential part of each unit, provision should be made for much supplementary and library reading on the part of all pupils. Such reading is of specific value in satisfying present interests and in discovering new ones.

c. *To Develop Greater Power and Efficiency in Various Fundamental Phases of Reading.* We are concerned here with a series of problems for the solution of which, basic instruction in reading is primarily responsible. The chief aim of the guidance provided is to promote the orderly development of the basic attitudes and habits on which increased power and efficiency in both silent and oral reading depend. The training provided should promote greater ease and understanding in all the reading activities in which pupils engage both in and out of school. The specific suggestions offered relate to six different phases of reading.

(1) Accuracy and Independence in Pronouncing Increasingly Difficult Words. Unfortunately the vigorous emphasis on silent reading during the last decade has resulted in an attitude on the part of some pupils of carelessness or indifference toward word recognition. If pupils are to make intelligent use of the important ideas or concepts a passage presents, they must be able to pronounce accurately and independently the words that represent them. To this end systematic training must be continued during the middle grades in recognizing words (a) through contextual clues; (b) through word analysis, including phonetics; and (c) through the use of the dictionary. Definite time should be reserved in which important word difficulties are considered and needed help is provided in overcoming them. Furthermore, systematic training in the use of the dictionary should be given beginning with the fourth grade and continuing until pupils can use it independently and efficiently.

(2) The Enlargement of Meaning Vocabulary. Thorndike [1] has emphasized the fact that the extension and enrichment of the meaning vocabulary is one of the most important problems of reading instruction in the middle grades. It includes not only the development of meanings of new words but also the fostering of broader and richer meanings of known words. Experiments [2] show clearly that specific guidance is very much more effective than incidental training. Further-

---

[1] E. T. Thorndike. "Improving the ability to read." *Teachers College Record,* 36: October, 1934, p. 2.

[2] Eleanor Holmes. "Vocabulary instruction and reading." *Elementary English Review,* 11: April, 1934, pp. 103–105, 110.

more, guidance in the use of contextual clues, supplemented by training in the use of the dictionary, is far better than reliance on either method alone. Specific word training should involve also: (1) word analysis, including exercises in identifying prefixes, suffixes, roots, and other cues of word form; (2) the classification of words according to a given basis, such as synonyms or shades of meaning, (3) keeping word lists, such as vivid descriptive adjectives or words used with special meaning or effectiveness by writers; (4) conversational periods that direct attention to word values and uses; (5) drill in defining words from contextual clues; (6) selecting appropriate definitions from those given in the dictionaries. For additional suggestions see Chapter IX.

(3) Accuracy and Thoroughness in Comprehension. The wide use now made of reading to enrich experience emphasizes the importance of rapid growth in accuracy and thoroughness of comprehension. In general cursory reading, guidance should aim to direct attention to the content and to aid pupils in associating right meanings, in retaining significant items of information, and in reacting appropriately to what is read. Needless to say, the reading activities provided should always be challenging and purposeful. Among the purposes for which pupils should learn to read intelligently, the following merit special consideration: to discover what a story is about; to determine the sequence of events; to select the larger thought divisions of a story; to discover the main point or central theme of a selection; to identify specific items of information; to select details that support an opinion, explain an idea, or prove a point; to find answers to factual and judgment questions; to verify statements; to determine how to perform an activity; and to draw conclusions from the facts presented. The foregoing list may be indefinitely extended. In promoting desirable types of growth use should be made at first of materials that can be comprehended readily by the pupils. As they acquire ability to read effectively for different purposes the difficulty of the material should be increased. It is of major importance that teachers insist on as high a quality of performance as is possible in individual cases. Through systematic guidance, extending throughout the middle grades, the general efficiency of pupils in comprehension should be greatly increased.[1]

---

[1] For additional suggestions the following references should be consulted:

Fowler D. Brooks. *The Applied Psychology of Reading.* Chapters VII, XI, and XIV. (D. Appleton-Century Company: New York, 1926)

Arthur I. Gates. *The Improvement of Reading.* Part III. (The Macmillan Company: New York, 1932)

(4) Competence in Interpretation. Closely related to the development of comprehension is growth in ability to interpret. The latter implies not merely a grasp of the content read but also an appraisal of its worth according to some basis of judgment. As pupils secure experience through wide reading, they should learn to compare information and ideas from many sources and pass judgment on their value and significance. They should learn to weigh the evidence presented and distinguish what is sound and relevant from what is not. They should also learn to recognize the underlying meanings and implications of the statements made. In the field of recreational reading, pupils should be guided in selecting from the books and magazines read that which is interesting and satisfying to them. Through discussions, dramatizations, visual aids, and other means pupils may be led to judge the beauty and worth of good literature, as against the commonplace and worthless. If pupils are to grow in the directions indicated, lessons should be planned almost daily that will stimulate them to interpret the meaning of what is read and to sense its broader values and implications. Helpful suggestions are contained in the references listed in the footnote to the preceding paragraph.

(5) Speed of Reading. Records of progress in reading show that speed continues to increase steadily during the middle grades. Because of the great importance attached to speed of reading, pupils have often been urged to read very rapidly without due consideration to comprehension. The fact should be remembered that pupils differ radically in their capacity to read rapidly; also, that speed is influenced by the reader's purpose, his interest in the content, the difficulty of the material, his control over the mechanics of reading, and his capacity to interpret meanings readily. Without doubt the most effective way to

---

Julia M. Harris, H. T. Donovan, and Thomas Alexander. *Supervision and the Teaching of Reading.* Chapters IX and X. (Johnson Publishing Company: Richmond, Virginia, 1927)

Paul McKee. *Reading and Literature in the Elementary School.* Chapter VIII. (Houghton Mifflin Company: Boston, 1934)

Samuel W. Patterson. *Teaching the Child to Read.* Chapter XIII. (Doubleday, Doran and Company, Inc.: Garden City, New York, 1930)

Mary E. Pennell and Alice M. Cusack. *The Teaching of Reading for Better Living.* Chapter VIII. (Houghton Mifflin Company: Boston, 1935)

Clarence R. Stone. *Silent and Oral Reading.* Chapters VII and VIII. (Houghton Mifflin Company: Boston, 1926)

Harry G. Wheat. *The Teaching of Reading.* Chapter XIV. (Ginn and Company: Boston, 1923)

increase speed of reading is to provide pupils with abundant opportunities to read highly interesting but relatively simple stories. Of almost equal value is wide reading of simple informational material that will aid in solving a problem. On frequent occasions timed exercises with attention directed to the content are valuable for pupils who are not reading as rapidly as they might. In such cases, comprehension should be checked so that speed will not be increased at the sacrifice of comprehension. Only in the case of very slow readers are flash-card exercises of value at this level of advancement (see final section of Chapter IX).

(6) Quality of Oral Reading. The fourth stage of development is a particularly appropriate one for emphasis on interpretative oral reading. As a rule, children now read more rapidly silently than orally. Furthermore, most of them read aloud somewhat haltingly and ineffectively. To secure the desired improvement, they need carefully directed practice in highly motivated situations and opportunities for recognizing the standards that govern good interpretation. Accordingly, group activities should be organized at times in which pupils can discover under skillful guidance the characteristics of good oral interpretation and can make progress in applying the facts learned. Equally, if not more, important is the need for frequent opportunity to read to others in highly motivated audience situations. The principles underlying good oral reading and specific suggestions for securing improvement are considered in Chapter X.

d. To Increase Competence in Study Activities. The development of power and efficiency in general reading calls for increasing competence in study activities that involve reading. In this connection the relation between the work of the reading period and that of other fields of the curriculum is very close. Not infrequently the guidance provided during the reading period anticipates needs that will arise in various subjects, as, for example, ability to organize what is read. In such cases, training is given in the habits and skills required through the use of selections that lend themselves readily to the purpose. On other occasions, the reading period may be used for supplementing the guidance provided in the various subjects. As a rule, the reading materials used should be similar to, or selected from, the fields in which the problem arose. This procedure insures practice in situations in which the habits should function. The guidance provided should, of course, be given under the stimulus of motives that are real and compelling to the children.

Owing to the rapid increase in the demands made upon the child by the modern curriculum, the opportunities for increasing his competence in study activities are almost unlimited. In order to suggest some of the more important types of knowledge and skills that should be emphasized during the fourth, fifth, and sixth grades, the following list, compiled from various publications and reports by teachers and school officers, is included:

1. In locating information:
   a. Knowledge of the nature, location, and purpose of different parts of books.
   b. Ability to use an alphabetical arrangement.
   c. Ability to use the index, table of contents, and other parts of a book effectively.
   d. Ability to interpret maps, tables, graphs, and various types of information in books other than printed words.
   e. Ability to use a dictionary, an encyclopedia, and other sources of information in study activities.
   f. Knowledge of the types of material available in the classroom, the school library, and the public library.
   g. Knowledge of the function, organization, and operation of school and public libraries.
   h. Ability to use the library card file.
   i. Ability to scan material in order to locate specific facts and ideas.
2. In selecting and evaluating material needed:
   a. Ability to carry problems in mind while reading.
   b. Ability to discriminate between the relevant and the irrelevant.
   c. Ability to judge the appropriateness and validity of materials.
   d. Ability to prejudge and select books for specific purposes.
   e. Knowledge of how to determine the recency of a printed statement.
   f. Ability to recognize the difference between statements of fact and opinion.
   g. Ability to identify objective evidence.
   h. Ability to select information with discrimination from various sources.
3. In organizing material:
   a. Ability to recognize the author's aim, purpose, and organization.
   b. Ability to select the central topic of a paragraph or an entire selection.
   c. Ability to select main points and supporting details.
   d. Ability to grasp relationships.
   e. Ability to arrange ideas in proper sequence.
   f. Ability to summarize.

     g. Ability to outline.

     h. Ability to take notes effectively.

4. In solving a problem or making application of what is read:

     a. Ability to keep the problem clearly in mind.

     b. Ability to select relevant information or data.

     c. Ability to analyze the facts secured in order to identify relevant and irrelevant items.

     d. Ability to compare items of information for likenesses and differences.

     e. Ability to organize facts so that their implications are clear.

     f. Willingness to suspend judgment until sufficient evidence is at hand.

     g. Ability to support conclusions.

5. In remembering what is read for specific purposes:

     a. Knowledge of the purpose to be served.

     b. Recognizing the need for retaining facts.

     c. Ability to concentrate and use will power in work.

     d. Ability to select the relevant.

     e. Knowledge of efficient procedures in memorizing:

          (1) Relating old and new.

          (2) Taking notes.

          (3) Outlining.

          (4) Summarizing.

          (5) Learning by wholes.

          (6) Distributed recall.

     f. Ability to use an outline as an aid to retention.

The foregoing outline is far from complete. It should be supplemented in individual schools according to the needs of the pupils in following the curriculum used. The training provided should be related to challenging learning situations no matter from what source the materials read are drawn. The work should be so organized as to promote growth in the simpler phases of most study activities during the fourth grade and should increase steadily in difficulty during the fifth and sixth grades. As a result of carefully planned guidance throughout this period pupils should grow rapidly in ability to engage intelligently and effectively in study activities that involve reading.[1]

    e. To Determine the Needs of Pupils and to Provide Needed Corrective and Remedial Instruction. One of the important aims of guidance during the fourth stage of development is to promote a relatively

---

[1] Gerald A. Yoakam. *Reading and Study.* Chapter XV. (The Macmillan Company: New York, 1928)

See references in the preceding footnote for other valuable suggestions.

high level of reading efficiency. If this end is to be achieved, teachers should study the progress and deficiencies of their pupils regularly and adapt instruction to their varying needs. Methods of determining the needs of pupils are considered at length in Chapter XII and procedures for meeting individual differences are described in Chapter XI.

Many types of deficiencies are characteristic of the middle grades. Among the more important are: failure to comprehend accurately because of a careless, indifferent attitude toward the content; a limited meaning vocabulary; inadequate background of related experience; inability to recognize words accurately; unusual difficulty in word recognition, due to inadequate previous training in word discrimination and phonetic analysis; failure to make use of contextual clues; visual or auditory defects; lack of interest; poor habits with respect to speed of reading, due to inability to recognize words and interpret their meanings readily, to a careless disregard for content that results in an unduly rapid rate of reading, or to failure to adjust speed of reading to the purpose at hand. The foregoing list could be greatly extended if space permitted.[1]

5. Standards of Achievement

Pupils who complete satisfactorily the requirements of the fourth stage of development in reading exhibit the following characteristics:

1. They are familiar through reading with numerous aspects of human activity.

2. They have acquired strong motives for and keen interest in reading for information and pleasure, and devote time regularly to recreational reading.

3. They are able to recognize and pronounce new words independently or to find them quickly in the dictionary.

4. They have reached approximate maturity in rate and span of recognition, in rhythmical progress of perceptions along the lines, in eye-voice span in oral reading, and in speed of silent reading for recreational purposes.

5. They have greatly expanded their meaning vocabularies and have mastered various aids in deriving the meanings of words, including the intelligent use of the dictionary.

---

[1] For detailed discussions of types of deficiencies and appropriate corrective and remedial measures, see Chapter XIII and the following references:

E. A. Betts. *The Prevention and Correction of Reading Difficulties.* (Row Peterson & Company: Evanston, 1936)

Arthur I. Gates. *The Improvement of Reading: A Program of Diagnostic and Remedial Methods.* (The Macmillan Company: New York, 1935)

Marion Monroe. *Children Who Cannot Read.* (The University of Chicago: Chicago, 1932)

6. They have increased their power of comprehension and interpretation to the point where they are able to make a grade score of 7.0 in silent reading.

7. They have made rapid progress in acquiring independence and efficiency in a wide range of study situations that involve reading.

8. They are able to use economically and skillfully books, dictionaries, encyclopedias, and other sources of information that are needed in their reading and study activities.

Pupils who give evidence of satisfactory attainments at the end of the sixth grade are prepared for the fifth stage of development in reading; those who have not made sufficient progress should continue to receive instruction of the type outlined in this section whether they remain in the sixth grade or are advanced to the seventh.

IX. Stage Five: The Refinement of Reading Attitudes, Habits, and Tastes

(Junior and Senior High School and Junior College)

The National Committee on Reading was bold enough in 1924 to suggest that guidance in reading should be provided in junior and senior high schools. This was a noteworthy step in view of the fact that very little consideration had been given prior to that time to reading problems at the secondary-school level. Experience during the last ten years fully justifies the recommendation of the National Committee. Furthermore, evidence has been secured that shows the urgent need of further extending the period of training. Instead, therefore, of limiting the fifth stage of development in reading to the junior- and senior-high-school grades, the present report includes the junior college as well. As a result, provision is made for carefully planned guidance in reading throughout the period of general education.

It would probably not be out of place here to suggest that a sixth stage of development should be added to those outlined in this Yearbook. The chief purpose of the guidance at that advanced stage would be to promote a high level of efficiency in critical reading and library research among students pursuing specialized and professional programs.

1. Reading Achievement of Pupils at the Secondary-School Level

The fact was pointed out earlier that a majority of the pupils who enter the junior high school are prepared for a broad range of reading activities. But there remains in the minority an unfortunately large percentage of pupils (in the seventh and in subsequent grades) who are surprisingly deficient in ability to read. For example, in a study made in fourteen four-year high schools, reading tests were given to 5,705 freshmen. Approximately four percent of these pupils made comprehension scores no higher than those attained by average second- and third-grade pupils; five percent made scores equivalent to those attained by average fourth-grade pupils; six percent, by fifth-grade pupils; and seven percent, by sixth-grade pupils. In all, 22 percent, or nearly one-fourth of the total number tested, received comprehension scores below the norm usually attained by pupils at the end of the sixth grade. Previous studies have shown that high-school pupils who rank below this norm often encounter serious difficulty in doing the required reading and fail as a result.

The foregoing results are doubly significant in view of the fact that the median score of all the pupils tested was equivalent to the norm usually attained by eleventh-grade pupils. A further analysis of the results showed that approximately one-fourth of the pupils tested scored so far below the upper half of the group that the former were in no sense comparable in educational status to the latter. Furthermore, approximately one-fourth of the pupils made scores between the sixth-grade norm and the median score of the group. While such pupils are able, as a rule, to read the materials commonly assigned to ninth-grade pupils, experience has shown that they are not able to compete successfully with those of superior reading habits. The results of class-room experiments supply conclusive evidence, however, that most of them are capable of rapid growth in habits of intelligent reading if appropriate remedial work is provided.

Studies made also in junior high schools and junior colleges justify the conclusion that pupils at each of the levels of secondary education vary widely in reading achievement. An analysis of their needs shows that at least three different types of training in reading are essential. The first is developmental in character and aims to promote increased efficiency in reading and study activities on the part of all pupils, with especial reference to the reflective and interpretative processes involved. The second type includes systematic training to improve the reading and study habits of those who can read the assigned materials, but with far less ease and comprehension than the superior readers. In the study cited above, this group included those who ranked above the sixth-grade norm on the tests given but below the average of the group tested. The third type includes corrective and remedial instruction for those who rank below the sixth-grade norm. It is obvious that the training provided for this group must be adapted to the needs of individuals. Not infrequently, however, group instruction may be given to pupils whose needs are similar. Such training should be supplemented at times by individual help and guidance.

2. Specific Aims of the Fifth Stage of Development

Before discussing in detail the types of training and guidance essential, the specific aims of reading in junior and senior high schools and junior colleges should be considered.

1. To extend further the experiences of pupils through reading and to increase greatly their intellectual apprehension. To these ends each subject of the curriculum should provide stimulus and opportunity for wide reading of books, selections, newspapers, and periodicals that broaden the pupil's vision and increase his understanding of the problems studied.

2. To extend and refine reading interests and tastes that will direct and inspire the present and future life of the reader and provide for the wholesome use of leisure time. Special attention should now be given to the development of permanent interest in current events and of the habit of reading periodicals and books with reasonable speed and good judgment. In this connection a recent commission [1] identified the following specific motives that should guide the reader in seeking information:

(*a*) To keep informed concerning current events, as in reading news items, editorial comments, and book and play reviews in the daily newspapers or weekly periodicals.

(*b*) To learn more about events or questions of special interest, as in following the comments and predictions on the sports page or the articles in professional journals.

(*c*) To broaden one's range of information, as in cursory reading of articles in weekly and monthly periodicals or browsing in books.

The reader should also be guided by a strong desire to understand or comprehend. The commission illustrated such motives by two statements:

(*a*) To learn the opinions of others on civic, social, economic, and scientific problems, as in reading editorials, discussions in magazines, books on special topics.

(*b*) To discover guiding principles, fundamental interpretations, and the relative importance of various objectives or ideals in the social, economic, scientific, or other fields among one's intellectual interests.

---

[1] *An Experience Curriculum in English.* (English Monograph No. 4, National Council of Teachers of English. Pp. 101–106. D. Appleton-Century Company: New York, 1935)

If the foregoing purposes are achieved, pupils should become broadly acquainted with the sources and values of different types of reading material and should acquire standards that may be employed in the critical selection of materials to read.

3. To promote vigorously the further development of the habits involved in gaining an intelligent grasp of the author's meaning, in reading for different purposes, and in making keen critical interpretations of what is read. Reading at this level is largely a reflective and interpretative process and every effort should be made to stimulate and develop appropriate habits.

4. To develop a high degree of skill and efficiency in study activities, including the use of books, libraries, and other sources of information, and to extend and refine habits involved in locating, collecting, and summarizing printed materials.

5. To improve and refine habits involved in good oral interpretation, particularly of informational, literary, and dramatic selections, and in connection with public and class activities that require reading to others.

6. To provide corrective and remedial instruction in the fundamental habits involved in oral and silent reading whenever the need for it exists.

In order to accomplish these aims at least the following types of reading activities should be provided and carefully directed: intensive reading and study in practically all curricular fields; extensive reading of assigned or suggested references to supplement the information gained from intensive study and class discussion; group recreational reading and enjoyment of various types of good literature, including that found in recent books and periodicals; free reading in school, in the public library, or at home of current events, periodicals, and books for recreation, to satisfy an interest or curiosity, or to aid in solving a problem. The problems involved in directing such reading activities are discussed at length in Chapters V, VI, and VIII.

3. Types of Instruction in Reading at the Fifth Stage

In addition to the types of reading activities just mentioned, special periods should be reserved in which attention may be devoted specifically to (a) developmental instruction in reading for all pupils; (b) systematic guidance in reading for those who can read the materials regularly assigned but who encounter difficulty in doing so; and (c) corrective and remedial training for those who are seriously retarded in reading. These three types of training will receive special consideration here. Since they are closely related to the problems about to be discussed, important types of guidance in content fields will also be described briefly.

a. Developmental Instruction in Reading. The chief purpose of developmental instruction in reading is to stimulate growth in ability to comprehend and interpret with increasing depth and clarity, and to prepare pupils to engage more independently and efficiently in study activities that involve reading. For this purpose special periods should be reserved from time to time in which attention may be directed to significant types or phases of reading. Some schools utilize a part of the English or the social studies period for this purpose; others provide a special period on one or two days a week. The particular plan adopted in this connection is of minor importance. It is imperative, however, that the instruction provided be wisely conceived and carefully organized, and that it be directed by a capable teacher.

The nature of the developmental program has not been fully determined as yet but it is receiving serious consideration today in various sections of the country. Many schools are attempting experimentally to determine the types of guidance that will be most helpful at various levels. The results secured thus far make it possible to recommend with reasonable assurance certain types of training that promise to be of great value. The suggestions offered will serve their purpose if they stimulate further study of problems relating to developmental instruction in reading in secondary schools and junior colleges.

(1) Junior High School. As indicated earlier, the training provided in junior high schools may be closely correlated with such fields as English or the social studies, or it may be given during periods reserved in the time schedule for the purpose. The materials used should relate to problems of specific interest to the pupils, should provoke good thinking, and afford opportunity for promoting needed growth in essential reading attitudes and habits. Some schools are making use of recent texts that explain the nature of important reading and study procedures and that provide exercises designed to promote the development of appropriate habits. Among the teaching problems that arise, the following merit special consideration:

1. To expand the meaning vocabulary systematically and to develop greater independence in deriving or finding appropriate meanings of words.
2. To promote increased power of comprehension and interpretation. For example:
   a. Comprehending exact meanings.
   b. Recognizing the broader meaning or significance of what is read.
   c. Appreciating the quality or worth of the ideas presented.

    d. Making critical judgments concerning the relevance and validity of the facts presented.

    e. Sensing the author's aim or purpose, and the assumptions that underlie his arguments.

3. To develop an insight into the procedures involved in reading different kinds of material and for different purposes. For example:

    a. An interesting story versus a detailed description.

    b. Reading to identify a sequence of events versus reading to judge the quality or worth of an author's ideas.

4. To improve efficiency in study activities involving reading. For example:

    a. Selecting facts from different sources.

    b. Searching for relationships.

    c. Determining effects resulting from certain conditions or factors.

    d. Applying principles, facts, and ideas in interpreting new situations.

    e. Generalizing on the basis of the evidence secured.

5. To train pupils to adjust the speed of reading to the purpose at hand, varying from very careful reading to skimming.

The foregoing list of teaching problems should be expanded in each school according to the needs of the pupils and the difficulties they encounter. The teacher of reading should maintain close contact with the teachers in other fields in order to recommend types of training that will promote increased efficiency in the pupils' reading. At times training initiated by teachers of the content fields should be continued during the reading period; under no circumstance, however, should the teacher of reading assume full responsibility for the types of guidance in reading to be given regularly in the content fields.

(2) Senior High School. The types of training provided in the junior high school should be continued at a more advanced level during the senior-high-school period. In addition, special emphasis should be given to training in the critical reading of different types of material. For this purpose use should be made of a few excellent books illustrating different kinds of composition — for example, history, science, argumentation. Through comparative studies of good procedure in reading and interpreting various kinds of material, new insights may be secured and the efficiency of the pupils greatly increased. The chief aims of such guidance include:

1. To promote the development of those modes of thought and interpretation essential in particular fields. Such training should be provided in close coöperation with the teachers of the various content fields. Indeed, it is desirable that they participate in the comparative study of methods of reading materials selected from different fields including their own.

2. To promote increased efficiency in study activities involving reading. While achieving the preceding aim, an examination should be made of effective study procedures in various fields, including common elements and differences. Such problems as the interpretation of graphs and tabular materials, the use of tables of contents and indexes in different kinds of books, the use of card catalogues, reference books, bibliographies, and guides in different fields, and the techniques of summarizing and abstracting different kinds of material should receive specific attention.

Some may argue that the types of training outlined above should be given exclusively in the various curricular fields. No effort is made here to minimize the responsibility for guidance in reading of the teacher of a specific field. Experience shows clearly, however, that the types of studies here recommended promote clearer understanding and greater efficiency than can be secured through guidance provided in separate fields only. The program outlined has the unique advantage that it aids in coördinating the training given throughout a school and in increasing responsibility for definite guidance in each field.

(3) Junior College. The instruction in reading provided in the junior college should continue the types of training outlined for the senior high school and introduce new elements. For example, readings may be assigned and conferences arranged concerning the nature of historical and scientific writings, the elements of logic and scientific method, the characteristics of various patterns of thinking (such as inductive and deductive), and the relation of sentence form and structure to the expression of thought. As a means of applying to reading the facts learned, a few excellent books in several fields should be studied intensively. Special attention should be given to techniques involved in critical interpretation and evaluation, such as sensing the underlying assumptions, recognizing validity or error (that is, error of fact or error in logic of conclusions or assumptions), and drawing inferences from the facts presented. As a result, students should be far more thoroughly prepared than many are at present to engage in intelligent interpretation and critical study of various types of material. We face here an almost virgin field. Preliminary experiments supply striking evidence of the possibility of rich returns through well-conceived developmental training in reading for junior-college students. The next decade should witness notable developments at this level.

b. *Guidance in Reading in the Various Curricular Fields.* Supplementing the basic training that has been outlined, pupils should receive continuous guidance in reading and study activities in the various curricular fields. Such guidance is essential if pupils are to profit to the fullest extent from the intellectual opportunities the school provides. Each teacher has many responsibilities in this connection, of which three will be considered here.

(1) The first is to stimulate pupils to exercise those desirable reading and study habits that have been acquired before entering a given course or that are being emphasized at the same time through developmental training in reading. To this end, carefully planned assignments should be given to aid pupils in recognizing the purposes to be achieved and the most effective reading and study procedures to adopt. The use of a few minutes daily to consider desirable reading and study activities and to point out questionable practices has proved very profitable. During supervised study periods teachers should observe the reading and study habits of their pupils, identify misdirected efforts, and provide individual or group help as needed. Careful study should also be made of the reports presented by pupils in class to determine wherein their reading has been effective or ineffective. Only through constant attention to such matters can teachers promote maximal growth in their pupils.

(2) A second responsibility of each teacher is to promote efficiency in those reading and study habits that are more or less peculiar to each field. This step is essential if pupils acquire the habits and understandings that characterize capable students in specific fields. Examples of important types of training follow:

1. Clarifying the meanings and concepts that attach to important words in the general and technical vocabulary of a given field. As indicated in various recent reports, the development of an adequate meaning vocabulary presents a very urgent problem in practically every content field.

2. Comprehending a principle or an explanation, such as the principle of refrigeration in a general science text or the explanation given in a civics text of representation in the Senate.

3. Understanding a problem to be solved, such as grasping the essential conditions of a mathematics problem.

4. Utilizing in the interpretation of what is read the basic principles relating to a field, such as interpreting facts read in geography in terms of the relations between natural environmental conditions and human activities.

(3) A third responsibility of every teacher is to awaken interest in supplementary reading and to provide abundant opportunity for it. This type of reading is very important because it extends the experiences of pupils far beyond the limits of class discussions and of in-

tensive reading assignments. It quickens their thinking concerning numerous problems in a given field. It intensifies their interests in such problems and frequently leads to the discovery of avocational or professional interests. Each teacher who leads pupils into paralleling, contrasting, or enriching intellectual experiences through reading outside of textbooks should herself understand, and make her pupils understand, the differences between intensive and extensive reading. Many pupils who do not receive such help fail to adjust their habits of reading to the major purposes to be achieved.

The foregoing discussion has aimed merely to emphasize the importance of continuous guidance in reading in each content field. Various related problems and appropriate teaching procedures are considered at length in Chapter V.

c. Additional Guidance in Reading for Those Who Encounter Difficulty. The two general types of guidance in reading just described are essential for all pupils but they do not fully meet the needs of some of them. One such group includes pupils who are able to read the textbooks usually assigned but who encounter considerable difficulty in doing so. These pupils need more or less intensive guidance for a time in a wide range of reading and study activities. Two general plans have been adopted in providing for their needs. In schools in which there are several sections at a given grade level, those who are in need of special help are assigned to one or more sections and given systematic guidance in reading in a particular field, usually English or the social studies. A second plan is to provide special help in all classes for those pupils who are encountering difficulty in reading assigned materials.

The materials in either case are those regularly used in the classes or grades involved. The methods, however, are modified considerably to promote rapid growth in reading as well as satisfactory mastery of content. For example, many pupils have not acquired sufficient experience in a field to be able to interpret easily what they have read. Accordingly, more time and effort are required to develop an adequate background for each unit through the recall of related experiences, the use of pictures and illustrative materials, and the oral presentation of new and illuminating facts. Experience shows clearly the value of such steps in preparing pupils for reading and study activities. The amount of help needed varies with classes and individuals. The steps taken arouse interest, develop centers of interpretation, quicken thinking, and promote clear interpretation.

A second need relates to the vocabulary encountered. Investigations show conclusively that a limited meaning vocabulary is one of the chief causes of poor comprehension. More than the usual amount of attention should be directed to both the general and the technical vocabulary of the materials read. This can be done effectively during the preparatory step referred to above by introducing key words in the discussion, writing them on the blackboard, and commenting on their meaning and significance. Such steps have been found very valuable at the junior-college level as well as in the lower schools. Not infrequently teachers find that pupils need training in the use of the dictionary as an aid to greater independence in recognizing the meanings and pronunciations of words.

A third means of helping pupils is to provide guidance in reading for specific purposes, such as finding answers to questions of judgment, recognizing the author's organization of facts, and selecting materials relating specifically to a problem. The character and amount of such help varies widely among groups and individuals.

A fourth type of help needed relates to specific deficiencies in interpretation exhibited by individual pupils. Studies made by McCallister,[1] for example, identified many poor habits such as the following: " comprehension of only a part of a passage as shown by the omission of points of major importance," " misinterpretation because of lack of preciseness in comprehension," " failure to discriminate between relevant and irrelevant material," and " inability to recognize the relation between a known series of facts and an assigned problem based on those facts." Such deficiencies inevitably result in unsatisfactory progress. They should be recognized and made the basis of specific training.

The guidance provided should extend to all types of reading difficulties that the pupils encounter. Methods of appraising the attainments and needs of pupils are treated more fully in Chapter XI. Special guidance should be continued until pupils have corrected their chief difficulties and have materially increased their reading efficiency. An unpublished study shows that special help in reading during a semester resulted in distinct improvement in the case of over eighty percent of the pupils. Furthermore, the improvement gained was retained over a summer's vacation in over seventy-five percent of the cases.

d. Corrective and Remedial Training for Severe Cases of Reading Deficiency. Pupils who rank below the sixth-grade norm, or who are

---

[1] James M. McCallister. " Reading difficulties in studying content subjects." *Elementary School Journal*, 31: November, 1930, 191–201.

unable to read the materials used in the grades to which they are assigned, should be organized into special groups for both corrective and remedial training. Group guidance should be supplemented daily by much individual help. Because the deficiencies are so varied, the reading materials used should be selected with care, and should be sufficiently simple to be read with reasonable understanding. Similar provision should be made in all subjects to which these pupils are assigned. The instruction in reading that is given should not be in addition to a regular program of work; it should be one of the four or five units of a normal program.

The methods used should be adapted to the specific needs of the groups and individuals taught. The training and guidance provided, however, should be subordinated, as a rule, to the mastery of interesting content or to the solution of challenging problems. Not infrequently teachers attempt to secure improvement through the use of exercises that lack continuity and fail to arouse interest. Experience shows clearly, however, the wisdom of providing activities that help pupils to recognize their needs and that provide motives for vigorous effort to overcome them. Furthermore, most of the training given should be based on materials that are rich in content values. The statement should be added that other materials, such as standardized practice lessons, may be used on occasions to provide desirable types of practice and to measure progress.

It will be impossible here to discuss at length the numerous problems involved in diagnosis and remedial instruction. Detailed suggestions for measuring the attainments and needs of pupils are considered at length in Chapter XII; diagnosis and remedial procedures in the case of severe reading deficiencies are considered in Chapter XIII.[1]

4. Teachers of Reading

All high schools and junior colleges should have on their faculties one or more teachers thoroughly prepared in the field of reading. Such

---

[1] The following references will prove of special help to those who assume responsibility for deficient readers:

William S. Gray. "Reading difficulties in college." *Journal of Higher Education,* 7: October, 1936, 356–362.

James M. McCallister. *Remedial and Corrective Instruction in Reading.* (D. Appleton-Century Company: New York, 1936)

Ruth Strang. "Improving students' reading." *Journal of Higher Education,* 5: November, 1934, 426–432.

teachers should be responsible for continuous studies and inventories of the reading accomplishments and needs of pupils. On the basis of evidence available they should organize reading programs for their schools, including developmental training in reading for all pupils, supplementary guidance for those who encounter difficulty in reading the regularly assigned materials, and corrective and remedial instruction for seriously retarded pupils. In addition they should furnish information concerning reading problems to teachers in the other fields of the curriculum. Furthermore, they should stimulate and direct among staff members studies of problem cases in reading and should coöperate actively in helping to provide reading materials adapted to the level of achievement of poor readers. In these and other ways the reading teacher may render an invaluable service to the school as a whole, to the members of the staff, and to the pupils.

SUB–COMMITTEE ON CHAPTER V

Chairmen

ERNEST HORN, Professor of Education, State University of Iowa, Iowa City, Iowa

MABEL SNEDAKER, Supervisor Social Studies and Extension, University Elementary School, State University of Iowa, Iowa City, Iowa

Associates

CARTER V. GOOD, Professor of Education, University of Cincinnati, Cincinnati, Ohio

ALICE M. JORDAN, Supervisor of Work for Children, Boston Public Library, Boston, Massachusetts

MAXIE N. WOODRING, Professor of Education, Teachers College, Columbia University, New York City

CHAPTER V

READING IN THE VARIOUS FIELDS OF THE CURRICULUM

Mabel Snedaker
Supervisor of Social Studies
University Elementary School, College of Education
State University of Iowa, Iowa City, Iowa
and
Ernest Horn
Professor of Education and Director of University Elementary School
State University of Iowa, Iowa City, Iowa

I. Introduction

The fundamental importance of reading in serving the needs of contemporary life, the types and purposes of reading, and the place of reading in the school program have been discussed in earlier chapters of this Yearbook. The purpose of this chapter is to point out the significance of the relationship existing between reading and other fields of the curriculum and to suggest ways of developing and guiding reading in relation to other school subjects and activities. The discussion that follows is concerned, therefore, with the basic importance of reading as an essential tool in study, the relation of reading to literature, the contribution of an enriched curriculum to the development of ability in reading, the relationship of wide reading to the enrichment of the content subjects, and the subsequent problems of study growing out of this enrichment, the responsibility of all teachers for the effective direction of the reading pertinent to their curricular fields, and suggested methods and means for developing efficient reading habits.

II. The Nature of the Relation between Reading and the Various Curricular Fields

1. Basic Importance of Reading Ability in Study

Reading is so intimately related to all the work of the school that it is difficult to determine where reading leaves off and study begins. This intimate relationship is admirably expressed by Lyman:

. . . the activities of reading, of thinking, and of studying are considered as three aspects of the one process by which we learn to use materials which we find in printed form. All are activities of the mind. We *read* serious books to get ideas; we *think* about them to see what these ideas mean; we *study* ideas and their meanings, endeavoring to make them our permanent possessions and to get ready to use them in problems of our own.[1]

Reading and other curricular fields are reciprocally related. On the one hand, skill in reading is indispensable to the study of all subjects, and wide reading plays an important part in motivating and enriching thought. On the other hand, the various fields of the curriculum motivate, develop, and maintain the abilities essential to the use of books and create permanent interests in reading.

Although much has been written about the importance of reading in the various curricular fields, the degree to which reading limits learning does not in practice seem to be fully recognized. Under present conditions, and perhaps under ideal conditions, pupils must obtain from books a large part of their knowledge and much of their stimulation to thinking. Reading is therefore an essential tool in the study of most parts of the curriculum. Closely related to reading is the ability to locate books and articles that deal with problems met in and out of school; to select, understand, and appraise pertinent problems; to organize the data, often secured from a variety of references, so that the information will aid in the solution of their problems; and to provide for the retention, the improvement, and the use of what has been learned. Shortcomings in any of these types of abilities are quickly reflected in the quality of the pupils' work in all subjects studied from books. There is probably no single source of frustration in study that is so serious as that found in deficiencies in reading ability.

The effective use of any of the abilities cited in the preceding paragraph requires the exercise of many reading knowledges and skills. For example, in outlining, which plays an important part in the organization of data, the reader must be able to comprehend what is read, select the topic or heading of the paragraph, select the main points, choose subheadings, and decide between supporting and irrelevant details. If the outline is to be written, he must have a knowledge of the compositional skills involved, such as capitalization, punctuation, and form. All these abilities must be systematically developed.

---

[1] R. L. Lyman. *The Mind at Work.* P. 14. (Scott, Foresman and Company: Chicago, 1924)

The grade level at which training in the various types of study activities should begin depends on the needs and the previous training of the group. Even such difficult skills as those involved in outlining may need to be introduced in the primary grades. For example, elementary phases of outlining are useful to first-grade children who are planning an assembly program on " Our Trip to the Williams' Farm." The college student finds that skill in outlining facilitates clear thinking. As the ideas considered become more difficult and as thought processes applied in interpreting the ideas grow more reflective, the resulting outlines become increasingly complex. Training in organizing ideas in outline form should be given on progressively higher levels from the primary grades through college.

A statement of the desired outcomes in reading for each important division of the reading program will be found in Chapter IV. No attempt will be made in this discussion, therefore, to assign skills to specific grades. The important consideration is that definite training in effective reading habits should be given early and should keep pace with students' needs, even to the college level.

2. The Relation of Reading to Literature

" Literature is most appreciated and makes its best contribution when it is approached in a recreational mood of curiosity and not in the way of study and work." The foregoing statement by Sterling Andrus Leonard is descriptive of the best classroom practice in the teaching of literature.[1] Enjoyment is recognized as an essential factor in developing appreciation. Consequently, all teaching procedures are planned to help the student not only to comprehend but also to enjoy the experience that the author portrays.

The acceptance of the point of view that the reading of a literary selection should be a pleasurable experience has influenced reading instruction in several ways:

(1) Definite reading periods are given over to the enjoyment of literature. Many schools have a separate reading period devoted to recreational reading. Every effort is made to have this period one to which students look forward with eager anticipation. Much attention has been devoted both to the selection (from the world's greatest literature) of materials that students enjoy reading or hearing read, and to the organization of these materials into units closely related to children's interests and problems. The approach to any

---

[1] *Report of the National Committee on Reading.* Twenty-Fourth Yearbook of this Society, Part I. P. 143. (Public School Publishing Company: Bloomington, Illinois, 1924)

literary selection and the consideration of it are always recreative rather than analytical. A wide variety of reading experiences are provided: free reading, silent reading of a selection in order to share in later discussion, oral reading in an audience situation, dramatization, the singing of poetry set to music, book reviews, the memorization of poetry, and numerous other experiences.

(2) Since all the activities of the literature period are intended to promote the enjoyment of literature, the importance of good oral reading as a means of sharing experiences with others has become increasingly apparent. The improvement of oral reading is receiving much emphasis in the literature program through such procedures as informal dramatization and the informal reading of plays; book reviews in which the funniest, the most exciting, or the most interesting part of the story is read aloud; verse-speaking choirs; reading aloud by the teacher or by pupils who read well so that students hear good oral reading; and reading in groups in an audience situation. Grouping children for oral reading on the basis of reading ability and of interest has distinct advantages: first, materials suited to their reading ability may be supplied to each group so that no child is ever asked to stumble through a selection too difficult for him to read orally; second, the selection presented by each group may be new to the others, thereby assuring an interested audience. The stimulation afforded by interested listeners and the reader's knowledge that he can read a selection so that others will enjoy it are strong incentives to read well. It is taken for granted, of course, that the easy material supplied to a poor reader is below neither his own interest level nor that of the group, and that the material has been carefully prepared by the reader.

(3) The enjoyment of literature in the reading period, together with the broadening of interests and the stimulation to extensive voluntary reading provided by the enrichment of other curricular fields, has greatly increased the amount of independent reading for pleasure. This has served to emphasize the importance of skillful guidance of children's leisure reading so that it is wholesome and well balanced and so that there is consistent growth in the building of fine and discriminating reading tastes. It has served to emphasize also the mutual value of the close relation between literature and the other fields of the curriculum.

(4) Stress upon the enjoyment of literature has broadened the scope of pupils' interests and activities during the reading period as well as in leisure time. For example, a visitor to a sixth-grade class in literature that had become deeply interested in a unit on ballads found groups and individuals engaging in the following activities: searching ballads about Robin Hood for typical phrases that might be used to make the conversation in a play seem characteristic of the time; studying Strutt's *Sports and Pastimes of the People of England* [1] and other references to learn the part played by Robin Hood and

---

[1] Joseph Strutt. *The Sports and Pastimes of the People of England.* (T. T. and J. Tegg: London, 1833)

his merry men in the May Day Games; consulting the footnotes in collections of old English songs for information concerning the May Day ceremony known as the Hal-an-Tow; making a list of songs about Robin Hood that might be used in the play; sketching costumes for the characters in the play; reading directions for the old English dance, Sellenger's 'Round; attempting to relate experiences of their own in the style of the ballad; and comparing different versions of Robin Hood ballads.

3. The Contribution of an Enriched Curriculum to the Development of Ability in Reading

The contribution of effective reading habits to achievement in all fields of the curriculum is no more significant than is that of an enriched curriculum to the development of proficiency in reading. An enriched curriculum promotes the development of reading ability in numerous ways. First, it encourages extensive reading, both in connection with planned units or assignments and in connection with the voluntary reading that the curriculum motivates. Second, wide reading in the various fields of the curriculum to solve problems or to satisfy interests encourages a more aggressive and thoughtful search for meaning. Such reading results in an appreciation of the significance and the implications of ideas and cultivates a high level of interpretation. Third, an enriched curriculum creates and cultivates permanent interests. For example, the child who, through reading, discussion, and participation in various activities, becomes deeply interested in the conservation of forest resources continues to read and think about this subject.

The interrelation between reading and other aspects of the curriculum is well illustrated in the social studies. Every part of a well-planned program in the social studies exerts a favorable influence upon reading. The assignment stimulates interest, helps the pupil to set up specific purposes to guide his reading, and, consequently, leads to an aggressive search for meaning that is entirely lacking when pupils read material not pertinent to their interests and needs. It is a matter of general observation that pupils who are deeply interested in a problem will secure meaning from a selection that would otherwise be too difficult for them. For example, one group of elementary-school pupils, interested in learning how to destroy the tussock moths that were killing trees on the playground, secured information from books much more difficult than the textbooks designed for their grade. Moreover, a good assignment supplies the student with a logical basis for evaluating, selecting, and organizing the ideas presented in the selection, thereby encouraging the building of clear, accurate, and well-organized concepts and the development of efficient methods of work. Passive reading, on the contrary, is likely to result in inaccurate and poorly organized concepts and in ineffective habits of work. Lacking specific purposes to guide his reading, the pupil often misses the central thought of a selection and remembers only details that catch his attention.

Other steps in instruction contribute to the improvement of reading. The study period is largely a reading period and affords unusual opportunities for remedial work if pupils' efforts to understand, to appraise, and to organize the materials read are wisely guided. The class discussion also plays an important part in the improvement of reading, not only because it motivates reading, but also because it affords the pupil an opportunity to recognize and correct wrong impressions and to enlarge, clarify, and organize his ideas effectively.

Extensive voluntary reading is undertaken as a result of interests created or deepened by the social studies. During a study of relief maps the children in one geography class in the intermediate grades raised the question, How was the earth formed? During the leisure reading hour many books, such as R. L. Ditmar's *The Book of Prehistoric Animals*,[1] Edith B. Walker and Charles C. Mook's *Tales of the First Animals*,[2] and W. Maxwell Reed's *The Earth for Sam*,[3] were read by members of the group.

Reading, of course, is only one of many approaches to understanding in the social studies. For example, one group of children who were studying the history of American Indians listened to Indian music, and learned to sing Indian songs and to dance Indian dances. They studied Indian designs and used these designs in decorating the tepee, drum, pottery, and other articles in the making of which they duplicated as nearly as possible the materials and the processes used by the Indians. Many periods in which children were free to follow out their own interests were spent in painting a large backdrop for the stage. The backdrop was to be used during an assembly program about Indian life that had been planned in oral-composition periods. An excursion

---

[1] R. L. Ditmar. *The Book of Prehistoric Animals*. (J. B. Lippincott and Company: New York, 1935)

[2] Edith B. Walker and Charles C. Mook. *Tales of the First Animals*. (Farrar and Rinehart, Inc.: New York, 1930)

[3] W. Maxwell Reed. *The Earth for Sam*. (Harcourt, Brace and Company: New York, 1931)

to an Indian reservation resulted in firsthand information concerning Indians of today. During the literature period, the group enjoyed listening to Grace Moon's *Chi-wee*,[1] J. W. Schultz's *Sinopah, the Indian Boy*,[2] and Henry Beston's *Sons of Kai*.[3]

In a similar way, another group of children who were interested in pioneer life dipped and molded candles; leached wood ashes into lye and used the lye in making soft soap and hominy; washed, carded, spun, and wove wool into cloth; grated soft corn and made bread; parched corn; made apple leather, dried apples, and dried pumpkin rings; split out ' puncheons ' and ' clapboards'; demonstrated with logs methods of quarter-notching and half-notching; made models of well sweeps, a latch with a latchstring, and a hominy-block; held old-fashioned spelldowns; and dramatized the singing school. They made an excursion to the log cabins at the city park to identify ' puncheon,' ' clapboards,' ' chinking,' and similar terms. They consulted persons able to contribute information concerning the best methods of carrying out activities. For example, they interviewed a woman who could spin and make hominy and soft soap. They invited old people to speak to them about pioneer days and asked an old fiddler to play and ' call off ' the dances at a party given for their parents. Planning and evaluating the activities provided many opportunities for discussion and for organization.

As related lessons in other fields, the children learned to sing pioneer songs, to sing and play party games, and to dance the old square dances. They devoted art periods to drawing and painting pictures of pioneer articles for friezes, for illustrations in summary notebooks, for charts, and for other purposes motivated by a consideration of problems relating to pioneer life. Arithmetic was needed in solving such problems as the following:

1. A pound of paraffin will make eight large dipped candles. How many pounds will we have to buy if each one in our class of 24 pupils makes a candle?

2. An ounce of beeswax to every pound of paraffin makes better candles. How much will it cost for beeswax at 5¢ an ounce?

The stories, summaries, letters, and records for which a need arose as the unit developed provided lessons in composition. One lesson in

---

[1] Grace Moon. *Chi-wee*. (Doubleday, Doran and Company: Garden City, N. Y., 1925)

[2] J. W. Schultz. *Sinopah, the Indian Boy*. (Houghton Mifflin Company: Boston, 1913)

[3] Henry Beston. *Sons of Kai*. (The Macmillan Company: New York, 1926)

written composition consisted in the writing of individual summaries following the completion of a problem about pioneer foods, each child being responsible for a clear, concise, and accurate summary of a topic of his own choosing. One child, for example, wrote about " Pioneer Sweetening," a second about " How We Made Apple Leather," and a third about " Kinds of Wild Game Which the Pioneers Had." In one oral-composition lesson attempts were made to give good explanations of ' cracklings,' ' trying out,' and other terms from a " Pioneer History Vocabulary Chart," which had been compiled by the children themselves.

All these activities helped to enrich and to vitalize the social studies and, hence, contributed ultimately to the improvement of reading. Through the enlargement of experience and the creation of interest, they broadened understanding, built permanent interests, and encouraged the building of better reading tastes. Moreover, these various means of enrichment stimulated and involved reading. Extensive reading was essential both in securing the information upon which the activities were based and in checking accuracy as an activity was developed. One group of children wrote a play in which the scene was laid at a ferry where travelers by land compare experiences with travelers by water. The pupils not only read widely as preliminary preparation for writing the play, but they also checked with reference material as they wrote, in order to make sure that the experiences related by their characters were typical of the experiences of real pioneers. Other phases of reading were motivated by these activities. The study skills needed in locating, understanding, selecting, and organizing data were developed in lessons giving training in basic reading skills, while books and stories about pioneer life were enjoyed in periods devoted to recreational reading as well as in leisure time outside of school. For example, the study-reading period for one day was devoted to finding the answers in a basic reference book to specific questions, such as, " What games were played at pioneer parties? " The children spent the recreational reading period for the day in reading aloud carefully prepared stories about pioneer amusements, such as " The Dance at Grandma's " from Wilder's *Little House in the Big Woods*,[1] or " A Little Girl's Button String " and " A Quilting Party " from Shetter's *When Grandma Was a Little Girl*.[2]

---

[1] Laura Ingalls Wilder. *Little House in the Big Woods*. (Harper and Brothers: New York, 1932)

[2] Stella C. Shetter. *When Grandma Was a Little Girl*. (Rand, McNally and Company: Chicago, 1926)

The foregoing illustrations from the social studies showing how the enrichment of experience and the creation of interest promote the development of reading ability may be paralleled in other fields of the curriculum. In a town where an epidemic of smallpox caused the board of health to require vaccination of every child, the pupils of the sixth-grade class in health were eager to do something to convince doubtful pupils of the value of vaccination and to build morale in the school. They raised problems; read extensively; consulted the school nurse, doctors, and health officers. After much evaluation and discussion, they planned and gave the assembly program outlined below. In order that their talks might be easily understood by an audience ranging from third-grade children to parents, they made and used slides, large graphs, charts, illustrations, and cards on which were printed key words, such as *vaccination*.

How Smallpox Was Conquered

Announcer
  What Smallpox Is
  The History of Smallpox before Vaccination
  Objections to Inoculation
  Edward Jenner
  How Vaccination Was Discovered
  The Spread of Knowledge about Vaccination
  The Opposition to Vaccination
  The Acceptance of Vaccination
  How You Should Take Care of Your Vaccination
  Some Famous Smallpox Epidemics
  A Story about Vaccination in California When It Was a Part of Mexico
  Laws Regarding Smallpox
  The Success of Vaccination

Stage Managers

In Charge of Music

In Charge of Programs

III. The Relation of Wide Reading to the Enrichment of the Content Fields

1. Difficulties Growing Out of the General and Abstract Nature of the Textbook

A large number of careful investigations have shown that, in general, textbooks are poorly comprehended by pupils of the grades in which they are used. The poor comprehension results from two factors: first, the general reading ability of pupils in most schools is lower than it should be; second, the textbooks themselves have deficiencies that make them difficult to understand. The excessive number and the inherent difficulty of the topics that are included in typical textbooks, as well as the meagerness and the abstractness of the treatment, makes these books hard to read. It is not possible for the pupil, no matter how high his intelligence or general reading ability may be, to obtain an adequate understanding of a difficult topic from the brief and abstract statements that are made about it in the average textbook. Many ills follow from these shortcomings: the conscientious pupil, unable to get the meaning, may be driven to memorizing or paraphrasing the words of the book; the habit of attempting to understand what is read is discouraged; the impossibility of understanding the textbook, unless supplemented by the teacher's comments or by collateral readings, deprives the pupil of the satisfaction that comes from insight and builds progressively a distaste for reading. Either from the point of view of developing meaning or from that of building right habits of reading, the limitations of the textbook without amplification should be clearly recognized.

Recent textbooks in content subjects have shown some improvement in reducing the reading difficulty of the material. Efforts have been made to simplify the vocabulary, and the books have been somewhat increased in size in order that more details and illustrations might be included. These modifications do little, however, to solve problems arising out of the inherent difficulty of the ideas, and the treatment is still much too meager. There is great need for supplementary materials that are authentic; vivid and absorbing in style; rich in detail, anecdote, and incident; and generously supplied with pictures, maps, diagrams, and charts.

Various means of supplementing the textbook — or, perhaps better, of making it understood — have been suggested, such as visual aids, excursions, comments by the teacher, the use of objects, constructive activities, and collateral reading. The most important of these is probably collateral reading. Experiments have consistently shown the superiority of extensive reading over what is ineptly called 'intensive reading.' [1] The need of wide reading as a means of achieving clear and

---

[1] Carter V. Good. *The Supplementary Reading Assignment.* (Warwick and York, Inc.: Baltimore, 1927)

Francis D. Curtis. *Some Values Derived from Extensive Reading in General Science.* Contributions to Education, No. 103. (Teachers College, Columbia University: New York City, 1924)

Robert D. Weaver. "Extensive and intensive methods in history," *The Historical Outlook,* 23: October, 1932, 222–290.

accurate meanings, of giving a vivid sense of reality, and of developing interest in the problem at hand is generally accepted. Without wide reading and other sources of experience, instruction tends to become formal and verbalistic. Few of the practices that characterize the best modern instruction are possible on the basis of the textbook alone.

2. The Need for Collateral Reading as a Means of Achieving Clear and Accurate Meanings

Collateral reading is particularly important as a means of building the rich background of meaningful concepts that make possible the re-creation of experience. Perhaps no other content field illustrates this point more aptly than does that of the social studies. In reading history, the child must be able to live vicariously the lives of persons in times and places that are far removed from his experience if he is to interpret an historical period in the light of its own time. In reading geography, he must be able to enter into the essential realities of life in a region, if he is to understand the activities of its people. In each subject collateral reading can supply much of the wealth of detail, anecdote, and illustration necessary to give the vivid, concrete impressions that lend reality to life and provide an appropriate background when the child is concerned with distant lands and with peoples who lived in other times and under other conditions.

3. The Importance of Collateral Reading in Providing for Individual Differences in Reading Ability

Materials that range widely in reading difficulty are essential in order to prevent injustice to both the poor and the excellent reader. The reading abilities within an intermediate-grade group studying the westward movement may vary from that of the pupil who reads with difficulty a fifth-grade book, such as Clark's *Westward to the Pacific*, to that of the pupil who reads easily a college textbook, such as Riegel's *America Moves West*.[1] If the poor reader is not to build ineffectual reading habits and if the good reader is not to become intellectually lazy, the reading list must include books easy enough to be readily understood by the poor reader and books difficult enough to challenge

---

[1] Marion Clark. *Westward to the Pacific*. (Charles Scribner's Sons: New York, 1934)

Robert Riegel. *America Moves West*. (Henry Holt and Company; New York, 1931)

the interest and the best efforts of the most competent reader. Collateral readings are a valuable means of supplying materials that provide for individual differences in reading ability.

Attention should be called to the fallacy upon which many so-called ' easy ' references seem to be built; namely, that material can be simplified by giving less space to each topic. On the contrary, books intended for the poor reader should be rich in interesting details, pictures, and illustrative anecdotes, for these concrete elements hold his interest and challenge his thinking.

4. Types of Collateral Reading

Although collateral reading is probably the most widely used means of enlarging understanding, its values are not always fully secured because of errors in the selection and use of materials. Failure to distinguish between different types of collateral reading and to evaluate the contribution made by each is a common cause of difficulty. A detailed discussion of the values of various kinds of collateral reading is beyond the scope of this chapter, but a few principles concerning the selection and the use of recognized types may be suggested.

a. Reference Materials. It is generally recommended that reference reading include reading from additional textbooks, encyclopedias, yearbooks, atlases, government and state bulletins, and similar materials containing indispensable information in adequate detail. The selection of reference materials is assumed to be governed by such criteria as authenticity, clearness, interesting style, pertinence to the unit of subject matter, well-organized index, and good mechanical make-up. However, teachers of content subjects are constantly being annoyed by discovering that many of the references suggested in the lists at the ends of chapters contain only a paragraph or a few pages that are pertinent to the problem at hand and that the information given in these pages is sometimes out of date. Since the references are seldom annotated, the teacher in the school where funds or library facilities are limited finds the task of selection unnecessarily complicated. Moreover, there is often no indication of the comparative reading difficulty of the books in the list. At best, the teacher's task of acquiring a thorough knowledge of essential reference materials is arduous. It would be greatly facilitated if the following points were observed in compiling a list of references:

(1) The list should be selective rather than extensive.

(2) Since funds for the purchase of reference materials are often

restricted, a minimal bibliography of books containing the most help on the largest number of problems should be suggested.

(3) References should be classified with respect to approximate reading difficulty under some such heading as, "For Grades III–V."

.(4) If the material is to be used by younger children, a topical arrangement of references is often desirable. For example, a class working on a problem in science dealing with the value of snakes as a means of helping to control harmful rodents and insects found it helpful to have references listed under the topical headings: kinds of snakes in our state, the food of snakes, habits of snakes, harm done by snakes, the good that snakes do, foolish notions about snakes.

Since reference materials vary widely with respect to arrangement, organization, and content, the pupil will not be able to use them effectively unless he is given an explanation of the type of information to be gained from each source and unless he receives instruction in the specific skills needed in order to gain this information economically. As various important sources, such as *The World Almanac, The Pageant of America,* bulletins from many national and state agencies, atlases, and encyclopedias, are needed in the solution of problems, the books should be shown to the pupils and the general plan of arrangement of each explained. Tables of statistical data from *The World Almanac* and other references may be copied on the blackboard and instruction be given in how to read and interpret such information with reference to the problem under consideration. During the assignment of a lesson pupils should be encouraged to suggest sources that they think are likely to contain helpful and reliable data bearing upon the problem or topic to be discussed. Occasionally a pupil who has checked his judgment of a source by finding and reporting information to the class may be called upon to demonstrate, step by step, exactly how he located and evaluated the data.

Since biographies, memoirs, journals, diaries, letters, and travel stories are at once history and the materials with which the historian works, they are included in collateral reading lists at all levels of instruction. However, the use made of such sources at the elementary-school level is far too meager, partly because some of these sources (particularly journals, diaries, and memoirs) are not commonly so accessible as are general reference books and partly because there is a tendency to underestimate the interest that such materials hold for younger pupils. One fifth-grade class, interested in westward expansion, read with deep interest Majors' *Seventy Years on the Frontier*,[1] and Steele's *Across the Plains in 1850*,[2] as well as numerous excerpts from Thwaites' *Original Journals of Lewis and Clark*.[3] A comparison of such firsthand accounts with the information given in the textbook arouses in the pupil a desire to consult sources in order to enrich the limited horizon presented by the textbook. He thereby acquires both a respect for source materials and a basis for evaluating books. A more extensive use of such source materials in both the reference and the recreational reading program should be encouraged.

b. Recreational Reading Materials That Supplement the Systematic Reference Reading. Books that are accurate in essential background and that have the virtue of being true to human experience often assist the child to live imaginatively in other times and places. For example, the child who is studying pioneer history may gain a clearer understanding of many pioneer activities through sharing the interesting experiences of Laura and Mary, as told in Mrs. Wilder's *Little House in the Big Woods*.[4] Smoking meat for winter use, loading the long rifle, harvesting oats with a cradle, and many other processes are described with a detail usually lacking in social-science reference books and in such a way as to show the significance of these processes in the lives of the people. *Early Candlelight Stories*, by Stella C. Shetter,[5] *Caddie Woodlawn*, by Carol Ryrie Brink,[6] and other well-written books with authentic background aid in giving a sense of reality to a period that is far removed from the child's experience.

Geography, no less than history, may be invested with reality through the reading of books that present such a vivid and accurate picture of life that the reader is able to enter vicariously into the essential conditions of life in a particular region. These books should be written by persons who have lived in the country of which they write, know it intimately, and possess a deep understanding of its people and

---

[1] Alexander Majors. *Seventy Years on the Frontier.* (Rand, McNally and Co.: Chicago, 1893)

[2] John Steele. *Across the Plains in 1850.* (Printed for the Caxton Club: Chicago, 1930)

[3] R. G. Thwaites. *Original Journals of Lewis and Clark.* Vols. I–IV. (Dodd, Mead and Company: New York, 1904–1905)

[4] Laura Ingalls Wilder. *Little House in the Big Woods.* Harper & Bros., New York, 1932.

[5] Stella C. Shetter. *Early Candlelight Stories.* (Rand, McNally and Company: Chicago, 1924)

[6] Carol Ryrie Brink. *Caddie Woodlawn.* (The Macmillan Company: New York, 1935)

its problems. Don Gopal Mukerji's stories of boy life in the small villages of India — *Hari the Jungle Lad*,[1] *Kari the Elephant*,[2] and *Ghond the Hunter* — are charming examples of books for young readers that meet these criteria. Among books recommended for higher grades may be cited Gertrude Atherton's *The Conqueror*,[3] which gives a description of a tropical storm far superior to that found in reference sources, and Rudyard Kipling's *Captains Courageous*,[4] which presents a vivid and authentic picture of the fishing industry off the banks of Newfoundland.

Certain precautions must be taken to prevent the misuse of fiction as collateral reading:

(1) The pupil must have clearly in mind the distinction between collateral reading of this type and the reading of reference and source materials. He must realize the purposes that each serves and he must use these purposes as a guide in deciding the type of reference he should consult. If his purpose is to assemble authentic information answering specific questions concerning life in the Middle Ages, he will read textbooks and reference sources. If his purpose is to people the Middle Ages with living persons, he may read Howard Pyle's *Men of Iron*[5] or A. Conan Doyle's *The White Company*.[6]

(2) The pupil must understand the limitations of such material. He must understand that vivid and absorbing fiction may not present a true picture because of the author's bias or lack of knowledge and penetration. He must understand, also, that fiction may be accurate in many of its details and yet create a wrong impression in the mind of the reader because the picture is incomplete.

(3) As in the case of reference materials, the reading lists should be selective rather than extensive. Recreational reading lists suggested as a means of supplementing systematic reference reading in geography are consistently poor in this respect. Many of the books included have slight merit either from the standpoint of broadening

---

[1] Don Gopal Mukerji. *Hari the Jungle Lad.* (E. P. Dutton and Company: New York, 1924)

[2] ——*Kari the Elephant.* (E. P. Dutton and Company: New York, 1922)

[3] Gertrude Atherton. *The Conqueror.* (Frederick A. Stokes: New York, 1934)

[4] Rudyard Kipling. *Captains Courageous.* (Doubleday, Doran and Co.: Garden City, New York, 1923)

[5] Howard Pyle. *Men of Iron.* (Harper and Brothers: New York)

[6] A. Conan Doyle. *The White Company.* (Harper and Brothers: New York, 1928)

knowledge or from that of deepening understanding. They seem to have been included in a bibliography about a country merely because the scene of the story is laid there, although no information about the geographical background of the region or about the lives of its people is presented. A far more serious shortcoming in these lists is the inclusion of books from which the reader acquires distorted and inaccurate ideas. Such books appear all too frequently in courses of study and in the bibliographies of supplementary readings recommended in textbooks in the content subjects.

c. Excerpts from Adult Literature Read Aloud by the Teacher. The children's increased understanding and appreciation well repay class time spent by the teacher in reading aloud carefully selected excerpts from books written for adults, which are too difficult for children to read for themselves. One of the most effective ways to give a child an appreciation of the hardships incident to providing the common necessities of life in pioneer days is for the teacher to read aloud, from *The Story of a Pioneer,*[1] the account of how Anna Howard Shaw and her brother Harry dug a well with spades and walled it with slabs of wood roughly joined together. To help the children gain an understanding of the relentless limitations of life in the wilderness, the teacher may read Chapter II from the same book, which gives vivid descriptions of life in a frontier home " one hundred miles from a railroad, forty miles from the nearest post office, and a half-dozen miles from any neighbors, save Indians, wolves, and wildcats." Sometimes entire books at the adult level may be profitably read to the children as a means of making subject matter concrete. The pupils in a second grade who were studying Indian history listened with interest to Frank Linderman's *Red Mother,*[2] and some sixth-grade children who were studying Latin America thoroughly enjoyed *Tschiffely's Ride.*[3]

Reading to the children excerpts from materials easy enough for them to read for themselves is an important means of introducing new books and of stimulating interest in source materials of unusual merit.

---

[1] Anna Howard Shaw. *The Story of a Pioneer.* (Harper and Brothers: New York, 1915)

[2] Frank Linderman. *Red Mother.* (John Day Company: New York, 1932)

[3] A. F. Tschiffely. *Tschiffely's Ride.* (Simon and Schuster: New York, 1933)

IV. Problems of Study Growing Out of the Enrichment of the Curriculum

1. The Responsibility of Teachers of All Subjects for Effective Study of Those Subjects

The present-day curriculum, with its emphasis upon organization in terms of problems and upon a rich collateral reading program, has directed attention to the extent to which achievement is limited by ineffective methods of study. The procedure of consulting references, assembling data from many sources, and using these data in the solution of problems has made evident deficiencies of study that were not apparent when children read from a single book. Teachers find that, no matter how skillfully they may use the assignment to give children strong purposes for reading, loose and rambling recitations are likely to result unless children are also taught how to achieve these purposes.

Growing recognition of the close relation between achievement and effective habits of study has influenced in two ways the point of view toward a program of training in study habits.

In the first place, the importance of skills involved in selecting, appraising, and organizing data has become increasingly apparent. Problem assignments that are broad enough in scope to provide challenge for the superior pupil and, at the same time, to encourage contribution by the poor pupil, tend away from questions that may be answered in a few brief statements toward those covering a wide range of information. How extensive the information may be is illustrated by the problem and sub-questions raised by a junior-high-school group interested in a study of " How the Race Has Put Itself on Record."

Problem III. *How important was the invention of hieroglyphic writing?*
  A. Where and when did the people live who developed hieroglyphs?
  B. How advanced in civilization were these people?
  C. What were the chief characteristics of the writing?
    1. What did the characters look like?
    2. How did the writing materials affect the form of the characters?
  D. How were hieroglyphics deciphered?
    1. Who did the work? When?
    2. How difficult was the task?
  E. What types of records have been deciphered?
  F. What were the advantages of hieroglyphics over pictographs and ideographs?

The data essential to an adequate discussion of this problem were secured from twenty-five books and periodicals. The references ranged in difficulty from relatively easy materials designed for use in intermediate grades, such as Ilin's *Black on White* [1] and *The Story of Writing*,[2] to books intended for adults, such as Mason's *History of the Art of Writing* [3] and Clodd's *The Story of the Alphabet*.[4] The amount of reading done by each pupil was dependent upon his interest and ability. To select from many sources the points bearing on a problem, to appraise their worth and interest, to compare and weigh the opinions of authors, to assign points to the sub-question to which they are relevant, to perfect their organization, and finally to plan a report to the class — all require greater efficiency in the selection, evaluation, and organization of ideas than does the preparation of a lesson from a single textbook. In extensive reading, moreover, there is not only a need for organization but a strong incentive for it. Some children read books that others in the group will not have an opportunity to consult. Since they have interesting and pertinent information that others may not have read, they see the necessity for organizing their information in such a way that it may be reported clearly and concisely.

In the second place, the increased awareness of the importance of effective study habits has directed attention to the importance of relating training in methods of study to the specific needs of each field of subject matter. Analysis of the skills that children need to use in preparing one day's assignments has shown that, in addition to skills involved in the study of most content lessons, there are special skills, knowledges, and abilities peculiar to different subjects. In order to solve a problem in geography, children may need to compare a map showing distribution of rainfall with a map showing length of the growing season. Undoubtedly such study abilities are most easily acquired in connection with the immediate need of them and with the materials in which they will be used. Furthermore, teachers are becoming convinced not only that the special skills and abilities peculiar to a subject are best taught in connection with that subject but also

---

[1] M. Ilin. *Black on White*. (J. B. Lippincott Co.: Philadelphia, 1932)

[2] *The Story of Writing*. Prepared under the auspices of the Committee on Materials of Instruction of the American Council on Education. (American Council on Education: Washington, 1932)

[3] William A. Mason. *A History of the Art of Writing*. (The Macmillan Company: New York, 1920)

[4] Edward Clodd. *The Story of the Alphabet*. (D. Appleton-Century Company: New York, 1915)

that skills common to the study of all content subjects function best in the situations in which they will be applied. Evaluation and interpretation are in a great measure affected by the purposes that direct the reading. The meaning a pupil will attach to a selection when considered in relation to a broad problem or a large unit of subject matter may be different from that which will result when the selection is read as unrelated material, even if the reading is guided by detailed questions. Moreover, the relations between ideas and the implications that may be drawn from these relations are likely to be better interpreted if the pupil is able to apply principles, generalizations, and knowledges recalled from previous experience in a specific field. This principle applies to the study of pictures and illustrative materials as well as to reading content. To the child who has been trained to look for things that indicate the geographic personality of a region, a picture of the harvesting of a crop on a farm in central Chile showing mountains in the background suggests implications concerning the probable impossibility of increasing the amount of land under production and the extent to which modern farm machinery is used. If the child has been adequately trained, he will want to check the validity of his tentative conclusions by consulting reference sources.

One result of the growing realization of the importance of relating training in methods of study to the specific needs of each field of the curriculum has been to place the responsibility for the efficient study of a subject squarely upon the teacher of that subject. In effect, every teacher becomes a teacher of reading. Such a plan has distinct advantages, not only for the motivation of drill in reading skills, but also for guidance in the application of the skills to specific fields.

Introducing skills when they are needed leads children to appreciate their usefulness and provides an immediate check on accomplishment. For example, pupils who find it difficult to locate materials in an attractive new set of encyclopedias are easily led to appreciate the need for lessons dealing with the use of the index volume; the pupils in a science class who have tried with only partial success to make a small trial sundial and who hope to be allowed to build a large one on the playground, work carefully on a reading lesson that gives training in how to follow accurately directions for making a sundial; and the children in an arithmetic class who are eager to raise their scores on a progress chart are keenly interested in a series of reading lessons that provide guidance in understanding verbal problems. In a similar way, drill to maintain skills previously introduced is readily motivated.

A class of pupils who have decided that graphs would be helpful in presenting committee reports upon the forest products of Latin America vigorously attack a drill lesson in which the essential features of every graph are reviewed and then checked with various types of graphs.

The fact that teachers of all subjects assume responsibility for efficient study of their subjects does not obviate the necessity for systematic teaching of study skills in definite reading periods. Since the specific functions served by a separate reading period have been developed in detail in Chapter III, it will be necessary to mention here only those phases bearing on the direction of study in all the work of the school. From the point of view of teachers of all subjects, provision for training in study skills in separate reading periods is important for several reasons. First, many reading skills are basic to the study of all subjects, and it is economical to teach such skills in a reading period. Second, many abilities need to be developed progressively, and this development can be accomplished more easily if the knowledges and skills involved are presented in the reading period than if they are introduced only when they are needed in the study of content subjects. For example, a knowledge of the sequence of the letters in the alphabet is the first step in teaching how to use the index. When facility in alphabetical arrangement has been acquired, children are instructed in the usefulness of the index, its location, its organization, finding words in it, deciding upon the key words in questions that are to be answered from the index, and other activities concerned in effective use of indexes. Third, emphasis upon study skills in a separate reading period serves as a constant reminder to both teacher and pupils of the importance of good reading habits.

Although reading periods are given over to systematic training in efficient methods of study, the work done in such periods should be closely related to the needs of the other fields of the curriculum that not only motivate the development of reading skills but also provide for their application and maintenance. Such integration is indispensable to a carefully planned remedial program. When one teacher is responsible for most of the instruction at any grade level, reading is readily integrated with the other work of the school. Even when instruction is departmentalized, however, there should be as close a relation as possible between the work of the reading period and that of geography, history, and other subjects.

Competent teachers assume responsibility for contributing to efficient methods of study in the following ways:

1. **Painstaking** effort is directed toward discovering whether pupils possess the background of ideas that make it possible for them to get meaning from the materials to be studied. Provision is made for extending inadequate experience through talks or explanations by the teacher, excursions, constructive activities, visual aids, collateral reading, and other means. All of these contributions to understanding are reflected in improved reading ability.

2. Provision for training in resourceful and independent thinking and for refining modes of interpretation determines procedure in all phases of instruction. Furthermore, pupils are constantly urged to attempt to apply the principles and generalizations gained through previous experience to new situations. For example, the teacher of algebra encourages pupils to use the knowledges gained concerning equations stated in one way to equations stated in different ways.

3. Every assignment is carefully analyzed as to study skills required for its completion and training in these skills is given. Each teacher is particularly concerned with types of reading and study procedures that are peculiar to his subject or that have special significance in relation to it. The teacher of geography may find that the assignment requires the reading and interpreting of a kind of graph that the children have never before used, or the teacher of algebra may find that pupils have never before changed quantities from a tabular to a graphic presentation. The teacher of science may find that students cannot explain a science experiment clearly; or the teacher of industrial arts, that boys cannot follow directions in sharpening a tool. The teacher of high-school physics may discover that pupils need much help in understanding the concepts important in the use of the equation, or the teacher of college history, that students need training in the proper use of quotations from sources. Teachers of most subjects at all levels of instruction find that pupils need much guidance in acquiring the meaningful vocabulary essential to achieving insights in a particular subject, in attaching to familiar words new meanings that are basic to understanding, or in recognizing and attaching meaning to technical words used only in that subject. For training in the use of all such new or special skills, class time must be used whether the pupils concerned are at the elementary, secondary, or college level. Smaller amounts of class time will be required for guidance in the application of basic skills in which pupils have had considerable practice during the reading period. For children in the elementary school, careful supervision in the

use of these skills during the study period must be provided. Whenever a teacher finds students deficient in the basic reading skills needed in his field of work, he has no responsibility that is more important than removing these deficiencies.

4. Every possible opportunity is utilized to develop in pupils: first, a realization of the significance of books and articles as a source of information in the solution of their problems; and second, a respect for effective and accurate use of study skills because of the extent to which they govern achievement. Students' attention is constantly directed to reading as a means of satisfying their interests and needs whether their purpose is to answer their own questions, such as *How can you tell the difference between a butterfly and a moth?* or whether their purpose is to find information needed in solving problems or in carrying out activities in which a group is coöperating.

2. Methods That May be Used by the Teacher for Encouraging Effective Reading Habits

The most challenging problem facing any teacher is that of directing all the work of his field toward developing and refining modes of thinking and interpretation. Ways in which all phases of instruction may contribute to this outcome in reading and elsewhere are suggested in the following sections.

a. In Setting Up Problems. The essence of the provision for intelligent reading is to focus the reading upon problems to which the textbooks and collateral readings are supposed to contribute. Effective study is conditioned, therefore, by an assignment that is highly motivated and sharply focalized, that provides for individual differences, and that sets the pupil to work under the guide of specific purposes he has helped to state. In such an assignment the pupil plays an active part. He assumes responsibility for helping to state and to organize the problems that are to guide his reading, for suggesting and discovering sources of information, and for planning methods and means of reporting the information in concise and interesting form. Furthermore, the pupil's ability to state a problem clearly is the best evidence that he is ready to read about it; and interest in the problem is the best guarantee of his interest in the reading. Many types of approach to a problem are possible but all are likely to be most effective if the teacher has the following points clearly in mind: (1) detailed, accurate, and thorough knowledge of the subject matter underlying the problem; (2) the knowledges, appreciations, and attitudes that are desirable outcomes of study; and (3) a planned organization of problems and sub-problems to be covered.

The statement of problems by the pupils need not, and seldom will, follow this organization exactly. Such a plan is important to the teacher, however, in guiding pupils' thinking so that important points are not overlooked and in securing a problem broad enough in scope to challenge the best efforts of the strongest pupil in the group and yet adequately provide for the slower ones. As pupils proceed in their study of a unit, each problem may grow out of the preceding problems and no special approaches may be necessary.

b. In Directing Study. A number of factors in the administration of the study period are important to the development of effective and independent methods of study. The suggestions in the following paragraphs relate largely to the direction of study in the elementary school, but the principles involved and many of the procedures described are applicable at higher levels of instruction:

(1) *Provision for individual differences in the assignment of materials and special activities.* The teacher must have a thorough knowledge of the references bearing on a problem. This is essential in caring for the wide range in reading ability within a group. Helping each child to secure books that he can use efficiently is one of the most important of the teacher's functions during the study period. Books commensurate with his ability may be unobtrusively passed to each child at the beginning of a period. As children come to the reference shelves for additional materials, certain books may be suggested as the next references for them to read. A thorough knowledge of the references is necessary, also, in directing individual study and as a basis for directing special reports or special interests in a problem.

(2) *Provision for training in study skills that the class is using for the first time or in which the pupils are not proficient.* Attention was called to this point in the discussion of the teacher's analysis of the assignment. Unless the study skills are taught during a related reading period or as a part of the assignment, open-book instruction should be used during the study period to insure that students will employ these skills efficiently.

(3) *Provision for individual aid and for work with small groups.* Careful supervision and help on individual difficulties during the study period are important to growth in the mastery of effective study habits. The teacher should move about among the children, noting difficulties and helping to overcome them. One pupil may need help

with outlining in taking notes, another may be returning a reference book to the shelves before he has found half the important points that the book contains about the problem, a third may be copying into his notebook phrases that he does not understand, a fourth may be omitting important data from a graph that he is making. Sometimes the teacher may work with a small group of children all of whom are having the same difficulty. However, the teacher should not spend too much time with the slow students and thus neglect the better students, who also profit from stimulation. One precaution to which a teacher must be constantly alert in the supervision of the study period is that direction of study must not be allowed to degenerate into unnecessary interruptions of wholesome effort on the part of the pupil.

(4) *Provision for definite techniques in taking notes from reference materials.* Much careless and ineffective note-taking is prevented if, in addition to the training in study skills involved in comprehension and organization, certain restrictions are set up concerning the taking of notes. Under this category come: Take as few notes as possible. Take notes in your own words. Write down nothing that you do not fully understand. Never copy any statements concerning a topic from a book until you have read the entire discussion of the topic, have weighed the information critically in relation to the problem, and have re-checked the material to be sure that you have selected the most important points. Plan to use your notebook for reference only. If a book tells something so well that you want your classmates to hear the exact words, place a strip of paper in the book to mark the excerpt so that you can read it to the class.

(5) *Provision for thinking-through what has been read and planning how to report it clearly to the group.* Many rambling, poorly organized, and inadequate contributions to class discussion might be avoided if the last five or ten minutes of the study period were reserved for re-reading notes, thinking through the materials read with reference to the problem, and planning how to report the data in concise, well-organized form. This point is crucial with reference both to intelligent study and to effective participation in group discussions.

(6) *Provision for definite techniques in the construction and use of illustrative materials.* Certain empirical rules may be set up to further the effective use of graphs, maps, charts, and pictures, in addition to skills involved in making, reading, and interpreting them. These may include: Make all illustrative materials large enough that the class can see them clearly. Use the blackboard, large sheets of brown wrapping

paper or newsprint thumbtacked to the worktable or to the floor, or make slides that may be enlarged by the projector. If you wish to call the attention of the class to an illustration in a book, put a marker in the book, list the pictures topically on the blackboard under the section marked " Pictures," and return the book to the shelves. Members of the class may then consult the book in turn. If you think a picture is important to the understanding of a problem, plan to ask for time during the discussion period to pass the picture about and to explain it.

(7) *Provision for placing responsibility for efficient study squarely upon the pupils.* The group should feel responsible for suggesting ways of making subject matter concrete and interesting, reporting study difficulties, and attempting to weigh and evaluate the discussions of different authors in the light of the problem.

c. In Guiding Group Discussions. A group discussion period is usually rich in opportunities for critical evaluation, for organization, and for resourceful and independent thinking. The importance of skillful guidance on the part of the teacher in order that pupils arrive at sound understandings and discover new problems is generally underestimated. Scholarly knowledge of the problem, a planned summary of the important knowledges and appreciations that are desired outcomes of the discussion, and adeptness at questioning are requisites of success in guidance. In addition, the following attitudes and procedures have been found helpful in guidance:

(1) The teacher should encourage a scientific attitude when data are reported. Pupils should feel responsibility for reporting data accurately and should be called upon to cite and to quote from sources when differences of opinion arise.

(2) Critical evaluation of data reported is crucial to right habits of thinking. Every effort should be made to lead pupils to weigh information carefully, but not skeptically, and to accept no statement that they do not understand without asking for an explanation. It is wholesome to encourage pupils to state frankly that, although they read a selection carefully, they did not understand it.

(3) The discussion period provides many opportunities for training in organization. Attention is always centered in the attempt to report information so clearly that others who have not read the references will be able to understand the points contributed. Pupils should be held sharply to the point under discussion. They should be encouraged to be intolerant of rambling, of repetition of information, or of the introduction of irrelevant material. Real interest in solving the problem

under discussion is, of course, the best means of helping the children
to assume responsibility for holding to the point. Attempts to improve
upon the organization of information and to state more clearly the facts
given in a stumbling recitation may well be encouraged.

d. In Summarizing and in Making Records. A summary of important points brought out in a discussion is indispensable not only as
a means of clarifying and clinching understandings, but also as a basis
for raising problems for further study. This summary may be an outline of important principles and generalizations dictated by the class
as a group, prepared by a small committee, or written by each pupil.
It may be the report of an activity or of a plan for an assembly program. Whatever form the summary takes, it should stress the selection
of important points rather than the reiteration of what has been told
in class. Thus developed, the summary will supply many opportunities for critical thinking and for practice in organization.

V. Factors Affecting the Teaching of Study Skills in the Reading Period

The importance of close integration between training in study skills
in the reading period and applying these skills in the study of content
lessons has been discussed earlier in this chapter. Several other factors,
however, determine the effectiveness of a program of training in study
skills. These factors include the materials of instruction, important
items of method that should operate in the administration of lessons
that give training in study skills, provision for individual differences,
and the diagnosis of study difficulties.

1. The Materials of Instruction

Since the avowed purpose of training in study skills is to increase
efficiency in all the work of the school, it would seem reasonable to base
such instruction upon materials comparable in all essential points to
those used in the actual study of lessons. This principle implies, first,
that the materials should be of as many different types as there are
study needs to be met in the various curricular fields and activities, and,
second, that the materials should be largely informational in character
(science, history, geography, arithmetic, biography, and similar factual materials). Naturally, the materials should satisfy standards
that characterize good literature, that is, authenticity, clear and interesting style, and good organization. Furthermore, the materials will
better serve as a basis for learning how to study effectively if they

meet certain additional requirements. Perhaps the most important of these requirements is that the materials should be easy enough to be read fluently by the pupils using them. When the objective is to gain command of an ability, such as the ability to select a paragraph heading, attention should not be distracted by excessive reading difficulties. Since textbooks in geography and other subjects that supply the basis for much training in study skills are often hard to read, additional easy materials are desirable.

Books containing a wide range of such materials systematically graded to insure orderly development of basic reading abilities are particularly helpful in the introduction of new skills and serve to simplify practice upon skills already introduced. One complete set of these books, supplemented by smaller sets of from six to ten, the number depending upon the size of the class, may be used to advantage in the study reading period. A second important requirement is that books intended primarily to teach pupils how to study should contain aids to efficient work, such as (a) directions for study, preferably addressed to the pupils; (b) approaches to lessons or suggested activities that motivate study and help the pupils to set purposes to guide their reading; and (c) adequate means of measuring the results of study that are comparable to those commonly used in study situations. Since materials should be pertinent to the interests and needs of the group, books with content relevant to the units of work carried on in the grade are preferable.

2. Important Items of Method That Should Operate in the Administration of Lessons That Give Training in Study Skills

Some teachers, and unfortunately some pupils, also, have the impression that a study reading period possesses many of the features of a necessary but unpleasant duty, that it must be attacked grimly and its goals accomplished because they are essential even though uninteresting. Quite the contrary is true. Children should be interested and alert, and experience the satisfaction of success. Several means are helpful in bringing about this desirable situation. A good assignment is, unquestionably, one of the most essential of these. The extent to which comprehension and the ability to remember what is read are affected by the assignment has been emphasized throughout this discussion. In no part of the curriculum is an assignment that stimulates interest and helps the pupil to set up specific purposes to guide his reading more crucial than in study reading, where achievement is affected in so large a measure by the ability to understand what is read. Perhaps no other single cause is so responsible for ineffectual teaching in the reading period as is a poor assignment. Typical of such bad practice is the lesson described in the next paragraph.

Having instructed the children to open their books to a lesson about the Cecropia, the teacher asked, " How many of you have seen a Cecropia? " Not many had, and the teacher continued, " Then you will be interested in learning about the Cecropia. Read the lesson carefully because when you have finished you will be tested to see how well you understand what you read." When the children had finished reading, books were closed and questions such as the following were asked: " Upon what kind of trees and shrubs is the cocoon spun? " When the children failed to remember the answers to some of the questions, the teacher reproached them, saying, " You did not read carefully. It told in the lesson."

Contrast this purposeless reading with the following assignment:

A bowl of water containing newts brought from the aquarium was passed about among the children, who asked many questions, including:

" How can they stay still in the water so long? "

" Are they baby newts or grown up newts? "

" Will they eat the goldfish? Will the goldfish eat them? "

" Are they related to a dinosaur? " (This from a child who had been examining a picture of prehistoric animals.)

The teacher inquired, " Wouldn't you like to find the answers to your questions? Let's write them on the blackboard."

After their questions had been written, books were opened to a lesson about newts, which the children read with interest under the guidance of specific purposes that they had helped to set.

When all the information bearing on their questions had been reported, one child remarked that the lesson told other interesting things. The teacher suggested that the lesson be read a second time to discover new questions. The children then read the lesson a second time, and again with interest, because they worked under the stimulus of a new purpose. Moreover, they decided to read further about newts, since some of their questions were not fully answered in the material. Possible sources of information were suggested and pupils volunteered to try to find and report this information to the class.

Many ways of relating study reading to children's interests and needs may be utilized, including the integration of training in study skills with immediate needs, as suggested earlier in this chapter. Some carefully planned means of motivation will always be used by the competent teacher.

A number of other factors in the administration of a reading period promote growth in the abilities involved in study. These include the following procedures:

1. Insuring that *all* pupils in a group understand clearly how to apply a skill. For example, if only a part of the class succeed in locating a given word in the index of the book, the teacher calls upon some child who found the word to explain how he found it while the others follow his directions step by step.

2. Referring pupils back to the reading content as a basis for making decisions. One teacher used the method described below to secure this outcome. Two possible headings for a paragraph about cooking in a pioneer fireplace were written on the blackboard as the pupils suggested them:

The Dutch Oven
How Cooking Was Done in a Pioneer Fireplace

When pupils disagreed as to which of the two headings was the better, the teacher said, " A good paragraph heading covers all the important ideas in a paragraph. Re-read the material to see if you can find an important idea not covered by the first heading." The children cited several methods of cooking to show that " The Dutch Oven " did not cover all the important ideas. The second heading was checked in the same way.

3. Emphasizing meaning rather than speed in reading. The purposes for which a pupil reads, his interest in the material, its difficulty, and his command of fundamental reading habits and skills will determine in large measure his speed of reading. While every effort should be made to keep pupils alert and concentrating upon the immediate reading objectives, a pupil should seldom be urged to try to increase his rate of reading: " read as fast as you can and get the meaning." Attention should rather be centered upon providing opportunities for extensive reading of easy materials and other reading situations that have been found to develop speed as a concomitant.

4. Introducing skills in an orderly arrangement of successively difficult steps. Discouragement and consequent lack of interest in improving study habits result from asking pupils to apply reading abilities without having laid the background of knowledges and skills that makes it possible for them to succeed. For example, pupils often fail in attempting to make outlines because they have not received adequate training in skills that build the ability to outline. A ladder

of organization skills that has been found helpful in teaching pupils to outline selections is included in the last section of this chapter.

3. Provision for Individual Differences in the Reading Period

Success in teaching study skills is conditioned by provision for individual differences in assignments, in materials, and in exercises that measure accomplishment. The most widely used of these various means is the differentiated assignment that sets up a minimal requirement for the less competent pupils and suggests enriching activities for the better pupils. A great weakness in many of these assignments lies in the quality of the additional activities suggested for the best readers. These are often merely entertaining chores, which neither promote growth in reading ability nor offer any challenge to critical thinking. Sometimes drill in applying a type of skill may be based upon materials at varying levels of difficulty so that, although all children are filling in skeleton outlines, the class has been divided into several groups, each group using a set of books commensurate with its ability. Exercises used to test comprehension and other abilities may provide for individual differences by suggesting activities for the pupils who finish before the majority of the class; for example, at the end of an exercise testing comprehension of " The Story of Picture Writing " was found this direction: " When you have completed the test, try to write a picture sentence of your own. See if the class can read it." Care should be used to avoid making such assignments an additional task that seems to penalize accomplishment. Probably the most satisfactory method of caring for individual differences is to allow children who seem to have acquired facility in using a skill to test their mastery in extensive reading while the teacher carries on remedial work with those who need it. This plan results in a constant shifting of groups, since children progress from class practice to extensive reading as fast as they are individually able to do so.

4. The Diagnosis of Study Difficulties

The discovery of reading disabilities is the first step in planning remedial procedures. Both standardized and informal tests may be given to discover each pupil's reading difficulties. Informal tests should be used frequently to determine which students have acquired proficiency in employing certain reading skills and which ones need additional practice. The teacher should strive to enlist the pupil's active coöperation in attempting to diagnose his own deficiencies in reading and in planning ways of overcoming them. Convincing the pupil that skillful reading can be developed and making it possible for him to succeed through adapting training in study skills to his particular needs are basic factors in securing this wholesome attitude toward reading. For the most part, pupil's should correct their own papers in an informal test and should regard this work as a useful means of discovering their own reading disabilities and as a guide in choosing remedial exercises. Of great value in furthering the pupil's progress are files of practice exercises that the pupil may withdraw and use as he does practice cards in arithmetic.

VI. Conclusion

The preceding discussion leads to the conclusion that reading is essential to successful study in all fields of the curriculum and that the various curricular fields in turn motivate reading and provide a basis for acquiring efficient reading habits. A record of poor reading ability in a school is an unmistakable indication of a general low level of thinking and study in all the subjects of the school. Hygiene, history, geography, and civics could not have been studied efficiently without definite training in reading skills as they were needed for specific purposes, and such training would have improved the ability to read. Nor could these subjects have been well taught without stimulating new and permanent interests, encouraging thoughtful and extensive reading, affording opportunities for critical thinking, and giving broad training in organization and interpretation.

VII. Exercises That Have Been Found Helpful in Developing Reading Abilities Important in Study

We include only a limited sampling of exercises that have proved helpful in developing specific reading abilities. In many instances, also, just enough of the exercise has been given to illustrate its type. Attention should be called to the fact that these illustrative exercises were used in situations where they met specific needs. They would have had far less value as isolated drill. In general, skills should be developed in relation to the materials and the problems with which the pupils are concerned.

The illustrations are assembled under five topics: (I) Reading in Relation to Mathematics, (II) Locating Materials, (III) Reading Maps, (IV) Organizing Materials, and (V) Reading and Interpreting Graphs and Tables.

I. Reading in Relation to Mathematics

1. Illustrations from Grade IV [1]

Major skill: Comprehension and evaluation
Arithmetic skill: Ability to interpret fundamental processes

1. Jean bought a book for 35¢ and two notebooks at 15¢ each. How much money must she pay the clerk?

( ) A. Which of the following facts are you asked to find out?

1. The number of books Jean bought.
2. The change she should receive.
3. How much they cost her altogether.
4. How much money Jean had.

( ) B. Which of the following facts is given?

1. The price of each article.
2. How much money Jean had.
3. What kind of notebooks she bought.
4. How much she gave the clerk.

( ) C. Which of the following is the most reasonable answer?

1. 60¢. 2. $1.50. 3. 30¢. 4. $5.00.

D. Write the hidden question in this problem.

2. Frank sold 50 papers on Thursday, 44 on Friday, and 62 on Saturday. What was the average number of papers sold per day during the three days?

( ) A. Which of the following facts are you asked to find out?

1. How much money Frank made.
2. The total number of papers he sold.
3. The average number of papers sold a day.
4. The number of days Frank worked.

( ) B. Which of the following facts is given?

1. The number of papers Frank sold altogether.
2. The price of each paper.
3. How many papers he sold each day.
4. How much money Frank made.

( ) C. Which of the following is the most reasonable answer?

1. 50. 2. 150. 3. 25. 4. 13.

( ) D. What is the first step in solving this problem?

1. Add. 2. Subtract. 3. Multiply. 4. Divide.

---

[1] The six illustrations, 1 to 6, showing work-type reading lessons, were developed by teachers in the schools of East Waterloo, Iowa, under the direction of Miss Hazel Prehm, Supervisor of Elementary Grades.

3. It takes 5 pounds of cotton seed to make 1 pound of oil. How much oil can be made from 1320 pounds of seed?

( ) A. Which of the following facts are you asked to find out?

    1. How much oil will come from 1320 pounds of seed.
    2. How many seeds in 5 pounds.
    3. How many plants there were.
    4. How much oil in 5 pounds of seed.

( ) B. Which of the following facts is given?

    1. The number of pounds of oil.
    2. The number of pounds of seed it takes to make 1 pound of oil.
    3. The amount of oil in a pound of seed.
    4. How many seeds each plant produces.

( ) C. Which of the following is the most reasonable answer?

    1. 5000. 2. 250. 3. 16. 4. 50.

( ) D. To solve this problem what must you do?

    1. Add. 2. Subtract. 3. Multiply. 4. Divide.

2. Illustration from Grade IV

Reading skills: Comprehension and evaluation

Arithmetic skill: Use of fundamentals — to tell what process must be used to solve the problem

Number papers 1–15. Read each problem carefully. Decide what process you would use to solve problem. Write the letter *a*, if you would add; *s*, if subtract; *m*, if multiply; and *d*, if divide.

( ) 1. Our play circus had 5 dogs, 3 cats, 6 white rats, 1 gnat, and 4 rabbits. How many animals were there?

( ) 2. One of the big elephants had 175 lbs. of hay, 16 lbs. of bread, 18 lbs. of lettuce, and 50 lbs. of cornstalks. How many pounds did he have?

( ) 3. Roy found 25 balls on the golf links this season. He sold 19 of them. How many balls were left?

( ) 4. On our route the postman has to drive 58 miles each day. How many miles does he drive in 6 days?

( ) 5. Mr. King, the janitor, cleans 157 erasers each day. How many does he clean in 5 days?

( ) 6. Jerry sold his father 2 tickets to the game for 80¢. How much did each ticket cost?

3. Illustration from Grade V

Skill: Vocabulary used in arithmetic work with common fractions — matching terms and definitions

Directions: There are three parts to this lesson. In each part are seven words or terms used in arithmetic work with common fractions. These terms are numbered 1–7. Below them are ten definitions lettered a–j, inclusive.

Number the lines on your paper to correspond with the seven terms in Part 1. After each, write the letter of the definition which matches that term. Follow this same plan in Parts 2 and 3.

Part 1:

1. Fraction
2. Numerator
3. Reciprocal
4. Simplify
5. Common denominator
6. Proper fraction
7. Cancellation

a. The term of a fraction which tells into how many parts a quantity has been divided.
b. The division of a numerator and a denominator by the same number when multiplying fractions.
c. A number that can be exactly divided by each of the denominators of two or more fractions.
d. Multiplication or division of both terms of a fraction by the same number.
e. The inverted form of a number.
f. One of the equal parts of anything.
g. A number that is complete or entire, that does not contain a fraction.
h. The term of a fraction which tells how many parts are taken.
i. To change a fraction to its lowest terms.
j. A fraction in which the numerator is less than the denominator.

Part 2:

1. Least common denominator
2. Whole number
3. Reduction
4. Even number
5. Odd number
6. Mixed number
7. Divisible

a. A number that is not divisible by 2.
b. The multiplication or division of both terms of a fraction by the same number.
c. The division of a numerator and a denominator by the same number when multiplying fractions.
d. A number that is divisible by 2.
e. A number containing a whole number and a fraction.
f. Capable of being divided without remainder.

g. A number that can be exactly divided by the denominators of two or more fractions.

h. The smallest number that can be exactly divided by the denominators of two or more fractions.

i. One of the equal parts of anything.

j. A number that is complete or entire, that does not contain a fraction.

4. Illustration from Grade VI

Specific reading skill: To select hidden questions

Arithmetic skill: Measurements involved

Write the numbers from 1–15. Read each problem carefully and write the hidden question after the corresponding problem number. If a problem has more than one hidden question, write both or all of them.

1. In 2 feedings Joe fed his calf 13 qts. of skim milk. How many pints did the calf have at each feeding?

2. Mrs. Kay made 2 cloth rabbits for Baby Nell. She used 4/9 yds. of flannel for each one. How many inches did she use in all?

3. How many yards of ribbon are needed to bind the 4 edges of a blanket 40 inches long and 36 inches wide?

4. One day a man who runs a lunch room bought 3 dozen pies at 40¢ each. He cut each pie into 6 pieces, selling each piece at 10¢. He sold the pies for how much more than he paid for them?

5. Five loads of coal weighed 2200 lbs., 1800 lbs., 2400 lbs., 2540 lbs., and 2460 lbs., respectively. Find the cost of the five loads at $8.50 per ton.

6. Find the total cost of 8 lbs. of sugar at 5½¢ a pound and 1½ doz. oranges at 40¢ a dozen.

7. When a man drives his car 52 miles in 12 minutes, what is the rate per hour?

8. Mr. Allen wants to build a fence around a lot 150 feet wide and 165 feet long. At 75¢ a rod, how much will the fence cost?

Key: Hidden questions. Measurement involved.

1. a. How many quarts did he feed at one time?
   b. How many pints in a quart?

2. a. How many yards did she use?
   b. How many inches in one yard?

3. a. How many inches around the blanket?
   b. How many inches in one yard?

4. a. How many pies did he buy?
   b. How much did he pay for all the pies?
   c. How many pieces in 36 pies?
   d. How much did he receive for 216 pieces?

5. a. How many pounds did he buy?
   b. How many pounds in a ton?

6. a. How much did he pay for 8 pounds of sugar?
   b. How much did he pay for 1½ dozen oranges?
   c. How many in a dozen?

7. a. How many minutes in one hour?
   b. 12 is what part of 60?

8. a. How many feet around the lot?
   b. How many feet in one rod?
   c. How many rods of fencing will it take?

5. Illustration from Grade VI

Major skill: Remembrance

Arithmetic skill: Knowledge of units of measurement

Number paper 1–25. Select the words in column II that match the ones in column I. Write the letter after the corresponding number.

I.		II.	
1. three feet		a. ten cents	
2. 2000 lbs.		b. 24 hrs.	
3. one gallon		c. 1728 cu. inches	
4. a day		d. a ton	
5. one dime		e. four quarts	
6. twelve		f. to the cu. ft.	
7. sixteen ounces		g. a pound	
8. 7½ gallons		h. one dozen	
9. a cu. ft.		i. 3 ft.	
10. 36 inches		j. a yard	
11. 365 days		k. one sq. mi.	
12. a bushel		l. 160 sq. rods	
13. a minute		m. a dollar	
14. a sq. ft.		n. a year	
15. an acre		o. 144 sq. in.	
16. 640 acres		p. 4 pecks	
17. ten dimes		q. 60 seconds	
18. 30 days		r. 52 weeks	
19. 1 pt.		s. a peck	
20. 1 cent		t. 4 gills	
21. 8 quarts		u. 10 mills	
22. a year		v. one month	
23. ninety degrees		w. circle	
24. one meter		x. one right angle	
25. 360 degrees		y. 39.37 inches	

1. j.	6. h.	11. n.	16. k.	21. s.
2. d.	7. g.	12. p.	17. m.	22. r.
3. e.	8. f.	13. q.	18. v.	23. x.
4. b.	9. c.	14. o.	19. t.	24. y.
5. a.	10. i.	15. l.	20. u.	25. w.

6. Illustration from Grade VII

Major skill: Comprehension and evaluation

Arithmetic skill: Ability to solve problems in percentage

1. The wages of Henry Adams have been $140 per month. They are to be increased 12½%. What will his new wages be?

( ) A. Which of the following facts are you asked to find out?

    1. His annual salary
    2. How much his salary was increased
    3. How much he can save
    4. What his new salary is to be

( ) B. Which of the following facts is given?

    1. His new wages
    2. How much his wages are increased
    3. The per cent of increase
    4. His annual salary

( ) C. Which of the following is the most reasonable answer?

    1. $150 2. $55 3. $1400 4. $250

    D. Write the hidden question in this problem.

2. Clara weighed 90 pounds before she became ill. During her illness her weight decreased 5%. What did she weigh then?

( ) A. Which of the following facts are you asked to find?

    1. How long her illness lasted
    2. How much she weighed after losing 5% of her weight
    3. How much she lost
    4. What fraction 5% is

( ) B. Which of the following facts is given?

    1. The per cent of decrease in Clara's weight
    2. How much she weighed after her illness
    3. How many pounds she lost
    4. How long she was ill

( ) C. Which of the following is the most reasonable answer?

    1. 45 2. 95 3. 65 4. 83.5

( ) D. What is the first step in solving this problem?

    1. Addition 2. Subtraction 3. Multiplication 4. Division

3. The Frank Fruit Exchange sold 85 boxes of apples for Mr. Carter at $2.25 per box. They kept for themselves a commission of 5% and also $25.00 they had spent for freight. How much did they send Mr. Carter?

( ) A. Which of the following facts are you asked to find?

    1. The amount of commission
    2. How much money Mr. Carter received
    3. How much the apples sold for
    4. How much the Fruit Exchange made

( ) ( ) B. Which two of the following facts are given?

    1. The selling price of a box of apples
    2. The amount of the commission
    3. How much the Fruit Exchange kept altogether
    4. The rate of commission

( ) C. Which of the following is the most reasonable answer?

    1. $2500 2. $10 3. $500 4. $160

( ) D. How many steps must be taken to solve this problem?

Key: *Exact answers*

  I. A. 4, B. 3, C. 1, D. What was the amount of increase? $157.50
 II. A. 2, B. 1, C. 4, D. 3.   85.5 lbs.
III. A. 2, B. 1, 4, C. 4, D. 4 steps $156.69

7. Illustration from Grade IX [1]

Reading skill: Comprehension and evaluation
Algebra inventory test of ability in reasoning

Directions: You will find five methods suggested for solving each of the problems in this exercise. *Only one* of these methods is correct. Select the method you believe to be correct and place an " X " before it on the blank provided. *Read each problem carefully.*

1. If you know the number of crates of oranges ordered by a fruit dealer and the price of a single crate, how would you find the cost of the entire order?

    _____a. Divide the cost of the entire order by the number of crates.
    _____b. Subtract the price of a single crate from the cost of the entire order.
    _____c. Multiply the number of crates by the price of a single crate.
    _____d. Divide the number of crates by the price of a single crate.
    _____e. Multiply the price of a single crate by the cost of the entire order.

---

[1] This exercise was furnished by Dr. Harry Newburn, Principal of University High School, Iowa City, Iowa.

2. On a long journey a man traveled a certain number of miles by train and the remainder of the distance by airplane. How would you find the distance traveled by train?

_____a. Divide the total distance by two.

_____b. Subtract the distance traveled by train from the total distance.

_____c. Add the distance traveled by airplane to the distance traveled by train.

_____d. Subtract the distance traveled by airplane from the total distance.

_____e. Divide the total distance by the distance traveled by airplane.

3. A milkman sells a certain number of quarts of milk per day. If you know the profit he makes per quart, how would you find his daily profit on milk?

_____a. Divide the number of quarts by the profit per quart.

_____b. Add the profit per quart to the number of quarts sold per day.

_____c. Divide his daily profit by the profit per quart.

_____d. Multiply the profit per quart by the number of quarts sold per day.

_____e. Add his daily profit to the profit per quart.

4. If you know the distance between two towns and the number of hours it takes to drive that distance by automobile, how would you find the average rate of speed an hour?

_____a. Divide the number of hours by the distance.

_____b. Multiply the distance by the number of hours.

_____c. Multiply the average rate by the number of hours.

_____d. Divide the distance by the average rate.

_____e. Divide the distance by the number of hours.

5. Our principal received a bill from a book company stating the number of algebra books purchased and the total cost of the order. How would you find the cost of one book?

_____a. Multiply the total cost of the order by the number of books.

_____b. Divide the total cost of the order by the number of books.

_____c. Subtract the number of books from the total cost of the order.

_____d. Multiply the cost of each book by the number of books.

_____e. Divide the number of books by the total cost of the order.

II. Locating Materials

8. Illustration from Grade IV

Skill: The use of the index

  1. Drill on alphabetical order

    What letter in the alphabet comes just before:

      s _____; h _____; f _____; u _____; k _____?

    What letter in the alphabet comes just after:

      o _____; l _____; g _____; v _____; t _____?

Arrange these letters in alphabetical order: i, t, n, x, e, d, v, h

Write the first names of the pupils in your reading group in alphabetical order.

Write the following words in alphabetical order: *biscuit, butter, berries, ball, black, bottle*

Write the following words in alphabetical order: *bitter, big, bind, bicycle, bill, bible*

Write the following words in alphabetical order: *bitten, biting, bite, bittersweet*

  2. Drill in using the key to the index, noting punctuation, etc.

Find the word *Alaska* in your index

    Alaska, 186, 203–207, 229, 231 (220)

Find the Key to the Index at the top of the page. It will help you to answer the following questions:

Upon which pages would you expect to find the most important material about Alaska? Why?

Which of the following pages would you choose as likely to contain the most material about Alaska: (1) 203, 207, (2) 203–207?

Why is the last page number about Alaska enclosed in parentheses?

  3. Drill in choosing from a question the word needed to locate information in an index

Directions: Underline the word which you would locate in the index in order to answer each of the following questions.

What state leads in the production of boots and shoes?

What color are the flowers on a cotton plant?

What are the chief fruits raised in Florida?

Why are trains in Europe quieter than ours?

Test your judgment by finding the answers to the questions.

9. Illustration from Grade VI

Skill: The use of the index

Find the answers to the following questions. Refer to the index of the same book you have been using.

  1. For what is the vicuna valuable?

2. Why has the number of sheep in Germany fallen off?

3. What three conditions make the western part of Czechoslovakia the most important iron and steel region of that country?

4. What part of our cotton crop does Great Britain use for its manufacturing?

5. What are four minerals for which Spain is noted?

6. How long has tin been mined in the British Isles?

7. How do Chinook winds affect the temperature?

8. In what river is the Iron Gate?

10. Illustration from Grade IV [1]

Skill: Locating information in an encyclopedia

1. How an encyclopedia is arranged
   A. In what order are the articles of an encyclopedia arranged?
   B. What other book is arranged in the same way?
   C. How do you tell which volume to use?
   D. Since the topics are arranged alphabetically, what is the value of an index volume?
   E. When would you use the index volume?

2. Practice in choosing the correct volume
After each word write the number of the volume which you would use to find information on the topic:

alligators _____   spiders _____
elephants _____   mice _____
snakes _____   ducks _____
swallows _____   mammals _____

3. Practice in selecting the correct volume for answering a question
Write the number of the volume in which you would expect to find an answer to each of the following questions:
   A. When was the printing press invented? _____
   B. What is the size of the Amazon River Basin? _____
   C. What are the names of the hawks that injure the farmers' property? _____
   D. How did the pioneers make soap? _____
   E. According to the index, a reference to salmon is given on page 3113. What volume should you use? _____
   F. Information concerning the making of ink is given on page 1779. What volume should you use? _____

---

[1] Illustration 10 was developed by Mable Cummings, Supervisor of Elementary Grades, Rapid City, South Dakota.

Key Words from *Compton's Encyclopedia*

Volume 1 — A–Bro 1–516   Volume 5 — Mar–Par 2145–2686
Volume 2 — Bro–Edi 517–1082   Volume 6 — Par–Sno 2687–3262
Volume 3 — Edi–Has 1083–1596   Volume 7 — Soa–Zwi 3263–3842
Volume 4 — Hat–Mar 1597–2144   Volume. 8 — Index 3843–4410

11. Illustration from Grade II

Skill: Rapid reading to locate the answers to questions

1. Take a copy of the book *How the Indians Lived,* by Frances Dearborn.
2. Find the chapter on page 153.
3. What is the chapter about?
4. What sign meant " buffalo in sight "? On what page is it?
5. Find the page of the chapter which tells about paths and trails. Write the page number.
6. Why did the Indians mark trails?
7. Why did the Indians sometimes burn spots on trees?
8. Find a picture showing how an Indian might mark a path with stones. On what page is it?
9. Find a picture in your book of Indian picture-writing. On what page is it?

12. Illustrations from Grade VI

Skill: Answering questions by using an appendix

Directions: When you have a question that may be answered by using an appendix, the first thing to do is to glance over the names of all the tables and decide which one is most likely to give the information you are looking for. Otherwise you will probably waste several minutes reading through many pages before you come to the right table.

Since you have already had some practice in using the appendix in your geography, you should be able to answer the following questions very quickly. Head your papers in your usual way and number down the side from 1 to 8. Write each answer as briefly as possible. Remember to decide which table to use for each question before you begin to look for an answer.

1. Which one of the possessions of the United States has the largest population?
2. Asia is the largest continent in area. Does it also have the greatest population?
3. Does the capital city of your state have a population of 30,000 or more?
4. How deep is Lake Superior?
5. Texas, California, Montana, New Mexico, and Arizona are our five largest states. Which of these are also densely enough populated to have a population of over 5,000,000?

6. What was the second largest city in the United States in 1830?

7. Does Europe or North America have the larger population? Which continent is larger in area?

If you finish answering the questions before the other pupils, make a list of questions, similar to these, that may be answered by studying the appendix.

Skill: Deciding upon the best reference source

Write the name of one book in our room or science library that would be likely to give a good answer to each of the following questions.

1. How far from the earth is the moon?
2. How do you multiply decimals?
3. How do you pronounce ' bacteria '?
4. Who discovered the cause of yellow fever?
5. Where is the Sahara Desert?
6. How is rubber obtained?

III. READING MAPS

13. Illustration from Grade IV [1]

Skill: Reading rainfall and growing season maps

Directions: Yesterday we were talking about the conditions necessary for raising wheat. Can you sum up what we said about rainfall and length of growing season?

Rainfall: Needs annual rainfall of from twenty to forty inches

More than forty inches is too much

Some varieties grow with only ten inches if rain comes at right time

Growing season: At least three months

Turn to the maps showing rainfall and growing season on page 54. Let's see what we can tell from maps about what sections of our country have good conditions for raising wheat.

Questions for oral discussion and study

1. Look at the key. How is the section which has too little rainfall for wheat shaded?

2. How much rainfall does this section have?

3. What states have some parts that get less than ten inches of rain in a year?

4. Look at the wheat map on page 84. Can you find much wheat growing in these parts that get less than ten inches of rainfall a year?

---

[1] Illustration 13 was developed by Evelyn Benzler, Teacher of Fourth Grade, University Elementary School, Iowa City, Iowa.

5. Can you tell from the map on page 101 (shows irrigated land) why some wheat can be raised there?

6. Which shading shows too much rainfall for wheat?

7. In which parts of the United States is there too much rainfall?

8. Can you find much wheat grown in these sections?

9. What is the average rainfall in the big wheat belts?

10. Notice how much wheat is raised along the twenty inch rainfall line. What does this line mean?

11. What do we mean by the *growing season?*

12. Which marking shows too short a growing season for wheat?

13. Which states have this very short season?

14. What reasons can you find from these two maps for not raising wheat in western Montana?

15. What other reasons might there be?

16. What reasons can you find from this map for not raising wheat in Nevada? in eastern Oregon? in Mississippi?

Concepts Important to the Map Interpretations Developed in This Lesson. (To be emphasized throughout the discussion.)

1. A little wheat is often grown even though conditions are not good.

2. The lines do not mean a sudden change in amount of rainfall or length of growing season.

3. Other needed conditions for raising wheat, such as soil and rain at proper time, are not shown on these maps.

4. A section may have the necessary conditions for raising wheat but find some other industry more profitable.

14. Illustration from Grade VI

Skill: Reading a dot map

1. What does each dot stand for, as shown by the key?

2. What are the four greatest cattle raising regions of the world?

3. In which one of these three regions are the fewest cattle per square mile?

4. What country with a warm climate produces very many cattle?

5. Are many cattle raised in eastern Europe?

6. Are there more cattle per square mile in Ireland or Scotland?

IV. ORGANIZING MATERIALS

15. Illustration from Grade I [1]

Skill: Arranging sentences under topic headings

Oral directions: On the sheets I have given you are sentences from stories

---

[1] Illustration 15 was developed by Emma Watkins and Mable Root, Teachers, University Elementary School, Iowa City, Iowa.

dictated by committees. Here on the blackboard are four topics. Can you choose the topics about which each sentence tells? (Each sentence was considered in turn and the number of the sentence written on the blackboard under the proper topic heading.)

Farm — Garden — Dairy — Poultry

1. We saw a silo and a tractor.
2. The sweet peas are up.
3. We set out onion plants.
4. We made a seed corn tester.
5. Bottles are sterilized by steam.
6. The Second Grade came in to eat vegetable soup.
7. We made butter.
8. Most seed corn is not good this year.
9. We whitewashed the chicken house.
10. We candled eggs at our assembly.
11. Pat and Ed hitched the horses to the manure spreader.
12. Much of our food is raised on Iowa farms.
13. Cracked eggs are broken, beaten, or frozen before they are shipped.

16. Illustration from Grade VI

Skill: Arranging paragraph headings in a logical order

Directions: A composition on "Coffee" that followed the outline below would be quite a 'jumbled' affair. Number the paragraph headings so that they would make a good composition. If some of the headings seem to be sub-topics under others, arrange them so.

(Note: This lesson followed the discussion of the problem: To what extent do we depend upon Latin America for coffee?)

Transplanting the young plants to permanent situations
Sorting, sacking, and preparing for shipment
Picking the berries
Cultivation of the young trees
The conditions of soil, climate, and topography that favor coffee-growing
Pulping
Washing
Drying
Planting the coffee seeds in nursery beds
Harvesting the crop
The principal coffee-producing countries
Description of the coffee tree
Need of shade for the young trees

17. Illustration from Grade II [1]

Skill: Selecting material and organizing it about problems

Directions given orally: Read the chapter to find information about the problems that you raised. The questions will help you. As you find and read material about each question, decide which of the problems the information tells about.

Problems: (1) Did the Indians have any ways of communicating with each other except by talking? (2) Did they keep any records of what they had done, or of what the Indians before them had done?

1. What chapter in the book [Dearborn, *How the Indians Lived*] will be most likely to answer the question?
2. Did the Indians have written and printed words as we do?
3. What different kinds of signals did the Indians use?
4. Why did the Indians of the forest and of the plains differ in the kind of signals they used?
5. What were some of the messages that smoke could carry?
6. How many of these things were used by Indians in giving messages to other Indians? *stones, smoke, notches, blankets, beads, bark, skins*
   How was each used?
   Can you add any to the list?
7. How did the Indians measure time?
   What were *steps?*
   How long was a *sleep?*
   How long was a *moon?*
8. What kind of records did Indians keep?
9. What materials were used for making records?
10. Make an Indian sign that carries a message of some kind.

Something for those who get through early:
11. See who can find something about how the Indians kept records of bravery.
12. Who can find anything about Indian messages or records in any other book on the library shelves?

---

[1] Illustrations 11 and 17 were developed by Maud McBroom, Principal, University Elementary School, Iowa City, Iowa.

18. Illustration from Grade VIII [1]

Skill: Making an outline and using it in writing a summary paragraph

Directions: Your reference reading dealt with the problem *Why was England ready to become a great colonizing power about 1600?* What points did you find bearing on this problem?

The following points suggested by the students were written on the blackboard:

> The English farms were changing from diversified farming to sheep farming.
> The change to sheep farming was crowding people out of employment.
> Wealthy Englishmen had surplus money to invest.
> The English had developed the Trading or Charter Company as a type of coöperative enterprise.
> A rising standard of living had created a demand for luxuries.
> England was not self-sufficient for luxuries.
> England was lacking in naval stores.
> England was jealous of Spain.
> By the defeat of the Armada, England had overthrown Spain's sea power.

Discussion and evaluation of these suggested points led to their reorganization into the outline which follows:

Why England Was Ready for Colonization about 1600
1. England wanted to be self-sufficient
   a. England needed naval stores
   b. England did not want to depend upon other countries for luxuries
   c. Colonization would supply these needs
2. England had a surplus population
   a. The enclosure movement had crowded people out of employment
   b. This surplus population was anxious to better its condition
3. England had surplus wealth
   a. The result of profits from sheep farming
   b. Rich men had learned to form Trading Company organizations and so pool their wealth
      Examples: London, Baltic, and Levant Companies
4. England was envious of Spain's wealth

With this outline as a guide, each student was then asked to write a summary paragraph without notes. Fifteen minutes were allowed for the writing. An example of the summaries is given on the next page.

---

[1] Illustration 18 was developed by Dr. Howard Anderson, Head Department of Social Studies, University High School, Iowa City, Iowa.

" Why Was England Ready to Become a Colonizing Nation about 1600? "

Around 1600 England begins to realize that if England wishes to be a powerful nation she must be self-sufficient. In 1600 they are depending on other countries to supply them with their luxuries, such as spices, silks, and on Norway and Sweden to provide them with their naval stores. Consequently they hope and practically believe that in the new world they will find these needed necessities of theirs Due to the enclosure movement there is a surplus population in England. This means that if England wants to plant a colony in the new world it has the people to do it. Also due to the enclosure movement there are many wealthy men in England. These wealthy men pooled their money to form trading companies such as the London, the Baltic and the Levitt (Levant) companies. Such companies would be able to send men to trade and to colonize in the new world. England also realizes that Spain has much more wealth than she does. They are very jealous and envious of Spain and plan to find wealth in the new world so that England will be just as rich as Spain or richer than Spain. All these reasons account for the statement that England is ready to become a colonizing power about 1600.

19. A Ladder of Organization Skills Which Has Been Found Helpful in Developing the Ability to Outline and to Summarize [1]

These six skills should be developed in the order listed.

1. *Skill in selecting paragraph headings*

   Exercises to be used in developing this skill:

   a. Choose the best of several suggested headings.
   b. Match paragraph headings with paragraph.
   c. Rearrange in proper sequence paragraph headings listed out of order.
   d. Choose the topic sentence in a paragraph.
   e. Make paragraph headings.

2. *Skill in asking a question which covers all the important ideas in a paragraph*

   Exercises to be used in developing this skill:

   a. Change paragraph headings made by the class into questions.
   b. Choose the best of several questions, etc., as suggested under 1.
   c. Decide upon and list the important question for each paragraph in a selection. Check back through these questions to see whether you can answer them adequately. Use the questions as a guide in deciding where you need to re-read the material and as a check upon how well the selection is prepared.

3. *Skill in distinguishing between the main idea and supporting details*

   Exercises to be used in developing this skill:

---

[1] This material was developed by Mabel Snedaker.

a. Choose from a list of sentences the topic sentence or paragraph heading, and then decide which of the remaining sentences should be listed as important subtopics.
b. From an unorganized list that contains both steps in a process and supporting details, choose and arrange in proper sequence the important steps in the process of making or doing something.
c. Choose the steps in a process from a written account, then list supporting details for each step.

4. *Skill in dividing material into sectional headings*
Exercises to be used to develop this skill:

a. Decide in turn the number of paragraphs in a selection that tell about each one of sectional headings listed in order.
b. Match sectional headings with sections of material.
c. Divide material into sectional headings.

5. *Skill in outlining*
Exercises to be used in developing this skill:

a. Fill in a paragraph heading for each paragraph of a selection under the sectional headings recently made by the class.
b. Fill in skeleton outlines when the paragraph heading is given.
c. Fill in a skeleton outline when the paragraph heading must be supplied.
d. Use outlines which the class has made for various purposes: (1) as an aid to remembrance in giving a report; (2) as the basis for a summary of a paragraph; (3) as a guide in reviewing important points.

Note: Begin with one-step outlines of single paragraphs that are easily organized. Do not proceed to more complex outlines until students can make one-step outlines with facility.

6. *Skill in summarizing*
Exercises to be used to develop this skill:

a. Change outlines recently made by the class into summary statements.
b. Choose the best of several suggested summary statements for a paragraph.
c. Match summary statements with paragraphs.
d. Make summary statements for paragraphs.

V. READING AND INTERPRETING GRAPHS AND TABLES

20. Illustration from Grade V [1]

Skill: Changing statistics from tabular to graphic form
This drill lesson should be developed step by step, as directed, each step being discussed by the class.

---

[1] Illustration 20 was developed by Lucy Scott, Director of Practice in City Schools, Towson State Teachers College, Towson, Maryland.

The following table from *The World Almanac, 1936* gives information that will be helpful in your study of the forest resources of the United States. Can you show this information in a bar graph? What are the advantages in using a bar graph instead of a table?

Standing Timber in Chief States

State	Billion Board Feet	Number of Squares
Oregon	396	20
California	282	
Washington	256	
Idaho	81	
Montana	50	
Colorado	49	
Louisiana	41	
Maine	40	
Michigan	40	
Minnesota	36	

What materials will you need to make a graph for this table? (A sheet of squared paper, a ruler, a pencil, and a red, black, or blue crayola.) Before you start to make the graph, you should recall some of the requirements for a good bar graph. Those you will need to remember for this graph are:

A horizontal bar graph should read from left to right with the table at the left. The bars should be *uniform in width* and should be of the same color. The spaces between the bars should be the same. Figures for the scale should be placed at the top and the bottom. The title should be clear and complete.

Count the squares in the length and width of the paper and plan the scale, the margins at top and bottom and left before you begin to draw the bars. On a sheet of paper that is 33 by 42 what is the best scale to use for this table? Use a scale that can be computed and read easily. If one square represents 20 billion board feet, how long should the bar for Oregon be? When 20 is divided into 396 the answer is 19⅘. When the fraction is more than ½, as in this case, you may use the next whole number. If the fraction is less than ½ you may drop it. The bar for Oregon should be 20 squares long. Will a bar of this length leave enough space for margins at the left? Find the length of the bars for the other states in the same way.

If you have ten bars two spaces wide with one space between, will that leave enough margin space at the top and bottom of the page? How much space should be left at the top? After you have blocked out these spaces for margins, count the squares accurately for the bars, draw the lines and color evenly. Write in the table, the title, and the scale figures.

Questions for Study: Compare this graph with the one made yesterday showing production of lumber in the United States. What two states rank high on both graphs? What states that have standing timber do not lead in production of lumber? In what sections of the United States are these states? Why do they not lead in lumber production? You will probably need to consult references to find the answers to some of these questions.

SUB–COMMITTEE ON CHAPTER VI

Chairmen

JEAN BETZNER, Assistant Professor of Education, Teachers College, Columbia University, New York City

R. L. LYMAN, Professor of the Teaching of English, University of Chicago, Chicago, Illinois

Associates

FRANKLIN T. BAKER, Professor of English, Teachers College, Columbia University, New York City

FLORENCE E. BAMBERGER, Professor of Education, Johns Hopkins University, Baltimore, Maryland

ANGELA BROENING, Assistant Director of Research, assigned Head of the English Department, Forest Park High School, Baltimore, Maryland

LOU L. LABRANT, Associate Professor in English-Education, The Ohio State University, Columbus, Ohio

J. PAUL LEONARD, Professor of Education, College of William and Mary, Williamsburg, Virginia

HELEN K. MACKINTOSH, Associate Professor of English, School of Education, Miami University, Oxford, Ohio

ANNIE E. MOORE, Associate Professor of Education, Teachers College, Columbia University, New York City

ROBERT C. POOLEY, Assistant Professor of English, University of Wisconsin, Madison, Wisconsin

ELOISE RAMSEY, Wayne University, Detroit, Michigan

HOWARD FRANCIS SEELEY, Professor of Education, The Ohio State University, Columbus, Ohio

DORA V. SMITH, Associate Professor of Education, University of Minnesota, Minneapolis, Minnesota

CHAPTER VI

THE DEVELOPMENT OF READING INTERESTS AND TASTES

JEAN BETZNER
Assistant Professor of Education
Teachers College, Columbia University
New York City

and

R. L. LYMAN
Professor in the Teaching of English
The University of Chicago
Chicago, Illinois

This chapter sets forth factors that are affecting the reading interests and tastes of school children, college students, and adults, and records types of guidance that are attempting to utilize such factors. The discussion considers pertinent conditions in contemporary life, such as our increased need for understanding world affairs so that the individual may participate intelligently in social reconstruction; new developments in radio, cinema, and other devices for duplicating language that complicate the reading situation; the increased quantity of all kinds of printed materials, including the many books in translation; increased leisure and other basic changes in the social pattern. To these conditions must be added the prevalent confused and narrow concepts of culture and the exceedingly inferior reading experiences of the average citizen.

The discussion avoids an elaborate analysis of the terms ' interests ' and ' tastes,' and accepts the workable concept that *taste* is the integrated sum total of an individual's interests, likings, and choices as manifested consistently at any given period of his life. In any important field, such as reading, both emotional and intellectual elements enter into the constitution of a person's developing or relatively permanent tastes. The other major term in the title of this chapter, *development,* is interpreted as synonymous with *growth* as the individual advances from period to period in his educational experiences. Important is the consideration that *growth* is gradual; boys and girls go through normal stages of social, intellectual, and emotional development. It is just as necessary to recognize natural stages of development in tastes, beginning for all with immaturity and advancing for some (not for all, to be sure) to superior preferences, as it is to recognize gradual growth in specific reading habits and skills from one level of maturity to the next.

This chapter considers the development of interests and tastes primarily as a problem of the literature and free reading periods of the English classroom and library. However, it cannot be too often repeated that tastes and attitudes, like habits and skills, are the products of all related experiences. The widened range of reading of materials in all the content fields, as presented in Chapters III and V, is of course exceedingly potent in the development of reading tastes and interests.

I. STUDIES IN THIS FIELD: INFERENCES AND LIMITATIONS

The numerous investigations of the preferences of children and adults in reading materials, some informal and others made under carefully controlled conditions, have contributed general information, especially about the choices of children in stories, poetry, and certain aspects of book format. One condition needs to be noted. For the most part the reading choices reported are the results of conventional school courses, which often represent vital reading interests very imperfectly. It will be unnecessary to review or revaluate here the various investigations, since this has been done so recently.[1] For present purposes the most significant conclusions with respect to the preferences of young children are these:

1. There is evidence that elementary-school children will read what is accessible to them.[2] Probably the most significant single factor in the development of wholesome reading habits and tastes is the informal exposure of children to an abundance of good books and magazines in the home, school, and public library.

---

[1] A. I. Gates. *Interests and Ability in Reading.* Pp. 3–88. (The Macmillan Company: New York, 1930)

P. McKee. *Reading and Literature in the Elementary School.* Pp. 472–515. (Houghton Mifflin Company: Boston, 1934)

White House Conference on Child Health and Protection, *Children's Reading,* Pp. 8–11. (D. Appleton-Century Company: New York, 1932)

National Education Association. *Better Reading Instruction.* Pp. 309–310. (National Education Association: Washington, D. C., 1935)

[2] C. W. Washburne and L. Vogel. *Winnetka Graded Book List.* (American Library Association: Chicago, 1926)

2. Children enjoy the records of human experience dealing with content that is at least partially familiar to them.[1]

3. They prefer material that is presented graphically with action and dramatic quality.[2]

4. They enjoy reading material that is read under pleasant, agreeable conditions, with teachers whom they admire. The evidence indicates that children enjoy poems that a well-liked teacher herself enjoys.[3]

5. Certain aspects of format influence the choices of books by children.[4]

6. The average preferences of elementary-school pupils differ considerably from the choices made for them by adults directing their reading.[5] The correlation between what high-school pupils like and what their teachers think they like is .39. But naturally, we find among teachers some very capable judges of what pupils prefer.[6]

It is always to be borne in mind that the tastes of children and young people, as expressed in most of the studies, are immature, undeveloped. While caution must be exercised against formulating programs of formal aims in terms of predetermined teacher aims, as contrasted with programs in which pupil development is basic; nevertheless, there is the obvious necessity, never to be overlooked by those who guide children's reading, of teaching them what has been suggestively called " patience with books."[7] If immature likes and dislikes are gradually to be changed for the better in a developmental program, what children like must always be considered as useful guidance, but not as the determinant for continued practice. Rewards in the form of improved capacities are seldom if ever attained without effort, but effort need

---

[1] W. L. Uhl. *Scientific Determination of the Content of the Elementary School Course in Reading.* University of Wisconsin Studies, No. 4. (University of Wisconsin: Madison, 1921)

H. K. MacIntosh. " Recent data on children's interests in poetry," *Elementary English Review,* 8: January, 1931, 18–20.

[2] A. I. Gates, C. Peardon, and I. Sartorius. " Studies of children's interests in reading," *Elementary School Journal,* 31: May, 1931, 656–670.

[3] Alice Coast. " Children's choices in poetry as affected by teacher's choices," *Elementary English Review,* 5: May, 1928, 145–149.

[4] F. E. Bamberger. *The Effect of the Physical Makeup of a Book upon Children's Selections.* Johns Hopkins University Studies in Education, No. 4. (Johns Hopkins University: Baltimore, 1922)

[5] White House Conference. *Op. cit.*

[6] G. A. West and F. P. Caldwell. " Student and teacher preference in literature," *California Quarterly of Secondary Education,* 9: October, 1933, 19–22.

[7] Luella B. Cook. " Reading for experience," *English Journal* (High-School Edition), 25: April, 1936, 274–281.

not be dissipated upon reading materials beyond the maturity of the child.

Such studies as have been made, although of questionable validity, indicate that both the native and the developed tastes of high-school pupils are at a relatively low level.[1] While this is true, recent evaluations of experimental programs indicate that native reading interests and tastes, used as a starting point for guidance, can be greatly improved.[2]

1. Among high-school pupils of all ages interest in fiction greatly predominates. For recreation high-school boys select serial stories, tales of boy life and school life, stories of adventure and mystery. Their favorite authors are Doyle, London, Burroughs, Wright. Girls prefer mystery associated with romance; their favorites are Alcott, Porter, Bailey, Lutz.[3]

2. Pupils' reading preferences in newspapers reveal major interests in news, comics, and sports. Only five percent of the pupils read magazines and the better magazines are absent from the list. *Colliers* and *Liberty* are first in popularity; *American Boy* and *Boy's Life,* together with certain domestic magazines and science periodicals, are second; *Detective Stories* and *True Stories* rank high. Here the problem, as with younger pupils, is to take such preferences into account, to start with the learners where they are, and to guide them in the selection of worthier materials in line with their expressed preferences.[4]

The voluntary reading of college women is somewhat more satisfactory.

1. Women's reading is estimated as sixty percent fiction; twenty-five percent drama, poetry, biography, travel; fifteen percent science, art, history, religion, philosophy, and natural science. Titles most frequently withdrawn for voluntary reading from a well-stocked college library include *The Good Earth, A White Bird Flying,* Emily Post's *Etiquette,* and Shakespeare's plays.[5]

---

[1] Ruth Byrns and V. A. C. Henman. "Reading interests of high-school seniors," *English Journal* (High-School Edition), 25: January, 1936, 61–64.

[2] Lou L. LaBrant. "An Evaluation of the Free Reading in Grades Ten, Eleven, and Twelve." (Graduate School Series, Ohio State University, 1934)

[3] F. M. Hughes.. "Survey of the reading interests of pupils of the Madison, Wisconsin, high school," *Education,* 54: March, 1924, 437–438.

Anna Peterson. "Leisure reading of high-school pupils," *Education,* 54: January, 1934, 296–300.

[4] Anna Peterson. *Op. cit.*

Elsie S. Hanswald. "Training for classroom or for life," *English Journal* (High-School Edition), 22: November, 1933, 764–766.

[5] B. Lamar Johnson. "Stephens College library experiment," *Junior College Journal,* 4: April, 1934, 358–361.

2. The amount of library reading done by college students bears no relation to sex, intelligence, or scholarship.[1]

3. Fifty-six percent of college students do no optional reading of books; sixteen percent occasionally read newspapers and magazines; women do more required, men more optional, reading.[2]

Recent studies of the voluntary reading of adults indicate preferences of relatively low quality.

1. There is a marked preference for romance and five- or ten-cent detective magazines.

2. Cheap sex novels represent almost the entire stock of many rental libraries.

3. The depression has driven people to the public library, where they find somewhat better books.

4. Racial and social interests are prominent in the better titles read.[3]

The reported investigations of children's tastes and interests up to the present cannot be accepted at their face value. At best, they have disclosed only broad average trends in the preferences of somewhat narrowly selected groups. Moreover, they have been concerned mainly with the compiling of choices under different conditions, seldom under conditions of adequate exposure to wide varieties of reading materials. Little or no light has been thrown on the changing tastes of individuals or on the specific determining factors that affect changes in the tastes of individuals.[4] Since tastes and interests are predominantly individual matters, generalizations expressing the preference of a majority of a race, a sex, an age, or a group of given reading-ability are not sufficiently specific to furnish valid criteria. Moreover, many of the studies have been so loosely controlled that the results probably do not indicate the free choices of the groups studied. Adequate techniques for determining such choices have not been discovered.

A second limitation of the studies, especially those considering the preferences of young children, is related to the first. It is true that some of the investigations have led to definite improvement. For ex-

[1] Alvin C. Burich. "Student use of the library," *Library Quarterly*, 3: January, 1933, 87–94.

[2] J. R. Gerberish and Charles Jones. "The optional and required reading of college students," *School and Society*, 38: July 15, 1933, 93–96.

[3] Douglas Waples. "Community studies in reading, I. Reading in the Lower East Side," *Library Quarterly*, 3: January, 1933, 1–20.

[4] Helen Ferris. *Women and the Social Sciences.* Chapter VI, "The Young Girl and Reading." (John Day: New York, 1932)

ample, more books about normal childhood experiences have been produced in response to demand for such experiences; artistically better books — simple, clear colors and bold outlines — have grown out of the studies in that field. But it would be a mistake to regard the tastes and preferences found in such investigations as absolute standards of excellence in children's books; many of the values of art in literature would then be overlooked and new and valuable developments in bookmaking for children would be checked. Reading materials can scarcely be expected to exhibit qualities of vigor and integrity when prepared under the rigid limitative criteria that might be based on studies of children's interests.

The findings of investigations of the voluntary reading interests of secondary-school pupils, college students, and adults indicate that school guidance has not been successful. Preferences exhibited in voluntary reading, perhaps as a relief from the extensive amounts of required reading in various school subjects, are mainly for inferior materials.

At best, then, the accumulating studies of average tastes in reading — even those showing commendable preferences — can be used only as points of departure. Such studies, however, throw some light on the progress in taste reached by a given group of learners. They also lay new emphasis on the vital principle that the materials and the methods of guidance must always be in accord with the learners' capacities. The studies may help curriculum-makers and teachers to avoid the unspeakable educational waste, especially in the development of emotional responses, of exposing children to experiences far beyond their mental and spiritual levels of interpretation.

One school of thinkers insists that any rigid regimentation in the field of reading experiences, even if based upon seemingly reliable analyses of average tastes, is exceedingly dangerous. They believe that development in tastes is possible only when individuals continuously examine their own preferences in the light of their purposes, make use of the results of their own selections, and gradually arrive at a clearer conception of what is of genuine value to them. They champion varied and illuminating reading experience.

Others though they heartily agree that abundant unregimented reading is a valuable means of enabling readers to establish criteria of taste, nevertheless believe that the actual teaching of literature is justified in order to show learners how to read and to develop inductively, under guidance, fairly definite standards of merit that can be applied more or less generally. Many a classroom teacher has faced the question, What makes a good story, a good novel, a good play? She replies, " Come, let us find some of the qualities of excellence in this poem, story, or drama."

The distinction between teaching literature (the purpose of which is showing learners how to read intelligently) and guiding pupils' reading (the purpose of which is unanalyzed satisfaction in the reading itself) is fundamental and emerges from distinctly differing concepts of how human beings learn; and the more clearly educators see the distinctions, the more consistent and unified will their practices become. At proper times and places we *teach* pupils *how* to read, at others we *guide* them in the selection of *what* they may read pleasurably. Any growth in tastes other than haphazard individual progress is the result of emphasis on both.

II. FACTORS OUTSIDE THE SCHOOL THAT AFFECT READING TASTES

The purpose of this section is to indicate certain aspects of the environment to which pupils are exposed outside the school that must be taken into account if suitable guidance in reading tastes is to be made operative.

1. National Attitudes Toward Culture

The prevailing attitude toward the arts, and toward literature in particular, surrounds children and is absorbed by them even from their birth. The character of our nation's institutions and programs becomes so intimately associated with the lives of youth that their interests and tastes reflect the national ideas and ideals. Recent sociological studies throw light on the American attitude toward the arts. The facts presented as to the reading tastes of the population of one community offer little encouragement to those looking to general cultural advance or a more developmental educational program in the arts.[1] Surveys and analyses of the place of the arts in American society, and the part that art plays and might play in developing culture,[2] suggest that many changes are needed before art and its enjoyment can flourish. Various

---

[1] Robert S. and Helen M. Lynd. *Middletown: A Study in Contemporary American Culture.* Pp. 229–242. (Harcourt, Brace and Company: New York, 1929)

[2] G. S. Counts. *The Social Foundations of Education.* Pp. 347–387. (Charles Scribner's Sons: New York, 1934)

Lewis Mumford. *Technics and Civilization.* Pp. 364–435. (Harcourt, Brace and Company: New York, 1934)

workers suggest ways in which the school may become the effective agency in rendering it possible for people to make more satisfactory choices in the fields of art.[1]

2. Varied First-Hand Experience

The innumerable sensory experiences to which young people are exposed may, for some, serve to stimulate new motives for reading and for others act as substitutes for reading. The day is passed when, perforce, youths stayed at home and read books in their leisure time because they had nothing else to do. The contrast today is obvious. With the rapid expansion of transportation facilities, ' going to see,' ' going to hear,' ' attempting to handle,' are part of the normal life even of elementary-school pupils, and certainly of older youths. To their direct observation is exposed the construction of bridges, roads, dams, buildings, boats, airships. To them city, country-side, woods, shores, and mountains are easily accessible. Toy-makers reproduce on a small scale many of the tools of modern life. The modern museum gives children opportunities both to observe and to manipulate models of machines, instruments, and other products of past and present civilizations. To all such sources of first-hand experience young people readily respond. No one can deny the educative values that lie in multiplied first-hand experiences. For those interested primarily in the development of traditional culture, however, they present a new challenge. The world is so full of possible first-hand experience that young people need wise guidance, a portion of which can be given by reading. For most youths reading is no longer something apart from life, but intimately associated with it.

3. Readily Available Recorded Experience

The extent of the opportunities for young people to come in contact with printed verse, stories, and information provides either real danger or real opportunity. A mere listing of some of the sources from which these materials come will suggest how far-reaching are the problems relative to developing taste and interest in reading: increased production of children's books; expanding library programs with branch libraries; book vans; rental opportunities; extended loan privileges; museum and art gallery libraries; children's clubs; church schools; Boy and Girl Scout reading programs; summer camps and organized playground work with their libraries and story hours; organized adver-

---

[1] F. L. Keppel and R. L. Duffus. *The Arts in American Life.* Pp. 203–208. (McGraw-Hill Book Company: New York, 1933)

tising with numerous low-priced or gift booklets; stories and verses printed on containers of household products, on signs and signboards; motion and sound pictures; children's and adults' radio programs; syndicated comic strips and stories in daily and weekly newspapers; increased distribution of religious papers and magazines; books, story-telling, and reading in the home; book counters in chain stores; expanding sales in book shops; junior book clubs; and adult programs of parent education with available materials on books for children. All of these sources are furnishing various forms of recorded experiences in some communities, but in other communities only a few contribute to the experiences of children.

Many of the agencies listed above are primarily concerned with exposing youth to worthy materials. Unfortunately, an immense amount of trash is included among accessible books, magazines, and radio programs. A recent study involving 4,300 pupils in thirteen public schools of New York City [1] disclosed that twenty-eight percent of the pupils had no magazines in their homes. The types of magazines reported to be in the homes of seventy-two percent were, in order of frequency, (1) general story, (2) household, (3) serious popular, (4) detective and mystery, (5) science and mathematics, (6) movie and theatre, (7) literary, (8) children's. The magazine racks at any railway station or rental library reveal a none too inviting picture.

The conditions under which exposure to these materials takes place may be as potent in forming taste as the character of the material itself. The specific conditions that appeal to children need much more investigation before generalizations can be made, but on examination of the voluntary utilization of such out-of-school means for getting at the recorded ideas of others certain factors repeatedly appear. Some of these may be suggestive of lines for investigation, such as absence of coercion as to when, how, or what to select and use; opportunity to select from many distinctly different offerings; opportunity to share experience with adults or with mixed age-levels; or the combination of attractive elements, such as are found in radio programs with their regularity and dependability, continuity in characters, popular story-teller or reader, combination of music and speech, opportunity for some participation, and continual presentation of new incidents.

The ease with which children can voluntarily approach the abun-

---

[1] May Lazar. "The Reading Interests, Activities, and Opportunities of Bright, Average, and Dull Pupils." (Unpublished Doctor's thesis, Columbia University, 1936)

dant available literature, with its wide range in ideas, characterization, information, vocabulary, form, function, artistry, and appeal, presents problems that those concerned with the development of taste and interest in reading can neither evade nor examine from the angle of the school alone; and none of these problems is thus far solved.

III. FACTORS INSIDE THE SCHOOL THAT AFFECT READING TASTES

The purpose of this section is to call to attention curricular trends that are in accord with the purpose of developing tastes and interests.[1]

1. Changed and Changing Curriculums

a. Unified Purposes. One of the most conspicuous trends in the curriculums is the growing unity of purpose throughout the school. The specific content of each grade or group in a school may differ, but the general ends sought are the same in successive grades. For example, the sharp differences in purposes between primary and intermediate grades are disappearing. The once prevalent notion that primary grades are to furnish reading skills to be utilized in the intermediate grades, that the intermediate and upper grades are to refine and perfect such skills for use in still higher grades, is seldom acknowledged today. The responsibility of considering children's gradual growth over a period of many years contributes balance and perspective to the problem of developing tastes and interests. And at every level of advance the skills so far developed are to be used extensively and immediately in natural, normal reading experiences.

b. Widened Scope. The scope of the elementary-school curriculum, especially, is widening. Art, music, literature, communication, social studies, and science are reducing the time devoted to drill in reading, writing, spelling, arithmetic. In remedial work the teacher must give attention to details, but in guidance of general reading she must take into consideration widened interests. Reading is one of the primary means of supplementing direct experience in creating new understandings and interests in the enriched curriculums.

c. Emphasis on the Reader's Purpose. The generally accepted plan

---

[1] Claire Zyve and Marie Merrill. "Analysis of trends in an informal unit teaching program," *Teachers College Record*, 35: January, 1934, 293–309.

Laura Zirbes. *Curriculum Trends.* (Association for Childhood Education: Washington, D. C., 1935. Pp. 39)

Mary E. Pennell and Alice M. Cusack. *The Teaching of Reading for Better Living.* Pp. 122–144. (Houghton Mifflin Company: Boston, 1935)

of utilizing centers of interest or units of work is also leading pupils to seek voluntarily available reading materials of all sorts bearing upon the theme or core of the work. Moreover, the activity program, with its emphasis on the reactions of children to their environments and on their increasing responsibility for modifying these environments for the needs of themselves and others, tends to develop personal and social responsibility. Such actual participation in real problems that concern classroom, school, and community sends pupils voluntarily to records of human experience in order to secure a more adequate conception of current phases and conditions of life, including human motives. This means multitudes of normal reading experiences. Formerly our elementary schools were called 'reading schools,' with emphasis on the skills of reading; today, with their enriched curriculums, they are 'reading schools,' but with emphasis on reading for vicarious experience with many phases of life.

The trend in elementary-school instruction to extend the range of the pupils' understanding through vicarious reading experiences in line with group and individual interests is found also, to a somewhat lesser degree, in the secondary schools. More enlightened high-school procedures today are based on the key idea that " the major experience in using literature is reading it, abundantly, with enjoyment, under normal reading conditions." Several tendencies of enlightened high-school instruction pointing in this direction may be mentioned.

d. Reading, an All-School Function. Reading is rapidly coming to be considered an all-school function in the secondary school, and not the particular function of the English department. Any reputable book, the reading of which adds profitably and pleasurably to a student's interpretation of life in any field — history, social studies, science, art — is now considered an appropriate part of the high-school curriculum. This refers both to books commonly called non-literary and to *belles-lettres*, stories, essays, dramas, and poems, which, since Whitman at least, have vividly interpreted important aspects of life. The increasing use in the content subjects of supplementary bibliographies entitled " Story, Essay, Poem, and Verse " is indeed a wholesome sign.

e. The Free-Reading Movement. A second trend, influential in the gradual development of interests and tastes, known as the free-reading movement,[1] has two important aspects.

---

[1] Dora V. Smith. *Instruction in English.* Pp. 46, 56. National Survey of Secondary Education Monograph No. 20. (Government Printing Office: Washington, D. C., 1932)

Within English departments themselves the conventional intensive study of a few masterpieces is being greatly reduced. Historical treatment, biographical considerations, and minute literary analysis are introduced casually and incidentally in lower classes, and intensive study of literature, as such, is now generally postponed until the senior high school. Immature minds are mainly concerned with the functional or content values of literature. The traditional college-entrance emphasis is, in the best school practice, reserved for the few who are preparing to be English specialists in college.

A second aspect of the free-reading movement is inherent in the rapidly increasing use of the unit organization of literature courses. A central theme or literary form, like *Adventure* for a ninth grade, or *Drama* for a twelfth grade, is selected. Certain core materials are read and discussed by pupils and teachers, but a very considerable portion of the pupils' energies is expended in parallel or supplementary reading. With the central theme or the literary form of the unit in mind, the pupil reads supplementary materials. The aspects uppermost in such reading are finding and evaluating, and, to a somewhat lesser degree, the aspects of interpreting, using, and reporting (as the pupil brings back for class consideration the results of his exploration).

The Committee, in general, approving the free-reading movement as interpreted in the preceding paragraph, and commending the wide reading of supplementary materials in all classes, desires to express one necessary caution. An occasional pupil may read fiction far too voluminously, may enjoy what have been called 'reading debauches.' Such experiences may seriously interfere with other school and home duties and may even impair health. A conscientious teacher needs to be aware of this possible danger, which exists, of course, only in exceptional cases.

f. Varied Patterns of Experience with Literature. A third promising trend in curriculum-making, as yet largely in the experimental stages, may be mentioned. In various ways this trend endeavors to supplant with something better the deadly monotony of procedures that characterized English curriculums in the past. Bound by the idea that the term ' literature ' must include nothing but *belles-lettres,* and by the idea that literature units, as such, are most satisfactorily organized by literary forms, the curriculums have presented year after year an organization of poetry, short story, drama, essay. Some curriculums for six successive grades have followed that organization with slight modifications. Conspicuous among experiments in another direction is the varied curriculum that organizes content units in the junior high school, associates literature with certain problems of the social studies in the ninth or tenth grades, considers types of literature in the eleventh grade, and world literature in the twelfth. The larger schools are offering an increasingly wide range of electives in the upper years, with special provisions for contemporary writers. Closely allied, also, are the experiments in integrated courses in which literature, art, music, and history are fused, whether taught by one teacher or by associated specialists.[1] Even more promising are the non-college-credit courses in literature with which some secondary schools are experimenting, in which the traditional *belles-lettres* English courses are definitely modified for pupils who are unable to carry them creditably. Such undertakings, in theory at least, are based upon the idea that leading pupils to see and understand relationships may directly assist in developing intelligence, which in its final analysis is the understanding and utilization of relationships.

2. The Selection of Reading Materials

The term ' selection ' is here interpreted in two different ways: it may mean the selection by teachers of literature to be studied by the entire class, or it may mean the pupil's selection of reading he wishes to do independently or as part of class projects. Selection as exercised by schools in general and by teachers of English in particular is lamentably inefficient in both senses of the term.

a. Selection by the School. Satisfactory selection of reading materials is seriously hampered by the limited range of materials to be found in many schools and the uniformity of their quality, appearance, and use. The majority of elementary and secondary English classes throughout the country are one-textbook reading classes. The over-regimentation that may often accompany a closely prescribed textbook series cannot be too heartily condemned. Furthermore, adequate library facilities are available in only a relatively small number of favored communities. As long as this shortage of suitable equipment exists in a school, any adequate guidance in reading tastes will be impossible, however capable and inspired the actual teaching may be.

---

[1] *The American Epic,* Part I, Themes I–IV. (Los Angeles School District: Los Angeles, California, 1936. School Publication No. 276.)

Ruth Mary Weeks. *A Correlated Curriculum.* (English Monograph, No. 4. D. Appleton-Century Company: New York, 1936)

Almost as regrettable as the dearth of suitable materials is the failure of some educators to recognize the fact that children of elementary and high-school age are being exposed to a great variety of reading materials outside the school and that, since these materials are definitely influencing the children's tastes, they should be recognized in programs planned for guidance in the development of taste and interests.

Appropriateness is another important consideration in the selection of reading materials. Pupils whose immaturity and lack of reading skills make them unable to read intelligently a single page of simple narrative are often asked to study and recite literature that challenges cultured adults. Ninth-grade pupils read standard ninth-grade literature with average comprehension of 49.79, as measured by the best study yet made in this field, and twenty-five percent of ninth-grade pupils read such literature with an understanding less than .25.[1] 'Appreciation' is not at all identical with ' comprehension,' yet it is preposterous to think that readers can enjoy if their understanding is wholly inadequate. It is no wonder that such assignments too frequently lead to positive dislikes. Equally important, too, is the possibility that pupils of superior ability may also develop strong dislikes if they are presented with over-simplified material that fails to stimulate their capacity. Thus poor selection of a large share of reading content precludes the retention of desirable inherent tastes or the development of acquired ones. It violates the basal principle that learning experiences, even of factual matter, must be accompanied by at least reasonable feelings of satisfaction and achievement on the part of the learner — a principle that applies especially to all growth in which emotions are prominent.

Fortunately the facts are not entirely discouraging. Quite generously authors and publishers are responding to demands for materials in line with the interests and capacities of the younger pupils at least. An increasing number of children's books present contemporary life both at home and abroad.[2] Skilled authors and artists are creating

---

[1] Theo. W. H. Irion. *Comprehension Difficulties of Ninth-Grade Students in the Study of Literature.* (Bureau of Publications, Teachers College, Columbia University: New York, 1925)

Mary C. Burch. *Determination of a Content of the Course in Literature of a Suitable Difficulty for Junior and Senior High School Students.* Genetic Psychological Monographs, Vol. IV, Nos. 2 and 3. (Clark University Press: Worcester, Mass., 1928)

[2] Eloise Ramsey. "Children's books of the year," *Childhood Education,* 12: December, 1935, 114–120.

graphically and vividly an abundance of stories, poetry, and informational material.[1] Marked improvements are appearing in the size, shape, binding, color, and printing of children's books. Moreover, the supply of suitable, inexpensive children's books is constantly growing, and will make possible generously stocked reading tables in the home, class, and school library.

Unfortunately, less attention is being paid to the production of books suitable for young people of high-school age. However, intelligent selection of materials, even among the classics that still predominate in the more conventional courses, is somewhat generally stocking libraries with literature of fairly easy comprehension. Literature for all the readers is chosen with reference to the reading capacities of the middle group in mixed classes. Materials dealing with contemporary life now constitute fifty percent of many curriculums and anthologies. Some attention is being given to materials of local and seasonal interests. Regular use of reputable current magazines is increasing. In the better equipped schools, generously supplied classroom libraries lead pupils to many exploratory reading experiences. In equipping and expanding such libraries, attention is being given to a wide range of individual tastes and capacities, and to a wide range of contacts with life.[2]

The association of reading with meaningful experience, especially in the early years, cannot be too strongly emphasized. An appreciation of poems is developed by reading poems in which pupils are interested at the moment. Half the battle is won when reading experiences are made pleasurable by associating content with the daily experiences of life. The reading program of the future will assume the world view of interests rather than the racial or national view, and the world view will dominate at all points of the program.

b. Selection by the Pupil. The second meaning of selection, namely, the exercise of the pupils' individual choices, under wise guidance, depends primarily on abundance of acceptable material. By his voluntary choices the individual reveals his preferences; by his ability and willingness to choose ever more worthy materials he shows his developing

---

[1] A. E. Moore. *Literature Old and New for Children.* Pp. 352–388. (Houghton Mifflin Company: Boston, 1934)

[2] Committee on Home Reading, National Council of Teachers of English. *Leisure Reading:* A List for Grades Seven, Eight, and Nine. *Books for Home Reading for High Schools.* (National Council of Teachers of English: Chicago, 1930 and 1932)

taste.[1] Only by generous equipment can the danger of single textbooks and limited courses of study be avoided. The regimented reactions to a given limited content, if they do not lead to actual distaste in literature, at least may lead to an impersonal and standardized taste. In the honest effort to secure equal chance for all pupils to come in contact with well-chosen materials lurks the danger of depriving them of the benefits that can come only from the opportunity to exercise choice. Most promising, then, is the expansion of classroom, school, and public libraries — with all of the possible prescribed and voluntary uses.

Promising, also, and in accord with the principle that learners must assume responsibilities for their own growth are the encouragements given to pupils to contribute their own books for use in school, the more frequent use of the results of reading, and the breaking down of standard grade placements.[2] Schools and libraries are challenging readers to make their own selections, to establish their own valuations of reading materials over a range that steadily widens with their expanding capacities. These are all commendable phases of the effort to relate reading to experience, and to emphasize experiences *through* literature as well as *with* literature. Promising also is the trend for the newer courses of study to become encyclopedic rather than prescriptive, thus supplying teacher and pupils with abundant materials from which they may choose in accordance with the personnel of the class.

3. Methods of Guidance

Recent trends in the teaching methods of elementary schools reveal a tendency to develop children's abilities to select reading experiences that yield them satisfaction.

1. There is far greater concern for the individual child's strength or difficulties in learning to control reading techniques for his own use. The widespread attention to reading readiness and to remedial reading programs is eliminating the distaste for reading too often aroused in the past by baffling, disagreeable experiences.

2. There is a departure from uniform methods of teaching reading; novelty and the personal approach help to make a selection be long remembered.[3]

---

[1] Russell Thomas. *English Instruction in the University High School.* Chapt. V. "Voluntary Reading." Pp. 164–172. (University of Chicago Press: Chicago, 1933)

[2] *An Experience Curriculum in English.* (D. Appleton-Century Company: New York, 1935)

[3] Angela Broening. *Developing Appreciation through Teaching Literature.* Johns Hopkins University Studies in Education, No. 13. (Johns Hopkins Press: Baltimore, 1929)

3. Again we note the substitution of creative, constructive, investigative methods of working in reading, as in all phases of the curriculum, taking the place of memorization and reproduction common to older methods of guidance. There is less coercion as to what, and when, and where to read. Constructive enterprises often necessitate the reading of materials for information, verification, and inspiration, and offer occasion for sharing pleasurable library experiences with class groups. Unquestionably the guidance of recreational reading described in Chapter VI is potent in developing both reading tastes and reading habits.[1]

4. Above all, the literature period, the book period, and the story or poetry hour are filling a very important need. The group experiencing of the pleasures that lie in good literature, at definite times and places, usually through motivated listening and informal discussion, is exceedingly valuable in every grade. The literature period, although definitely related to it, is, of course, quite distinct from the formal reading period, in which the mechanics of reading are taught the few who are below grade standards while their classmates are occupied with other duties. In well-equipped schools the classroom tables for the literature period are piled with children's books, to which the children have guided access, with resultant informal chats about pictures and stories they enjoy. As they sit in the listening circle, they become absorbed in the rhythm and swing of poetry read to them and revel in the stories told by the teacher, often with book in hand.

Most of these promising trends in guidance appear also in the best secondary-school and college practices.

1. Instead of the deadening recitation method associated with half-hearted and inadequate home study, teachers and pupils are together during the class period reading and discussing the literature chosen for that period. Classroom experiences point ahead; they are preparation for reading, rather than quiz periods covering reading already done.

2. Frequently also the exhaustive analytical study of masterpieces is greatly reduced in amount, or abandoned entirely in lower classes of the high school. For it is substituted extensive reading both by groups and by individuals. The class period becomes a round-table meeting, the clearing house in which groups and individuals reveal what they have read through book talks, interpretative readings, and informal dramatizations. Pupils recommend good books to one another. Evidence derived from carefully controlled classroom experiments in wide reading culminating in group sharing, as contrasted with antiquated recitation methods characterized by fragmentary pretenses at expression, is conclusive that such extensive methods produce far more satisfactory comments and discussion on the part of pupils, are about of equal value in yielding per-

---

[1] Angela Broening. *Op. cit.*

manent detailed information about books, and cultivate decidedly superior attitudes of enjoyment and appreciation.[1]

3. Even when a class uses a single basal textbook, free reading of supplementary materials, in which browsing, finding, and evaluating are objectives of the readers, is often stressed even to a half of the pupils' time devoted to experiencing literature. The pupils' choices, under guidance, in association with their individual tastes and interests, are kept foremost.

4. Many cities are experimenting with reading programs in which several copies each of a few books are supplied to classes instead of many copies of a single title. Fully stocked school and classroom libraries, with a constantly changing supply of books in keeping with the content of the course as planned by the teacher, are gradually supplanting the one-textbook procedures. The result is that classes are kept together by a minimal core of materials that the pupils read and discuss together, and from this core, and in keeping with it, individual exploration among many books is at a premium.

5. Commendable innovations also appear in junior-college instruction in English. Formal lecture courses in which students diligently fill notebooks with second-hand facts and judgments are gradually being supplanted by programs of group and individual reading under the guidance of the instructor as a co-worker. Students are challenged to formulate their own judgments, to explore widely in lines of special interest to themselves, and generally to develop independence, instead of parrotlike repetitions of ready-made opinions.

6. The national survey of secondary schools revealed many unique practices designed to win the interest of students.[2] An innovation of school architecture indicative of the greater informality of procedure in certain English classes throughout the country is the ' English laboratory ' for study and informal discussion. In one high school is a large room with movable seats and easy chairs at one end, tables and reference materials in the center, and a small stage for dramatization at the other end. Bookcases, pictures, maps, and charts suggest that this is a study room as well as a place for discussion. A bulletin board shows clippings of literary and dramatic interest, and an exhibit case presents interesting work of the pupils or illustrative materials prepared for a selected unit of work.

Illustrations of lively discussion abound, both in modern literature and in work with the classics. A group of seniors in another school, led by one of their own number, discussed treasures in art and architecture in their own city that might call forth reactions such as Keats's " Ode on a Grecian Urn." A class of juniors, becoming skeptical concerning Emerson's advice regarding self-reliance, discussed the possible effect upon themselves and society at large if every individual in the world followed Emerson's suggestions to their logical

---

[1] Nancy C. Coryell. *An Evaluation of Extensive and Intensive Teaching of Literature.* (Teachers College, Columbia University: New York, 1927)

[2] Dora V. Smith. *Op. cit.* P. 59.

conclusions. A ninth-grade group reviewed the characteristics of the epic by selecting Lindbergh as the possible subject for a modern *Odyssey*. Another compared methods by which one becomes acquainted with people in fiction and in life.

Examples could be multiplied from all sections of the country to show that many teachers are making literature vital to their pupils.

Some teachers of literature in the upper high-school classes still believe that their primary obligation is to develop inductively the standards by which excellent literature can be distinguished from inferior. With their upper classes of the secondary-school, such teachers turn from mere exposure to reading to a directed and purposeful study of literature. Unguided reading experiences may for some superior individuals gradually disclose standards, but for many, even of the capable, guidance in intelligent discrimination is a more economical and profitable procedure. To lead pupils to change their immature likings for lyric poetry, essays, dramas, short stories and novels, into intelligently made judgments, to induce them to discover such criteria and then quite definitely to formulate the standards for themselves still remains one of the chief obligations and privileges of the teacher of literature.

4. Ways of Recording Achievement and Progress

a. Desirable Methods. How a school values any phase of its work may be estimated by the means used for recording the achievement of its pupils. If a school believes that the development of taste is made evident as individual pupils over a period of years select reading that gives them what they are searching for; as they manage with sacrifice of time and money to add books to their own libraries; indicate, as they use their own and borrowed books, that they regard some of them as especially valuable to themselves; share fittingly with others some of their experiences with reading materials; use their reading for their own benefit; and discard books that have ceased to be useful to them — that school will suitably measure its teaching processes. A fair picture of the functioning of tastes may then be secured by the use of individual and group cumulative reading records with provisions for reëxamination, by the starring of selections marked as favorites, by the recommendations made for the fall supply for the school library, by the yearly contribution of one or two books to the library, by the seasonable review of new books for parents' buying lists. Such records evaluate pupil progress, not in exact numerical terms, but in terms of the quality and continuity of normal reading achievements.

Of the somewhat more formal and yet commendable methods of evaluating achievement in secondary schools, the following may be listed, approximately in order of preference. First, on opportune occasions, reports to the class group made by individuals on materials they have read. Such reports, closely articulated with class work, are probably of highest merit. Second, periodic round-table meetings, book-club days, reading-circle meetings, in which pupils converse somewhat informally about their individual readings of the preceding fortnight or month. (It may be pointed out that a rich program of literature, such as is suggested in this chapter, minimizes the need of adjuncts like extra-curricular clubs and helps to break down the unfortunate curricular and extra-curricular dualism.) Third, when pressure of time precludes the two natural ways of reporting just mentioned, informal conferences with the teacher are appropriate, in which the teacher satisfies herself that reading has been done. Reading records kept on cards in a class file in charge of a class committee; brief written quizzes; informal personal essays on reading done; occasional informal oral reports, with the caution that only a brief portion of any one class hour should be so used — all these may be utilized occasionally. Fourth, in advanced classes only, especially classes studying the excellence of book-review pages, occasional written book reviews may be profitably utilized.

b. Undesirable Methods. In contrast with desirable methods of recording achievement certain deadening procedures all too common should be abandoned. Especially objectionable are forms of prizes or rewards in which the satisfactions of successful competition are substituted for the satisfactions inherent in the reading itself and the social use to be made of it. Reputable studies of motivation demonstrate that the most worthy incentives are intimately associated with learning activities themselves. Questionable indeed are class honor rolls, publicly announced school marks, and the like — all of which may be contrasted with pleasurable experience in the reading itself, motivated by the desire to share such pleasure with the social group when occasion offers. Even if the publicity of a high reward could be considered desirable for the winners, the inhibiting effects on those who do not win must also be taken into account. This is especially true because in the literature classes, as in all others that utilize the competitive motive, certain gifted children are almost certain to be habitual winners; certain handicapped children, to be habitual losers.

Another method of measuring achievement in reading, or at least recording progress in reading, is the formal, written book report. This device is almost always badly managed. Teachers fail to realize that a written report to which is attached too great scholastic importance may hang with deadening weight in a pupil's consciousness all the time he is reading. If a standard form of report has been prescribed, the outlines of that ultimate product obtrude themselves in the pupil's mind as he reads every chapter. Indeed, the skillful pupil may read the book only for answers to questions suggested by the impending record. Possibly English teachers make no greater error, in their laudable desire to have some composition associated with appreciation, than to load their pupils with written reports on reading.

Under various forms appears another method of securing data for teachers' class books, the ' new-type ' examination in literature, whether on class assignments or outside reading choices. When such tests are more or less informal, are intelligently made by the individual teacher to fit her own class and subject matter, and are used as essential parts of the reading program, they may be useful.[1] However, the danger is that true and false alternatives, best-answer choices, and the like may test a reader's memory or judgment of certain minutiae of language, or factual background, or isolated character traits, or distributed word meanings, or figures of speech, or other details, the mastery of which is either incidental or accidental, and often but remotely associated with the grasping of the author's message. When the outcome to be measured is the mastery of information about factual material in a content subject, the new-type examinations may have a place. Conceivably also, the teacher who thinks that a piece of literature is to be studied as if it were a chapter of history may establish that erroneous idea even more firmly by the use of such examinations. By such measuring devices pupil achievement is simply made and easily recorded, but the results in the development of tastes are often very unsatisfactory.

Those who guide children's reading experiences must realize that proof of developing interests and tastes does not lie in any external evidence that the reading has been done. Growth in appreciation cannot be numerically recorded. The evidence of developing interests and tastes is inherent in the satisfactions arising within the individual when he finds in books that which recalls, refines, reveals, or reaffirms ideas or feelings that seem to him to be valuable.

---

[1] Angela Broening. *Op. cit.*

SUB–COMMITTEE ON CHAPTER VII

Chairman

WILLIS L. UHL, Dean, College of Education, University of Washington, Seattle, Washington

Associates

B. R. BUCKINGHAM, Ginn and Company, Boston, Massachusetts

EDGAR DALE, Bureau of Educational Research, Ohio State University, Columbus, Ohio

E. W. DOLCH, Assistant Professor of Education, University of Illinois, Urbana, Illinois

GILBERT W. KELLY, Scott Foresman and Company, Chicago, Illinois

PHILIP A. KNOWLTON, The Macmillan Company, New York City

BERNICE E. LEARY, Department of Education, St. Xavier's College for Women, Chicago, Illinois

WILLIAM F. RASCHE, Principal, Milwaukee Vocational School, Milwaukee, Wisconsin

CARLETON WASHBURNE, Superintendent of Schools, Winnetka, Illinois

IVAN R. WATERMAN, Chief, Division of Textbooks and Publications, California State Department of Education, Sacramento, California

GERTRUDE WHIPPLE, Elementary Curriculum Section, Public Schools, Los Angeles, California

ETHEL C. WRIGHT, Supervisor, Work with Children, Toledo Public Library, Toledo, Ohio

CHAPTER VII

THE MATERIALS OF READING

WILLIS L. UHL
Dean, College of Education, University of Washington
Seattle, Washington

In earlier chapters of this Yearbook the Committee has emphasized its broad interpretation of reading as the use of printed materials for all purposes, both in and out of school. Thus ' reading materials ' comprise not only basal readers and related equipment but also supplementary texts, reference books, recreational books, pamphlets, periodicals, charts, strips, maps, and all other printed materials that can be used profitably by school children. Hence, this interpretation of the term ' reading materials ' greatly exceeds in scope that given in the Society's Thirtieth Yearbook, Part II, on *The Textbook in American Education*. This enlarged scope includes both the wider range of materials themselves, and increased flexibility of their use under modern educational theories and curricular patterns.

I. TYPES AND CONTENT OF MATERIAL AND EQUIPMENT ESSENTIAL TO AN ADEQUATE READING PROGRAM

Until comparatively recent times, school programs of reading were devoted almost exclusively to three purposes: first, the mastery of technical reading skills to insure literacy; second, proficiency in the oral rendition of meanings and the oral conveyance of rhetorical values; and, third, familiarity with a limited and arbitrarily chosen body of literature conventionally recognized as ' standard ' or ' classic.' Today, school reading is far broader in function; it is an aspect of rich and abundant living and a preparation for future growth. Thus greatly enlarged in significance, the reading program presupposes and requires materials of greatly increased variety and scope. The basal textbook, both in reading *per se* and in other recognized school subjects, remains with us in a large majority of schools as a common core, but around it is massed in some schools a body of extensive reading materials that vary with the requirements of individual readers. In many schools today, the whole range of the library serves in the capacity of a rich, expanded text.

The school's intimate dependence on conditions and activities outside itself is necessary and obvious. Before pupils first attend school, after school hours, and after school attendance is completed, they engage in numerous activities to which reading is related. These activities supply interests and readiness for pertinent reading. In turn, the reading done in school can affect these activities and can make them more satisfying. These facts enable the school to demonstrate clearly to pupils the value of the reading program.

Examples of relating the reading program to activities outside the school are available for all grades. In the kindergarten and first grade, materials are adapted by authors and teachers to the vocabularies and activities of the children. Many of the informal activities of the school day grow out of the materials that are read by the children or read or told to them; also, pupils are preparing for much of the reading of Grade I by similar informal activities. Often, reading materials based on such activities are created by pupils and teachers. The success of teachers is sometimes great enough to cause the pupils to continue school activities in their play at home. Richer opportunities arise in later grades for relating the reading program to out-of-school activities, because the pupils have greater command of reading and wider interests. For all types of schools and pupils such relating of local resources to the reading program is possible. Thus, city pupils have written sketches of their parks, water supply, police departments, and other civic conditions; and Navajo Indians of Arizona have prepared reading materials on soil erosion. Such work is an adjunct to the reading program, for pupils read the sketches they have prepared, and they read other related books and selections.[1]

The preceding paragraphs reëmphasize the comprehensive reading program that the Committee recommends throughout the Yearbook. The term 'materials of reading' definitely includes everything the children read, both within and without the school. Although this present discussion frequently reiterates the function and value of a rich and varied reading program, the treatment in the present chapter relates primarily to basal reading materials and textbooks, together with a relatively small number of types of supplementary reading materials.

---

[1] Fannie W. Dunn (Chairman). *Materials of Instruction.* Eighth Yearbook of the Department of Supervisors and Directors of Instruction. (Bureau of Publications, Teachers College, Columbia University: New York, 1935)

This plan was adopted in view of the fact that the nature of the materials for extensive reading is discussed elsewhere in various sections of the Yearbook, as in Chapters V, VI, and VIII.

Any summary of reading materials must take account of the maturity of the readers. Five scholastic levels may be distinguished: primary, middle-grade, junior-high-school, senior-high-school, and collegiate.

1. Reading Materials in the Primary Grades

The printed materials used in the primary grades are exceedingly diversified. They usually consist of a basal series [1] of readers, with certain accessories, and one or more supplementary books for each grade. Although sharp contrasts in function between different levels of the reading program are no longer recognized, reading instruction in the first three grades is expected to give normal pupils, by the beginning of the fourth grade, the ability to master new vocabulary sufficiently well to enable them to read unfamiliar materials with relatively little dependence on the numerous adjuncts required by beginners.

There is available today an abundance of basal readers and related equipment in series form, any one of which can be used effectively by normal or even moderately handicapped pupils. A brief survey of features common to many of these reading systems reveals certain current trends. A minimal conventional basal-reading equipment of the first three grades consists of a primer and a first reader for the first grade and one reader each for the second and third grades, each one, in many cases, preceded, accompanied, or followed by a consumable workbook closely related to it in content and vocabulary. Beginners are commonly provided with one or more preprimers — the trend is toward the use of several — to promote reading readiness; though, in systems in which workbook materials are used preparatory to the primer, preprimers are sometimes dispensed with. Large illustrated wall charts are often provided; they function not unlike preprimers.

---

[1] Here and elsewhere the assumption that 'regular' or 'basal' textbooks are prevailingly used is based upon a recent inquiry conducted among advocates of the activity school by a member of the subcommittee for this chapter. The estimates given indicate that only from five to ten percent of American pupils are enrolled in schools operating on the activity basis. Even in schools featuring integrated programs, textbooks in subjects involving the improvement of skills are likely to be used in the portion of the school day set aside for 'skills and drills.'

Word, phrase, and sentence cards are provided with many systems to insure pupil recognition of isolated portions of what is read.

Primary reading materials vary through many degrees of formality. The more formal programs place great reliance upon accessories like reading charts; word, phrase, and sentence cards; materials to facilitate word analysis; and workbooks. Less formal methods subordinate such accessories, so far as the printed equipment is concerned, and place a greater reliance upon capitalizing the interests that the children display in the classroom. Perhaps the distinction between formal and informal reading methods is, after all, chiefly one of emphasis. Different published systems of reading vary in formality by almost imperceptible degrees. It is probable that slow children need a more detailed method with greater reliance upon accessories than bright children do, though bright children occasionally respond especially well to relatively formal methods, like word analysis, that give them keys to be applied readily to new situations. Those who administer remedial reading programs for upper-grade and secondary-school children frequently find that the ' shortages ' of the poor readers may best be met by drills in word and syllable perception and related types of instruction.

Basal-reading materials for the primary grades have been perfected to such a degree that any one of many systems can be used successfully under ordinary conditions. Schools are courting disaster in their selection of such materials only when, in a misguided effort to distribute commercial patronage, they adopt for different primary grades portions of several systems that are essentially incompatible and hence virtually incapable of sequential use.

At the earliest stage, commonly called the preprimer, there is an increasing disposition to relate reading materials to the children's environment and experiences. This trend, already manifest in published readers, is particularly noticeable in school systems in which an activity curriculum prevails. In such systems, as well as those in which reading is taught as a distinct subject, teachers sometimes prefer to prepare their own preprimer materials, based upon bona fide classroom experiences of the children, and to issue the supplementary materials to their classes in mimeographed or dittoed form. The requirements of this procedure upon the teacher's time, initiative, and skill are heavy. To be most effective, such homemade materials must conform, to a reasonable degree, with the recognized principles of preprimer construction as to vocabulary control and the like. Moreover, they must articulate properly with later reading materials for which they are expected to lay a foundation. At the preprimer level, such materials may be particularly valuable. Above that level, individual teachers or local groups of teachers are increasingly unlikely to improve upon the product of professional textbook-makers. At best, reading matter thus prepared locally as an outgrowth of class experiences is valuable only in the classroom in which it was produced or in classrooms in which nearly identical experiences can be repeated. Efforts to substitute it in other classrooms for published material having a more universal appeal are seldom justified.

In the primary grades, the distinction between a basal reader, which, with its related equipment serves as a definite tool for the original mastery of a new skill, and the supplementary reader, which merely affords additional practice in the exercise and perfection of that skill, is sharply drawn. In content, however, the two may closely resemble each other at this level, and their differences be found chiefly in matters of emphasis. Basal reading is more *consciously* devoted to the attainment of accepted reading outcomes. Supplementary material, however, is used more discursively, more fluently. Most schools in which children, either as classes, groups, or individuals, read many books each year, regard only one of those books as the basal tool of instruction. It is clear, therefore, that in such schools the amount of supplementary reading greatly exceeds that which is basally required in carrying out whatever reading method has been adopted. A generation ago the primary child who could read a half-dozen books a year was indeed fortunate. Today that is a low number; the reading of twenty or thirty books in a single year is not unusual. A liberal equipment in more progressive schools is likely to include several sets of readers of standard or more than standard length, and many short, relatively inexpensive books. Such booklets may scarcely exceed in scope individual units in the basal reader, but they often provide an abundance of related reading matter. Indeed, there is an increasing tendency to reinforce basal-reader units with materials of this type, constructed with a nearly identical vocabulary and hence a minimum of reading difficulty. Other things being equal, a supplementary book that utilizes a high percentage of the vocabulary of a basal book is a more effective learning instrument than a book that has only a small proportion of its word list common to the basic list.

The present trend to increase the amount and range of supplementary reading is doing much to give children a sense of mastery in the early grades. Probably no other movement in reading is of greater importance, provided the extensive reading matter is purposefully selected. Aimless reading of numerous books, haphazardly assembled, may prove discouraging and confusing to average pupils.

The themes emphasized in the selections now commonly included in primary readers are more varied than formerly. Because of children's love of the fanciful, stories rich in imaginative appeal are ever popular. Animal stories abound. Purely fanciful material, however, though still commonly given more space at this level than factual material in literary or quasi-basal readers, receives relatively less emphasis than formerly. There is today a greater appreciation of children's interest in what is plausible and familiar as well as in what is fantastic and remote. Many readers now provide fascinating accounts of occupations that, to children, are romantic, such as those of the fireman, policeman, and postman. The milkman, the baker, the locomotive engineer, and the carpenter share the stage with the gnome, the elf, the knight, and the prince. The best juvenile books of today can be classified as juveniles only because they are simple in content, vocabulary, and sentence structure. They are fascinating and significant to people of all ages.[1] In a word, the child of today is given the impression from his earliest years that reading is a key to the world about himself rather than merely to a treasure house of infantile bedtime tales.

But this trend toward realism is not confined to literary readers and recreational or semi-recreational books. Books of work-type reading, closely related in vocabulary to the basal reader, are now in demand as virtual textbooks in content subjects throughout the first three grades. Such subject-matter texts are supplementary to the reader, and at the same time lay the foundations of instruction in the arts and in the sciences, social and natural. It is the careful vocabulary coördination with the basic reader that has made possible this relatively new development. The former notion that subject-matter texts in the primary grades were not feasible has been due largely to the lack of serious efforts in vocabulary coördination.

The provision of adequate recreatory reading is especially important at this stage. No modern primary classroom is complete without its ' browsing table ' or library shelf of juveniles. Such books, with their attractive pictorial features and relatively meager text, are sel-

---

[1] Cf. May Massee. "If a book is good enough for a junior, it is good enough for anybody." *Horn Book Magazine*, 12:1936, 227.

dom edited with a view to vocabulary correlation with the basal text. That fact, however, may not be wholly a disadvantage, since pupils who can read, with true enjoyment and reasonable mastery, books not rigorously restricted in vocabulary gain an early appreciation of the richness and variety of our native language.

2. Reading Materials in the Middle Grades

In the middle grades, except for children requiring remedial work, the character of the reading material rather definitely changes. The period for developing the elementary mechanics of reading, which has necessarily required so much emphasis in the first three grades, is passing. The period also of the undifferentiated curriculum is finished for schools of the traditional type. Indeed, even third-grade children, in a large majority of schools, have been given a book in arithmetic and, very likely, one in geography, and another in language. Elementary science similarly is making its claim for recognition as a subject, and in some schools has already gained a place in the primary period.

These tendencies become clearer as the child passes into the fourth grade. If he has not already had a geography book and a language book in his hands, he will receive them at this time. He also begins a history book or one embracing the social studies. And these books are not small. In the fourth grade, the total number of pages of reading matter in basal textbooks, entirely exclusive of books used in the reading course, may well total nearly two thousand.

Each of the curricular fields in which basal books are furnished — arithmetic, geography, history, language, health, science — will be likely to call for additional readings or for workbooks. Then there are also the basic and supplementary reading books. Even the conservative school today is requiring from rather young pupils an astonishingly large amount of reading.

In the middle grades important reading materials are found in the regular reading books — the fourth, fifth, and sixth readers. These books should articulate with the readers for primary grades — should build on their vocabulary, their types of content, and their degree of maturity of concepts. Within this middle-grade period there will be a gradual transition from predominantly fanciful to predominantly realistic subject matter. History, biography, and serious poetry of a simple sort find a larger place. At this stage the distinction between recreatory and work-type reading is becoming so pronounced that series of strictly work-type readers have been made available. Though such readers are not basal in the sense of presenting a well-balanced program of reading content — fanciful and realistic, literary and non-literary, prose and verse — many schools find them valuable for co-basal use because their content resembles the reading materials encountered in content-subject textbooks. Books of this type lend themselves to more minute dissection in the pursuit of reading skills than would be appropriate with strictly literary selections, which are likely to be spoiled by overanalysis.

When he reaches the middle grades, the child's vocabulary and conceptual background have been increased to such a degree that far more latitude in the choice of supplementary reading materials is justified, and the latter need not be correlated so closely with the basal reader. At this level, above all others, it is important that the child's reading mastery be increased in every possible way. Consequently, there has sprung up a wide variety of supplementary readers, both in related sets or series and in the form of isolated books. Some of these volumes give the child alluring specimens of material from standard juvenile books in the hope that he may be attracted to them for further reading through the library. For the mentally less mature pupils, who require a more vivid interest appeal, other readers are provided featuring stories rich in dramatic incidents. Anthologies of juvenile poetry are available, with emphasis upon modern verse. Other subject-matter fields are drawn upon, with the result that series of books in the social sciences, in the fine arts, in health, and in natural science are rapidly displacing the sets of quasi-basal literary readers formerly so popular. Thus is reading intimately correlated with the work in other subjects even in schools that still adhere to the traditional type of curriculum.

In schools having an integrated program, this lowering of the bars between reading and the other subjects is, of course, carried still further. In such schools the nature of the reading program is almost completely determined by the subject matter of the unit or activity that at the moment forms the core of the class work. Under ideal guidance and with abundant reading materials — and they must be far more abundant and therefore more expensive than in the traditional school — the child acquires a competence and resourcefulness as a reader that equip him well for secondary-school work.

Scattered reading of this kind, however, is fraught with dangers. So difficult is it to find reference material accurately gauged to the large variety of reading aptitudes found in any one class, that teachers in activity schools are seeking constantly to provide their own activity textbooks. Such materials tend to become summaries of subject matter, couched in language that can be read by the poorest readers in the class and that consequently fail to challenge the abler pupils. Obviously, such ' activity books ' represent a negation of the philosophy that produced them, since genuine pupil activity, in so far as it concerns reading, consists of the search for these items of information in a variety of sources, such as encyclopedias and miscellaneous library books.

At this level all but the dullest children receive much help from standard juvenile works of reference. Children's encyclopedias have in recent years been greatly improved. Efforts are being made to keep them up-to-date and to adapt them to the reading ability of the children most likely to use the various articles they contain. Children's dictionaries have also been greatly improved in recent years. From them much useless matter has been removed. Efforts have been made to concentrate upon the vocabulary most commonly met by children. Above all, definitions have been brought within children's grasp, in welcome contrast to the practice formerly so common of defining a simple term in words far more abstract and difficult than the word defined.

In the middle grades, as at all stages, supplementary reading merges imperceptibly into reference and recreatory reading. Perhaps the chief difference between the supplementary reader and the recreational or reference book relates, not to its content, but to the machinery of its distribution. The supplementary reader was formerly provided in classroom sets on a quasi-adoption basis, and even now, if not so provided, is circulated in smaller than classroom quantities from schoolroom to schoolroom or from school to school. It is therefore a book of which at least several copies are available but, of the library material for reference or recreation, there is likely to be but a single copy or at the most two or three. Group work, therefore, is possible with one, but only individual work with the other. It is imperative that individual pupils in the middle grades have access to a variety of books of all kinds. At this level, if any, they are likely to acquire a permanent taste for good reading.

The importance of the middle grades, and the vast amount of service the reading materials of these grades must perform, can be recognized only when one contrasts the reading matter of the third grade with that of the seventh. Only then does it become apparent that the school is remarkably exacting in its requirements during these three years.

The child must develop the mechanics of his reading and increase his reading vocabulary and speed. Such requirements are fundamental. He must also learn to read geographically, historically, scientifically, and mathematically. Geographically, he must read maps, and must grasp the relation of man to his earthly environment. Both geographically and mathematically, he must read graphs and statistics, but before he can do either he must read numbers and apprehend their significance as symbols of quantitative relations. Reading historically makes yet another demand in which time depth and time sequence — in short, time sense — are to be developed and used. Reading scientifically, whether it has to do with the subject called elementary science or whether it cuts across all the subjects, means reading with an appreciation of the concepts, themes, and generalizations that characterize even a rudimentary scientific attitude.

For all these purposes, the content of the middle grades should be carefully chosen and wisely administered. Whereas there is a general tendency to regard these grades as relatively less important than those which precede and follow them, a case could be made for regarding these grades as of critical importance.

3. Reading Materials for Upper Grades and Junior High Schools

a. A Fundamental Fallacy. A fallacy that perhaps has disrupted American education more seriously than any other is the assumption generally made until recent years that at the end of the sixth grade a normal child should be considered fully and completely to have learned to read. According to this assumption, a child was expected to have progressed from the mere rudiments to virtual adulthood in the three intermediate grades. As recently as fifteen years ago, seventh and eight readers were usually supplied to 'top off,' as it were, complete series. The eight-four plan was still in general vogue and a separate period was still devoted rather generally to practice in reading as such. These readers, however, were prevailingly built on the assumption that pupils had sufficiently mastered general reading skills and were prepared, therefore, to assimilate material of adult literary quality. In more recent years, the growing ascendancy of the six-three-three plan brought with it a strong propaganda for types of instruction in junior high schools differing sharply from the traditional elementary-school curriculum. One unhappy result of this trend was the gradual disappearance of the period specifically devoted to reading as a subject.

The doctrine that children entered the seventh grade as competent readers — able, with occasional reference to the dictionary, to read almost any English book — was reflected in the reading difficulty of subject-matter texts in all fields. Histories and geographies made but slight concessions to reading immaturity. The assumption that difficulties of vocabulary and sentence structure could safely be disregarded carried with it, in many places, a callous disregard of conceptual difficulty. As a result, textbooks in all subjects were badly overgraded. When, as was once the case, high-school pupils were for the most part a select group, the results were not so serious. By the time secondary-school education had become well-nigh universal, the situation became intolerable, and the necessity for corrective measures was seen by all. Today, therefore, many forward-looking schools are beginning to provide a continuation of the specific reading period throughout the junior-high-school, and even in some instances the senior-high-school, years.

b. The Content of Junior-High-School Reading. Of what shall junior-high-school reading consist, if indeed it is to be differentiated, as many now believe it should be, from English with its emphasis upon form and analysis, and literature with its emphasis upon esthetic values? Many teachers believe that the answer lies in a program of remedial reading — in diagnostic and remedial exercises of various kinds that afford carefully guided self-drill and self-criticism in the acquisition of reading comprehension and speed. In such programs the content value of the selections read is likely to be relatively simple; junior-high-school anthologies, individual classics (to a decreasing extent), and books of contemporary literature are used apart from the remedial program to give vitality to the work. Where ultra-analytical methods of reading improvement are not favored, work-type or factual readers are used, in many instances as the counterpart of the upper-grade basal reader. In many schools a tendency is observable to use reading materials in the social sciences, whether studied separately or included in fusion or integrated courses, as texts for the improvement of reading techniques.

c. Informal Reading Programs. A notable tendency of today is the comparative informality of many junior-high-school reading programs. This results in part from the earlier repudiation of reading as a formal subject and in part from the fact that the junior high schools, ever faced with the challenge to develop innovating courses of study, have been fertile breeding grounds for programs of the activity, unit, or integrated type. To meet these newer requirements, small unit books or paper-bound pamphlets on a variety of topics related chiefly to the social studies have been brought out by several agencies. Such pamphlets, for example, as those brought out under the auspices of the American Council on Education in 1932 and 1933 increase the latitude of teachers in the choice of reading materials. More are provided for any one year than any one class could read. In each, some detailed aspect of the social studies is treated rather exhaustively on approximately the junior-high-school plane of difficulty. Also, as in the middle grades, many junior high schools are providing, for strictly local use, their own unit readings in the social studies in mimeographed or other non-book form. Materials thus produced vary from conscientiously and competently written brochures well adapted to pupil requirements, to excerpts hastily thrown together from published books in violation of copyright laws and of recognized ethical and educational standards. Other unit publications, such as the pamphlets of the American Council on Education just mentioned, are edited with the care and finesse of commercially marketed books.

d. The Juvenile Encyclopedia. In schools at this level, the juvenile encyclopedia is a particularly useful tool of instruction. Indeed, when integrated courses are conducted in a manner consistent with the theory upon which they are based, even basal textbooks become largely encyclopedic in function. Here, again, we meet one of those apparent anomalies in which the newer education abounds: the encyclopedic textbook, rich in detailed subject matter but largely lacking in the motivating devices and study helps characteristic of the so-called ' progressive ' textbook of a decade ago, is revived in the guise of a modernistic schoolbook. It lacks impedimenta that presuppose consecutive reading of it by the entire class, and hence its domination of classroom procedure. Nevertheless, it gives teachers what they are seeking — a convenient thesaurus of information to be consulted when and if needed in the course of class work that differs from year to year and even from pupil to pupil.

Regardless of the system followed, however, a modern reading equipment for these grades should include not only multiple copies of several textbooks in each of several subjects, but also reference books of all kinds ranging from encyclopedias to unit pamphlets.

e. Recreative Reading. At this level, it is highly important that the child's taste in recreative reading be further developed. His social interests are relatively mature, although he may or may not be able to read books of mature reading difficulty. By this time also there have arisen sharp differences among pupils in reading ability. It is particularly necessary, therefore, that easy reading materials be accessible along with those that are more difficult. These are two sorts — well-graded books originally designed for adolescent and pre-adolescent youth, and simplifications and adaptations such as will be discussed elsewhere.

In the field of recreatory reading, in addition to recognized classics, whether in their original or in adapted form, there should be provided a copious amount of contemporary fiction, essays, and periodicals of varying degrees of seriousness and merit as judged by sophisticated standards. As was pointed out in Chapter VI, the child must be given an opportunity to participate actively in the development of his own literary taste. This he cannot do if all but the 'best' readings are withheld from him. Modern teachers who seek to guide the reading tastes of junior-high-school pupils are reluctant to assume a censorious attitude toward any but positively degrading contemporary literature. Lack of literary merit as judged by the accepted standards, which it is hoped the pupil will himself sometime learn to apply, need not always bar a book from truly modern school libraries.

4. Reading Materials for the Senior High School

The fallacy that pupils who have finished the sixth grade have mastered the skills of reading and are, without further training, competent to deal with materials of departmentalized subjects has, naturally, influenced also the senior high school. Today, when our schools contain many pupils who ten years ago would have left through lack of academic interest, instruction in the various subjects has been perceptibly slowed down because of the inability of students to master the concepts presented. Poor reading ability inevitably slows down the progress of the whole group. Often the entire student body is retarded to the speed possible of attainment by the pupils of less than medium ability.

Again, as in the case of the present junior high school, the materials with which reading must concern itself comprise practically the whole curriculum. This situation demands the coöperation of every teacher in the school in the effort to help pupils acquire sufficient reading ability to deal with the various subject-matter texts.

Each of the subjects studied in the secondary school presents its own problem in reading, and in the pursuit of these other subjects directed practice in reading is perhaps most effective. Many subjects have a technical vocabulary that must be mastered if the material is to be understood. Educators are trying to provide texts that, by association of ideas in the treatment or by actual definition embodied in the discussion, make the reading easy. To any pupil to whom the subject is new and technical, such texts are useful. By the rapid reader, however, in a non-technical subject such as history, a loss of interest is felt when such a method is pursued. Either the provision of separate, simpler texts for the slow reader who retards the rate of progress of the group must be extended, or below-average pupils must be given remedial work, preferably related to the content subjects, that will increase their abilities. Otherwise, such pupils should be segregated in special groups that will allow the regular student body to proceed at a normal rate.

Materials for high-school reading should continue to be drawn from all sources that minister to the academic and extra-scholastic interests of pupils. The field should be extended — at least for extensive reading — even beyond the point to which it has yet been carried. If, to secure the attention of pupils, reading lists must include material that seems of less permanent value than the standard works that made up the bulk of such lists even ten years ago, it is encouraging to reflect that the skill gained in the process of wide reading may gradually extend itself to a finer appreciation of literary values and to a keener understanding of subject matter. For those pupils who cannot respond to such natural evolution, some remedial work must be provided with subject matter mature enough to hold attention.

Not even a cursory survey of reading materials for secondary schools would be complete without at least a brief reference to the implications of the increasingly popular integration program. Such programs tend to minimize the function of textbooks as such; in fact, textbooks are seldom present in class quantities, though several small sets of books may be used by the pupils in their semi-independent search for materials concerning the problem in hand. Reference books, however, become increasingly essential as the curriculum becomes more informal. An effectively administered integration program at the secondary-school level requires a reference library, large, varied, wisely chosen, and, incidentally, expensive. Schools not prepared to undertake the labor and expense of acquiring such a library would do well to adhere to more traditional methods of instruction.

The pupil who is required in a fusion unit of English and social studies, for example, to acquire extensive knowledge on a specialized problem must piece together bits of information from several reference books. Rarely will he find in scattered sources materials that are adapted in gradation to the limitations of his reading ability. If, therefore, the great bulk of his work is of this sort, the slow reader is likely to suffer a serious handicap. Unless all such pupils are conscientiously coached with the use of remedial devices, their school work may be seriously impaired. Because of the difficulty encountered by slow readers in the use of the school library, some teachers, notably of the social studies but also of the natural sciences, tend to replace book materials with lantern slides, motion pictures, and artificially simplified extemporized readings of the tabloid type. Their pupils may gain some understanding of the subject, but they will certainly lack opportunity to become thoroughly literate. Thus subject matter, in complete defiance of the progressive philosophy, is sometimes permitted to overshadow one of the most important aspects of pupil growth. The abundant use of visual devices to support and supplement a rich and varied reading program is, of course, highly valuable. Likewise, a fusion or integration program that encourages student initiative and substitutes understanding and appreciation for mere memory may prove of solid worth. When, however, sound methods become perverted and educational responsibility is shirked through encouraging pupils to become non-readers, the result is not progress but reaction.

5. Reading Materials for the Junior College

As viewed by an English teacher, the junior-college reading problem is an extension of the twelfth-grade problem. Certainly, with the task of providing technical and cultural courses, it is very late to teach the mechanics of reading. A few colleges, however, recognizing that deficiencies in reading are the most frequent accompaniments of low scholarship, are providing remedial work in reading with surprisingly favorable results. Précis work has become a much-used device in many junior colleges. The lists of reading, both in the English course and in other academic fields, cover all subjects and cater to all interests. Biographies, books of travel, fiction of all types, scientific works, and many books dealing with the social sciences are the materials from which most college students must secure wider reading skills and closer correlation of academic work with the realities of life.

It should be borne in mind, however, that a reading program as discussed in this Yearbook is understood to comprise all reading materials, wherever and however used and for whatever purposes, and that the English course is only one of many. Aside from a growing number of so-called ' orientation courses ' within restricted, or at any rate related, subject-matter fields, junior colleges have as yet experimented little with the informal types of curriculum that are now engaging the attention of educators in lower levels of instruction. This means that in junior colleges textbooks are required for use in connection with most academic courses. A word, therefore, with reference to the character of books used in junior college may here be appropriate.

Educators who are deeply interested in the junior-college movement often assume that there is a qualitative difference between junior-college texts and textbooks for secondary schools on the one hand and for senior colleges or universities on the other. This assumption is correct only with very definite limitations. Junior colleges are of two kinds: one preparatory to upper-class work of full collegiate or university grade, the other an extension of the secondary school for such students as will not continue their academic work beyond the fourteenth year. Colleges of the latter kind are introducing an increasing number of so-called ' terminal ' courses, thus differentiating their work qualitatively from that of the first type of institution at the same academic level. Junior-college textbooks for terminal courses may be somewhat briefer and less formally organized than college textbooks of the traditional type, and to this extent constitute a new type of text intermediate in character between secondary-school and college texts. The number of terminal courses, however, is limited. Far more numerous are the so-called ' regular ' courses, which differ little, if at all, from those given in the four-year colleges and universities. The notion that a somewhat simpler and shorter textbook will be appropriate for use in such junior-college courses is quite erroneous.

II. The Relation of Reading Materials to the Maturity and Ability of Readers

It is obvious that books must be suitable for the readers who are expected to use them. Children's books should correspond in difficulty to the level of growth of boys and girls. It is equally important that books intended for adults of limited reading ability should be readable by such adults. These two requirements are by no means the same. Children's books, though obviously written with sufficient simplicity for adults who are poor readers, are unacceptable in content either for adolescents or for adults. The problem of dealing in simple language with themes, interesting and pertinent, for relatively mature human beings is being attacked by the American Library Association, by the

American Association for Adult Education, and by many other groups of educators.

1. Books for Beginners

The making of books for the use of young children has perhaps never engaged serious attention of more people than it does today. Thought bestowed on this subject has led to a refinement that sharply distinguishes the children's books of today from those of yesterday. The idea is no longer accepted that a poem or story *about* a child is necessarily a poem or story for children. The investigations of Dunn long ago revealed the fact that reading materials judged by adults to be of high interest for children were often regarded by the children themselves either with indifference or with positive distaste.[1]

a. *The Problem of Vocabulary.* The difficulty that beginners have in learning to read is largely a matter of acquiring a reading vocabulary. This is not to say that the thought and even elements of style other than words may be disregarded. It simply means that the one primary essential in learning to read is to associate meanings and pronunciations with written or printed symbols.

Accordingly, the vocabulary of books for primary grades is exceedingly important, and this importance is today steadily and intelligently recognized. Increasing attention is being given to the number of different words employed in writing beginners' books, to the distribution of the words throughout the text, and to the repetition of the words in order that they may be learned.

A modern preprimer contains about one thousand running words and about sixty different words. The different words are introduced very gradually — not more than a small number per page. The new words also recur again and again in order to give children familiarity with them in different settings. Primers that build upon preprimers may have one hundred fifty to two hundred additional new words in a setting of five or six thousand running words. Similar standards as to rate of introduction and amount of repetition are maintained as in the case of the preprimer.

The first reader, the second reader, and even the third reader, carry out in principle the procedure with respect to vocabulary just indicated as prevalent in the preprimer and the primer. In each case a restricted

---

[1] Fannie W. Dunn. *Interest Factors in Primary Reading Material.* Contributions to Education, No. 113. (Teachers College, Columbia University: New York, 1921)

number of words constitutes a controlled advance upon the vocabularies of the previous books, and the new words are handled as to initial appearance and subsequent occurrence in much the same way as before.

The days are gone when textbooks in reading are permitted to contain a large number of words that occur but once. Moreover, there is in the better class of primary books an integration with respect to vocabulary from book to book. The carry-over from primer to first reader and from first reader to second is complete, or nearly so. Furthermore, the words introduced into a given book are often consciously preparatory to the use of the same words in a subsequent book or books.

b. The Doctrine of Frequency. This introduces a new slant that has been given to some of our ideas about vocabulary. The tendency in America has been to rely almost exclusively upon the doctrine of frequency of occurrence as establishing the importance of words. Furthermore, it has been too often assumed that the more times the word occurred, the more useful it was, and, indeed, the more likely it was to be known to young children. But the correlation between frequency of use and gradation, though marked, has many exceptions, some of which have produced ludicrous results when their exceptional character has been overlooked.

c. The Doctrine of Power. An important supplement to the doctrine of frequency of use is the doctrine of power. Words should be selected for use in primary-grade reading materials, not only because they are common, but also because of their expressive power. The first-grade words, selected on the power basis, permit stories to be told that have meaning and movement, plot, and suspense. They are useful words. They play into the books for the second grade, just as the vocabulary of that grade, if chosen for its power, makes better books possible in the third grade.

How far a recognition of the doctrine of power may be carried is already illustrated in " Basic English." [1] Here is a vocabulary of eight hundred fifty words that is said to have the ' power ' of twenty thousand words. This vocabulary, however, is not a vocabulary for the primary grades. It simply serves as an illustration of what can be done in vocabulary selection when principles other than frequency of use are employed.

d. Sentence Structure. The making of suitable books for beginners implies more than a well-selected and a well-controlled vocabulary.

---

[1] C. K. Ogden. *The System of Basic English.* (Harcourt, Brace and Company: New York, 1934)

Sentence structure — to continue on the level of form alone — must be appropriate. Sentences without inversions are desirable. In books for the beginners, phrases should not be broken. Relational words should be used sparingly, as, indeed, they are likely to be if sentences are kept short. An occasional complex sentence or prepositional phrase, however, is not necessarily a blight on the style appropriate for even the earliest reading materials, as some persons seem to think. In general, remembering that the child is learning to recognize words visually presented, we should avoid in the earliest reading materials the rapid introduction of words of confusing resemblance.

2. Books for the Middle Grades

a. Content. In these grades it is proper to insist upon the primary importance of the thought content of reading materials as determining their difficulty. If the vocabulary of the first three grades has been well chosen, and if the child has acquired ability to identify new words by analysis or by other means of word perception, or by intelligent inference from context, then he is able to go forward on a new level. The vocabulary should continue to be basically within his grasp, which means that most of the words should be known to him as auditory symbols. But it is no longer necessary that all the words should be of this character. This is the period in which the pupil is expected rapidly to acquire new meanings. He takes on new subjects in his curriculum. It is to be noted that he is expected to learn from print some words that he never heard before. He is expected to give new meanings to some of his old words.

b. Ranges of Reading Interest and Competence. Two kinds of differences of pupil ability and advancement are found in these and in all later grades: differences among pupils of different school grades and differences among pupils of the same school grade. Consequently, some pupils read widely, while others read but little. A brief analysis of these differences will show their bearing upon materials of reading. Provision is made in all schools for a graduated series of reading selections as pupils proceed from grade to grade. But provision is lacking generally for the numerous pupils who, though in different school grades, have similar abilities and interests in reading. Just as adults, some who are extensively trained and others who are not, read the same popular novel, so pupils of Grade IV are interested in and able to read certain materials intended for Grade VIII. The farther a pupil advances in school, the greater his range in ability and interest in materials that lie outside his grade status. This range of ability and interest reaches downward as well as upward. By the time pupils reach Grade VII, some will read a full-length novel written for adults and follow this novel by Andersen's tales for their next reading. A balanced reading program for such pupils must extend, therefore, far beyond the limits generally indicated in classified lists of books.

Within a given grade, many other pupils lack the ability and interest needed even for books of their own grade. Such pupils often respond better to materials intended for grades below their own than they do to the books usually recommended for their grade. In extreme cases, pupils of Grade V and upward can read intelligently only the materials intended for two or more grades below their own. It follows that reading materials for any grade should include materials that are appropriate for three types of pupils: for pupils whose abilities and interests run both above and below their grade, for pupils whose effective reading is only below grade, and for pupils who merely conform with their own grade expectancy. Only by such a diversity of materials can the continuous development of all pupils take place.

Accordingly, the problem of writing suitable books for middle-grade children is one in which increasing attention must be given to the wide spread of pupils' maturity and ability as well as to the concepts with which the books deal. These concepts, especially the new concepts, must not be too pretentious, nor can they be introduced too rapidly. Generalizations should be built up; interesting detail should be provided. The fourth- or fifth-grade history, for example, cannot be a mere abridgment of the history for the seventh and eighth grades. It must have different *genre*.

c. The Problem of Vocabulary. At the same time, the problem of vocabulary is still to be kept in mind, even though it assumes a character in the middle grades somewhat different from its character in the primary grades. Perhaps the time may come when, at least in the basal reading books of these grades, a vocabulary control like that which is now gained in primary grades will be developed.

Then there is the question, applicable not only in these grades but also in earlier and later grades, of *vocabulary integration*. One of the surest ways by which the technical vocabulary of a given subject can be controlled and brought clearly to the reader's attention is to make sure that the words used in the books on that subject do not get out of hand. If vocabularies are selected for power, this can take place. The words that children learn will be usable in many different connections. Thus the books in science, geography, history, reading, and health will support one another.

Suitable books for the middle grades should continue to be simple in all the ways proper to the themes under discussion. In general, words that are known to be in the vocabulary of the children of the grades in question should be used. At present, there is great difficulty in determining what these words are, because the basis for selecting vocabularies has been something different from the grade knowledge of children. Another difficulty appears in the gradation of vocabulary. Our vocabulary specialists have been singularly forgetful of the fact that, truly considered, a word is not a form but a meaning. Whether or not the word *blaze* may be used in a fourth-grade book depends on the meaning you attach to it. If the blaze of a fire is meant, you are safe. If the blaze on a tree made with a hatchet to indicate the trail is meant, you will either have to teach the word or use a substitute. A simple word like ' get ' may have a dozen or more meanings, not just one.

3. Books for Secondary Schools

As we pass into the junior and the senior high schools, the relative importance of vocabulary continues to fall as the importance of conceptual matters continues to rise. Neither can be absent from consideration at any time, but the appropriateness of books for secondary schools will be judged mainly from the ideas that the books seek to convey.

For this reason a word of caution may rightly be spoken in regard to the various formulas that have been devised for appraising the difficulty of reading materials — the Johnson, the Lewerenz, the Vogel-Washburne, and the Gray-Leary. It must be understood that they are concerned entirely with matters of form. They do not consider the nature or difficulty of the concepts involved. It is proper to say that their authors do not pretend to do this, but it is equally proper to say that users of these formulas have forgotten the limitations of which the authors are well aware.

Distinctions among these various formulas would be invidious, but one cannot avoid the belief that some of them have been developed on insufficient, not to say trivial, bases. Moreover, even the best formula seems to be subject to a regrettable degree of unreliability. One needs but apply the formula several times to the same books to realize this fact.

In closing this section, reference may properly be made to the rather widespread movement of offering easy reading materials for upper-grade and high-school pupils, both in and out of school. The effort to treat topics of interest to boys and girls in their teens in language that children of nine or ten could understand is a praiseworthy endeavor. Even if the objective is not attained, the author may find that he has written an excellent book for normal and even superior children in their teens. Everybody likes to read an easy book, especially if it deals with topics that are not trivial.

Yet, the simplifying of a children's classic merely with reference to vocabulary and length of sentences is a procedure that many competent people refuse to approve. There is a sentimental indignation on the part of the *literati* that probably need not be taken too seriously. To simplify the diction of a work of literature to a degree that permits it to be enjoyed by children of a degree of maturity — or rather immaturity — proper to appreciate its content seems eminently worth while. The real question is not the desecration of a classic. It is the growth of the children.

A classic that will almost certainly be 'reached' by normal children in time to be appreciated probably ought not to be simplified, although it appears to be true that the reading of a simplified version often stimulates good pupils to reread the classic forthwith in its original version. But if a classic that has content value for children is couched in language that few children of the age to appreciate the story can understand, then it ought to be simplified. Perhaps it was mistakenly written in the first place. A number of such books have survived in their original form largely because of an adult belief that they were children's books. Not long ago an eminent schoolman confessed that he disliked *Alice in Wonderland* when he was a boy. He went on to say that most people of his acquaintance also disliked it when they were children. He expressed the belief that the book was not a child's book, for its qualities were such as to make it inappropriate for coevals with Alice. Yet he pointed out that the book continues to be purchased in large quantities by aunts and uncles, grandfathers and grandmothers, for the children of the family. Whether or not *Alice in Wonderland* is the sort of book this critic described it to be, some children's classics probably should be either abandoned or simplified, and other classics should be left alone.

Finally, we hazard the opinion that a book for normal children of a given grade, say the seventh or eighth, is unsuitable for slow children of a grade three or four years later. To be specific, we have in mind a

United States history for the seventh and eighth grades that has proved
to be suitable for its grades by large sales over a long period of years.
This book, however, when used for the teaching of United States history
to slow pupils in the senior high school, was not satisfactory. It was
too difficult! Not too hard in language — here we have evidently
passed beyond the question of vocabulary — but too hard conceptually.
The things that a normal child of the seventh and eighth grades can do
are beyond the capacity of a dull child of almost any age or grade. The
making of books for slow children in the secondary school is, therefore,
a task, to be done *ad hoc*. Such books cannot be transferred from lower
grades, either because they will then deal with topics that are too
juvenile or because they will actually be too difficult in point of
themes, generalizations, and concepts. The making of suitable books
for these children and for the remedial treatment in reading they so
greatly need is a problem by itself. This problem must be solved, not
merely by making language easier, but by a less-demanding conceptual
treatment and by a selection of topics that are socially important to
this class of children.

III. Mechanical Features

Purchasing departments have a growing tendency to specify the
standards they will accept for schoolbooks. For example, some state
boards of education issue to educational publishers detailed specifica-
tions for the textbooks they will consider for adoption. Such minimal
standards for the physical make-up of books provide in considerable
detail for items like paper, printing, sewing, forwarding, and covers.
Mechanical features of this kind are not within the scope of the sub-
committee treatment, but certain other mechanical aspects of textbooks are of decided concern. One of these is the typography of the
book. A definition of reading — though an inadequate one unless a
great deal is read into it — is the getting of meaning from the printed
page. Plainly, this definition regards typography, which is sharply
conditioned by the character of the printed page, as a central fact in
reading.

In connection with the type page, there are three important elements — *the type, the line,* and *the space between lines.*

1. Design of Type

Although the design of a type page is individual with every book,
and while its various aspects must be appraised as a whole, the con-

sideration of type alone is entirely possible, although somewhat artificial.

There are many designs of type, known as series or families, each
having certain characteristics of form. Each also has individuality as
to width of stroke, relation of heavy to light strokes, expansion, and
certain other matters. The larger series of type have sub-series that
differ from one another mainly in width of stroke and expansion. It is
possible to have nine varieties of a given series — average, medium,
and narrow expansion, each with heavy, medium, and light stroke.

All these matters have much to do with the legibility and pleasing
appearance of a page. Educators are prone to regard the *size* of type
as the only important matter in this connection, whereas nothing could
be farther from the truth. Clear legibility requires that type be firm
and clear — that there be plenty of white within the outlines of the
letters and between the letters — in short, *clear* type is needed more
than *big* type.

In an unpublished thesis by Marion Wiles a report is rendered in
which the speed of reading of two different 12-point types was compared. One of these types was bold in stroke and of wide expansion
(Century Schoolbook). The other was rather conservative in these
particulars (Monotype No. 8). The result showed a considerable
superiority for the Century Schoolbook type in point of ease of reading
— so far, of course, as speed of reading indicates ease of reading.

2. Size of Type

For many years printers have used the point system for designating
different sizes of type, a point being 1/72 of an inch. In any given
series, the largest type is likely to be 18-point or even larger and the
smallest perhaps 4-point.

But the designation of type in points is really not a good measure
of size. Type is cast on bits of metal, large type on large bits and small
type on small bits. It is these bits of metal, called slugs, to which the
number of points refers and not to the type that is cast upon them;
that is, 12-point type is cast on a 12-point slug. But there is always
some space left both at the top and at the bottom of the letters, and
that space differs decidedly as between series of type. We present here
two 12-point n's, one in the series called **Bodoni** and the other in
Century Schoolbook. The difference in the height of these two *n*'s
is striking. Yet they are both 12-point *n*'s! The fact is that points

to designate sizes of type are unreliable unless the series of type is specified.

A great many so-called ' standards ' have been offered as to the best sizes of type for pupils of different ages. The most prevalent standards are those which Shaw first gave in 1902. Where he got them he did not say, and diligent search has failed to disclose. His standards, how- ever, have been so often repeated that they have almost acquired the force of truth. They demand very large type for first-grade children and diminishing sizes thereafter.

The standards of the British Association for the Advancement of Science (1913), although they differ somewhat from Shaw's standards, agree with his in demanding an almost perfect inverse relationship be- tween size of child and size of type — big type for little children, middle-sized type for middle-sized children, and small type for big children and grown-ups. The British Association, like Shaw, had no experimental data to support its figures. In fact, it admits this in its report.

It would be strange — indeed, contrary to experience — if the rela- tion of type to physical maturity were such as these standards imply. The physical mechanism involved in reading is that of the eye. In- stead, therefore, of trying to relate the size of type to size or age of the child, it seems more reasonable to relate it to the maturation of the eye. Ophthalmologists are agreed that the eye reaches its physical maturity earlier than almost any other organism in the human body. They are not agreed as to the life age at which the full maturity of the eye takes place, but it is a fair interpretation of their opinion to say that full, or nearly full, maturity is reached by the time the child is eight or nine years of age or earlier. Translated into grades, this would mean about the third grade. It is probable, therefore, that, merely from the point of view of the physical receptor in reading, no change in the type page is required due to maturation after the age of eight or nine. In other words, it is probable that a third-grade child can ' see ' as well as an adult.

Before we go farther in this discussion, we need to make clear that if type is large, the space between lines, or ' leading,' must likewise be large. The two go together. The effort that some publishers have made to present large type with deficient leading has met with deserved failure. Large type implies much leading and consequently a page of relatively few running words. Clearly the educator cannot select books with little reading matter per page without accepting disadvantages inextricably involved in the choice.

One of these disadvantages is cost. A given amount of matter set in large type costs more than the same amount of matter set in smaller type. For example, a twenty-thousand-word reader may occupy eighty pages of 12-point type in moderately long lines well-leaded. Such a book would occupy more than twice as many pages if set in 18-point type of the same series with the same length of line and degree of leading. Three factors enter into the cost of manufacturing a book; paper, presswork, and binding. In the example just given, the cost of paper and of presswork would be doubled for the book set in 18-point type. Owing to the differential in cost, a choice between 12-point and 18-point type is not a free choice.

But another and even more serious disadvantage is involved if the penchant for artistically large type is allowed to have its untrammeled way. This disadvantage affects the reading program itself. Nothing is clearer than that the modern school and modern life are based upon an enormous amount of reading. Brief allusion was made on earlier pages in this chapter to the surprisingly broad reading program of the primary and middle grades. A language book, let us say, cannot be chosen because of its large type without at the same time choosing a meager program. In the case of an arithmetic, one cannot indulge his liking for tall and wide type and much white space on the page without at the same time defeating any purpose he may have of enrichment. A teacher cannot yield to his preference for a first reader of wide margins, broken lines, 18-point type, and many pictures without denying to the pupils half the reading experience that they might receive from a book of less pretentious appearance.

The widespread belief that young children need very large type is founded upon the idea that relatively small type is harder for little children to read and less attractive. The conviction is also entertained that relatively small types violate the principles of eye-hygiene.

As to the question of the relation of size of type to difficulty, we have evidence to show that current beliefs are ill-founded. An experiment on this matter was conducted under the joint auspices of four large publishing houses. The general conclusion derivable from these investigations is that young children read fairly small type more easily than they do large type. This was found to be true both for first-grade children and for second-grade children. The small type used in both grades was 12-point, and the large type was 24-point in the first grade and 18-point in the second grade. Other intermediate sizes of type were likewise employed — 14-point and 18-point in Grade I and 14-point in Grade II.

The full nature of the evidence from this coöperative study can be secured by consulting the reports themselves.[1] It is hard to maintain in the face of this evidence, as well as other reputable evidence, that, within any limits likely to be applied, young children find greater difficulty in reading small type than large type. Furthermore, a point could be made that *a priori* there would seem likely to be some advantage if children learned word forms in type that did not differ greatly in appearance from the type they would be employing a few months later in most of their reading.

On the score of attractiveness to children, there is no direct evidence bearing on our question. Let us grant that pupils, like their teachers, prefer large type. But is this preference so strong — or rather, is the emotional repulsion in the presence of small type so great — that we are obliged to forego in deference to it a richer reading program, an ease of reading at least as great, and lower cost?

Is it not enormously more important that the child should be interested in his reading as such than it is that he should be interested in its outer garb? There was abundant evidence in the joint experiment referred to above — an experiment using unillustrated stories set in all sorts of ways — that the children found their interest imaginatively and intellectually in the content of the material. The Sub-committee is prepared to say that the amount and quality of the reading matter greatly exceed in importance any differences in the type page that are likely to be encountered in schoolbooks.

But what about hygiene? What about eyestrain and fatigue? Again, as in the case of the emotional response of the child, no direct evidence is available. The assumption that a child in the primary grades will grow tired in reading 12-point sooner than he will in reading 18-point type is purely gratuitous. One may argue with plausibility that the same factors, whatever they are, that make the reading of 12-point type easier than the reading of 18-point type, will also work in favor of 12-point on the basis of strain or fatigue. In other words, it seems reasonable that the type that may be read more fluently will also be less tiring. If the same subject matter is read in 12-point and in 18-point type, the 18-point type necessitates far more eye-

---

[1] See *Thirtieth Yearbook*, Part II, of this Society, 93–125; also "Type sizes of first-grade textbooks," *The Nation's Schools*, 12:1934, 45–48.

movements, and it becomes necessary to pick up the beginnings of far more lines than with 12-point. The unproved presumption is that 12-point is easier on both counts. In this connection, it may also be worth while to restate the fact that the eye reaches its maturity long before the other organs and the body in general have done so.

Within limits — and this phrase is exceedingly important, though we do not as yet know just what the limits are — it is plausible and scientifically justifiable to argue for a conservative size of type in comparison with the sizes that attract those who judge books superficially.

3. Length of Line and Leading

Type size is given a prominent place in this discussion, because (in the popular mind) it stands as a symbol for the entire type page. People say of a book, " It is printed in large type," when in reality the impression made by the page may be created quite as much by the length of line and the white space between lines as by the tallness of the type.

As a matter of fact, length of line and interlinear space are indissolubly connected with type size. A lone line in small type is intolerable in comparison with the same line in large type. Effects upon the eye of the untechnical reader may be the same whether a point is added to the size of type or to the interlinear space.

The evidence is rather clear that short lines of printing are desirable. It is generally stated in the literature that a line should not exceed four inches. As with most general statements, there are many exceptions (for example, the distance the line is supposed to lie from the eye or the number of lines), but a four-inch line is not an unreasonable maximum unless special conditions prevail.

The truth of the statement that a four-inch line is a desirable maximum rests not so much upon the difficulty of reading a long line as upon the difficulty of locating instantly the left-hand end of the next line. Moreover, this difficulty is great only when there is a succession of long lines — a long paragraph or a page of such lines. People do not object to a six-inch line as a legend under a picture or as a direction to the pupils extending across the page of a workbook. It is doubtful if an objection to two or three successive lines of five, or even six, inches is valid. Moreover, length of line, as has been said repeatedly, is bound up both with size of type and with leading. A long line is much more tolerable when there is plenty of space between lines and somewhat more tolerable when type is large.

We may say, then, that the superiority of relatively small type, as found in the joint investigation, was most apparent when that small type was set on a short line with a generous space between lines. The line with the best showing was about two and one-half inches long. This specimen was a page set in 12-point type with four points of leading. A line one inch longer also gave a very good account of itself when presented with 12-point type and good leading. Light on the optimal length of line had previously been shed by a study of Gates,[1] which tended to show that a reader's pleasure or displeasure as to length of line results from habituation; readers prefer a length of line to which they are accustomed.

There is an indication in this that the short line set in double column on large pages may have even greater usefulness than we have hitherto attached to it. Such pages would permit the offering of extensive reading matter at a low cost. The theoretical objection that children, particularly young children, will read across the division of the page is without evidence.

4. Differentiation in Type

In connection with the efforts that both educators and publishers are making to increase the readability of books, certain other aspects of the type page are worthy of mention. Much effort is being expended to make textbooks look less ' textbookish.' So far as this means the deterioration of the really superior type page found in many textbooks to the level of the page of the popular novel, this effort may be misdirected. To the extent that restraint is exercised in the elaboration of headings, italics, and boldface, these efforts are in the right direction. There is ground for belief that some textbooks are overorganized. Very likely one cannot have an arithmetic or a language book without a variety of type, centered and side headings, change of interlinear space, and the like. But as textbooks approach the kind of book that is to be read straight along, these outward evidences of the pedagogy of the book should be dropped. They persist as a reminder of the days when the textbook was to be memorized and reproduced. They were intended to assist that process. Today, when emphasis is placed upon meanings and background, upon attitudes and emotional responses, such trappings are not only outmoded; they are a positive obstruction.

[1] Arthur I. Gates. "What do we know about optimum lengths of lines in reading?" *Journal of Educational Research*, 23:1931, 1-7.

IV. ILLUSTRATIONS AND OTHER VISUAL AIDS

Despite the mechanical attractiveness of certain recently published European schoolbooks that have been widely displayed in this country as examples of modern bookmaking, there is no reason to question the validity of the oft-repeated statement that, as composites of educational and mechanical values, American schoolbooks lead the world. They were elaborately illustrated long before the bookmakers of other countries gave serious attention to the problems of textbook illustration. Children in the primary grades of American schools have for many years been given reading textbooks more and more lavishly illustrated both in colors and in black and white, while children in other English-speaking countries have for the most part been required to achieve comparable results with a few illustrations in black and white or with no illustrations at all.

The child's first schoolbooks are likely to be the most copiously illustrated books that he will use in his entire school course. Studies of the effect upon reading mastery of various degrees of lavishness in illustration have not yet been made.[1] Results secured in Canadian and English schools with the most drab reading materials offer *prima facie* evidence that the pictorial equipment in American readers is determined more by the competition of publishers than by known educational requirements. However that may be, no American publisher would dare to produce a new basal series of primary readers lacking such equipment. Accordingly, the primary reader of today has a picture, more often than not in three or four colors, on nearly every page. Artists and engravers vie with one another in the production of beautiful results. Colorful books appeal to many teachers, as to children. The question arises whether a colored illustration so striking as to dominate a page may stimulate interest in itself to the extent of distracting interest from the text. Whatever may be the educational value of elaborate illustrations, expert teachers are demanding that illustrations in primary books be not only beautiful, but simple and appropriate as well.

The futility of inserting pictures at regular intervals, regardless of function or need, has long been recognized. Each illustration should have a *raison d'être* other than mere page requirements — a focal cen-

---

[1] See on this point and on certain other problems mentioned in this chapter, Guy M. Whipple. " Needed investigations in the field of the textbook." *Elementary School Journal*, 35:April, 1935, 575–582.

ter of interest directly related to the accompanying text. Irrelevant items are taboo. Pictures accompanying a story should conform accurately with the imagery ideally aroused by the text in young minds. In the case of primary readers of the work type, as in the social sciences, factual accuracy is demanded in the smallest details.

In readers for the middle grades the use of color is less lavish. It is assumed that, as children mature, color appeal is less necessary. Pictures in two or more colors have in recent years been used more commonly than heretofore in basal readers for the middle grades, but color in middle-grade textbooks in the content subjects is commonly confined to a frontispiece and a few colored inserts. Competition has not forced its more general use; competitive prices will not permit it; and, in any event, color might not greatly aid instruction.

We have seen that books in several of the content subjects are usually placed in the hands of the middle-grade child. These books vary in the extent to which their visual apparatus has been improved. Thus arithmetics are likely to be more perfunctorily illustrated than readers are, probably because, in the singling out of numerical or quantitative aspects of a picture for special attention, realism and attractiveness become subordinated or forgotten. There has been marked improvement in the illustration of school histories. Formerly, they were loaded with small, drab portraits of historical characters of no possible interest to the child; with reproductions of old prints *ad nauseam* because of their ready accessibility; and with maps so complex as to be of little value in the intelligent reading of the text. Today, a middle-grade history often rivals the reader in attractiveness. Imaginative drawings have nearly replaced perfunctory photographs, and simple maps, often of the animated type, are found where most needed. Noteworthy improvement has been made in the illustration of geographies: contrast the books of fifteen or twenty years ago, with their badly engraved photographs of almost any conceivable scene or building, relevant or not to the region under discussion, with modern geographies whose carefully selected photographs for directed picture study aid in the mastery of geographical principles. In other social-science books of today for the middle grades and above, graphs and cartoons, to say nothing of ingenious mergers of the two, are likely to be abundant.

Reference has already been made to a wide endeavor in the designing of present-day schoolbooks to avoid a so-called 'textbookish' appearance. Most teachers favor the modernistic application of the bookmaker's art. Greater liberties, of course, can be taken with supplementary books than with basal books, and with those that can be read quickly and laid aside than with those that must be used day after day. Excessively long printed lines, for example, reminiscent of the oversize preschool picture book, would not be appropriate in books requiring long and serious reading, though they do not disqualify juveniles from the primary-grade browsing table. Yet, a bright pictorial cover design extending over both the front and the back cover, ' bled ' pictures (*i.e.*, pictures extending into the margins), and decorated end papers or modernistic two-tone cloth are never inappropriate.

Deserving of passing mention in this connection, is the interest of certain teachers in books written and illustrated wholly or in part by their own pupils. The coöperative production of such books is an excellent academic exercise for all participating and perhaps, if the products are made generally available, of value to other teachers as an educational exhibit. But an effort to place books so written and so illustrated in the hands of children in other classrooms represents a naïve confusion of means with ends. There is no more experimental evidence to show that children are interested in pictures drawn by other children than there is to show that they are attracted to the symbolical drawings sometimes introduced into juveniles to catch the eye of sophisticated adults.

The pictorial equipment of schoolbooks, beginning with the seventh year, becomes relatively less important, until by the eleventh or twelfth year the pupil has read a good many books having few or no illustrations. The tendency is to limit the number of illustrations in such books as those of fiction in the literature course, in which the reader's own imagination may to advantage be allowed free rein. It is doubtful whether the allegorical poster-like drawings, photographs of murals, and the like, now so common in secondary-school books, relatively incapable of intimate illustration, serve a useful purpose. High-school textbooks in science are illustrated more abundantly today than ever before, obviously for the reason that illustrations in such books can be made really to function in the acquisition of important concepts.

V. The Relation of Reading Materials and Equipment to School Administration

Preceding pages have been concerned with reading materials, chiefly without reference to the relation of such materials to the schools in which the materials are to be used. This section calls attention to the intimate and necessary relationship that exists between reading materials and the administration of the schools.

Special consideration is given here to five administrative problems of reading materials and equipment: (1) the location of the school, (2) the teaching staff, (3) the promotion system, (4) the amount and quality of materials and equipment that can be made available, and (5) the practicality of providing essential reading materials and equipment in schools. Obviously, the support of education affects all these points.

1. The Location of the School

The amount and quality of reading materials and equipment needed depend on the location of the school with reference to facilities that are provided by agencies other than the school itself. Where circulating libraries are available, with special arrangements for school service, many books that schools would otherwise need to buy can be had for little or no cost. Similar additions can sometimes be made through other channels. City or community libraries and library policies may enable schools to augment their supply of books. Local interest in education and home conditions, especially with reference to libraries, influence the number of books that schools must provide to make their reading materials adequate. Administrators should be aware, however, that pupils are likely to have increased interests in reading as a consequence of excellent conditions outside the schools, and that, in communities where homes are the best equipped, the school's budget for books may need to be greater than in schools where general conditions are adverse to the promotion of a reading program.

2. The Teaching Staff

Teachers are the immediate administrators of schoolbooks. They are also curriculum-makers in fact whether or not they are in name. Consequently, a well-selected staff increases pupils' interests in reading and leads to stronger demands for adequate materials than would be true with an ineffective staff. The demand by teachers will be increased also by any campaigns that may have been conducted for the betterment of reading.[1] Teachers' attitudes and relationships with pupils

---

[1] Cf. William S. Gray. *Improving Instruction in Reading.* (University of Chicago: Chicago, 1933) Chapter III is a detailed account of a procedure used in an initial survey of teachers and teaching.

also affect their ability to stimulate pupils in the direction of reading: [1] the better the teaching staff, the greater the need for reading materials to satisfy the broader interests developed. From another point of view, the poorer the teaching staff, the greater the need for informing, inspiring reading materials.

3. The Promotion System

Some schools now promote pupils on the basis of achievement, while others promote them on the basis of chronological age. In either case, differentiation in reading materials is necessary. In schools that promote pupils on the basis of chronological age, greater differentiation of equipment is needed than in other schools, because, by the time pupils reach Grade V, some are able to read only as well as other more strictly classified pupils do in Grade II; the better members of a class sometimes exceed the norm for the grade in which they are classified. Mere maturity does not insure reading skill. Maturity does produce greater reading readiness, especially if suitable prereading activities are conducted. The type of promotion system affects, therefore, the range of difficulty of materials needed by the pupils of a given grade.

4. Amount and Quality of Materials and Equipment Available

The amount and quality of materials and equipment needed to enrich school subjects is only partly a problem of school support, for these materials, to be effective, must be selected with expert discrimination. To insure such discrimination, textbook committees must have both time and training for their work. This point is elaborated in the next section of this chapter. The careful planning and equipping of buildings and reading rooms is also necessary if the program is to function (see Chapter VIII). Book and periodical selection and classification and the quality of editions of standard books are further issues in this problem.

5. Practicality of the Provision of Essential Reading Materials and Equipment in Schools

The value of reading materials and equipment depends on the actual use that will be made when the best available books are accessible to pupils. The comparative economy of the printed page is recognized. In no other way can materials be presented as cheaply and effectively

---

[1] Cf. E. K. Wickman. *Children's Behavior and Teachers' Attitudes.* (The Commonwealth Foundation, Division of Publication: New York, 1929)

to pupils. Besides, the well-read pupil has increased skill for all other school work, increased information and experience, and increased interest in further reading. These points, together with the relative permanence of reading materials and equipment, lead to the conviction that money spent for books is money well expended.

VI. PROCEDURES NECESSARY FOR THE SELECTION AND PURCHASE OF ADEQUATE READING MATERIALS

1. Principles Governing the Selection of Books

Reference has been made to the broad use of the term 'reading' in this Yearbook. This use gives the term an inclusiveness far in excess of the ground covered in the Society's Yearbook on " The Textbook " (*Thirtieth Yearbook*, Part II). Accordingly, in our consideration of methods and standards of textbook selection, it is both convenient and necessary to presuppose the reader's familiarity with the portions of the *Thirtieth Yearbook* relating to this subject, notably Chapters VII, VIII, XIV, XV, and XVII. The six years that have elapsed since the appearance of those chapters have, with a few marked exceptions, witnessed little improvement in the means employed or the results secured in textbook selection. However, gratifying evidence exists of a growing sense of responsibility for sound book selection. Possibly this attitude is a welcome by-product of the older Yearbook. With this awareness of the problem goes a praiseworthy disposition to solve it scientifically, and various studies have been made of what constitutes scientific procedure in book selection.[1] Less gratifying, but probably inevitable, is the failure in some cases to apply a liberal amount of commonsense in the use and interpretation of the scientific procedures.

At this point two outstanding studies of textbook selection that have appeared since the *Thirtieth Yearbook* may be appropriately summarized.

A survey of the procedures and criteria used in selecting reading materials for pupils in 135 cities shows that various practices are now employed.[2]

The difficulties summarized in Table I point to the need for thorough training of committees in the selection of books. Such training would reduce the dissatisfaction that comes from most of the items men-

---

[1] Willis L. Uhl. *The Materials of Reading.* (Silver, Burdett and Company: Newark, 1924) Especially Chapters XIII–XIV.

[2] Gertrude Whipple. " Procedures used in selecting schoolbooks." *Elementary School Journal*, 36:1936, 665–673, 760–775; and 37:47–57.

TABLE I. — CAUSES OF DIFFICULTY ENCOUNTERED IN BOOK SELECTION
AND FREQUENCY OF MENTION OF EACH (After Whipple) [1]

Cause	Frequency of Mention	Percentage of Total Frequency of Mention
Lack of adequate methods of selecting books	33	27.2
Incompetency of staff members who select or use the books	26	21.5
Lack of certain types of books	22	18.2
Lack of funds	12	9.9
Unfair practices of publishers' representatives	8	6.6
Lack of valid standards of evaluation	6	5.0
Limited time	6	5.0
Ill effects of certain state requirements	4	3.3
Dissatisfaction with previous selections	4	3.3
Total	121	100.0

tioned. The training would be warranted because in a majority of cases the number of persons on committees is small. Committees so trained, if given adequate time for the application of available standards of judgment, could select texts on a genuinely professional basis.

The bases of selection used in one or more of the 135 school systems are indicated by the items in Table II. This list of criteria, compiled

TABLE II. — ITEMS CONSIDERED IN SELECTING SCHOOLBOOKS
WHEN SCORE CARDS ARE USED (After Whipple) [2]

1. Content:

    a. Ease of comprehension
    b. Value
    c. Scope
    d. Abundance of material
    e. Unspecified

2. Physical make-up:

    a. Type
    b. Binding
    c. Paper
    d. Arrangement of page
    e. Lines
    f. Illustrative material
    g. Spacing of words and letters
    h. Size of book
    i. Width of margins
    j. General appearance
    k. Shape
    l. Size and clearness of marginal notes and index
    m. Weight of book
    n. Unspecified

[1] *Ibid.*, 773.

[2] *Ibid.*, 767–769.

3. Aids to instruction:

a. Study exercises
b. Graphic material
c. Index
d. Table of contents
e. Provision for efficient use by teacher
f. Reference and bibliography
g. Tests and norms
h. Preface
i. Pupil material accompanying book
j. Glossary
k. Appendix
l. Pronunciation aids
m. Introduction to pupil
n. Remedial material
o. Title-page
p. Drill material

4. Method:

a. Development of reading habits and skills
b. Correlation with other subject matter and activities
c. Recognition of group and individual differences
d. Variety in types of activities
e. Provision for enrichment of vocabulary
f. Flexibility of method
g. Recognition of principles of psychology
h. Opportunity to develop general principles
i. Opportunity for pupils to discover cause and effect
j. Attention to pupil interest
k. Opportunity for applying general principles
l. Topical emphasis
m. Provision for supervised study
n. Unspecified

5. Objectives:

a. Harmony with educational aims
b. Desirable attitudes and economical habits and skills
c. Strong motives for, and permanent interests in, reading
d. Objectives of the course of study
e. Rich and varied experience
f. Correct standards and ideals in use of English
g. Vision of man in relation to his environment
h. Unspecified

6. Organization:

a. Organization around significant problems
b. Psychological rather than logical organization
c. Possibility of omissions without destroying sequence
d. Organization within selections
e. Placement of pedagogical material
f. Distribution, amount, and balance of drill
g. Unspecified

7. Author or authors:

a. Experience
b. Reputation
c. Training
d. Previous publications
e. Scholarship

   f. Familiarity with scientific investigations
   g. Participation in scientific investigations

8. Adaptation of specific needs

9. Series to which book belongs:
   a. Plan
   b. Gradation in difficulty

10. Scientific basis for method and content

11. Type of book

12. Recency of copyright date

13. General merit

14. Special features

15. Publisher

16. Price

---

from twenty-four score cards, presents an impressive number of features subject to evaluation, but the compiler points out that " only 13 percent of the total number of items listed on the score cards may be considered objective." [1]

In this same study of the practices followed in selecting reading materials for pupils in 135 cities, eleven methods of evaluating books were found.   These methods are shown in Table III.

TABLE III. — METHODS OF EVALUATING SCHOOLBOOKS (After Whipple) [2]

Trying books in the classroom
Comparing and discussing personal judgments
Making personal examination
Consulting book reviews and other printed materials
Making score-card evaluation
Securing judgments of specialists
Making preliminary eliminations
Analyzing materials with respect to topics treated
Applying statistical procedures to content
Analyzing materials with respect to duplication of selections
Formulating guiding principles

Only the first five methods in this list are reported with considerable frequency, while book reviews and score cards are reported chiefly

---

[1] Gertrude Whipple. *Loc. cit.*, 766.   [2] *Ibid.*, 770.

for recreational books and textbooks, respectively. The conclusion seems justified that too often books are selected without the best available techniques.

Another study describes the California State Curriculum Commission's plan for the evaluation of textbooks.[1] This plan involves the development of a set of criteria by which the books can be judged; the formulation of a score card based on the assignment of numerical values to essential items; the completion of a series of studies, primarily objective in character, designed to secure data with respect to the relative merits of the books on all essential items; and the interpretation and utilization of these data in rating the books.

According to the findings of the earlier study, the first item in this plan, the use of criteria, or guiding principles, is among the least prevalent (Table III). The advantage of including this item is one of economy: " books which obviously fail to meet any single criterion of major importance "[2] can be eliminated at once from further consideration. The use of criteria is defended as a practical first step. In reply to the possible criticism that an attempt to apply criteria is unscientific or otherwise unsound, the same authors advance the following points: sound criteria represent conclusions from pertinent research as to methods and materials, and " when research is lacking," sound criteria have " the consensus of educational authority."[3]

In the opinion of the Sub-committee, the study here cited is extremely valuable in its insistence upon the formulation of major criteria or standards as the starting point in the preparation of a score card for the evaluation of reading materials, including textbooks. Accordingly, seven criteria are presented here by the Sub-committee, with no attempt to develop detailed topics and subtopics under the seven heads.

Criterion 1. Reading materials should be suitable for the reader himself.

Criterion 2. Reading materials should be correct in mechanical aspects.

Criterion 3. Reading materials should be authentic.

Criterion 4. Reading materials should be extensive in content.

Criterion 5. Reading materials should be varied in style.

---

[1] Ivan R. Waterman and Erving R. Melbo. " A plan of procedure for the evaluation of textbooks in reading." *Elementary School Journal,* 35:1935, 662–674.

[2] *Ibid.,* 664.　　　　　　　　[3] *Ibid.,* 662.

Criterion 6.   Reading materials should meet the demands of teachers who are as good as the school system can obtain.

Criterion 7.   Reading materials should meet the purposes of modern school organization and administration.

Much has been said and written about the value and limitations of
score cards and of all other formal, mechanical, and quasi-statistical
devices for appraising books.   Undoubtedly the conscientious preparation of a score card is excellent groundwork for intelligent appraisal.
It is unnecessary to state that even the relatively uncritical use of a
badly constructed score card is likely to give better results than the
awarding of book adoptions on non-educational grounds.   Uncritical
mechanics are better than politics or favoritism.

An ideal situation is one in which a textbook committee is making
an honest effort to choose the best books in a certain subject, without
undue concern about minor differences in price and with no interest in
the identity of the publisher.   A committee thus operating, especially
with the help of a competent research organization, can usually be
trusted to evolve a plausible and coherent set of standards.   Such a
committee cannot always be trusted to weigh these standards soundly
— an all-important factor — or to apply them to the competitive materials in hand with astute discrimination.   Furthermore, routine items
in which the differences between books are almost sure to be incon-
sequential are likely to receive disproportionate emphasis.   Thus, recency of copyright date is likely to be overemphasized — indeed, it has
become a ludicrous farce in some cases, particularly when dealing with
subjects in which there are relatively slow changes in factual content
and teaching method.   Again, granting that mechanical features of a
book are important, we must point out that it is a highly exceptional
text, as schoolbooks are now manufactured, that is deficient in any
significant mechanical respect.   Once again, teachers often go to naïve
lengths in ascertaining biographical details about standard authors.
Furthermore, unless the procedure of eliminating at once books that
fail to meet major standards is followed,[1] the attention devoted to

---

[1] Thus, in using a score card, provision could be made whereby failure to score
above some specified ' dead line ' in given items would automatically be equivalent
to a total sum of zero.

Referring to the final statements in the above paragraph, it may be suggested
that textbook committees seeking to develop a quantitative score card may profitably take a leaf out of the experience of the psychologists who developed the
" Officer's Rating Scale " during the World War.   In most such scales there was

unworthy contestants is likely to obscure the issue and cause the committee to be blind to the merits of really superior books. One of our chief purposes in reproducing *in extenso* the items in Table II above was to indicate how many criteria and subcriteria are likely to figure in the use of formal standards of textbook selection. There is distinct danger that any but the shrewdest and most critical committeeman may fail to see the forest for the trees.

One point should be borne in mind. The value, whether great or small, of score cards is confined almost entirely to the appraisal of basal textbooks competing for formal adoption. The more informal the curriculum, the less dependence there is upon the basal textbook and thus the less occasion for the use of formal and complex evaluating devices.

A word at this point seems necessary with reference to an increasing disposition on the part of would-be expert book committees to demand of publishers elaborate word counts and vocabulary studies of books on all subjects for use in grades above the primary. In view of the importance of the conceptual element in the determination of gradation, such a demand reflects naïve beliefs in the measurability of vocabulary difficulty for all grades and in its all-importance in the determination of gradation. To such teachers the suggestion may be made that the best way to appraise a schoolbook is, after giving due attention to formal evaluating devices, to read it and to imagine oneself teaching it; then, if one's critical faculties are keen, a sound choice is likely to follow.

One point that appears to be entirely absent in the literature of book selection is the desirability of securing a proper correlation between different texts to be used in the same school. Reference has been made to the folly of adopting ' split ' series of primary readers. Akin to such a procedure, though less harmful, is the choice of books in one subject — provided subjects are taught as such — in total disregard of choices made in other fields. Today such a procedure can be avoided. Various consistent programs of texts are now available that treat apparently unrelated subjects with a carefully correlated vocabulary.

2. Principles Governing the Purchase of Books

What constitutes an adequate book equipment? In theory there is virtually unanimous agreement that the book equipment of an elemen-

---

inserted a final category like " General Value to the Service " to which was assigned as many as 40 of 100 ' points.' This took care of the " forest." — *Editor*.

tary school is inadequate unless it includes (1) a copy, in good condition, for each pupil of each textbook, supplementary book, or workbook the use of which by all the pupils in a class is required or presupposed by the scheme of instruction locally in vogue; (2) sets, in good condition, in smaller than classroom quantities, of supplementary books in all subjects or fusions of subjects for such group work as is presupposed in the course of study; (3) reference books in good condition — dictionaries, large and small, encyclopedias, atlases, almanacs, and the like — preferably for every schoolroom, but at least for every school library or building, sufficient to meet the needs of all pupils who have occasion to consult them; (4) one or two copies each of a wide range of books, both of literature and of specialized information, to facilitate the so-called ' library ' method of study, as recommended elsewhere; and (5) small sets or individual copies of a wide variety of books for recreational reading. To this list must be added (6) charts, cards, and strips for the teaching of primary reading, and (7) wall maps for use in geography and history classes. For secondary schools, an adequate equipment may be similarly described with, of course, the omission of non-book materials used in primary reading and with far greater emphasis upon variety and extent of resources in the reference library. At the junior-college level, since free textbooks are seldom or never supplied, extensive library facilities are all-important.

The foregoing summary may appear so simple as to be virtually axiomatic, yet few schools approximate a literal fulfillment of these conditions. Both before and after the onset of the depression, general neglect of schoolbook budgets in favor of showier items has been a widespread scandal of school administration. As was pointed out in the *Thirtieth Yearbook*, Part II, pages 224, 226, and 227, expenditures for schoolbooks just prior to the depression ranged from 1.4 percent to 2.2 percent of total public-school expenditures (according to the method of computation). In spite of the fact that approximately two percent of the total public-school budget was altogether inadequate for the provision of a suitable supply of reading materials, and in spite of the fact that the base upon which the percentage was computed dropped sharply subsequent to 1928, by 1932 the average expenditures for books did not, according to the most liberal computation, exceed 1.5 percent of total public-school expenditures. The book famine of 1933–1934 was notorious. Even since the beginnings of economic recovery, various large school units, notably cities, have failed to relieve this condition. Cases are on record in which cities having a population of a hundred thousand or more, whose supplies of reading materials are sadly de-pleted through several years of neglect, have book budgets ranging from nothing whatever to thirty cents per pupil. Various articles and editorials have been published in school journals and lay papers decry-ing this condition.[1] In conclusion the situation may best be summa-rized by the statement that, whereas it is extremely unlikely that a school's book equipment, if intelligently selected, will be too extensive or unjustifiably expensive, any shortage of equipment below a supply of all the books that can possibly be used to advantage is indefensibly extravagant. The financial saving that it represents as an item in the total educational budget is sure to be insignificant. Its cost in slowing down and generally defeating the reading program and through it the entire program of school work is sure to be excessive.

This discussion of inadequate reading materials should not be con-strued, however, as a plea for immediate and indiscriminate large-scale expenditure. It is far wiser for each individual school unit, large or small, to define its needs on a long-term basis, planning additions to its materials for several years in advance with a view to building up an ample and well-balanced equipment.

---

[1] See especially " War starts against dirty, frayed schoolbooks," in the *Boston Sunday Post,* September 9, 1934; "What shall we do about schoolbooks?" by Mary L. Langworthy, in the *National Parent-Teacher Magazine,* January, 1934; " Crusading for better schoolbooks for our children," in the *Boston Evening Tran-script,* January 9, 1935; "Move for better schoolbooks rapidly gaining friends," in the *Christian Science Monitor,* June 2, 1934; "Dirty textbooks," by Herbert Blair, in *Education,* September, 1933; "Textbooks often obsolete, dirty, and ragged," in the *Chicago Daily News,* July 11, 1934; "Skimping on schoolbooks," by Stuart Chase, in the *New York Herald Tribune,* May 13, 1934; "Schoolbooks and Supplies: Recent Trends on Expenditures and Policies," in *Educational Re-search Service* (Department of Superintendents and Research Division, National Education Association); "Printed material: Economy or extravagance?" by Arthur I. Gates, in the *Journal of the National Education Association;* "Books," from the *Educational Research Service* (Department of Superintendence and Re-search Division, N. E. A.), Vol. XII, No. 5, April 12, 1933; "Save the schools with books," editorial in *Journal of Education;* "For the love of books," by Lewis Worthington Smith, in *Child Welfare;* "Book tide has turned," editorial in *Journal of Education;* "Publishers give service plus," editorial in *Journal of Edu-cation;* "Next to the teacher — books," by Anson W. Belding, in *Journal of Education;* "Bricks without straw," "One class, three texts," "Not enough books," "Lack of reading material," "Out-of-date geographies," from "The Problem Box," by Augustus O. Thomas, in *Journal of Education.* (These articles have been collected and published in a booklet, *Dirty, Worn-Out, Out-Moded School-books.* The Macmillan Company: New York.)

References [1]

1. On Both Elementary and Secondary School Materials

Dunn, Fannie W. (chairman). *Materials of Instruction.* (Bureau of Publications, Teachers College, Columbia University: New York, 1935. Department of Supervisors and Directors of Instruction of the National Education Association, *Eighth Yearbook.*) Discussions of discovery, selection, use, and administration of materials for elementary and high schools (chiefly elementary schools). Classified bibliography of supplementary materials for various elementary and high-school departments.

Edmonson, James B. (chairman). *The Textbook in American Education.* Thirtieth Yearbook of this Society, Part II. (Public School Publishing Company: Bloomington, Illinois, 1931.) Discussions of the place of textbooks, costs, and standards of selection.

Gray, William S., and Leary, Bernice E. *What Makes a Book Readable.* (University of Chicago Press: Chicago, 1935. 115 pp.) On the elements of difficulty in adult reading material.

Hatfield, W. Wilbur (chairman). *An Experience Curriculum in English* — a report of the Curriculum Commission of the National Council of Teachers of English. (D. Appleton-Century Company: New York, 1935. 323 pp.) Basic principles, integration, and selecting and providing materials for various purposes of reading and literature are discussed on pp. 3–106.

Jordan, Arthur M. *Children's Interests in Reading.* (University of North Carolina: Chapel Hill, 1926.) Report of a series of investigations of elementary- and high-school reading.

Norton, John K., and Norton, Margaret Alltucker. *Foundations of Curriculum Building.* Ch. VII. (Ginn and Company: Boston, 1936. 599 pp.) Summarization and evaluation of many investigations. Bibliography.

Terman, Lewis M., and Lima, Margaret. *Children's Reading.* (D. Appleton-Century Company: New York, revised ed., 1931.) On the effects of individual differences on reading. Bibliography of children's books.

Uhl, Willis L. *The Materials of Reading; Their Selection and Organization.* (Silver, Burdett and Company: Newark, 1924. 386 pp.) On children's interests and comprehension of reading materials in elementary and high schools, standards for selecting materials, and physical conditions of reading.

Washburne, Carleton, and Vogel, Mabel. *Winnetka Graded Book List.* (American Library Association: Chicago, 1926. 286 pp.) Discussion of books read by pupils with reference both to enjoyment and reading ability.

---

[1] See also the references in Chapter VIII.

2. On Elementary-School Materials

Beust, Nora (compiler). *Graded List of Books for Children.* (American Library Association, 1936. 161 pp.) An annotated list of about 1000 titles of books.

Dunn, Fannie W. *Interest Factors in Primary Reading Material.* (Teachers College, Columbia University, Contributions to Education, No. 113: New York, 1921. 70 pp.) Report of an investigation of reading interests of children.

Gates, Arthur I. *Interest and Ability in Reading.* (The Macmillan Company: New York, 1930. 264 pp.) On the influence of vocabulary, kind of material, and the reading situation.

Huber, Miriam B. *The Influence of Intelligence upon Children's Reading Interests.* (Teachers College, Columbia University, Contributions to Education, No. 312: New York, 1928.) Results of experimental studies of children's interests in different types of materials.

Huber, Miriam B., Bruner, H. B., and Curry, C. M. *Children's Interests in Poetry.* (Rand, McNally and Company: Chicago, 1927. 233 pp.) Report of a study to discover the most suitable poetry for children.

McKee, Paul G. *Reading and Literature in the Elementary School.* (Houghton Mifflin Company: Boston, 1934. 591 pp.) This contains a section on the study and teaching of children's literature. Pp. 506 ff. are on criteria for judging materials.

Miller, Eleanor Olmstead. "Study of the preschool child's picture and story books by the battery of tests method." *Journal of Applied Psychology,* 13: 1929, 592–599.

Shuttleworth, Frank K. *A Critical Study of Two Lists of Best Books for Children.* (*Genetic Psychology Monographs,* Clark University: Worcester, Mass., 1932, Vol. 11, No. 4, pp. 247–320.) A comparison of Washburne and Vogel's *Winnetka Graded Book List* with Starbuck's *A Guide to Literature for Character Training* as to grade placement and general value and interest.

Sister M. Celestine. *Survey of the Literature on Reading Interests of Children of the Elementary Grades.* Catholic University of America Educational Research Bulletin. (Catholic Education Press: Washington, D. C., 1930, Vol. 5, Nos. 2 and 3.) Both secular and religious materials are included.

Weekes, Blanche E. *Literature and the Child.* (Silver, Burdett and Company: Newark, 1935. 456 pp.) Discussions of the nature and purpose of literature, selection of materials, illustrations; contains a classified list of supplementary, recreational, and reference books.

Wilkinson, Mary S., Weedon, Vivian, and Washburne, Carleton. *The Right Book for the Right Child.* (John Day Company: New York, 1933. 357 pp.) Principles of selection of books.

3. On High-School Materials

Center, Stella S., and Herzberg, Max J. (co-chairman). *Leisure Reading for Grades Seven, Eight, and Nine.* (National Council of Teachers of English: Chicago, 1932. 132 pp.) Lists of books classified by grades as to content.

Crow, Charles S. *Evaluation of English Literature in the High School.* (Teachers College, Columbia University, Contributions to Education, No. 141: New York, 1924.) Discussion of data obtained from 1999 pupils in 29 high schools.

Foster, Mary Elizabeth (chairman). *One Thousand Books for the Senior High School Library.* (American Library Association: Chicago, 1935. 96 pp.)

Rasche, William F. *The Reading Interests of Young Workers.* (Milwaukee Vocational School: Milwaukee, Wis. 102 pp. Vocational Educational Monograph, No. 9.) Reports upon book, magazine, and newspaper reading of 7065 workers, aged fourteen to eighteen years.

Woodring, Maxie Nave, and Gilbert, Harold. *Enriched Teaching of Commercial Subjects in the High School.* (Teachers College, Columbia University: New York, 1930. 389 pp.) This reference and the five that follow contain classified, annotated lists of readings.

Woodring, Maxie Nave; Jewett, Ida A.; and Benson, Rachel T. *Enriched Teaching of English in the Junior and Senior High School.* (Teachers College, Columbia University: New York, 1934.)

Woodring, Maxie Nave, and Sabin, Frances E. *Enriched Teaching of Latin in the High School.* (Teachers College, Columbia University: New York, 1930. 144 pp.)

Woodring, Maxie Nave, and Sanford, Vera. *Enriched Teaching of Mathematics in the High School.* (Teachers College, Columbia University: New York, 1928. 128 pp.)

Woodring, Maxie Nave, and Schwendener, Norma. *Enriched Teaching of Physical Education in the High School.* (Teachers College, Columbia University: New York, 1929. 143 pp.)

Woodring, Maxie Nave; Oakes, M. E.; and Brown, H. W. *Enriched Teaching of Science in the High School.* (Teachers College, Columbia University: New York, 1928. 374 pp.)

4. On College and Adult Materials

Gray, William S., and Munroe, Ruth. *The Reading Interests and Habits of Adults.* (The Macmillan Company: New York, 1929. 305 pp.) Discussion of reading interests of children and adults and of case studies of adult reading. Annotated bibliography.

Townsend, Atwood H. (chairman). *A Thousand Interesting and Significant Books.* (National Council of Teachers of English: Chicago, 1935. 79 pp.) A guide for college students and adult readers.

5. On Illustrations and Physical Make-Up

Bamberger, Florence E. *The Effect of the Physical Make-Up of a Book upon Children's Selection.* (The Johns Hopkins University Studies in Education, No. 4: Baltimore, 1922. 113 pp.) Report of an investigation of children's preferences as to size of books, color of bindings, illustrations, and attractiveness of the page.

Freeman, G. La Verne, and Freeman, Ruth S. *The Child and His Picture Book.* (Northwestern University Press: Chicago, 1933. 102 pp.) On the purpose and character of picture books for the nursery age.

Martin, Helen. *Children's Preferences in Book Illustrations.* (Western Reserve University Bulletin, New Series, 34, No. 10: Cleveland, 1931. 58 pp.) Presents an historical summary of book illustrations, and reports investigations of preferences of children in Grades I–IX.

Mellinger, Bonnie E. *Children's Interests in Pictures.* (Teachers College, Columbia University, Contributions to Education, No. 516: New York, 1921.) Summarization of children's preferences in Grades I, III, and V.

Mendenhall, James E., and Mendenhall, Marcia F. *The Influence of Familiarity upon Children's Preferences for Pictures and Poems.* (Lincoln School of Teachers College, Columbia University: New York, 1933. 74 pp.) Deals with preferences of children in Grades VII and IX.

CHAPTER VIII

THE SCHOOL LIBRARY

B. Lamar Johnson
Librarian and Dean of Instruction, Stephens College
Columbia, Missouri

I. Introduction

1. Assumptions Basic to the Reading Program

Throughout the Yearbook three assumptions are considered fundamental to the entire reading program:

(1) Opportunity to read widely is essential in learning to read. Furthermore, the development of motives for reading contributes to rapid growth in reading efficiency.

(2) Reading is developed in large measure through its application in the various curricular fields. Indeed, each teacher is responsible for efficient reading in his field, and, to that extent, every teacher is a teacher of reading.

(3) Many materials, other than the textbook, should be used in the classroom. " Under the old conception, the job of the teacher was to get the children through the textbook for the grade; under the new conception, both teacher and pupils are bringing into the classroom materials from all available sources." [1] This use of books not only vitalizes instruction but contributes to reading efficiency as well.

A reading program based upon these assumptions obviously requires a wide range of appropriate reading materials and will accordingly place heavy demands upon the school library. The purpose of this chapter is to consider the place of the school library in the broad reading program recommended in this Yearbook.

2. The School Library — What It Is

At least three concepts of the school library may be identified when considering its relation to the reading program. The library may be thought of as a room or suite of rooms in which are housed books and

---

[1] State of California, Department of Education. *The Library in the Elementary School.* P. 1. (Department of Education Bulletin, No. 18. September 15, 1935)

periodicals for the use of pupils and teachers; it may be regarded as a unit of the school organization that supplies reading materials to classrooms, study halls, home rooms, and laboratories; or it may be conceived as including all aspects of the pupil's environment (home, public library, and school) that supply him with reading matter.[1] The third of these concepts receives special emphasis in this chapter.

Studies of the reading behavior of entire communities, both urban and rural, have shown many uses and abuses of reading, some of which lie beyond the school's province as generally conceived. The need for attention to extra-curricular and accidental reading is probably no less than the need for attention to curricular reading, since the former will constitute the bulk of the pupil's reading throughout life. An effort is made in this chapter to consider the total reading environment of the pupil; however, the situation provided by the school receives the most attention.

3. Objectives of the School Library

One of the fundamental aims of the library is to bring to the school the products of the best minds of the present day and of past ages, for in books are recorded the best thoughts of the leading thinkers of all times. Statements of the objectives of the library usually, however, include more specific aims. The three most commonly accepted objectives are:[2] (a) to enrich the curriculum and to supply needed reference material; (b) to provide for worthy use of leisure time; and (c) to train pupils in the use of books and the library.[3]

a. *To Enrich the Curriculum and to Supply Reference Materials.* The expansion of the school curriculum and the adoption of teaching methods requiring extensive reading place on the school library heavy responsibilities and provide it with many opportunities for service. The library must supply, and make readily accessible, the needed materials for reference and materials that will help to enrich the curriculum. It can serve the reading program by guiding individual pupils to mate-

---

[1] The school library may properly contain printed materials, music, phonograph records, pictures, and slides. Since this Yearbook is concerned primarily with reading, only reading materials are considered here.

[2] B. Lamar Johnson. *The Secondary School Library.* P. 7. (National Survey of Secondary Education, U. S. Office of Education Bulletin, No. 17. 1932)

[3] Although this statement of objectives applies to the secondary school, it is strikingly similar to a widely accepted statement of the aims of the elementary-school library: C. C. Certain. *Elementary School Library Standards.* American Library Association, 1925. Pp. 4–5.

rials suitable to their reading ability, by guiding the reading of the pupils in such a way as to extend their fields of interest, and by training the pupils to turn to the library for assistance in any reading problem.

b. To Provide for Worthy Use of Leisure Time. As a result of the increasing recognition of the importance of leisure-time activities, the school curriculum is coming to include activities formerly assumed to be extra-class in character. Whether the leisure-reading activities in a given school are largely curricular or extra-curricular in nature, the school library must make adequate provision for reading materials adapted to the interests of the group that it serves. Its first task, then, obviously consists in learning what these interests are. Having determined the interests and having supplied appropriate materials for the particular group, the next task of the school library is to influence the pupils to think of the library as a place where satisfying leisure-time activities can be provided for.

c. To Train Pupils in the Use of Books and the Library. Broadly conceived, instruction in the use of books and of libraries includes instruction in all phases of reading considered in this volume. As this purpose relates to the school library particularly, it includes training in ability to use such aids as the card catalogue, the *Reader's Guide*, encyclopedias, and dictionaries. The importance of these library tools to any reading program is obvious, for the ability to read is not complete if the reader is unable to locate needed materials. But such training is not equally needed by all pupils. To identify those who respond to the training is one of the responsibilities of the library.

In short, the modern reading program proposed in the Yearbook places a twofold demand on the school library:

(1) An adequate amount of reading material must be available, appropriate both for the instructional needs of the school and for the pleasure reading of the group served.

(2) These materials must be so organized and administered that they contribute effectively to the educational program of the school.

The remainder of this chapter is devoted to a consideration of ways in which these demands may be met.

II. PROVIDING ADEQUATE READING MATERIALS

The provision of adequate reading materials involves a proper supply of materials appropriate for the specified purposes.

1. Securing an Adequate Amount of Reading Materials

The first problem that arises in connection with securing an adequate quantity of reading materials relates to support of the school library. The space reserved for this chapter will not permit a detailed discussion of the details of school library financing.[1] Suffice it to say that, if the school administrator is fully aware of the contribution that the library can make to the educational program of his school, he will see that the provision made in the school budget for reading materials is as adequate as the provision for other material facilities. In fact, the administrative steps taken should agree with the policy expressed by an educator who stated, " If I were an educational administrator in charge of a college, a high school, or even an elementary school, the first charge against the budget of the institution following the faculty would be funds for the library." [2]

Instead of buying large numbers of certain books, some schools are purchasing a limited number of copies of many different titles. In other words, these schools use the money formerly spent for a few textbooks in purchasing a far wider range of reading materials. In a high school in Ohio, for example, textbooks are used only by classes in mathematics and languages. Each pupil in this school pays a textbook fee. After the textbooks in mathematics and the languages have been purchased, the remaining funds are used for library books. This fund supplements the library expenditures provided in the school budget. In another high school, where pupils buy textbooks for most courses, some of the English classes use no textbook. In these classes each pupil contributes one dollar to a fund that the class uses for the purchase of appropriate books for the school library. The fact should be pointed out, however, that the foregoing plans are make-shift arrangements. Whenever pupils must contribute money for the purchase of library books, they are merely making good the failure of the school administration to provide adequate support for the library.

Although the school library is a most important and obvious source of reading materials, it is not the only source. The alert school administrator, teacher, and librarian can draw upon a number of other local agencies to obtain books essential for the effective functioning of

---

[1] For a discussion of school library finance, see: Lucile F. Fargo. *The Library in the School.* Pp. 415–421. (American Library Association, 1933)

[2] W. W. Charters. *American Library Association Leads,* **10**: September, 1933, 46.

the reading program. For example, coöperation between the school library and the public library often results in such practices as the following:

(1) The school borrows books from the public library.

(2) School reading lists are sent to the public library.

(3) Books needed by school pupils are put on a reserve shelf in the public library.

(4) The school principal notifies the staff of the public library of assignments that may result in the use of their books.

(5) Teachers take their pupils to the public library, where they are given instruction in how to use the library.

Schools may also establish helpful relations with county librarians.

> For the rural school and the small school system, affiliation with the county library is the best working plan yet devised. Through pooling funds in this manner, the average individual school has the use of at least five times as many books in one year as could be purchased with the single library fund.[1]

One rural community has a county library service that has been described as " the nearest approach in the demonstration counties to a single coördinated library system for all the schools, urban and rural. . . ." The plan used is described as follows:

> The parish board of education contributes approximately $3,000 to the annual budget of the library. This is used for the purchase and preparation of books, payment of custodians in the school stations, and general service. . . . Branches for combined school and community service are located in each of the nine rural white schools and in twelve of the thirty-three Negro schools. . . .
>
> Negro teachers in schools without branches secure classroom collections from the library of the county training school.
>
> The school service rendered by [this] . . . library is undoubtedly far superior to that which a school board could provide with the same funds under its own administration.[2]

Many schools, however, have no access to city and county libraries. Nevertheless, several possibilities are open to them. In most states traveling libraries, usually under the supervision of the state department of education or of the state library commission, are available to

---

[1] State of California, Department of Education. *Op. cit.* P. 9.

[2] Louis R. Wilson and Edward A. Wight. *County Library Service in the South.* Pp. 159–160. (University of Chicago Press: Chicago, 1935)

schools.¹ Ordinarily the only expense involved in the use of this service
is the cost of the transportation of the books borrowed. " Local circulating collections " are also available to some communities.

One of the most effective adaptations of the circulation collections
for rural schools in an area without public library service is in Placer
County, California. Two of the school supervisors have organized the
system. Each school that wished to join paid $15 the first year (later
$10) per teacher. All the money was used for purchasing books for
recreational reading. The entire collection was assembled in units composed of books suitable for pupils in each grade in the rural schools.
Thirty-four schools, twenty-six of which are one-teacher, belonged to the
organization in June, 1934. There is no duplication of titles in the
thirty-four groups of books.

The advantages of this plan for schools in areas without libraries are
numerous, particularly in view of the small amount which each school
spends. After the books are put into circulation, the success of the
scheme depends to a considerable extent on the coöperation of the individual teachers. The original book selection is important and should
be made only by a person familiar with children's literature and the
school curriculum. In counties where such a person is not available, the
advice of the state library commission, the state department of education, the state library association, or the American Library Association
should be sought.²

The circulating-collection plan may well be used in many counties
to supplement other reading material available.

Another source of books is the home library. The home always has
an important influence on reading. Books in homes may, on occasion,
be lent to the school. This practice can perhaps be used best in the
field of literature. An English teacher in one high school with an
enrollment of approximately two hundred pupils reports that, when his
classes were studying fiction, the books available in the school library
were totally inadequate. He appealed to his pupils and within two
days they had brought from their homes scores of appropriate books

---

¹ According to a report from the American Library Association, dated March
20, 1936, the following states have traveling libraries or direct mail borrowing
service: Colorado, Connecticut, Delaware, Georgia, Idaho, Illinois, Indiana, Iowa,
Kansas, Kentucky, Louisiana, Maine, Maryland, Michigan, Minnesota, Missouri,
Nebraska, Nevada, New Hampshire, New Jersey, New Mexico, New York, North
Carolina, North Dakota, Ohio, Oklahoma, Oregon, Pennsylvania, Rhode Island,
South Dakota, Texas, Vermont, Virginia, Washington, Wisconsin, and Wyoming.

² Louis R. Wilson and Edward A. Wight. *Op. cit.* Pp. 162–163.

that materially enriched the study of fiction. The practice of securing books from pupils' homes must, of course, be used with discretion; in many communities the quality of books in homes would make this practice impossible.

The foregoing paragraphs describe a number of methods of supplementing the books available in the school library. Such supplementary practices cannot, however, satisfactorily take the place of an adequate library budget. Unless the library receives adequate financial support, it cannot hope to make its optimal contribution to the reading program of the school.

2. Securing Appropriate Reading Materials

If a library is to serve the school effectively, it must have a sufficient quantity of reading materials and the materials must be adapted to its needs. When the library needs of a school are being determined, several factors must be considered: (*a*) the school curriculum — its present content, its growth, and its development; (*b*) the teachers — their interests, their emphasis in teaching, and their methods; (*c*) the pupils as a group and as individuals — their interests, their abilities, and their book needs; and (*d*) the reading background provided by the home and other aspects of the pupils' environment.

The study of these factors and the selection of appropriate books requires the coöperation of the librarian and the teacher. The librarian is in a position to make a vital contribution to the selection of materials; she knows aids to book selection and she knows what materials pupils use in the library. The teacher, however, must be given a major responsibility in book selection; the teacher knows his objectives, his course content, his method, and his pupils. His knowledge, combined with that of the librarian, provides the basis for procuring a collection of appropriate reading material.

A few schools are adding a third member — the pupil — to the group that participates in selecting books. A hundred dollars from the book fund is given to the senior English class in one school for the purchase of books of recent publication. The request that the money be spent for recent material is made because of the interest of the group in ' new ' books and because of the value that will accrue from a study of contemporary reviews and literary criticism. The class divides into committees to study new books in various fields, and these committees report their findings to the class. In the autumn of 1935 a class of sixty-three pupils reviewed one hundred fifty books and studied the list until a selection of fifty-eight titles was made. With only a hundred dollars to spend the class found it necessary to reduce the list even more. After prolonged discussion and much weighing of the value of one book against another, thirty-nine titles were finally ordered. Certainly the pupils in this class had a highly valuable experience, and undoubtedly they selected books appropriate to the school's needs.

Many schools without a librarian find the problem of selecting books particularly difficult. School-library supervisors, usually affiliated with the state department of education or with the state library commission, will assist schools that appeal to them for assistance. Gradually, the cumulated experience of librarians and teachers in all sections of the country has been made available in printed form to those confronted with the problem of selecting books. The following is a partial list of such aids to book selection:

1. For Guidance in Choosing Sets of Books in Any Library or School:

Subscription Books Bulletin. (American Library Association. $1 a year.) This quarterly bulletin describes and evaluates encyclopedias and sets of books that are sold to libraries by agents. One person cannot adequately examine these comprehensive publications, and, even though he may have leisure and background for careful examination, he is seldom able to compare the publication with other similar material. The bulletin presents the results of examination and comparison. More than 250 publications have been reviewed since 1930, and the files of back numbers are available for consultation in many school and public libraries.

2. For Guidance in Choosing Books for Elementary-School Libraries:

Graded List of Books for Children. Joint Committee of the National Education Association and National Council of Teachers of English. (American Library Association, 1936. $1.75.) This list prescribes about 1,500 books, giving publisher and price, brief descriptions of the books, and suggestions about the types of children to whom the books appeal. It is divided into sections for Grades I–III, IV–VI, and VII–IX. A complete index makes it possible to find any particular title or to locate easily all books on one subject.

Children's Catalog, Siri Andrews, editor, 5th ed. rev. (Wilson, 1936.) Sold on a service basis. A list of books recommended by librarians for use with children from the youngest through junior-high-school age. It gives publisher and price of desirable editions of each book and indicates the grade levels at which each can be used. It is indispensable in selecting books and is valuable also for reference use, since, in addition to listing books under author and title, it gives under each small subject the names of books and chapters of books on that subject. This feature makes the list especially useful to the teacher in locating information and fictional material on any subject touched in class. The *Catalog* is kept up to date by a yearly supplement.

Realms of Gold in Children's Books. Bertha E. Mahony and Elinor Whitney, compilers. (Doubleday, Doran and Company, 1929. $5.) An annotated and illustrated list of books for children. Books are classified under unconventional but helpful headings, according to type and subject.

Five Years of Children's Books. Bertha E. Mahony and Elinor Whitney. (Doubleday, Doran and Company, 1936). This book supplements and brings to date the *Realms of Gold* by the same compilers.

The Right Book for the Right Child: Graded Buying List. (John Day, 1933. $2.50. Supplement, 1935. 25¢) A list of 1,500 children's books selected and annotated by children's librarians and graded by the Research Division of the Winnetka, Illinois, Public Schools. Books are arranged by grade according to a formula that considers vocabulary difficulty as well as range and complexity of structure. The list is indexed by author, title, and subject.

3. For Guidance in Choosing Books for Junior- and Senior-High-School Libraries:

1000 Books for the Senior-High-School Library. Joint Committee of the National Education Association, American Library Association, and National Council of Teachers of English. (American Library Association, 1935. $1.) Suggestions for a basic collection arranged by subject, with an index by author, title, and subject. Includes information about publishers, price, desirable edition, as well as a brief comment about each book.

Standard Catalog for High-School Libraries. Zaidee Brown, editor. 2nd ed. (Wilson, 1932.) Sold on service basis. A list of about 3,000 books for junior- and senior-high-school libraries. Like the *Children's Catalog*, it serves the double purpose of helping in the selection of books and of answering reference questions. Books and parts of books about any subject are also listed. Information is included about publisher, price, desirable editions, as well as a short description of the contents of each book. It lists many pamphlets. It is kept up to date by a yearly supplement.

Leisure Reading for Grades Seven, Eight, and Nine. (National Council of Teachers of English, 1932. 20¢) An attractive illustrated list for children to use themselves. The notes are planned to interest young people. It is arranged by subject.

Books for Home Reading for High Schools. (National Council of Teachers of English, 1930. 20¢) An illustrated list arranged by subjects, planned to interest high-school pupils in books for pleasure reading.

Background Readings for American History. Jean C. Roos, compiler. Reading for Background, No. 1. (Wilson, 1935. 35¢)

What Shall We Read Next? A Program of Reading Sequences. Jean C. Roos, compiler. Reading for Background, No. 2. (Wilson, 1935. 35¢)

These pamphlets are examples of lists carefully selected to serve one field or a particular purpose. They give suggestions of material to be added to the library and call attention to new uses of books already in the library.

4. For Guidance in Selecting Current Books:

The Booklist: A Guide to New Books. (American Library Association. $2.50 a year.) A monthly selection of books for libraries, giving full buying information and descriptions of the books. The notes about each book indicate how it may be used and at what age level it will appeal. The selection of books for young people is made largely from the adult list.

Horn Book. (270 Boylston St., Boston, $2.50 a year.) This magazine, issued bi-monthly, contains lists of books distinctively annotated and articles about authors and books. It is planned for children, teachers, and librarians. It considers books of interest to children through the junior high school and sometimes through the senior high school.

Wilson Bulletin. (Wilson. 50¢ a year.) Each issue of this monthly library magazine contains a brief selection of books, a book preview, and frequent special lists.

To these publications should be added local and state lists, some of which have been carefully prepared. Only if aids in book selection are made available to teachers and pupils, and are used by them can these important groups actively participate in the choice of books, and only through such participation can the aim of the selection of appropriate reading material be attained.

III. CONTRIBUTION OF THE LIBRARY TO THE EDUCATIONAL PROGRAM

The effective use of the library in a comprehensive reading program involves two main types of contribution: (1) using reading materials in classroom instruction; and (2) using reading materials in recreational reading.

In discussing the use of reading materials, this section will not consider in detail specific techniques used by the classroom teacher, for this subject is treated in other chapters, particularly Chapters IV and V. The chief purpose of this section is to consider how to make the materials available, to the end that they may be most useful. This purpose is not, however, the sole responsibility of the librarian or the teacher-librarian. The teacher's responsibility for providing his pupils with ample opportunity for using books is fully as significant as the librarian's responsibility for making books available.

1. Using Reading Materials in Classroom Instruction

The coöperation of principal, librarian, and teacher is essential in any instructional program in which reading is to function adequately. In too many schools the administrator, in his educational planning, fails to consider the library; too frequently the librarian and the reading materials remain in the library, while the teacher and pupils remain in the classroom. The comprehensive reading program presented in this Yearbook demands that the principal aid and encourage pupils, teachers, and librarian to put the library to effective use. Furthermore, pupils, teachers, and librarian should coöperate in promoting the appropriate use of books. Teachers and pupils (as individuals, as committees, and as classes) should go to the library, and the library should extend at all times to the classroom. Such coöperation results in making the library an important element in the educational program; it makes the classroom a real center for work with books; and it increases the use of the library as a real center of class work.

a. The Principal's Responsibility. The responsibility of the principal extends to all phases of the reading program. However, he has special responsibilities for promoting the contribution of the library to the educational program of the school. He must make provision in the school for adequate funds for books and magazines and funds for the employment of a capable librarian — a librarian who knows books and libraries, who knows the school and its educational program, and, more important, who knows boys and girls.

The principal should use the library as an aid in instructional supervision, the term ' supervision ' being interpreted to include all activities that have as their purpose the improvement of instruction. In meeting this responsibility, the school principal should use many procedures. He may visit the library regularly and confer with the librarian. He may study the use pupils are making of the library facilities. He may study the use made of the library during succeeding years. He may study the use made of the library by pupils of various teachers. He may ask the librarian at each faculty meeting to call the attention of faculty members to library materials of general interest. He may arrange that instructional problems involving the library be studied by faculty committees and be considered at faculty meetings. He may see that a long-term (five-year, for example) plan for the development of the school library is instituted and carried out just as carefully as is a similar program for curricular development.

Many principals spend time at the circulation desks of their school libraries and find this procedure particularly valuable in the supervision of instruction. Work at the circulation desk gives the supervisor an opportunity to observe the results of teaching: he sees pupils preparing the assignments that develop from class periods. If a teacher makes vague and indefinite assignments or is using a stereotyped textbook method, these facts are discovered through contacts at the circulation desk. If a teacher is an inspiring guide, a leader of boys and girls, a short time in the library acquaints the supervisor with the situation. Some supervisors find the time spent in the library so valuable that they are including the library more and more frequently in their regular schedules of instructional visits.

b. The Librarian's Responsibility. The first responsibility of the librarian is to administer the library in such a way that teachers and pupils can find the materials they need. If careless administration makes it difficult to locate specific books or periodicals when they are needed, the library cannot contribute effectively to the reading program.

A second responsibility of the librarian is to become acquainted with classroom instruction. An excellent method of gaining this acquaintance is to visit classes. In most schools, however, the librarian's schedule will not permit her to make many class visits. In a large number of schools outlines of all courses offered are available in the principal's office. A study of such outlines, supplemented by conferences with instructors, is an effective means of becoming acquainted with instructional plans and procedures. The importance of informal contacts with teachers cannot be overlooked.

A third duty of the librarian is to acquaint the teachers with what is available in their respective fields. An adequate collection of books on biology is likely to render no real service if the biology teacher does not know of these books. Book lists are an obvious aid in encouraging teachers to become acquainted with library materials. Some librarians provide teachers with lists of new books in their particular fields; some supply every teacher with lists of all new books added to the library. Reading lists, including old books and periodical literature, as well as new materials, are of special value. Reading lists on subjects of class interest are invariably appreciated and used by teachers.

Book lists are necessarily impersonal. There can be no substitute for the informal method of calling the attention of teachers to new materials or to other materials with which they may not be acquainted. At times a brief note may suffice; at other times a casual word may be desirable; on still other occasions it may be helpful to give the teacher a book or a group of books with the suggestion that he may wish to examine them. Faculty meetings also offer excellent opportunity for the librarian to call the attention of the faculty as a whole to interesting materials.

Any device that brings teachers to the library is, of course, helpful in acquainting them with library resources. Some schools hold faculty meetings in the library; others report that a faculty reading corner proves popular with teachers. In a few schools instructors themselves prepare lists of all books in the library in their respective fields. While these lists have value *per se*, their particular value lies in the fact that they have made the teachers aware of the available materials.

A fourth responsibility of the librarian is to administer the library in such a manner that it serves the requirements of every teaching situation that makes use of library materials. The problem of discovering how best to adapt the library to classroom instruction is difficult. The librarian may await passively the request of teachers for special privileges or she may look actively for opportunities to assist in the instructional process. One librarian addressed the faculty somewhat as follows: " The library is here to serve you and your pupils. I am eager to adapt our library to you and your needs. I should, therefore, appreciate it if you will study each course that you are teaching — its objectives and its methods — and ask yourself the question, ' How can the library aid me in better attaining the objectives of my course? ' After you have done this, let me know what I can do. I am eager to do everything possible to aid you, even though your request may involve departure from what has been our usual library procedure." The response to this invitation was immediate. Some teachers felt a need for classroom libraries. The granting of these requests (most of them for temporary loans to classrooms) had an immediate influence on instruction, for the classrooms soon became centers for work with books. Some teachers indicated their desire to take their classes to the library in order that groups might work on common problems. A number of teachers indicated that at times they wished to have groups or committees of pupils go to the library for conference work. Several teachers suggested the possibility of spending some of their vacant periods in the library where their pupils could confer with them about appropriate books immediately at hand. The simple device of inviting the faculty to study its library needs and make them known led the teachers of this school to give intelligent consideration to the use of reading materials in their courses.

Many of the newer methods of classroom teaching demand that teachers and pupils have the opportunity of working together in the presence of appropriate books, both during and outside of regular class periods. As a result, classroom libraries are used widely in schools employing new methods of classroom instruction.[1]

> The effective use of the school library involves provision for withdrawing units of books from the library to classrooms for limited use. This may be in the way of supplementary reference books or free reading books to be used for a single hour, for a day, or for a week or more. The important thing is to have the books mobile, so that the books and the children can be got together easily. Any arrangement which facilitates easy access to books heightens their use and effectiveness.[2]

The type of classroom library referred to above is a collection charged out from the central library of a school to a classroom in the same building. In many cases, particularly in elementary and rural schools, the classroom library is the only unit of school library service.

> These unit libraries are usually provided by the school system or by the public library. While they are to be preferred to no library facilities, they have great limitations. . . . This is inevitable in view of the necessarily limited nature of the book collection and in the absence of the facilities and organization which go to make up typical library service.[3]

Classroom libraries of the permanent type do, of course, have real value in small schools or in schools having no central library service. In general, however, a school should aim to provide for the classroom library as a supplement to, and not as a substitute for, the central library. Thus employed, the classroom library is a useful aid in enriching the educational experiences of the pupils.

Having classes spend class periods in the library has proved of great value in many schools. This plan is frequently used in elementary schools where scheduled library hours are a regular part of the week's program. If classes are to spend class periods in the library, careful consideration must be given to the seating capacity of the library. To have a group spend a class period in the library of some schools would

---

[1] B. L. Johnson. *Op. cit.* P. 55.
[2] State of California, Department of Education. *Op. cit.* P. 26.
[3] *Ibid.* P. 23.

mean that library privileges would be denied to other pupils during the same period.

A number of devices have been mentioned that have proved helpful in making books contribute effectively to the educational program of the school. The important factor, however, in adapting the library to instruction is not the device or the devices that may be used; rather, it is the desire and the willingness of all concerned to make the library serve the needs of the educational program. Given this desire on the part of both teachers and librarian, specific methods of attaining the desired ends will be discovered.

c. The Teacher's Responsibility. The effective use of library materials in instruction depends in large measure upon the teacher. Fortunate indeed is the school with adequate library facilities and with a librarian who is acquainted with classroom teaching, who does everything possible to acquaint teachers with available reading materials, and who is eager to individualize library administration in harmony with the needs of each teacher and each class. Even this situation, however, would result in no progress if the teachers did not take advantage of the opportunities thus offered.

In schools with library facilities the responsibilities of the teacher include becoming acquainted with all available materials in the school library that are appropriate for the use of his classes, assisting in determining what books should be added to the library, and using available reading materials in such a way that they make their optimal contribution to teaching objectives. This use of library materials depends, fundamentally, upon the instructor's philosophy of teaching (see Chapter V). There are, however, a number of devices the teacher may use to advantage.

The teacher will find it most helpful to go frequently to the library and browse among the books. Teachers in several schools, as has already been mentioned, have prepared lists of all library books relating to their courses. The teacher may encourage the optimal use of library materials by making clear and purposeful assignments. The effects of a vague and purposeless assignment are most clearly seen in the school library, where pupils come to seek for something — they know not what.

In making assignments, the teacher must know and keep in mind the materials available in the school library. It is a waste of time for pupils to be sent to the library to study books that are not and never have been in the library. Meticulous care in ascertaining that assigned materials are available will make for increased library and instructional efficiency.

Many teachers find that instructional efficiency is increased when they work with their pupils in the presence of books. Individual guidance in reading and learning is facilitated if teacher and pupil can cooperatively select appropriate reading material, rather than talk about materials that are in a library in another part of the school building. The desire to teach in the presence of books may lead to the establishment of classroom libraries (through either permanent or temporary loans of books to classrooms); it may lead to library reading hours (groups spending class periods in the school library); or it may lead to the teacher's spending office hours in the library. The specific device adopted is relatively unimportant; however, the desire to work with pupils in the presence of books will undoubtedly lead to the adoption of some devices that will lead to the desired end.

The discussion of the teacher's responsibility has largely been based upon the assumption that the school has an adequate library. What are the teacher's responsibilities if the library is inadequate or entirely lacking in his school? In such a case the instructor, in addition to his usual responsibilities, must assume those ordinarily assumed by the librarian. He must devote a rather large amount of time and effort to procuring needed materials (see Section II, above, for a discussion of traveling libraries and other sources of reading materials). He must attempt to locate appropriate reading materials that may be borrowed from other libraries. Oftentimes, the task of securing adequate reading material will be extremely difficult.

d. A Joint Teacher-Librarian Responsibility: Teaching the Use of Books and of Libraries. No mention has thus far been made of an extremely important function of the school of any type — elementary or secondary, rural or urban — namely, teaching pupils how to use books and libraries. Any school that wishes to embark upon a reading program will, of course, provide instruction in the use of books and libraries. In the school without a library this instruction resolves itself into teaching the use of the dictionary, possibly an encyclopedia, and certainly such mechanical features of all books as the table of contents and the index. In a school without a librarian the problem of determining who should give this instruction is simple; it can be given by no one other than the teacher. In many schools having librarians, however, the problem of whether the librarian or the teacher shall give instruction in how to use the library is a real one, concerning which there is much difference of opinion. Persons who believe that librarians should give this instruction state that most teachers do not know enough about the use of libraries to meet the responsibility. If this accusation is true (and, unfortunately, evidence seems to point in that direction), the situation offers a real challenge to teacher-training institutions.

> Opposition to having instruction given by librarians is largely based upon two contentions: First, that most school librarians have little, if any, training or experience in teaching; second, that having librarians teach the unit will cause pupils to regard the use of the library as something " extra " and as a matter of but little importance as compared with what is studied under the direction of the regular teacher.[1]

No matter who is in charge of library instruction, constant effort should be made to give this instruction, not as an end in itself, but as an aid to the solution of problems that pupils are facing as part of their regular class work.[2] Practice exercises, whether given by librarian or by teacher, are not sufficient. The crucial point is that the location of materials, both books and periodicals, must be constantly emphasized by the teacher in his regular instruction. The ability to locate materials cannot be taught and then forgotten. Repeated application must be made as a part of regular teaching.

In any program of instruction in the use of libraries, the problem of measurement arises. Tests of the informal type have long been given, but little has been done in setting up tests that measure all those abilities necessary for the effective use of the library. Such tests will prove helpful in charting the direction that library instruction must take for the individual pupil.

Throughout the discussion of the joint responsibility of the teacher and of the librarian in making the library function in the teaching program, emphasis has been placed upon the coöperative relation that must be maintained. The teacher, in a sense, assumes the rôle of librarian, for he works with his pupils in the presence of appropriate books (in the classroom library or in the school library, for example) ; the librarian thus becomes a teacher, for she guides and stimulates pupils as they study and learn. The library staff and the teaching staff merge into a united instructional staff in promoting the use of books and other library facilities in the improvement of teaching.

---

[1] B. L. Johnson. *Op. cit.* Pp. 46–47.
[2] For examples of carefully planned courses of study in library instruction see those published by the boards of education of Cleveland, Denver, and Detroit.

2. Using Reading Materials for Recreational Purposes

a. Importance of Recreational Reading.[1] All uses of printed matter other than those specified by school assignments, whether by English teachers or by teachers of other subjects, are generally designated 'recreational reading' and are properly encouraged as such. Such reading deserves special comment in this chapter for several reasons. First, materials that the individual reads from free choice represent the type that he will most likely read after he leaves school. Second, there is abundant evidence to show that three-fourths of the adult population read material that is mediocre, or worse, by any respectable standards of fidelity to fact, literary merit, intellectual maturity, sincerity of purpose, and social idealism. Third, such mediocre writing — whether propaganda, slushy sentiment, convincing statement of half-truth, or any other violation of what Aristotle understood Ethics to mean — will have an effect on any youngster who has not been systematically taught how to discover and escape his enemies in print.

For this reason the sociologist, the political scientist, the psychiatrist, and many others attach great importance to the values of recreational reading — a phase of reading that many schools disregard. Certainly a case can be made for more adequate attention in the schools to general reading for hearty enjoyment. The fact that recreational reading is distinguished from reading for study purposes does not imply that the latter may not be enjoyable and have significant implications for recreation. Indeed, the more effective the classroom teaching, the more important is its rôle in developing reading habits that carry over into pleasure reading.

b. The Library's Contribution to a Recreational Reading Program. Recreational reading is not, of course, confined to the school. It includes all the reading of the pupil, whether the source of the material be the home or the school, the public library or the news stand. As educators come to realize the importance of out-of-school influences on the reading habits of boys and girls, school librarians may be expected to take active part in influencing the pupils' extra-school reading environment. To this end, school librarians can aid parents in selecting books for pupils; they can consult with book stores and news stands

---

[1] For ideas and for many of the statements in the following two paragraphs, the Committee has, with permission, drawn upon an unpublished manuscript by Douglas Waples.

regarding appropriate reading materials for children; and they can co-operate with the public library in selecting books for boys and girls.

Ideally, if the school library is to assume leadership in guiding recreational reading, it should take two steps not ordinarily taken in schools. First, it should initiate a continuous study of the reading done by each pupil in the school, securing, of course, all possible assistance from other school departments. Second, it should interpret the reading records of pupils for staff members, who can motivate the reading that individual pupils can do to best advantage at a given time. Such procedures are most important, but at present they are beyond the possibilities of most school libraries.[1]

Several steps may be taken in almost any school by the school librarian who is awake to the importance of the problem of recreational reading. She can make informal studies of the reading of pupils in order to learn their interests and habits. The extent of such studies must be guided by available time and resources. To be most valuable, they must include reading from all sources that comprise the pupils' reading environment. The results of such surveys should be used in selecting materials for the recreatory reading of pupils and in guiding their reading.

The school library should surround pupils with books and magazines at every opportunity. Appropriate reading materials should be made a natural and ever-present part of the pupils' environment. The methods for accomplishing this result will vary materially in different schools. Frequent and regular presence in a library, of course, does much to adjust pupils to an environment of books. Schools having central libraries will attempt to make their libraries so pleasant and so attractive that pupils will wish to spend much time in them. Book exhibits and book posters add to the attractiveness of the library and also aid in directing attention to interesting books. Schools often make specific arrangements whereby pupils spend regular periods in the school library. In many elementary schools various grades come to the library for regularly scheduled reading hours. In some secondary schools homeroom groups likewise come to the library for regularly

---

[1] These steps are actually being taken in the eight-year study begun in 1933 under the sponsorship of the Progressive Education Association. In this study the development of freshmen in some thirty secondary schools is being carefully followed until they have graduated from college. The results of this study may well point the way to procedures suggested above.

scheduled reading during homeroom periods. A number of schools have abolished study halls and now require pupils to spend their vacant periods in the library. Evidence indicates that this particular plan of making books a part of the pupil environment results in a marked increase in the use of library materials for recreatory reading as well as for class use.[1]

In many schools it is impractical to schedule groups of pupils for regular periods in the library. Books can then be brought to the classroom, laboratories, homerooms, and study halls. In schools with inadequate library facilities, it is important that teachers and administrators utilize every opportunity to obtain reading materials from other sources, such as the public library, the county library, the home, or the state traveling library. It is obvious that the methods used in making books a part of the environment of pupils will vary materially from school to school.

IV. CONCLUSION

The school library is not an end in itself; it succeeds only to the extent that it contributes to the educational program of the school. If the library is to contribute effectively to the reading program, it must supply adequate and appropriate reading materials; furthermore, a united staff of teachers and librarians must coöperate to the end that these materials may be used both for instructional purposes and for recreatory reading.

---

[1] B. L. Johnson. *Op. cit.* Pp. 40–43.

SUB–COMMITTEE ON CHAPTER IX

Chairman

PAUL McKEE, Professor of Education, State College of Education, Greeley, Colorado

Associates

WILLIAM A. BROWNELL, Professor of Educational Psychology, Duke University, Durham, North Carolina

EDWARD W. DOLCH, Assistant Professor of Education, University of Illinois, Urbana, Illinois

ARTHUR I. GATES, Professor of Education, Teachers College, Columbia University, New York City

CAROL HOVIOUS, Head of the Department of English, San Benito County High School and Junior College, Hollister, California

FRANCES JENKINS, Assistant Professor of Education, University of Cincinnati, Cincinnati, Ohio

CHAPTER IX

VOCABULARY DEVELOPMENT

PAUL McKEE
Professor of Elementary Education and Director College Elementary School
State College of Education
Greeley, Colorado

I. INTRODUCTION

In the discussion of the nature of reading presented in Chapter II, emphasis was placed upon the fact that reading involves the realization of accurate meaning. If a child or an adult is to achieve this fundamental value through the various reading activities proposed in this report, great importance must be attached to the development of an adequate reading vocabulary.

As the term is used in this chapter, a ' reading vocabulary ' consists of the words, phrases, and other printed symbols that can be utilized by the reader in securing meaning. The school's responsibility in building such a vocabulary involves two major instructional tasks. First, opportunities must be provided through which the child builds concepts, understandings, or meanings, and becomes efficient in using the spoken symbols of these concepts. Second, training must be given to equip the child with the ability to identify the words, phrases, and other printed symbols that are used to represent these concepts or meanings in reading matter.

The first task is commonly known as the development of a rich meaning vocabulary, and as such is discussed in Section II of this chapter. The second task, commonly known as training in word recognition, is considered in Section III. Throughout the chapter the attempt is made to consider vocabulary development in the light of the total problem of reading instruction. Suggestions offered are based upon the hypothesis that vocabulary is, and must be, an agency for the realization of meaning in reading.

1. Two Fundamental Principles

Recent evidence shows that verbalism — mere word recognition and word reproduction — is prevalent in much of the reading that goes on in school, and that teachers are easily misled into accepting the child's oral or written reproduction of word forms as valid measures of satisfactory understanding of what he has read.[1] Additional evidence shows that too many children do not know the meanings of words, that they do not realize their deficiencies, and that they make little if any effort to discover the meanings of unknown words.[2] These facts indicate the need for school authorities to come to a clear understanding of the importance of the development of meaning vocabulary and of training in word recognition and the relationship between the two. The following statement of two fundamental principles, upon which the discussion in this chapter is based, attempts to provide this understanding.

a. Principle 1. It is clear that one achieves meaning in reading only insofar as he has concepts, or meanings, to associate with printed symbols. It is impossible for one to read printed symbols that represent unfamiliar concepts, even though he is able to recognize and pronounce the word forms accurately. Printed symbols do not give meaning to the reader; they merely stimulate him to recall familiar concepts. Then the reader, through utilizing these concepts, and frequently by combining them to build new concepts, achieves meaning by making it rather than by getting it from the printed page. Thus, meaning in reading comes from the reader's recalling and manipulating the concepts he possesses, rather than from the printed symbols at which he looks.

Furthermore, the degree and quality of the meaning one achieves in reading are dependent upon the richness and the accuracy of the concepts he possesses. With rich concepts, full comprehension can be secured; with partial or vague concepts only partial or vague meaning can be attained. Correct concepts make correct comprehension a possibility; false concepts can produce only misunderstanding. Likewise, with reliable concepts new meanings can be acquired during reading; with unreliable concepts misconceptions result.

Since one's concepts are the source of meaning in reading, and since the character of the understanding that one achieves in reading is determined by the richness and accuracy of his concepts, it is evident that the most fundamental task in the development of an adequate

---

[1] These data were obtained through a series of investigations made under the direction of Dr. Ernest Horn, State University of Iowa, Iowa City, Iowa.

[2] Evidence for this statement is found in an unpublished study by William S. Gray and Eleanor Holmes, made at the University of Chicago, Chicago, Illinois.

reading vocabulary is the building of many accurate concepts, or meanings, in the child's mind.

b. Principle 2. The possession of many dependable concepts does not in itself enable one to read. One must also learn to recognize familiar printed symbols quickly and accurately, and he must acquire effective methods of identifying unfamiliar word forms. The fact must be remembered that adequate teaching of word recognition does not necessarily enable the child to understand what he is reading. Thus, while training in the skillful use of effective methods of developing word recognition is an essential task in the development of a reading vocabulary, such training is important only when it is closely associated with the realization of meaning. Furthermore, training in word recognition should be subordinated to the development of concepts, or meanings. Constant application of this principle must be made in all instruction pertaining to vocabulary development if children are to learn to make correct meanings rather than merely to recognize word forms in their reading.

II. THE DEVELOPMENT OF A RICH MEANING VOCABULARY

The fundamental task in the development of a meaning vocabulary is the building of concepts, understandings, or meanings. These concepts necessarily include those of a general nature that are useful in all reading and, quite necessarily, concepts of a technical character needed in reading in a given field. A secondary but very important task is the development of the ability to utilize these concepts correctly in oral activities. The present discussion offers suggestions relative to the development of meaning vocabulary from the pre-school or kindergarten through the junior college.

1. Development of Vocabulary During Early Periods of Training

During the period of preparation for reading, at least two things should be done to enable the child to develop a meaning vocabulary.[1] First, means must be provided by which the child may acquire accurate concepts that will later serve as the source of meaning in reading. Second, there must be ample opportunity for him to become familiar with the common sound symbols of these concepts.

---

[1] For a more detailed discussion of the development of meaning vocabulary during the preparatory period, see L. Harrison. *Reading Readiness.* (Houghton Mifflin Company: Boston, 1936)

Several procedures may be used in developing needed concepts. Among these are the following:

1. Provision must be made for many worthy and concrete experiences through such means as effective activities, projects, excursions, construction work, dramatization, and the like.[1] It is well to keep in mind, of course, that inasmuch as the meaning one achieves in reading is determined by the nature of his concepts, these concrete experiences must develop accurate meanings. Experiences that provide the child with misconceptions probably lead to misunderstanding in reading. It is also important that the experiences provided be varied rather than limited in scope. Furthermore, such experiences should be thought about, interpreted, and used by the child in further work.

2. Pictures, including photographs, movies, and drawings, that present concepts truthfully should be used frequently in developing meanings to be realized through various activities.

3. Numerous opportunities should be provided under the direction of the teacher for the children to carry on informal discussion among themselves, to exchange experiences and ideas, to question one another concerning experiences spoken about, and to engage in conversations, story-telling, simple explanations, and other important oral language activities.

4. There should be much simple explanation by the teacher of new and partially familiar concepts. These explanations must be given in such a way that much detail, already familiar to the child, is used in explaining the new concept.

5. Every effort should be made to enable the child to feel dissatisfied with lack of meaning concerning anything he encounters, and to encourage him to ask frankly for such meaning.

6. There should be much oral reading and story-telling by the teacher. The material read, of course, should present new concepts and meanings in sufficiently familiar settings to insure clear understanding.

7. During the early stage of the period of initial instruction in reading the meaning vocabulary that the child has acquired is utilized in first reading experiences, presented usually in the form of 'home-made' materials. Soon, however, the child begins to read preprimers, primers, and other books. Consequently, during the preparatory period the teacher should begin to look ahead to discover what concepts must be developed in order that the child may realize meaning when reading this material. This looking ahead may well involve an examination of first books to be used, and it should lead to the discovery of needed concepts or particular meanings required rather than word forms. With a knowledge of the meanings that are needed, the teacher may then set about making provision for the acquisition of those which the children do not already have.

---

[1] Throughout this discussion, the use of experiences is emphasized as the most potent procedure in developing a meaning vocabulary.

In order that the concepts, or meanings, developed may become familiar to the child when expressed in spoken form, provision must be made for the development of his speaking vocabulary and his ability to use this vocabulary readily both in his own speaking and in following that of others. The following suggestions are appropriate:

1. In connection with all school activities, provision should be made for children to talk about the concepts that are being developed through any one or all of the means described above.

2. A rich and meaningful program of guidance in oral language should be followed. This very informal program will be closely related at times to the content of the first reading to be done; it will be based exclusively upon the child's experiences, and will provide for frequent use of the sound symbols of familiar meanings and growing concepts. Among other things, this program will include rich opportunities for (a) informal conversation about common, familiar experiences; (b) simple story-telling and relating of experiences; and (c) the giving of simple directions, explanations, and descriptions. This means that the importance of effective instruction in language as it relates to the development of a meaning vocabulary should not be overlooked. Available evidence shows that some supposed reading difficulties are probably language difficulties.[1] Furthermore, the speaking vocabulary of a young child is the vocabulary he thinks with, and speaking and listening to reliable content undoubtedly aid in the development of meanings.

The development of a meaning vocabulary should continue, of course, throughout the period of initial instruction in reading. Procedures to be used are much the same as those employed during the preparatory period. The following suggestions merit consideration:

1. The curriculum should be greatly enriched in all fields.

2. Many real and varied experiences should be utilized.

3. There should be much opportunity for children to engage in valuable types of oral expression, providing for the development of concepts through exchange of experiences and for securing familiarity with the spoken symbols that represent them.

4. Suitable pictures should be employed.

5. There should be much simple explanation, story-telling, and oral reading by the teacher.

6. The various activities that relate to reading experiences and grow from them should be arranged for.

---

[1] W. E. Young. *The Relation of Reading Comprehension and Retention to Hearing Comprehension and Retention.* (Doctor's Dissertation. College of Education, State University of Iowa: Iowa City, Iowa, 1930)

2. Development of Vocabulary through the Elementary School

At every grade level in the elementary school, children are frequently unable to achieve meaning because of the presence of unfamiliar concepts in the material to be read. Technical terms are a source of difficulty. Figurative language is particularly misleading.[1] Much difficulty is caused by the child's lack of familiarity with concepts referring to such matters as time, space, quantity, latitude and longitude.[2] Most startling, however, is the difficulty caused by the child's lack of familiarity with the various and particular meanings for given word forms, many of which, such as *get, run, aside,* and *with,*[3] are so well known to the teacher that the child's limitations are overlooked.[4]

Several different procedures may be used in developing a meaning vocabulary during the elementary-school period. All of these should be characterized by informality and reality. The fact that drill upon words, isolated from context, does not bring desired results [5] indicates that all terms should be taught in contexts that enable the reader to derive the meanings intended. The advantages of some of the functional or indirect procedures described below were summarized in a recent discussion.[6]

1. The elementary school should employ a curriculum that is increasingly enriched in the sense that children may have many more desirable experiences than is usual in most schools. These experiences must gradually build accurate concepts, and they must occur in different fields of human activity. For

---

[1] A. Ayer. *Some Difficulties in Elementary School History.* (Bureau of Publications, Teachers College, Columbia University: New York, 1926)

[2] Most of these data were collected through a series of investigations made under the direction of Dr. Ernest Horn, College of Education, State University of Iowa, Iowa City, Iowa. See also: L. Harrison. *Nature and Development of Time Concepts among Young Children.* (Master of Arts Thesis. Department of Education, The University of Chicago, 1935)

[3] E. W. Dolch. *Reading and Word Meanings.* (Ginn and Company: Boston, 1927)

[4] J. C. Dewey. *A Case Study of Reading Comprehension Difficulties in American History.* (Doctor's Dissertation. College of Education, State University of Iowa: Iowa City, Iowa, 1931)

[5] H. K. Newburn. *The Relative Effect of Two Methods of Vocabulary Drill on Achievement in American History.* University of Iowa Studies in Education IX. (State University of Iowa: Iowa City, Iowa, 1934)

[6] E. L. Thorndike. "Improving the ability to read," *Teachers College Record,* 36: October, 1934, pp. 1–19.

the child who has a wealth of worthy experiences in social studies, science, art, music, and in many other fields, a meaning vocabulary will develop rapidly.

2. The program of instruction in oral language should be so arranged that children will exchange experiences orally as a means of gaining new concepts and meanings. It is most important that the content of these language activities be concerned with many different fields of human activity, and that conversations, story-telling, explanations, and all other important oral language activities include topics to be read about.

3. Opportunity should be provided for the child to read a great deal of varied simple material. There can be no doubt that this is one of the most potent means of developing and refining meaning vocabulary. But the material used must be simple in the sense that only a few strange concepts are included. The only hope that a new concept may be developed, or that a new meaning may be added to a partially familiar concept through wide reading, occurs when that concept is surrounded with a large amount of familiar detail, sufficient to enable the child to build the meaning of the strange or partially familiar concept. Furthermore, such material must be selected with regard for the wide range of reading ability among children within a given class. Each pupil should have access to much material that is simple and that has sufficient familiar detail for him.

4. Beginning in the fourth grade, there should be definite and vigorous teaching of the use of the dictionary as an aid in the acquisition of meaning. The great difficulty here is that dictionaries too often define words by using strange concepts. There is little hope that this condition can be improved greatly until more is known about what words children understand at a given grade level.

5. Teachers of various fields, such as science, social studies, and literature, must do a better job than is usually done in preparing the child to read a given piece of material in these fields. Many concrete and real experiences should be acquired in sensible construction work, excursions, activities, projects, and so forth, that are related to the content of the material to be read. Furthermore, assignments should be concerned with the building of concepts that are required in reading, making frequent use of carefully selected pictures, simple explanation, and any other means that may be employed successfully. This careful building of concepts preparatory to the reading of a given selection is important, not only because of the need of successful reading in a given field, but also because if it is not done, the teacher, since she permits pupils to become satisfied by mere verbalism, is guilty of helping to produce careless readers who do not insist on understanding what they read.

6. In connection with the teaching of a given field, much of the class discussion or recitation should be concerned with the clarification of meanings and the removal of misconceptions. Teaching should be done in such a way that every child is encouraged to ask concerning the meaning of any strange

word he has encountered. This statement implies that the discussion should be considered as an opportunity for teaching rather than for testing.

7. Sound-motion pictures provide an excellent opportunity for developing concepts.

8. Materials for informal reading activities, constructed by the children and the teacher on the basis of familiar experiences, should be used throughout the elementary school. It is a mistake to discontinue the use of such material when book-reading is introduced. This is particularly true for the child whose meaning vocabulary is meager.

9. Every attempt should be made to develop among pupils worthwhile interests to be followed through reading. Because a child makes a determined effort to acquire concepts needed in reading about an interest of his own, this provision should go far in improving both the quantity and quality of his reading.

Some attention has been paid to more direct ways of developing meaning vocabulary by attacking words in more or less isolated form. The possible advantages and limitations of such procedures have been presented elsewhere.[1] Among the procedures of this type are:

1. The study of antonyms, synonyms, prefixes, and suffixes
2. Direct explanation of words appearing in important word lists
3. The use of exercises involving selection of synonyms, opposites, etc.
4. The keeping of a vocabulary notebook
5. The use of vocabulary games
6. The construction of pupil word lists of various types

3. Development of Vocabulary in the Secondary School [2]

By the close of the sixth grade, the child who has enjoyed continuously the advantages of an enriched curriculum, numerous real and varied experiences, and suitable wide reading should have developed an extensive meaning vocabulary. Unfortunately, at present, such pupils in the secondary school are too few in number. Verbalism is widespread at this school level.[3] Furthermore, teachers of the so-

---

[1] E. L. Thorndike. "Improving the ability to read." *Op. cit.*

[2] The discussion of this topic presupposes familiarity on the part of the reader with the pages that precede it.

[3] For example, see: (a) H. Short. *Concepts of Certain Qualitative Terms Used in Seventh-Grade Social Science Materials.* (Master of Arts Thesis, College of Education, State University of Iowa: Iowa City, Iowa, 1933.) (b) M. King. *Pupil Comprehension of Place Location Data in Junior High School American History.* (Master of Arts Thesis. College of Education, State University of Iowa: Iowa City, Iowa, 1934)

cial studies, science, literature, and other fields, everywhere report that they are unable to teach effectively because of the pupil's lack of reading vocabulary. The great majority of the difficulties are concerned with lack of meanings rather than with ineffective word recognition. Evidence collected to date shows that difficulties occur with words used frequently in all reading matter, with the different meanings associated with given word forms, and with figures of speech, technical terms, and qualitative terms.

There is no doubt that in order to improve instruction in the secondary school, concerted and determined action must be directed at the problem of developing meaning vocabulary. Emphasis should be given to the following suggestions:

(1) Because the achievement of meaning in reading in a given field depends upon the student's possession and use of concepts needed in that field, and because it is quite possible, therefore, for one to read with reasonable comprehension in one field and with very little in another, each teacher must recognize clearly his responsibility for enabling the student to build the many concepts required for intelligent reading in his field. A major task in the teaching of any given field is concerned with developing in the student the ability to read intelligently in that field, and the basic, although not the only, responsibility in performing this task is the development of meanings. It is well to remember, too, that the student who attempts to think in a given field without possessing dependable concepts is capable of doing only that type of thinking which leads to false conclusions and undesirable prejudices. Apparently the secondary-school teacher must engage in the task of developing the meaning vocabulary needed in his field if he wishes to insure acceptable achievement by his students, and if he wishes to be free from the guilt of producing students who are satisfied with verbalism rather than understanding in their reading.

When the teacher has discovered the concepts needed in his field the following procedures may be used to enhance their development.

1. Every effort should be made to utilize representative concrete experiences in the form of projects, excursions, construction work, experiments, and the like.

2. Frequent use should be made of the dictionary and encyclopedia in connection with the teaching of various fields.

3. There should be much wide reading in connection with the learning in all fields. It is understood, of course, that the material used will be composed of much familiar detail rather than of summary statements. This is essential

in order that the construction of a new concept, or the addition of a new meaning, may be possible. The materials will also cover a wide range in terms of reading difficulty.

4. Pictures, graphs, familiar illustrations, and simple explanations should be used frequently.

5. Assignments should include the clarification of unfamiliar concepts in the reading to be done.

6. Much time in the class period should be used for pupil discussion, for the utilization of important types of oral expression, and for the clarification of concepts and the removal of misconceptions rather than for the conventional types of quizzing.

7. Serious effort should be made to develop among students interests to be followed through reading. It is difficult to keep a student from developing concepts needed for reading in a field in which he is intensely interested.

(2) All secondary schools should secure much closer coöperation with respect to vocabulary development than commonly exists between English and the work in other curricular fields. Meanings encountered in various fields should serve as content for some of the conversations and other important types of oral expression. This practice is essential in providing familiarity with the spoken symbols of these concepts, and in promoting their growth through the oral exchange of experiences.

(3) The English teacher may make a more direct and formal attack upon the development of meaning vocabulary. Among the most commonly used procedures are the following:

1. Providing training in the use of the dictionary.
2. Teaching the meaning of isolated words found in formal word lists. This procedure is likely to be successful only with the intelligent and earnest student.
3. The teaching of synonyms and antonyms.
4. Training in building words from stems, prefixes, suffixes, and other words.

4. Development of Vocabulary in the Junior College [1]

The fact that reading without meaning persists into and through college is clear evidence that previous teaching and much college teaching is superficial and verbalistic.[2] Every college teacher whose stu-

---

[1] The discussion of this topic presupposes familiarity with what has been said in the preceding pages of this chapter.

[2] See: A. Atchison. "'Torrid, Temperate, and Frigid Zones' — Sources of Error in Children's Thinking." *Thirty-Second Yearbook* of this Society. Pp. 483–485. (Public School Publishing Company: Bloomington, Illinois, 1933);

dents must engage in considerable reading should be aware of this problem.

The task of developing meaning vocabulary at the college level is quite similar to that encountered in the secondary school. Emphasis is placed upon the following suggestions:

1. Each teacher in a given subject must assume this responsibility, not only with reference to the concepts needed for reading technical words in that field, but also for ordinary words unknown to a student at a given time.

2. There is a need for the use of concrete experiences, wherever possible, as a means of developing needed concepts for reading.

3. Great care should be used in all assignments to do whatever can be done to develop concepts needed for reading, bearing in mind that these concepts should be taught in the contexts in which they are met.

4. Many class discussions should be concerned with the building of concepts and the removal of false notions.

5. A given content course should make use of multiple references for wide reading, provided materials that include much illuminating detail are available to be used in building new meanings through reading. This does not refer to the use of multiple 'summary' textbooks.

6. College teaching should encourage the student to ask concerning the meaning of strange concepts, make him dissatisfied with verbalism, and foster frequent use of the dictionary and encyclopedia.

III. THE DEVELOPMENT OF WORD RECOGNITION

If the principles outlined in the preceding sections of this chapter are observed, the reading material provided for each child in the primary grades will contain few if any words of unknown meaning except those whose significance can be derived readily from the context. If the materials as a whole, as well as the particular words, are intelligible, silent reading may be a thoroughly meaningful experience, provided the pupil can recognize words with sufficient ease, speed, and accuracy to permit him to direct his attention primarily to the thought. To read orally with understanding and appropriate expression the pupil must be able to recognize and pronounce the words with ease, speed, and accuracy. Effective methods of recognizing and pronouncing words, therefore, must be developed. Since learners at all levels of advancement are often baffled by new and difficult words, many of the principles developed in this section have wide application.

A. C. Eurich. *The Reading Ability of College Students.* (University of Minnesota Press: Minneapolis, Minnesota, 1931)

1. Characteristics of Word Recognition by the Skillful Adult

A brief description of the techniques of word perception employed by the moderately competent adult reader will indicate some of the skills that the school must seek to develop. The adult can recognize several words, especially if they form familiar thought units, in a single glance comprising a fraction of a second. In such a brief exposure, the adult does not really see specifically the individual letters, or syllables, or even the words. He merely secures an 'impression of the whole phrase — a whole of significant parts. This high level of skill in perception makes rapid reading possible. Recognition of single, familiar words is even quicker, easier, and more accurate. Less familiar words may require more time — occasionally a brief ' looking-over ' in which, perhaps, the initial part is observed first, then the following parts, with or without another glance at the whole. A quite unfamiliar and difficult word may require deliberate effort to pick out, see, and sound (usually inaudibly) in order the several parts that catch the eye. Usually, the word comes to mind as soon as all these steps have been taken, or even before. Occasionally a very unusual word may cause considerable difficulty and may require, in addition to the observing and sounding of syllables, the sounding of some of the individual letters. In brief, the competent adult can recognize common words by a rapid and apparently superficial view of the word form; he has a variety of methods of working out the recognition and pronunciation of difficult words. To decipher unfamiliar words he begins typically with the quickest and easiest analysis but shifts to other devices when these fail. If the word is quite unfamiliar, he may be uncertain about the pronunciation even though he is reasonably satisfied concerning the meaning. In this case, he may go forward with his reading, or may look up both meaning and pronunciation in the dictionary. Provision must be made in school for developing the techniques that are essential parts of the adult's reading equipment.

2. Characteristics of the Child's First Attempts at Word Recognition

The child's first perception of words is very different from that of experienced readers. The beginner sees the word as a strange, complex, puzzling form. It is more complicated to the child than Chinese or Voodoo symbols are to adults, since the latter are aware of certain general principles of word composition and have had years of experience in studying many kinds of symbols. The child may not know that words contain definite letters or that they must be viewed consistently from left to right; otherwise *was* when viewed leftward becomes *saw*, or from the middle to end to beginning, *asw*. What the child typically sees is either a funny-shaped form with certain features, such as length or general outline, or certain details such as a hole (letter *o*), or a chair (letter *h*), or a tail (letter *y*), or high parts (tall letters like *l*, *k*), or dots over the *i*'s, or pairs (*oo*, *ee*), or other items that catch his eye. The child's first ways of perceiving words are never so useful as those of adults; they are not adequate to avoid confusing such forms as *boy, bag, toy, tag, dog,* or *there, their, them*. The child's method of seeing words must be improved gradually in the most serviceable directions.

3. Essentials of Effective Word Recognition

Effective techniques for word perception must be developed to enable the pupil:

1. To learn new words when they are first encountered or introduced by the teacher in order to develop a reading vocabulary.
2. To work out the full recognition and pronunciation of words that cannot be recognized instantly at sight during reading.
3. To recognize familiar or previously studied words with increasing ease, speed, and accuracy during reading.

In selecting techniques of word perception and methods of developing them, the teacher must take care to see that the techniques taught for one purpose do not conflict with those needed for another. For example, although children can learn to recognize a word by merely naming or sounding the individual letters in order, this method hinders, rather than aids, the quick and accurate identification essential to rapid reading. Similarly, although pupils can be taught to recognize most words merely by seeing the total shape or configuration, this device, employed exclusively by beginners, leaves them handicapped when the word cannot be recognized ' at sight,' or when a new word has almost the same configuration as an old one. The pupil needs a variety of techniques to meet the three major needs listed above, and these techniques must be developed so that they supplement rather than conflict with one another.

4. Statement of Principles for a Program in Word Recognition

School experience and our knowledge of learning suggest the following guiding principles as basic to a program in word recognition.

(1) Pupils should be helped through 'ear training' to discover that spoken words, despite their apparent unity, are composed of distinctive sound elements or syllables, in order that when they begin to observe and study printed words, they may more easily see word parts that correspond to the sound. Some children at the time of entering school have never learned to identify distinguishing sound elements in many simple words of wide usage; other children have never discovered that *enter* is composed of two sounds *en-ter,* much less that *sing* contains the *s* and the *ing* sounds, and that *string* ends like *sing* and begins like *strong.* A sufficient sense of the sound character of words can usually be derived from word-sound games based on telling words beginning like *boy,* or ending like *fine,* which may be introduced in the kindergarten or later. The recognition of words that rhyme is also helpful. Extensive, formal instruction is not required. Except for some special guidance and for demonstration involving the prolonging and repeating of sounds for the less apt pupils, instruction carried beyond enjoyable sound games is unnecessary. The habit of hearing the most obvious sounds in words is sufficient.

(2) The pupil must be shown that printed words (unlike almost all other objects in the world), when viewed in detail, must be perused from left to right. The difficulty of many beginners lies in viewing words from right to left, from middle to end to beginning, or in other random directions, as well as from left to right; that is, their eyes wander back and forth over a word. Reversal errors (*on* for *no*), wild guesses, and general confusion result.

(3) The pupil must be helped to acquire the habit of reacting attentively to words, if the meanings represented are to be recognized accurately. He must look sharply, and note the whole and its significant features. The failure of many children to learn and remember words is due to their passive, inattentive attitude toward the individual word.

(4) The pupil who is learning to read should acquire the habit of comparing words in order to note differences and similarities. Even if the pupil reacts to each word individually, he will not progress rapidly unless he compares and contrasts words with each other. Significant elements of words are often identified by comparing one word with others, especially with those that are similar in one or more respects.

(5) The pupil must develop the habit of discovering and seeing the most significant aspects and parts of words. English words are

very diverse in character. Since certain word features or parts are more helpful in some words than in others, the pupil must be trained to identify several:

(*a*) *The total shape or configuration.* Whatever other means of perception may be used, a sharp, quick eye for the total figure is essential. Although pupils must learn to see the elements within words, they should not perceive them in isolation but as parts-of-the-whole.

(*b*) *Larger component parts.* Such parts include terms in compound words (*policeman, upon*), or in words composed of a familiar word plus a letter or syllable (*darker, seeing, seen*), or of syllables and phonograms (*window, after, family*.) Ability to break words into the larger parts is particularly useful for several reasons. Fewer steps and less time are required than when smaller elements are employed. Since components of those types represent units of pronunciation, they are more easily sounded than other elements represented by such divisions as *sc-h-ool* or *ch-ildr-en*, which may be seen with equal ease. Furthermore, such components as syllables and large phonograms usually form effective basal clues for quick recognition in rapid reading when perceived as parts of the whole word rather than independently.

(*c*) *Smaller components.* Since some words can be worked out only in terms of smaller units, and since such units form the distinctive features of many words of which a large element or elements form the major portion, pupils must learn to see certain smaller parts. For example, familiarity with *th* assists in working out *this, that, they, then.* Since the distinctive features of *bring* and *sting* are the elements *br* and *st*, which appear with high frequency in primary words, the pupil is helped by learning to use them as recognition clues.

(*d*) *Letters.* Familiarity with letter sounds is very helpful, or even necessary, in analyzing many words. Knowing the sound of the letter *s* is helpful in making out such words as *say, sing, sight*, which are composed of this letter combined with frequently appearing phonograms. Such words cannot always be recognized at sight. The habitual analysis of these words, even words such as *run* and *big*, into all the single letter sounds is usually undesirable. By keeping attention directed to the content, many words may be recognized as soon as the sound of the initial letter is identified.

(6) Visual analysis must precede the sounding of word parts. The beginning reader will usually recognize a word as a sight word by observing its general appearance, together with some feature that strikes his attention. In some cases recognition may be the prompt result of a single glance; in others the recognition may be the delayed outcome of a search for a tell-tale visual clue or clues, such as those mentioned above.

If a rapid visual survey fails to reveal the identity of a word to a pupil who has learned to sound word parts, the following steps occur: first, the pupil sees separately the parts of the word that represent sounds; second, he thinks these sounds, or says them audibly or semi-audibly; and third, he unifies, blends, or combines them to suggest the word as a whole. Of the three steps, the seeing and breaking up of words into usable parts by visual analysis is primary both in the order of events and in importance. The child cannot give the sounds of phonograms, syllables, and letters until he has seen them in a word. Consequently, early stages of guidance should be directed to help the pupil learn how to discover in words the parts that are useful for ready recognition and, when possible, for sounding as well.

(7) Visual analysis should isolate word parts readily sounded. As the pupil acquires ability to analyze the visual form, he should be shown that the parts correspond to definite sounds. For example, when he sees in *baby* the two parts *ba* and *by*, the teacher can show him, if he does not discover this fact himself, that each part represents a sound combination. In this way is initiated the habit of supplementing the parts seen by the sounds they suggest. One of the difficult tasks thereafter is to make this habit function only when it is necessary and useful, without leading the pupil to employ it when a glance or visual study is sufficient and superior.

(8) Early work in word perception should be done with words the meanings of which are known to the children and which have already been introduced and will be used later. The learning experience should take the form of refining and improving perception of words already introduced by reviewing them frequently in comparison with additional words.

(9) Word elements should be recognized first by discovering them in words, not in isolation. To find *th* and *ing* in the words *thing* or *thinking* is very different from recognizing them when alone.

(10) Guidance should help the pupil to detect the word features that have appeared most frequently in the words in his own reading vocabulary. To teach children word elements that, however frequent they may be in English in general, will not be encountered for some time in the child's own reading is to waste his time and lead him to distrust the value of guidance.

(11) After pupils have learned to see similarities and differences in words and to discover common visual components and phonograms, they may profit by making up families of their own from the words they are reading. Thus a child may assemble such families as *can, cap,*

care, cat; black, blow, blue; day, play, say, may, away, and add new words to them as suitable ones appear. This procedure gives pupils a motive for analyzing words, helps them to master new words by associating them with words already familiar,[1] provides effective lists for comparing words and for revealing the common elements and distinctive features, and automatically provides for limiting word analysis to elements that really appear in the words the pupil is reading.

(12) Certain types of intensive and formal phonetic practices should be avoided. For example, it is futile to try to teach beginning pupils to give exactly all the forty or more letter sounds. Children need early only the more obvious and frequent letter sounds. To insist on their sounding out all words fully and definitely is a great error. When the other sources of suggestion — the general context, the meaning of the particular sentence, and the general appearance of the word as a whole and in its parts — are well used, complete sounding of all the elements is seldom necessary. " Just a hint of the word sound as given by one letter will cause the sound of the entire word to flash in the child's mind." [2] Furthermore, it is unwise to insist on any sharp division of vowels and consonants or the use of any formal system, such as initial or final blends. In general, the most helpful means is a combination of both procedures. For example, *same* separated into the sounds *s-a-m-e*, presents a difficult task in blending and, when sharply divided into *s-ame* or *sa-me*, an unnatural task. It is highly desirable for the child to give a natural unbroken sounding of the word following a visual scrutiny of it. If he is not able to do so readily, it is usually better to sound the word slowly so that the vowel sound is prolonged, connecting both the preceding and following consonants, as in ' *sa-ame.*' [2] This more unified, continuous sounding suggests the word sound more fully. The formal rules concerning long and short vowels, the influence of doubling consonants, and the like are too complicated and too often inapplicable or misleading to be of value in the primary grades.[3]

---

[1] The special merits of this 'association category' device are discussed at some length in A. I. Gates, *Generalization and Transfer in Spelling.* (Teachers College, Bureau of Publications: New York, 1935)

[2] E. W. Dolch. *The Psychology and Teaching of Reading.* P. 92. (Ginn and Company: Boston, 1931) For comments on difficulties resulting from such practices, see: A. I. Gates. *The Improvement of Reading.* (The Macmillan Company: New York, 1935)

[3] I. C. Sartorious. *Generalization in Spelling.* Contributions to Education, No. 472. (Teachers College, Columbia University: New York, 1931) and E. W. Dolch. *Op. cit.* Chapter IV and pp. 110–113.

(13) Pupils must learn to use meaning or context clues to assist them in identifying unfamiliar word forms. When children begin to read, they already have formed the habit of using the meaning of what they hear. This experience aids them in *guessing* the unfamiliar or poorly heard spoken word. Unfortunately the pupil's tendency to carry over this habit to the reading situation is sometimes blocked. Of primary importance is the fact that the meaning of a passage must be kept in mind and used simultaneously with the observation and study of the printed word form. This association is necessary not only because it makes word identification easier and more accurate but also because neglect of meaning during word study reduces or entirely disrupts comprehension. Teachers should remind pupils that thinking of the meaning helps them to recognize the word and gives them such guidance as may be needed to develop the habit and keep it alive.

Some children may seem to depend unduly on this device. The difficulty in such cases is not that they use the meaning too much. It is merely that they fail to employ other methods of attacking the printed word form. The remedy lies in teaching them to check their guesses; that is, to use the latter technique along with the former. Such instruction must be organized to induce them to use contextual meanings as much as possible when studying word forms. Instruction should provide experience in which it is absolutely necessary to employ both types of clues.

5. Procedures in Developing Word-Recognition Techniques

A type of approach that embodies some of the principles enumerated above will be briefly outlined. The method illustrated is suited to an early stage of reading instruction, but with modifications the procedure is applicable at various levels.

a. Selecting Suitable Materials. The first problem is that of selecting materials suitable for instruction in word recognition. As a matter of fact, anything suitable for the children to read is serviceable for this purpose. By using the words already encountered by the pupils in their reading, material of a type highly useful in promoting growth in word perception may be constructed. Certain rhymes, puzzles, interesting "Silly Sayings," and other short selections provide opportunities for gathering into brief form and effective arrangements words that merit special comparison and analysis. Comprehension exercises may be made for any selection in form highly suitable for word study.

For purposes of illustration, a selection deliberately made up of a large proportion of similar words previously used and, therefore, very artificial in character has been selected. Such material could be rubber-stamped on a chart or written in print-script on the blackboard or, for certain lessons, typed or mimeographed for desk use.

> Jack is a big boy.
> He has a brown bag.
> He has a big dog.
> His dog is called " Nap."
>
> John is a little boy.
> He has a blue hat.
> He has a black bag.
> He has a bad dog.
> His dog is called " Nip."
>
> John and Jack like to
>   play with the dogs.
> Nip and Nap play with them every day.
> They will soon be playing tag.
> Then there will be lots
>   of running and shouting.

b. Methods of Procedure. In the following description several ways of dealing with this selection are suggested. The order of the different activities will vary with the competence of the class as well as with the special interests and purposes of individual pupils and with the teacher's procedures in meeting the needs of particular pupils.

Step 1. Reading for the thought. The teacher asks the pupils to read the material silently. She then asks the children to tell and discuss what they have read, and asks volunteers to read the content orally for some good reason. It is important that all the children get the content of the selection clearly in mind so that the meaning will be used along with word-form clues in the study that follows. After the selection has been read and discussed, the word-study activities begin.

Step 2. Searching to discover words that look alike. The teacher suggests that the pupils reread the material in order to discover words that look very much alike in some respect. The pupils are likely to pick out such words as the following:

Jack	John					
big	boy	bag	dog	bad	hat	tag
Nip	Nap					
brown	blue	black				
play	playing	running	shouting			

As these words are discovered, the teacher or a pupil reads the material that contains them and points them out. The teacher may then point to one after another to help the slower pupil see them in sequence.

Step 3. Discovering and identifying common visual, phonetic, and other elements. As similar words are pointed out, the teacher may ask the pupils to tell in what ways they are similar. Children will suggest that some words are very much alike in shape (*bag, dog*), or in initial letters (*little, like*), or in the middle (*boy, dog*), or in final parts (*bag, dog*), or in form and sound, *i.e.*, contain phonograms as in the case of *blue* and *black, bag* and *tag*, or syllables as in *playing* and *shouting*. As the pupil suggests these similarities or identical parts, the teacher should point them out clearly so that all members of the class may see them. Work of this type may continue for some time until striking examples of similarity in the lesson have been discovered and discussed. The teacher should exercise sufficient guidance to make sure that the most helpful comparisons are made and the most useful elements are identified. She should, in fact, have in mind a systematic plan for progressing from the rough and crude early stages to the more refined and subtle phases of visual and phonic analysis, as suggested in the preceding pages. This general plan is suited to all stages and all useful types of word study and word analysis.

Step 4. Discovering and discussing differences in words. This step consists of calling attention to the parts or characteristics of words that distinguish them from others. It may be combined with the activities suggested in Step 3. For example, the question may be raised concerning how one can tell *bag* from *bad*, or *tag* from *bag*, or *blue* from *brown*. Pupils should be encouraged to point out the differences they see. In this way, the teacher can discover the basis of their discrimination and bring out better distinctions. This activity helps the teacher avoid attempts to bring out distinctions so subtle as to confuse rather than assist the pupils at the time.

Step 5. Further experiences in locating and comparing words adjusted to individual needs. For many children, the foregoing activities may be sufficient; for others, they serve mainly as demonstrations and explanations. The latter include less advanced children who follow the reading, identification, and comparison of words, but who are unable to contribute much themselves. For these, and often for the abler pupils, too, additional experiences, varied in type to maintain interest, may be employed. For example:

a. Location of similar (confusable) words in the text. Here the teacher may give orally a word, such as *big* or *boy*, or certain phrases, such as *big boy* or *big dog*, and ask a pupil to point them out on the chart. The other children should find them and tell whether the pupil sent to the chart is right or wrong. The purpose of this exercise is to have the pupil identify at least two words or phrases that are likely to be confused with each other. It demands accurate discrimination between words and rewards success in it. It is more difficult than some of those that follow.

b. Matching word cards with sentences in the text. For example, the pupil may be given three cards containing the words *Jack, big, boy,* and sent to the board to place them over the words on the chart. The first line on the chart contains the sentence — *Jack is a big boy.* The pupil is to try to find this sentence, read it, and then place the proper words directly over the words in the line on the chart. If he makes mistakes, such as placing *big* above *boy,* further exercises like those following will be needed.

c. Superimposing words on transparent paper on words on the chart. For pupils who have special difficulties in seeing the differences between such words as *bag, boy, bad,* a helpful device is to reproduce these words on cellophane paper and have the pupil place each over the word or words with which it is confused. The teacher can assist the pupil to see the differences and the common parts.

d. Matching cards containing identical and similar words. This is an exercise for the slower pupil in which he is given several cards with words, such as *big, bag, boy, dog,* and a second lot of cards containing the same words. The child is directed to put together the cards that contain identical words. If he makes mistakes, the cards may be compared and discussed.

e. Putting word cards in blank spaces. The pupil may be given word cards, such as *Jack, big, boy,* to fit in the spaces of incomplete sentences, such as the following, which are provided on a chart or written on the blackboard:

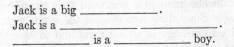

The pupil is asked to look at his cards and pick out and put in place the word or words that will complete the sentence so that it has the same meaning as the story on the chart. Any errors should be discussed and the child referred to the original chart containing the whole sentence. This exercise may be made more difficult by giving the pupil certain additional words easily confused with one or more of those previously used. Thus *bag* or *dog* may be used, as well as *boy,* and *John* may be introduced as well as *Jack.*

f. Reassembling sentences out of word cards. The pupil may be given cards containing all the words in a sentence from the chart and asked to arrange them to tell the story. If the pupil finds this very difficult he may be permitted to look over the correct sentence on the chart. After the sentence is constructed he may read it and compare it with the original one, or a strip of tagboard containing the proper sentence may be handed to him to place directly over the sentence he has assembled. This exercise may be made more difficult by giving the pupil extra cards containing similar words.

Step 6. Selecting comprehension exercises. This step may precede Step 5 for all pupils, be used by the abler pupils while the teacher pursues Step 5 with the slower, or be employed by the latter after Step 5. It employs various types of comprehension exercises based on the substance of the original text. For example, the following true-false statements may be placed on the board or on a chart.

> Jack is a big bag.
> John is a bad boy.
> Jack is a bad dog.

If the pupil misreads a sentence or misinterprets it, he may be asked to read it again more carefully, to study the individual words, or to compare the statement as a whole with the correct form. Any of the preceding comparisons and studies may be conducted on the basis of this material. Children may often be interested in making up similar true or false statements to show each other or to use as a class exercise. Such exercises may be developed as a coöperative enterprise. Seeking and finding the ideas and words that make good exercises afford very good training in word perception.

Step 7. Grouping words similar in general respects. This step consists of having children make their own families of words that contain common visual or phonetic elements or that are so much alike in general configuration or in details as to lead to confusion. On their own initiative, or assisted by the teacher as much as may be advisable, the children should scan the assignment for words containing ' old friends,' parts of compound words, syllables, phonograms, and so forth, and add them to the groups already arranged, or form new groups. As the children add a new word they should scan the members of the original lists. Since these lists contain the words most frequently confused, their ability to distinguish among them and to perceive the individual words quickly and accurately is improved. Since these lists provide easy recognition of the common elements, familiarity with these components is developed.

The general procedure just outlined may be employed, with obvious modifications, from the beginning stages to a point where further work on word recognition is unnecessary. After a pupil has learned to recognize a number of words, he may be assisted to identify and compare them and to point out similarities and differences. Obviously, the similarities and differences indicated at the beginning or at any other stage should be those that the pupil can readily see and utilize and that suggest the most useful types of clues to pursue at the time.

6. Special Problems Associated with Instruction in Word Recognition

As pupils progress in word mastery and word perception, they encounter special problems that merit consideration.

a. Syllabication. In working out the recognition and pronunciation of polysyllabic words, skill in dividing the words visually into syllables and, in many cases, in sounding them is essential. Although words encountered in the first year are predominantly monosyllables, many longer words soon appear. Ability to syllabicate is now helpful and can be acquired in some degree during the second and third grades. The sound analysis of monosyllables usually consists of giving two sounds for a word where only one exists in normal pronunciation, as in sounding *bat* as *ba-at*. This is a more difficult feat than pronouncing *baby* as *ba-by*. Thus any sensible seeing and sounding of word parts provide a basis for syllabication. The important consideration is that the pupil be assisted to adopt the easiest and most natural visual and auditory divisions.

Special difficulties arise in finding and using the syllables in long, polysyllabic words, such as *automobile*, merely because they are long and contain many syllables. The pupil, feeling helpless to deal with so complicated a total, may avoid an attempt, or he may proceed by dividing the total into a larger number of units — as *au-to-m-o-bi-le* — than he should, or he may observe the words carelessly, omitting parts.

Really astute guidance is needed to determine the rate at which to lead the pupil into the more exact types of syllabication. In general, the policy should be to move gradually from recognizing the whole word by sight, to seeing it as a whole of significant large parts, such as *auto-mobile*, and later to more detailed divisions, such as *auto-mo-bile* and *au-to-mo-bile*. To help the pupil with a particular word, the teacher may use such devices as pointing to or underlining the parts as she says them from left to right, or covering the whole and then uncovering each part just before saying it, and finally sweeping under the word as a whole.

b. Correlation with Spelling. At least two decades ago the advantages of spelling by syllables were pointed out,[1] and subsequent investigation and experience have confirmed the wisdom of this policy. The prevailing method of pronouncing the word part by part while looking at the equivalent portions in the printed word, then attempting to visualize these parts while sounding them softly or mentally, and finally writing them while recalling the appearance and sound, provides excellent practice in recognizing words as composed of syl-

---

[1] See the review by Ernest Horn in "Principles of Method in Teaching Spelling Derived from Scientific Investigations," *Eighteenth Yearbook* of this Society, Part II, 1919, pp. 283–290.

lables, in seeing the syllables clearly, and in combining them again into word-totals. When pupils are effectively taught to use this general type of attack in spelling, they are equipped to acquire the basal techniques essential for word study and syllabication in reading. Indeed, after this stage has been reached, deliberate word-form study may and should be largely confined to spelling. In reading, it is merely necessary to see that the pupil carries over the essentials of the technique and establishes the habit of using them.

c. Use of the Dictionary. All authorities agree that the pupil should learn to use the dictionary as soon as he is able to understand its content. Word-picture dictionaries restricted to the vocabulary of the basal reader are often employed to great advantage in the first year's work, and general dictionaries are usually introduced in the fourth grade. It is regrettable that the habit of using a simple, dictionary type of book, established in the first grade, remains undeveloped in some schools during the second and third grades. In other schools growth is promoted by exercises that provide for the classification of words as to meaning or in alphabetical order. Such activities in word perception as were suggested above also help pupils in learning to use the simplest 'regular' dictionary. Fortunately, books are now appearing that are much better suited to the needs and abilities of children who are completing the primary grades.

d. Perception by Thought Units. As stated earlier, the competent adult reader perceives words instantly in groups — often in thought units. Several types of misguided efforts to achieve this skill may occasionally be found in practice. The worst is the effort to force beginners to recognize a phrase at each fixation. It is impossible for children in the beginning stages to recognize groups of words in anything like the manner that adults do. To attempt to force them to do so is not only futile but likely to interfere with the development of any useful form of word perception as well. Another error is to emphasize phrase perception before word perception is reasonably well advanced in speed, accuracy, and general character. Phrase recognition is a complex habit that emerges from wide experience in reading simple interesting material. It is not required until very rapid silent reading is needed in everyday work.

Various devices have been employed for developing perception of words in groups. A first and essential feature is learning to isolate word groups that represent thought units. Work in observing such units, without pressure to perceive them in a single eye-exposure, may

be started some time before a reading grade score of **3.0** is reached.[1]
After pupils have achieved some skill in locating the thought units
and when the need for more rapid reading is evident, it is advisable to
demonstrate how such units may be read at a glance. For this purpose, quick exposures of flash cards or of phrases in sentences written
on the board or controlled by special apparatus, such as some form
of tachistoscope or lantern-slide or motion-picture projections on a
screen, provide helpful classroom demonstrations. Practice in reading
at a glance signs on the schoolroom walls, billboards, or placards in
stores is valuable.

Although these procedures help initiate desirable habits, real development must come through participation in natural reading activities. In the beginning stages, the use of reading material that is
divided by slightly longer blank spaces between the thought units or
in which alternative units are underlined is serviceable in making the
habit function. Later, experiences in attempting to read at a glance
the headings and subheadings of news columns and advertisements
in newspapers and similar materials in periodicals and books is excellent practice. By following such a program, ability to read ordinary matter should develop without extensive demonstration and
drill as the pupil experiences a real desire to read more rapidly.

7. Special Needs and Difficulties in Developing Word Perception

Growth from the uncertain, labored perception of the first words to
the easy and rapid perception of thought units, and from the use of
meaningless clues to recognition in which awareness of familiar syllables and common visual elements is implicit, is gradual and prolonged.
In the program that has been outlined, it is apparent that growth is
of a hierarchical character: skills of the higher level cannot be obtained until the underlying techniques from which they spring through
reorganization and combination have been developed. These habits
and skills are among the most difficult and subtle of all reading techniques. They are easily overlooked and readily upset by accidental
factors and unfortunate or inopportune guidance. To neglect their
development and leave them to trial-and-error learning is to assure
the appearance of many undeveloped and distorted habits. Scarcely

---

[1] For a variety of suggestions for this purpose, see: L. L. Zirbes, K. L.
Kellor, and P. Miner. *Practice Exercises and Checks on Silent Reading in the
Primary Grades.* (Bureau of Publications, Teachers College, Columbia Univer-
sity: New York, 1925)

less serious than neglect of appropriate guidance are several other common errors. One of these consists of overemphasis on one type of element or skill to the exclusion of others. Another is the sudden introduction of techniques without due degard to the pupil's equip-, ment at the time. For example, drilling on a large number of subtle phonograms or emphasizing rules concerning long and short sounds in the early stages will confuse or mislead most pupils. Another error is that of concentrating the training into a comparatively brief period, such as the second or third half-year. As recommended above, guidance should begin as soon as the pupil has learned to read a few words, and continue for several years to lead him forward gradually, not to push him violently, until he achieves versatility and competence. To do this effectively requires patience and intelligent guidance, not sporadic, violent drills. The plan suggested above contains features that make this policy easier to pursue, as well as more fruitful, than conventional, formal drill plans.[1]

---

[1] General discussions of methods of developing word recognition will be found in: E. W. Dolch, *The Psychology and Teaching of Reading.* Pp. 23–119. (The Macmillan Company: New York, 1931) and A. I. Gates, *The Improvement of Reading. Revised Edition.* Pp. 220–330, 357–371. (The Macmillan Company: New York, 1936.) Reviews of studies of the frequencies of various word elements in various word lists will be found in Anna D. Cordts and Maude M. McBroom, "Phonics," in *The Classroom Teacher.* Vol. II, pp. 420–432. (The Classroom Teacher, Inc.: Chicago, 1927) and A. I. Gates, *New Methods in Primary Reading.* (Teachers College, Columbia University, Bureau of Publications: New York, 1928)

SUB–COMMITTEE ON CHAPTER X

Chairman

Vera Alice Paul, Associate Professor of Speech, Whitworth College, Spokane, Washington

Associates

Alice M. Cusack, Director of Kindergarten and Primary Grades, Kansas City, Missouri

Ethel Mabie Falk, Madison Public Schools, Madison, Wisconsin

Arthur S. Gist, President of Humboldt State Teachers College, Arcata, California

Marjorie Hardy, Germantown Friends School, Philadelphia, Pennsylvania

M. Lucile Harrison, Colorado State College of Education, Greeley, Colorado

Ellen C. Henderson, Speech Specialist, Public Schools, Salt Lake City, Utah

Helen Mackintosh, School of Education, Miami University, Oxford, Ohio

A. T. Weaver, Chairman of the Speech Department, University of Wisconsin, Madison, Wisconsin

CHAPTER X

THE IMPROVEMENT OF ORAL READING

Vera Alice Paul
Associate Professor of Speech, Whitworth College
Spokane, Washington

The term 'oral reading' as used in this chapter designates the process by which the reader gives to others directly by speech the words and meaning of the printed page. Oral reading is, therefore, a social art involving the writer, the reader, and the listener. To have any excuse for asking people to listen to him, a reader either must be an interpreter, or he must be practicing the art to learn it. The basic habits of recognition and comprehension that are involved in fluent oral reading were discussed in earlier sections of this Yearbook. The purpose of Chapter X is to consider the social value of oral reading and the fundamental factors involved in good interpretation, and to present practical suggestions for improving and refining the oral interpretation of the printed page.

I. Social Values of Oral Reading

As compared with silent reading, the occasions for oral reading are comparatively infrequent. As a result, it has recently been given relatively little emphasis in many schools. However, both in and out of school needs arise for having someone read orally.

1. School Situations in Which Oral Reading Is Valuable

To name all of the school situations in which oral reading is necessary or advantageous would be neither possible nor interesting. A few typical examples should suffice; those given are not, of course, mutually exclusive.

1. To pool the findings on a subject for which several sources have been consulted by the group.
2. To read reports aloud to the group.
3. To read current events verbatim.
4. To read directions for the rest of the group to follow.

5. To read a problem for the group to solve or to read a riddle for them to answer.

6. To read stimulating contributions by worthwhile writers in order to enrich group discussions.

7. To substantiate statements or to prove a point by reading the opinion of an authority.

8. To have pupils in turn read entertaining stories, biography, adventure, travel.

9. To share favorite bits of literature that are valuable culturally, emotionally, and socially.

10. To read the lines of a play or of a dramatized story in order to add to the richness and pleasure of school life.

11. To read a letter or other communication of interest to the group.

2. Situations Outside of School That Require Oral Reading

The social advantages of oral reading are not limited to school activities. Many professional workers need to read aloud. For example, the lawyer, the preacher, the doctor, the scientist, the teacher, the dramatist frequently find themselves faced with the necessity of reading to others. Many other persons occasionally make real contributions by being able to read aloud effectively. Common situations in which this need arises are the following:

1. A secretary may read the minutes of his organization as a perfunctory routine or he may read them as though they were a record of importance.

2. A child or an adult may read the newspaper as a social service to an elderly person who cannot read it for himself.

3. A speaker may occasionally read from manuscript instead of speaking extemporaneously.

4. A member of a group may read interpretatively to a group of congenial people.

5. Parents may read to their children, thus giving them their first experience in story and verse.

6. Radio and forum speakers may greatly increase the value of their presentations by improving the clarity and quality of their oral reading.

We must not, however, lose sight of the fact that the social value of oral reading is in direct proportion to the quality of the presentation. If one's silent reading is inadequate, he himself is the main loser; but if his oral reading is faulty, both he and his listeners are losers. Society has no legitimate place for poor oral reading, and no excuse for poor oral reading exists in school — unless merely as a stage in the progress toward good reading.

II. Objectives of Interpretative Oral Reading

To teach oral reading as a perfunctory exercise in the program of the day is time ill spent; to teach it as a means to desirable ends, that of making for greater appreciation of literature, pleasanter social relationships, and richer living, gives it educational significance. Teachers should have both general, developmental objectives and immediate, teaching objectives.

1. General Objectives

We shall present briefly at this point some of the possible outcomes of oral reading that indicate general objectives toward which teachers should work from one school year to another.

1. Oral reading, especially in the early stages of reading, aids in the association of meaning with printed symbols.

2. When a pupil is learning to interpret, reading aloud facilitates the development of habits of accurate recognition and serves as a check upon the completeness of the associations formed.

3. Oral reading serves as a means for the development of pleasant, well-modulated voices. Much could be done to improve the frequently criticized American voice, if the potentialities of oral reading were realized in our schools.

4. As a result of teaching oral reading thoroughly, oral diction should be improved. The two requirements that the speech of the average person should meet are that it be easily understood, and that it approximate the cultural level of the section of the country in which he lives.

5. Wise teachers can make use of oral reading to help in the establishment of desirable personality traits. Among other advantages, the ability to read well orally tends to promote poise and confidence. Most children like to read and will accept personal criticism if it will increase their opportunities for reading. Most classes include the pupil who reads well, but who is impatient of the poor reader or is interested only when he himself is reading; the child who likes to show off but is a poor reader; the child who is too timid to do his best; the child who is nervous and tense whenever he attempts to read. Oral-reading situations offer many opportunities for overcoming such handicaps.

6. The oral-reading period presents an opportunity for inculcating a sense of social responsibility. The reader who realizes that he owes

his group the best he has to give, and listeners who realize that they owe the reader courteous attention until he finishes, have learned important lessons in pleasant social relationships. Oral reading is an excellent means of establishing group feeling. The mere fact that the same people frequently listen and interpret together seems to develop a valuable communal spirit.

7. Interpreting others' thoughts expressed in varied, well-formed sentences must inevitably give students a feeling for language structure. A sentence correctly read does for the ear what a diagram does for the eye; every word is correctly placed in its relation to the other words in the sentence. When a pupil is sensitive to the natural relations of the words, he cannot say *where* for *were* and remain unaware of his mistake. If pupils learn early to clarify by their reading the relations of the words in sentences, and the relation of sentence to sentence in the paragraph, they can hardly help expressing themselves orally and on paper with increasing ease and effectiveness. Oral reading is particularly valuable in initiating and refining language habits.

8. If a school has helped its pupils to acquire good taste, it has bestowed upon them something beyond price. Through their intimate experience with literature, and through standards of artistic interpretation built up through the years, students in their oral-reading classes should develop taste that will make for discriminating choices in what they read, what they select on the radio, what they enjoy in motion pictures, what speakers they like, and what theaters they attend.

9. Closely akin to good taste is appreciation. Someone has said that to read a poem well one must be a poet. One of the major aims of a teacher of reading should be to lead her pupils into the joy of creative thinking by helping them submerge themselves in the thoughts and emotions of the writer. This is appreciation.

2. Immediate Teaching Objectives

For teachers to have before them general objectives like the nine just mentioned is important; it is quite as important for them to have immediate teaching objectives in mind when directing oral reading.

1. A teacher of oral reading should insist that her pupils understand what they read; that they comprehend both what the writer says, and how he feels about what he says. To induce pupils to approach the printed page with the idea of getting complete meanings requires the building up of right attitudes.

2. The teacher knows that progress depends in part upon discriminating listening on the part of her pupils and of herself. No pupil can read his best when he knows that neither his teacher nor his classmates are listening attentively. Also, if teachers and pupils are keen listeners, many pupils who are fluent but mediocre readers will no longer enjoy the distinction of being considered good. When the class and the teacher listen alertly to the reader, and the reader listens to himself, progress will be made.

3. Effort is necessary to lead pupils to express emotion sincerely and without self-consciousness.

4. Concentration on the act of interpretation is essential to good reading. If a reader conscientiously does his best from first to last, his listening group will in all probability respond to his earnest endeavors.

III. FUNDAMENTALS OF ORAL INTERPRETATION

Oral reading, like silent reading, is essentially a re-thinking of the ideas on the printed page (see Chapter II). Such a conception of the reading process is a significant one upon which to base this section. The oral reader, however, has an additional responsibility; he has to express what he is thinking in such a manner that those who are listening will think with him. Just what the factors are that make it easy to listen to one reader and difficult to listen to another cannot be stated precisely. Nevertheless, because we believe that improvement of oral reading depends upon the insight that both teachers and pupils have into basic factors of interpretation, we may note some of the factors at least. The reading of most persons improves after they have learned something of the techniques involved in vocal expression.

1. Voice Control

Probably the most difficult factor with which teachers have to cope in oral reading is monotony of voice. The vocal apparatus is a sensitive, delicate mechanism, capable of revealing accurately what we think and what we feel. Most persons talk informally much less monotonously than they read. The reason is obvious; they are thinking what they are saying, and they are reacting emotionally to what they are thinking.

Meaning is carried by a variety of voice changes — changes in pitch, time, force, and quality. A few words about each of these aspects of speech:

a. Pitch. Pitch in speech has to do with the degree of elevation of voice tones. We have a speaking range as we have a singing range. One reason why our reading is monotonous is that we do not use our vocal range. If a stranger were to ask to be directed to the home of one of our neighbors, we might say, " Go to the end of this block and turn to your left. Mr. Blank lives in the second house on the right hand side of the street." If we gave our directions clearly, a trained listener would notice that we went up and down the scale from word to word, and that we definitely shifted the pitch on certain words and syllables — a pitch change called ' inflection.' If the stranger were obtuse, we might repeat our statement, but use even larger intervals and more decisive inflections. If a mother were to see her small child standing on a busy highway, she would probably call in a high pitch, " Richard, get off the road this minute." The rapid approach of a car would cause her to use a still higher pitch. If teachers can help pupils while reading to employ the pitch changes that they use when they talk, that will contribute much to the development of effective oral reading.

b. Time or Rate. Variety in time or rate of reading depends upon two factors: the length of pauses the reader makes, and the rate at which he utters the words between pauses. As we talk to our friends, we reveal both what we think and how we feel about the matter by variations in rate of speaking. Pauses help to make clearer the thoughts we express. By pauses of varying lengths we break up a sentence into thought units. If the person who was directing the stranger has said, " Gototheendofthisblockandturntoyourleft.Mr. Blanklivesinthesecondhouseontherighthandsideofthestreet," the inquirer would have gained a very indistinct idea of how to find his friend. To clarify his directions, the speaker must break up the sentences into idea units by intervening pauses, some so short they are scarcely discernible. What he would say would sound something as this looks: Gototheend‿oftheblock andturn‿toyourleft. Mr. Blank lives‿inthesecondhouse ontherighthandside‿ofthestreet. By pauses also, sentence is separated from sentence, paragraph from paragraph, and section from section. An audience follows with difficulty a reader who crowds idea units together.

Pauses also help reveal emotion; they often coincide with the pauses for meaning, as in the sentence, " For weeks and weeks we waited, and for months the candle burned at the window; but he never came back." Making the audience believe that the character interpreted by the reader had a heart-breaking experience depends partly upon the pauses between words and thought units.

Variety in the rate of utterance between pauses also reveals both thought content and emotional content. The person who directs the stranger must further clarify his meaning by prolonging certain words in each thought unit, and by quickening the rate of saying the other words in the group. The mother whose child is in danger is likely to show her terror by uttering all her words rapidly; the more frightened she is, the faster she is likely to speak. On the other hand, the one reading the illustrative sentence in the paragraph above would intensify the emotion by prolonging most of the words.

c. Force. Variations in force, in vocal energy, are significant in giving intellectual meaning and are most revealing in expressing emotional meaning. In order that his audience may hear, a reader applies energy to his words in keeping with the size of the room and of his audience. He also makes the thought content easy to understand by increasing the energy on the salient words and syllables. This method of strengthening points is called ' stress.' Many teachers labor under the misapprehension that stress and emphasis are synonymous. The result is that many untrained readers overstress the peaks of a thought unit and underinflect them. The effect of such reading is laborious and monotonous. Emphasizing a point in a unit does not involve stress primarily, but a combination of pitch, time, and force.

The fact was pointed out earlier that force is significant in revealing emotional meaning. Force to the reader is what touch is to the musician. To use as much force to direct the stranger to the neighbor's house as the frightened mother would use to call her child from the street would be insulting unless the man were deaf. To read " Four Little Foxes " with the same force as one would read " Hail to the Chief Who in Triumph Advances " would indicate that the reader had an inadequate understanding of the meaning of the poem.

d. Quality. Quality is that property of sound which enables us to recognize our friends by their voices as easily as we can by their faces. Perhaps the two media of expression most difficult to disguise are the expressions of the face and the quality of the voice. The sentences used by the person directing the stranger are purely factual; however, the listener can tell from the quality of the speaker's voice whether he is eager to be of service, or whether he is impatient at being interrupted. On the other hand, the mother's cry is a burst of fright. People hearing her can tell by the quality of her voice without distinguishing a word she says that she is frightened. By changes in quality the most personal and intimate meanings are communicated. Changes in vocal quality reflect emotional attitudes rather than intellectual meanings.

It does not matter whether one is reading of the influence of the Japanese current upon the climate of the Western coast of the United States, or Lear's defiance of the elements, the fullness of meaning that comes to the audience depends upon the reader's meaningful variation of pitch, time, force, and quality. In the interpretation of the first the most significant factors are sharpness of phrasing, definite pitch intervals, and strong pointing; in the second, quality, force, and tempo are of primary, phrasing and pointing of secondary, importance.

2. Bodily Control

Practically every part of the organism is used in effective speech. One expresses his thoughts and feelings by means of the body as well as by the voice. Oral reading can only be easy when there is proper freedom from tension and relaxation of the body. If the body is rigid, the voice is apt to be hard or metallic. If, on the other hand, the body is too relaxed, the voice has little vitality or energy.

Good physical poise suggests a sufficient self-possession and control to enable the reader to concentrate on the thoughts and feelings of the selection he is interpreting and to react emotionally to them. The effective reader must sit or stand in such a way that the body can show what the reader is thinking and feeling. If the shoulders are rounded or the head dropped or held too high, the balance of the body is incorrect. Bodily alertness increases alertness in oral interpretation.

The effective oral reader must be alert and active; he must reveal thoughts and feelings with face, head, and eyes. Inner meanings are conveyed effectively by various movements of the head, of the eyes, and of the shoulders, but these bodily expressions should be controlled and appropriate to the thoughts and feelings represented by the selection read. This will be accomplished if primary emphasis is placed upon the clear interpretation of meaning.

IV. TEACHING ORAL READING

1. Place of Oral Reading in the School Program

That oral reading has a place in the school program needs no confirmation. Even when enthusiasm for silent reading was at its height, most schools gave some time to reading aloud. However, the scope of oral reading has not been given enough consideration. The teaching of oral reading for its own sake means little. The case is much the same as that of teaching penmanship. If the writing period were the only time principles of good penmanship were observed, there would be little value in teaching it. Obviously, penmanship is taught in order that the students' writing in all subjects may be legible. The same situation holds in oral reading. Every curricular field that involves reading provides opportunity for good oral interpretation; consequently the teacher of each subject is in a sense a teacher of oral reading. Basic guidance in acquiring appropriate habits is essential; the use that pupils make of their instruction depends greatly upon the care with which all teachers direct oral reading activities.

For many reasons, it is impossible to outline a plan for fitting oral reading into the school program. Any system, however, in which progress in oral interpretation is expected must provide for both learning and practice in it.

a. Basic Instruction in Oral Reading. The quality of the oral reading in our schools today would be improved if these points were generally recognized:

1. That the techniques of oral reading should be developed for all pupils and taught specifically to some.

2. That the techniques cannot be effectively taught incidentally, but that a time must be set aside for learning the art.

3. That all pupils at a given grade level do not require the same techniques and therefore can often be taught more effectively in small groups than in large groups. The work of these groups must be geared into the reading program in terms of the objectives of a semester. Such groups should be flexible and should allow children to move from one group to another in terms of their needs. There must also be situations in which the whole group works as a unit.

4. That the teacher with a pleasant voice, accurate speech, and a knowledge of the fundamentals of voice production can do more for the oral reading of her pupils through the models that she presents than can any amount of practice or drill on the isolated techniques of speech.

5. That the coöperative setting up of standards by which oral reading shall be judged is more effective than a great deal of extemporaneous criticism of individual readers. Preceding an oral-reading period and early in the semester, the teacher and children should discuss what they know about oral reading. Then they should set up a list of things which they expect a good reader to do. Such a list might include such points as (a) speak clearly and distinctly;

(b) pronounce words correctly; (c) read in such a way that the audience will enjoy the story, and (d) sit in a comfortable position. These points should be modified and added to as they are used to evaluate the oral reading.

In addition to being taught to read aloud, pupils should be given frequent opportunities to put into practice what they are learning. When the school has one teacher to a grade, practice under observation is easy; but in a school of special teachers a spirit of close coöperation should exist between the subject-matter teachers and the reading teacher. The run of the school day offers many opportunities for audience reading. The periods for opening exercises and recreational reading, and the literature, history, and geography classes afford natural audience-reader situations.

b. Audience Reading. The value of audience reading will be increased if certain practices are observed.

1. The audience reading period should be unique among the periods of the school day. Children and teacher should approach it with pleasure and anticipation. The teacher or the children responsible for the period should stimulate curiosity and interest in the material to be used.

2. It is important that the material read should be something that the group actually wants to hear.

3. The word ' audience ' connotes listeners; in ' audience reading ' no book should be in evidence except the one held by the reader. If pupils are reading in turns at sight, the child who has read can easily pass the book to the child who is to follow, and if the teacher selects the logical breaks in the composition, the pause is not detrimental. The word ' audience ' also connotes a group seated in an informal manner. Teachers who are so fortunate as to have movable seats in their classrooms can arrange them in a double semicircle. In rooms where seats are fastened to the floor, children may sit together. In both cases the reader will sit facing the audience.

4. The laboratory, or practice, period and the audience reading period should be kept distinct. No reader can give himself over freely to the interpretation of a passage if he expects to be interrupted for corrections. Children who read to an audience are entitled to the same courtesy that should be shown an adult reader. Occasionally at the end of the period a few general comments may be made, such as, " I think Fred's pronunciation was much better; I did notice, though, that he still says ' ketch.' "

5. It is also important that no poor audience reading should be permitted. Every child should succeed. The teacher should know what each child is capable of doing and not allow him to attempt something for which he is not ready. Pupils should be encouraged to examine with the teacher or with another pupil, before reading, material with which they are not familiar, even

when the passage is to prove a point or to amplify a statement in a geography or history period.

6. Few questions should be asked during such a period. Questions should refer to character, situation, or central idea. Such a question as, " Why is this a good title for a poem? " illustrates the last-named type.

c. Oral Reading in Various Subjects. If oral reading is to be a factor in content subjects, the types of reading must be taught that will be needed in those subjects. In general, there are two occasions for oral reading: first, when the material is read at sight, and second, when the material is prepared in advance. However, there are gradations between the two. Sight reading, which requires quick, accurate recognition and a sentence sense, will be mere verbalism if it is attempted before mature reading habits are established. At any grade level, the material used should be easy enough to eliminate difficulty in word recognition, phrase grouping, and sentence structure. The material should be interesting to the readers and the audience. Even good readers differ in their sight-reading ability. Those who are inclined to have ' stage fright ' should be handled considerately.

Perhaps the most common situation involving oral reading for the average person in or out of school is the one in which he reads aloud after he has read the material silently once or twice. Such material may be more difficult structurally and in vocabulary than may be safely risked for sight reading.

Sight reading and the reading of partially familiar material have their place both in school and out. However, all formal reading should be carefully prepared. Such preparation demands that the interpreter read the selection aloud so critically that he knows exactly what inflections are best, where the pauses are, what parts he should speak slowly, what parts quickly, and how he can most effectively interest or stir his audience. The chief reason that supposedly prepared reading is poor is that people are not willing to pay the price of preparing adequately to read well. In all school activities that involve oral reading the line between casual preparation and thorough preparation should be clearly drawn, and under no circumstance should students be permitted to read at sight, or after only a hasty perusal, material that requires careful preparation.

2. Improving the Quality of Oral Reading

After oral reading has been fitted into the school program, the next step logically is to give some suggestions as to how the quality of the reading may be improved, and how the reading period may be made interesting and valuable.

a. Selection of Appropriate Material. The choice of material for oral reading can make the class period a success or a failure. In selecting material for sight reading, the vocabulary should be at least a grade lower in difficulty than the one in which the children are classified. New stories will probably succeed better than very familiar ones. If the teacher adopts the principle, " Begin with children where they are," she will choose material in which she knows the group is interested. For groups that do not yet enjoy reading aloud, humorous stories and poems serve as an excellent starting point.

However, the teacher should attempt to acquaint children with all types of reading material through the audience reading situations. They should come to know folk tales, fairy stories, poems, plays, letters, history, biography, travel, short stories, nature and science, myths, legends, fiction, newspapers, and magazines. The particular types selected depend somewhat upon the grade level of the children.

The teacher may find help in such well-known sources as those listed in the recent pamphlet from the United States Office of Education entitled " Aids in Book Selection." This bulletin will lead her to materials of known value. She should be guided also by the definitely expressed interests of her own group. These should be followed, but at the same time they should be broadened and strengthened.

b. Necessary Techniques. To discuss all the techniques that children should learn in order to read well is impossible here. Those who are teaching reading should familiarize themselves with recent texts on oral interpretation, several of which are to be found in the bibliography at the close of this chapter. In the next few paragraphs, therefore, we shall attempt to deal with only a few of the faults common to oral reading from the early elementary grades through the college.

(1) Pronunciation. — Oral diction is generally poor. A good reader first of all knows how to pronounce words. He knows the sounds of which the words are composed; he recognizes the English sounds by ear, and by sight when he looks words up in the dictionary. Such recognition requires ear training through the early and middle grades, and a knowledge of diacritical marks.

The pronunciation of polysyllabic words is a phase of diction to which special attention should be given. There is a simple principle of pronunciation that all teachers should know, and of which pupils should be aware as early as they are able to understand it. The principle is this: strong syllables should be strong; weak syllables weak. The word *municipality* will serve for illustration. Good pronunciation demands that *mu* be minimized by pitching it low, uttering it quickly and lightly; that *nic* be strengthened slightly by raising the pitch and increasing the time and force; that the *i* be scarcely audible; that *pal* be strengthened decisively by heightening the pitch well above the other syllables and by increasing the time and the force so that it is definitely the peak of the word; that the third *i* be scarcely audible; and that the *ty* be given slight value. The teacher of elementary-school pupils may indicate the rhythm of such a word, and the strong and weak syllables, by gently tapping with her pencil.

(2) Phrasing. — Oral diction has to do not only with pronouncing individual words, but also with putting words together into groups, or phrases. In reading the words of a phrase the same principle of peaks and depressions holds. *On the top of the hill* presents the same problem of weak words and strong words as *municipality* presents of weak and strong syllables.

Since the showing of the relative values of words by strengthening a phrase at one point and weakening it at others is of vital importance as an oral-reading technique, brief discussion of the subordination of words should not be amiss. Sometimes a teacher becomes diction conscious, and notices that her pupils are not saying *an, had,* and *was,* as the dictionary indicates they should be pronounced. She straightway goes about to improve their speech by insisting on definite *ăn*'s, *hăd*'s, and *wäs*'s. She fails to recognize that the function of the dictionary is to give the pronunciation of individual words, not the sound of the word as it is fitted into a sentence. In uttering the weak words in a sentence, the time element is important. Consequently, the vowels of weak monosyllabic words in a phrase tend to be uttered with what is known in phonetics as the neutral sound (sometimes called the relaxed *u*). It is a very quick vocalization that sounds something like *ŭ,* but is much more quickly and lightly uttered. Most dictionaries indicate this sound in polysyllabic words by italicizing the letter that takes the neutral sound. It is, therefore, not " thŭ book," but " th*u*-book "; not " *ŭ* boy " but " *u*boy." We do not say, " He came from thu house," but " H*i*came fr*u*mth*u*house." However, if the meaning should make *from* the peak, the *o* would become the kind of *o* that the dictionary indicates it should be. In general, articles, prepositions, auxiliaries, and personal pronouns are weak.

Some teachers are afraid that, by encouraging children to utter weak words lightly, they will be fostering slovenly speech. They need have no such fear. Anyone but a speech defective can say one-word-at-a-time, but it takes real vocal agility to touch the words just enough never to miss them, yet never to oversound them. The good reader might be compared with the pianist who never misses her grace notes, never blurs her tones, yet never gives a note more value than the rhythm justifies.

Coördinate with the reading of a single phrase is the breaking of a sentence into word groups. The majority of students, even in college, phrase poorly. Correct phrasing should be started as soon as the children put four or five words together to make a complete thought and should be continued with eternal vigilance as the learners' sentences grow increasingly difficult. The technique is essential for intelligible oral reading, and a teacher who finds a student who cannot phrase should start him on easy sentences and continue to help him until he can break up difficult ones.

(3) Significance of Punctuation Marks. — A word should be said about the relation of punctuation marks to oral interpretation. Teachers still say, " Let your voice fall at the period, let your voice rise at the question mark," and college students still say, when their phrasing is criticized, "But there is no comma." As soon as children encounter punctuation marks in their books, they should be informed that the author has placed them there to help his readers grasp his meaning; learners should never be allowed to think that punctuation marks are there to tell them how to *give* the meaning. From the early grades children should be taught to end a sentence naturally as they talk; that is, end it with the inflection that carries to a conclusion the complete meaning of the sentence.

(4) Use of the Voice. — In the reading of children, in particular, there are two common voice faults. First, the voice does not sound natural; second, the speaker seems to get out of breath. Every teacher is familiar with the typical reading voice, high pitched and strained. A reader with such a voice cannot express shades of meaning. He must be put at ease and induced to relax, particularly his throat and jaw. Students should be made to understand their problem and be taught to listen for strained quality in their voices.

A tight voice and inadequate breath often go together. If a reader is at ease, he is likely to know when he should take a breath, though not always. Many students need to be taught to keep enough breath in their lungs to insure their getting through a sentence effectively and in good form. To do this, unless the sentences are very short, they must inhale briefly during the longer pauses of the sentence.

Except in specialized classes of interpretation, voice training divorced from meaning has little place. From grade to grade students should grow in appreciation of the richness of meaning on the printed page, refine their techniques for interpreting meaning, and better their standards for evaluating their performance. The way to promote satisfactory growth is by carefully planned laboratory periods, in which both teachers and pupils experiment in the use of their voices to express meaning adequately.

Reading poetry well is important both for its intrinsic value and as a means of voice training. On the whole, from the elementary school to the senior college, students read poetry poorly. Here are three suggestions for training in this phase of oral reading:

1. Those reading poetry should be taught to ask themselves, " What is the poet saying? " In a measure the success of their interpretation depends upon the answer. When students realize that a poem says something about things that they have thought, felt, and imagined, the sentences become intelligible.

2. When readers get little meaning from the words of a poem, they are inclined to scan instead of to interpret. A poem is written in a pattern of weak and strong syllables; and that pattern is all the reader gives who scans: *ta DUM ta DUM ta DUM*. When he begins to interpret the poet's meaning, he phrases, inflects, prolongs some of the words, pauses for emotional meaning, and uses the force and quality that seem to him best to express how the author feels. The pattern of the poetry is still present, but the reader gives meter plus meaning.

3. The language of poetry troubles students. Inverted order, often a stumbling block, should be made clear; figurative language often obscures meaning, and students should be taught to distinguish between figurative and literal language. The run-on lines many times need special attention.

Through the group reading of poetry teacher and pupils can develop the techniques involved in good pronunciation, clear enunciation, and pleasing interpretation. This practice is known as ' verse speaking.' Children develop a genuine interest in it because they see a definite reason for reading correctly, clearly, and beautifully. In the past ten years verse speaking has been introduced into the United States, and in many centers it represents an important English activity.

In the typical elementary school the children of a given room or a group selected from various rooms comprise the verse-speaking choir. This work may be carried on also in the high school and in adult groups. The voices are first sorted to form high, low, and medium tone groups. Poetry selections are read in unison, antiphonally, or with narrator and characters. There are other possible variations. Sometimes a singing choir forms the background for the speaking choir by humming an appropriate accompaniment. The use of a simple stage setting, uniform costumes, and lighting effects adds to the interest of the presentation. Selections must be chosen from the standpoint of both audience and performing group. In practice periods children read the poems. In later periods they know the poems so well that a printed copy is unnecessary. In this fashion memorization is accomplished unconsciously. The fact should be pointed out that in concert work of any type the performance and needs of individuals are subordinated to the group activity.

c. Procedure for the Laboratory Period. The period in which teacher and children share reading experiences has many possibilities. It may be organized in two different ways. In one, the teacher, as leader or reader, may use a wide variety of methods to make the situation interesting and challenging. These may be mentioned:

1. Perhaps, as she reads a selection, she stops for comments or questions from children that call for interchange of experience.

2. She may read from section to section of a story for which headings in jumbled order have been placed on the blackboard. Children match the part of the story as it is read with the proper heading.

3. The teacher summarizes the early part of a book, reads to a point of high interest, has children suggest the ending, then reads and compares. Instead of the last step, children may read the book for themselves.

4. The teacher reads a story or a poem and has children suggest possible titles.

5. Sometimes it is interesting to read a group of poems. These may be poems entirely unlike, all of similar type, poems centered about a character, or poems centered about a period in history.

6. Toward the close of a semester, when children have enjoyed many poems, a poetry memory contest may be staged. Children write ten numbers on a page. The teacher then reads some lines from each of ten poems. Children try to recall the title of each poem and write it in the proper space.

7. Another possibility is a reading club, which will set up certain oral reading achievements as a basis for membership.

In similar fashion children may take the lead. They may use some of the schemes for creating interest that have been indicated for the teacher.

1. Children may prepare in advance to read a story. This may be done individually, in ability groups, or in mixed groups.

2. One group reads to the other as audience when there are two classes in the room.

3. Children read easy material, at sight, in turn.

4. A pupil summarizes, then reads the most interesting part of the story.

5. A pupil selects and prepares for reading material he will present to pupils of a lower grade. This is especially helpful to the pupil who cannot read material at his own grade level.

6. Pupils serve as exchange readers with other rooms.

7. A pupil reads while a group pantomimes.

8. Children give a conversational dramatization in which one child is the Book, and others read the character parts.

9. Children come prepared to read their favorite poems.

10. Children reread poems previously heard in order to do a variety of things, like creating pictures or bringing out the rhythm.

Group reading can be used from the early grades to the college. Students secure social and emotional satisfaction from participating, and many timid ones express themselves as they never would when reading alone. Teachers can give training in diction, phrasing, pausing, breathing, and emotional effects through voice changes, to the group as a whole that they could not possibly find time to give to individual members. Teachers should take care that the reading is really a group interpretation, not mechanical concert reading.

Time may be spent profitably on various phases of diction. Children enjoy ' tongue twisters ' occasionally. At least they serve to make the children think about their enunciation.

The elementary grades are the crucial periods in teaching oral reading. By the time pupils reach the sixth or seventh grades their oral reading habits are fairly well set. If these habits are serviceable, all of the pupils' subsequent study of interpretation will be a matter of deepening their power of expression and of enriching their minds and spirits. If the habits are not serviceable, then we should extend the training. High schools and colleges should give remedial work for those who have formed poor oral-reading habits, and should give to those who can read well opportunities, through class work in literature and through specialized courses in interpretation and in acting, to grow in culture and appreciation, and to acquire an enriched personality.

REFERENCES

Barrows, Sarah T., and Pierce, Anne. *The Voice and How to Use It.* (The Expression Company: Boston, 1933)
Discusses the vocal mechanism and its use. Has many exercises for the development of voice and diction.

Basset, Lee Emerson. *A Handbook of Oral Reading.* (Houghton Mifflin Company: Boston, 1917)
The philosophy underlying this discussion is that clear understanding is the basis of sane, convincing speech. Appreciation and feeling follow thought.

Case, Ida Mae W., and Barrows, Sarah T. *Speech Drills for Children in the Form of Play.* (The Expression Company: Boston, 1929)
A good book for teachers in the lower grades.

Corson, Hiram. *Voice-Spirited Education.* (The Macmillan Company: New York, 1918)
A most inspiring book for those interested in oral reading.

Fuller, H. H., and Weaver, Andrew T. *How to Read Aloud.* (Silver, Burdett and Company: Newark, 1935)
Principles of oral reading stated for the untrained reader. Has much illustrative material.

Henderson, Ellen C. *Reading and Speaking Techniques.* (Improvement Publishing Company: Chicago, 1936)
A book for teachers in junior-high schools and grade schools.

Kerfoot, J. B. *How to Read.* (Houghton Mifflin Company: Boston, 1910)
An excellent book on reading as an extension of experience.

Mearns, W. Hughes. *Creative Youth.* (Doubleday, Page and Company: Garden City, New York, 1926)
Discusses how, by developing a proper environment, the creative spirit in children can be freed.

Mosher, Joseph Albert. *The Production of Correct Speech Sounds.* (The Expression Company: Boston, 1929)
An excellent text for the untrained teacher. It takes up the sound as it should be made, and the common deviations from the standard. The study is based upon diacritical marks.

Parrish, Wayland Maxfield. *Reading Aloud: A Technique in the Interpretation of Literature.* (Thomas Nelson and Sons: New York, 1932)

Although the discussion and the illustrative material is on the college level, the underlying principles of oral reading are so well stated that a teacher in the elementary grades can get valuable help from this book.

Paul, Vera Alice. *Present Trends of Thought on Oral Reading.* (University of Iowa Bulletin, College of Education of Iowa Series, No. 31, 1932)

A survey of the attitudes toward oral reading during the past twenty or twenty-five years.

Woolbert, C. H. *The Fundamentals of Speech.* Chapters X–XIV. (Harper and Brothers: New York, 1927)

Makes application of principles of good speaking to the problem of oral reading. The subject is divided into the logical and the emotional content of material.

Woolbert, C. H., and Nelson, S. E. *The Art of Interpretative Speech.* (F. S. Crofts and Company: New York, 1927)

Discusses interpretation as an art which involves first the getting of meaning, and second of giving the meaning. A valuable text on the college level.

CHAPTER XI

INDIVIDUAL DIFFERENCES AND THEIR IMPLICATIONS WITH RESPECT TO INSTRUCTION IN READING

Donald D. Durrell
Professor of Education, Boston University
Boston, Massachusetts

Children of the same age differ greatly in their abilities, habits, and interests in reading. This chapter discusses the causes of individual differences, indicates how they may be discovered in the classroom, and suggests methods of providing for them.

Variations from the average are not to be considered as due mainly to extraneous causes that can be removed by appropriate treatment. The range of individual differences in reading will increase rather than diminish under an excellent instructional program. Children with superior mental endowments are capable of achieving high levels of ability and of pursuing a wide variety of interests in reading, while children with inferior ability are ordinarily limited to lower achievements and a narrower range of interests even under the best conditions. While a certain uniformity of interests within a learning group is desirable for developing social understanding, the infinite variety of things to be learned at any school level makes it important that differences in interests should be encouraged, to the end that the classroom may be enriched by the contributions of various members. Individualization in interests and abilities when properly utilized enhances the degree of socialization in the classroom.

The classroom teacher must bear most of the responsibility for providing for individual differences. While various types of ability grouping tend to make classes more homogeneous, particularly in general achievement levels, a wide variety of differences is always present. Children with like scores on achievement tests differ in certain phases of reading, such as amount of voluntary reading, interests in reading, rates of learning, understanding of word meanings and concepts, accuracy and completeness in oral and written recall, organization and retention of ideas, imagery in narrative reading, skills in word analysis, ability to adapt their reading to various types of assignments, ability to select suitable materials, expression in oral reading, speed and accuracy in silent reading, and many other skills. Ability grouping will generally decrease the range of reading levels in classrooms, but it leaves unsolved the major problems of providing for individual differences.

I. CAUSES OF INDIVIDUAL DIFFERENCES

There are so many causes of individual differences in reading achievement among pupils of the same age that only the outstanding ones can be summarized here. Chapter XIII includes a discussion of causes of individual differences in relation to extreme difficulties in reading. Some of the more important factors contributing to variations in reading skills are the following:

1. Intelligence

When measured by intelligence tests, children show a wide range of mental ages at each grade level. While intelligence is a highly important factor in reading development, it is not the all-determining condition that it is often assumed to be. Brightness does not guarantee correspondingly high reading achievement. A low mental age does not always indicate the limit of the dull child's reading achievement. One study indicated that of 1130 children at the close of the sixth year in school, twenty-nine percent had reading ages above their Stanford-Binet mental ages, fifteen percent had reading ages one or more years below their mental ages, and fifty-six percent obtained reading ages within one year of their respective mental ages.[1] Surveys usually indicate that dull children tend to have high accomplishment quotients while bright children have relatively low ones. Many studies indicate, however, that under superior instructional conditions children tend to achieve reading ages roughly equivalent to their mental ages.

2. Sensory Capacities

The possession of excellent sight and hearing is undoubtedly an asset in learning to read. These capacities not only affect the reading task itself but also affect the acquisition of a background of experience that makes reading more meaningful. A more complete discussion of sensory capacities may be found in Chapter XIII.

---

[1] Donald D. Durrell. "The influence of reading ability on intelligence measures." *Journal of Educational Psychology*, 24: September, 1933, 412–416.

3. Physical Condition

Physical well-being is an asset in any endeavor, and, conversely, temporary or chronic fatigue or illness interferes with learning. The physical condition of the pupil influences both the rate of learning to read and the degree to which the child profits from the experiences that contribute to reading. Physical condition affects attention to the task, the vigor and persistence of action, and other essential factors in learning. Many other constitutional factors, some of which are discussed in Chapter XIII, play a rôle in determining the reading achievements of individual pupils.

4. Language Equipment

The out-of-school language experiences of children also affect reading achievement. These experiences often differ widely for children of the same age and of the same community. The child's hearing and speaking vocabularies, his understanding of sentences of different degrees of complexity, the scope and nature of his interests, his desire and opportunity to read, write, speak, and listen, and his background for visual and auditory perception of words, as well as the activities that compete for his attention or supplant his desire for reading, are probably determined to a large degree by his out-of-school experiences, as well as by his intellectual, sensory, and physiological make-up. The language environment in the school will also tend to increase the differences in the reading achievement of children. Such factors as delayed speaking of English, or speaking chiefly or wholly a foreign language before entering school, or unfamiliarity with the pronunciation of the teacher exercise considerable influence upon the ease of learning to read.

5. Rate of Learning

A child is likely to progress more satisfactorily in reading when the difficulty of the material and the rate of introduction of new material are suited to his achievement level and his learning rate. Courses of study, textbooks, and classroom teachers often assume that there is only one level of achievement and one standard rate of learning for each school year. If the program offered happens to fit the child, his progress is likely to be satisfactory; if it is too difficult for him, he is likely to make little or no progress and to acquire many confusions and incomplete learnings. If the burden is too light, accomplishment is decreased and poor habits are likely to be acquired. The large gains in reading achievement shown in many recent studies of remedial and regular instruction are due in considerable degree to a careful adjustment of the instruction to the child's level and learning rate.

6. Response to Motivation

Many types of motivation are used in the classroom. They involve the utilization of interests already established, enrichment through preliminary activities and discussions, a variety of methods of presenting materials, records of accomplishment through the use of graphs and charts, discussions of ideals of workmanship, contests and rewards, deprivation of privileges, and fear of punishment and failure. A study of children's motives in school reveals that fear of unfavorable attention, punishment, or failure is present to a marked degree. There are differences among children in their responses to any form of motivation. Some are helped by a given kind of motivation, others are seriously hindered.

Recent studies of children's interests indicate that, while there is some uniformity of interests among children at different age levels, there are many differences in interests at each age level. The degree of a child's interest in stories of dogs, airplanes, fairies, or inventions depends partly on the types of previous experiences and the competing interests he possesses. An adjustment of the reading material to the child's interests will make for success while lack of adjustment will make for failure. This does not mean, however, that children have no interests in common. Practically all children are interested in animals, circuses, and numberless familiar topics. But within each field wide variations in interests appear. Success in reading depends in considerable measure on skillful adjustment to the pupil's vital interests and purposes.

The child's response to the personal habits of the teacher must be taken into account as a source of differences in reading achievement. The teacher's habit patterns — voice, methods of praise, response to the child's success or failure, choice of words, manner of presenting tasks, the telltale signs that reveal her feelings about the child, and any of the minute habits and mannerisms commonly implied under the somewhat vague term ' personality ' — may or may not stimulate the child effectively, and the amount of learning will be increased or diminished accordingly.

7. Other Factors

All specialists in remedial reading report that many more boys than girls have reading deficiencies. Two investigators [1] found that girls use reading as a recreation more often than boys do. Sex differences in reading may possibly be accounted for by environmental circumstances mentioned above under the headings "Language Equipment," and "Response to Motivation," or such differences may come from unknown underlying causes.

Personal characteristics, such as emotional blocking, persistence, attitudes toward school and home, are thought to affect the child's reading achievement. Such factors may be crucial in some cases, but it is often difficult to determine whether they are the cause or the result of difficulties in reading. The relation to reading of these and other factors is discussed in a monograph by Ladd,[2] and is also treated in Chapter XIII of this Yearbook.

Confusions and faulty habits are likely to appear when children with different backgrounds, learning rates, and interests are taught any complex skill. It is often impossible to tell in a particular case what factors are the primary causes of reading deficiencies. Indeed, it is difficult enough in the classroom situation to determine their present nature and significance. The outline of faulty habits presented elsewhere reveals the multiplicity of skills that are involved. A child is fortunate if he escapes confusions and difficulties in all these phases of reading. The success of children in acquiring many minor habits, skills, and understandings contributes to the complexity of individual differences in the classroom.

II. Discovery of Individual Differences in the Classroom

The first step in providing for individual differences in the classroom is the observation or measurement of the instructional needs of the children. Various means are available for use in observing or measuring such differences. Some of the general divisions presented below are most important in the primary grades, while others are more important in the intermediate grades or the secondary schools. The

---

[1] H. C. Lehman and P. A. Witty. "Sex differences in reference to reading books just for fun." *Education*, 48:1928, 602–617.

[2] M. R. Ladd. *The Relation of Social, Economic and Personal Characteristics to Reading Ability*. Contributions to Education, No. 582. (Teachers College, Columbia University: New York, 1933)

suggestions, then, are not meant to be followed exactly in all reading situations, but are to be considered as the elements of working plans that should be modified to fit the level of instruction and the objectives of the local course of study. If an individual pupil is severely retarded or if a more elaborate analysis of a single function is desired, suggestions for these purposes may be found in Chapters XII and XIII or in the chapters dealing with the various special topics.

1. Standardized Test Records

Standardized tests should always be included in a program for the analysis of individual differences. Their particular service lies in giving a reliable measure of the general level of achievement of each child and in measuring the amount of gain after a period of instruction. In addition, certain standardized reading tests contain diagnostic features that reveal strength or weakness in certain phases or types of reading. Standardized tests at present, however, do not measure a number of items important to the reading program. We have, for example, no standard tests of the extent and nature of the child's interests and habits in voluntary reading, nor are tests available for determining the child's ability in unaided oral or written recall after reading. Tests often do not indicate fully the particular meaning difficulties that any child will encounter in a given reading selection. Informal tests based upon the materials of instruction are usually the best means of revealing the suitability of materials for the child. When the skills are highly specific and complete mastery is important, inventory tests should be developed and used frequently. If an inventory test in recognition of new words taught were given monthly in the first grade, the onset of many reading difficulties would be made too evident to ignore. The program of standardized and informal tests must be planned in relation to the objectives for the particular grade. Suggested programs for each grade may be found in Chapter XII.

2. Attitudes and Interests in Reading

It is generally agreed that the most important outcome of reading instruction is the intensity and extent of reading interests. Objective tests have contributed little as yet to the measurement of this type of reading outcome. However, there are a number of fairly satisfactory methods for measuring interest that are coming into wider use.

a. Records of the Amount and Type of Voluntary Reading. Such records may be obtained from questionnaires as to the non-assigned reading done during vacation periods or during the previous week or month. These questionnaires should include various types of reading, such as fiction, stories or articles in magazines, sections of newspapers, books or articles on hobbies or sports, poetry, and other forms of reading.

Such a questionnaire should be more than the answer to the question, "What did you read during the spring vacation?" since many types of reading will be overlooked in the child's recall. It is better to make a list of suggestions to prompt the child's memory and to present them orally or in writing. Such items as the reading of directions for constructing things, of advertisements, of recipes, or of words to songs are worth noticing and might ordinarily be overlooked in the child's unaided recall.

If honest answers are to be secured, no rewards of any sort should be given for the reports. If high marks are given, praise or censure administered, or charts and graphs displayed, the teacher cannot expect honest answers on subsequent questionnaires. A teacher's attitude toward the questionnaire might be indicated in a comment like the following: "I should like to know what use you make of reading outside of school. Many of you find other things to do that you like better and some of you have very little time for reading. However, there are a great many uses for reading that you may not have found and which I should like to suggest if you have not already discovered them." If the accuracy of a child's response to such a questionnaire is doubted, it may be checked by engaging the child in informal conversation that brings in the information contained in the doubted items. An untruthful report is often an indication of an improper attitude toward the purposes of the questionnaire on the part of the teacher as well as of the child.

Tests of current information, following the completion and the multiple-choice procedure, are suitable for discovering the extent and depth of a pupil's reading about recent events. Such tests are easily built by scanning recent issues of news digests, such as are found in some newspapers, and in magazines such as *The Literary Digest* or *Time*. Such current-information tests are especially suitable for secondary-school and college students.

Weekly reports of outside reading, book reports, records from library cards, and other formal reports are not usually helpful in measuring the extent of voluntary reading. They cover only a narrow scope and are often tinged with a compulsory aspect that makes them of little value as a true measure of interest.

b. Rating Scales of Attitudes toward Reading as Evidenced in Classroom Activities of the Pupil. Rating scales of this sort are often merely expressions of opinion and as such are of doubtful validity, but they serve to keep to the fore the problem of interests and attitudes. A scale like the following has been found useful:

1. Takes obvious delight in reading. Is interested in stories, study-type reading, poetry, etc. Turns to reading at every opportunity. Talks with pleasure about materials read.
2. Likes to read certain things. Responds well to motivation, but often requires urging. Has narrower range of interests.
3. Reads required lessons. Shows low degree of interest in unassigned reading. Responds fairly well to motivation.
4. Is reluctant to read required lessons. Avoids reading whenever possible. Is indifferent to motivation.

3. The Level of Reading Ability

Do the materials of instruction fit the range of reading ability of the children in the classroom? One method of discovering this is to give standardized achievement tests to determine the differences in reading ability and then to see that the reading materials provided fit the range of abilities covered. Such a survey usually reveals wide differences in reading ability in each grade. Table I indicates the results of such a survey in the first six grades of a moderate-sized city.

TABLE I. — DISTRIBUTION OF READING-TEST GRADE SCORES (END OF YEAR) IN SIX GRADES

Grade	I Low	I High	II Low	II High	III Low	III High	IV Low	IV High	V Low	V High	VI Low	VI High	VII Low	VII High	VIII Low	VIII High	IX	Total Number Pupils
I	10	54	39	38	24	23												188
II	1	3	11	37	64	24	22	8	1									171
III			1	12	45	43	66	24	8	5	1							205
IV					5	12	46	46	35	16	8	2	3	3	2	2	1	181
V						2	18	19	39	68	45	22	15	6	1	3	4	242
VI							3	3	12	36	37	47	19	15	14	8	22	216

The spread of reading abilities in each grade is typical, except that lower levels of ability in each grade are often found in towns that make less provision for children with reading handicaps. A given classroom may not have the full range of reading levels indicated in the table. It will be noted that the range of reading abilities increases with each grade, indicating a need for a wider range of instructional materials.

After the standardized tests are given, the textbooks and supplementary materials should be studied to see that a sufficient supply is available for each level. It is often the case that the books provided are much too hard for the poorer readers, while the superior readers find little material that is challenging.

While the standard tests will indicate roughly the range of reading materials that should be available, there are many informal methods of determining the suitability of a particular book in regard to its difficulty. The chief difficulty that the child encounters in the primary grades is in accurate recognition of words, while in the intermediate and upper grades knowledge of word meanings is of primary importance. The suitability of a book for a child or a group of children may readily be tested in regard to these vocabulary difficulties.

a. Books for the Primary Grades. To determine whether the difficulties of word recognition in a given book do not make it unsuited for a particular child, the child may be asked to read orally from it a selection he has never read before. The selection should be approximately one hundred words long. A record should be made of the number of words that the child finds difficult. The child should be prompted on difficult words after an error or a five-second hesitation, so that he will not make errors through unnecessary confusion or delay on a single word.

We have no experimental evidence as yet in regard to the proper vocabulary load for children with different levels of mental ability. If the child's learning rate is determined experimentally by measuring the number of new words that he can learn daily, the number of difficult words in the daily lesson can be adjusted to that learning rate. In the usual classroom practice, it appears that children find difficulty in mastering material containing more than one difficult word in twenty running words. Some authorities hold that even this moderate number of new words is an unwise, and often unsafe, vocabulary burden for most children unless their reading development is checked and directed with exceptional frequency and skill. Independent silent reading ordinarily requires even easier material, unless the child has unusual skill in word analysis.

b. Books for the Intermediate and Upper Grades. While difficulties in comprehension at these levels depend on many factors, the basic difficulty is probably one of understanding words and concepts. This is particularly true in the case of textbooks in the content subjects. To determine the difficulties in word meaning of a particular textbook, a series of matching tests may be prepared in the following manner:

Select a chapter that has not been studied and pick out all the words and phrases that might not be understood. Not fewer than thirty of the most difficult words and expressions should be chosen. Divide the words into groups of seven or eight each and prepare definitions for them that the child can understand. To each group one or two extra definitions should be added so that there will still be choices of definition for the last word in the list. An example of such a test for one group of words from a history chapter follows:

____ put an end to	1. work harder
____ martial	2. stopped
____ derision	3. warlike
____ harangue	4. to treat badly
____ redouble his efforts	5. a noisy speech
____ symptom	6. scorn
____ persecute	7. a sign
	8. giving power

The child writes the number of the correct definition on the space before the word. Such tests may be written on the blackboard, and the child need copy only the word and the number of the correct definition.

The measurement of word and phrase difficulties usually gives a fair indication of the difficulty of a book for a group of children. A very heavy meaning vocabulary usually indicates the need for an

TABLE II. — WORD-RECOGNITION DIFFICULTIES OF THIRTY-SEVEN SECOND-GRADE CHILDREN READING ORALLY A SELECTION OF ONE HUNDRED WORDS FROM A SECOND-GRADE SUPPLEMENTARY READER

Number of Errors in Word Recognition	Number of Children
0	3
1–3	7
4–6	7
7–9	8
10–12	6
13–15	4
16–17	0
18–19	0
20–21	2

easier book. The difficulty may be checked further by some of the comprehension tests suggested later in this section.[1]

Table II shows the results of testing word-recognition difficulties in a second grade. If we assume that one error in twenty running words is the maximal difficulty of material for this grade, the results of this test indicate that the material of the supplementary reader was too difficult for at least twenty of the children. Twelve children made more than one error on every ten words.

TABLE III. — WORD-MEANING DIFFICULTIES OF THIRTY-TWO EIGHTH-GRADE CHILDREN IN A CHAPTER IN THE HISTORY TEXTBOOK USED IN THAT GRADE. (60-ITEM TEST)

Number of Errors	Number of Children
0–4	1
5–9	3
10–14	8
15–19	2
20–24	3
25–29	6
30–34	3
35–39	2
40–44	0
45–49	3
50–54	0
55–60	1

If we knew how many word meanings could be learned in a day by the pupils of the class represented in Table III, we should be able to state the relative difficulty of the chapter for them. However, the fact that so many children make twenty or more errors indicates that far too much time must be spent in the teaching of word meanings in order that the chapter may be clearly understood. An easier book would probably be more suitable for the group. Although some children are able to read intelligently in spite of a difficult vocabulary, they usually secure more meaning when they are less frequently confused by unknown words.

[1] An excellent treatment of the problem of vocabulary and sentence difficulties in reading appeared in a recent series of articles by E. L. Thorndike. "Improving the ability to read." *Teachers College Record,* 36: October, November, and December, 1934, 1–19, 125–44, 229–241.

4. Abilities in Comprehension and Interpretation

Comprehension is more than retention of the words of the story. It consists of many constituent abilities, such as the following: ability to understand word meanings, ability to understand different forms of sentence structure, ability to see the relative importance of ideas and to understand the total meaning or general purpose of the writer, ability in visualization and other forms of imagery, ability to supplement the thought correctly. Differences in ability to recognize words and in interest and attention should not be overlooked as possible causes of differences in comprehension.

Comprehension may be measured by the use of standard tests. If such tests are used, however, they should be examined to make sure that sufficient time is allowed so that the child has an opportunity to attempt exercises that tax his comprehension, and that the questions used require clear comprehension rather than mere verbatim report of the context.[1]

Informal tests may be used by the teacher for measuring the child's comprehension of classroom assignments. It is generally well to measure such comprehension by using both short and long sections of the material, since a child can often comprehend units of one or two paragraphs in length when he cannot comprehend several pages of the same material. In preparing questions for measuring comprehension, the usual multiple-choice or completion types found in standard tests may be used. No general agreement seems to exist among authorities in regard to the skills of comprehension to be measured. The teacher should build test items for the ability considered most important for her grade. The following tests of paragraph comprehension, organization of ideas, understanding of significant details, and comprehension of total meaning are taken from the silent-reading comprehension test of the 1936 Iowa Every-Pupil Tests of Basic Skills.[2] The questions are based on a selection of six paragraphs.

Paragraph Comprehension

(   ) What is the main idea of the first paragraph?
   1. Marco Polo was an explorer 600 years ago.
   2. Several expeditions have gone part way into Tibet.

---

[1] See Chapter XII for a further discussion of comprehension tests.

[2] Prepared by Ernest Horn and Maude McBroom. Distributed by the Bureau of Educational Research and Service, Extension Division, University of Iowa, Iowa City, 1936.

3. Very little is yet known about Tibet.

4. The country of Tibet belongs to China.

( ) What is the main *purpose* of the last paragraph?

1. To tell what the husbands do.

2. To give a definition of polyandry.

3. To describe a peculiar marriage custom of Tibet.

4. To explain that polyandry is practiced principally by country people.

Organization of Ideas

( ) ( ) ( ) Which three of the following belong under the heading: "Natural Barriers Which Separate Tibet from the Outside World"?

1. Lowlands	6. Himalaya Mountains
2. Malay	7. Military fortifications
3. Desert highlands	8. The Indian Ocean
4. Rivers and valleys	9. The large size of the country
5. China	

( ) ( ) ( ) Which three of the following ideas from this article are signs that the people of Tibet are backward?

1. Visitors are kept out by natural barriers.

2. The Tibetans have accepted no modern ideas.

3. Their farming is very crude.

4. Few people in Tibet live in towns.

5. The Tibetans do not resemble their neighbors.

6. Very little is known of their history.

7. They have many superstitions.

8. They look something like American Indians.

Understanding of Significant Details

( ) Why have the priests been able to gain such a hold upon the people?

1. The priests of Buddhism are called lamas.

2. There are many monasteries in Tibet.

3. The people are very superstitious.

4. The priests do not have to do any work.

5. The people practice polyandry.

( ) What accounts for the differences between the homes in the highlands and those in the lowlands?

1. It is colder in the highlands.

2. The people in the highlands are always moving about.

3. The people in the lowlands have crude implements for building.

4. Nearly all the people of the lowlands live in towns.

Comprehension of Total Meaning

( ) Which of the following do you think is the best title for this entire article?

1. How We Know about Tibet
2. A History of Tibet
3. How Tibetan People Make a Living
4. Tibet, Land of Mystery
5. Where Tibetans Came From

( ) What two main ideas do you think the writer of this article intended his readers to get from it?

1. Tibet is north of India and belongs to China.
2. We have been unable to learn much about Tibet.
3. The people of Tibet are not all alike.
4. The religion of Tibet is Buddhism.
5. Life in Tibet is very different from life in America.
6. There is no explanation for the way Tibetans live.
7. Tibet is almost twice as large as Texas.

Such questions may be prepared by the teacher in connection with the regularly assigned lessons in the classroom. When a low degree of comprehension is found, these tests might be followed by matching tests like those suggested above, in which word and phrase meanings are checked in order to discover whether they contribute to the difficulty. If a single type of question, such as those measuring organization of ideas, gives difficulty, several similar tests may be given to see whether the difficulty indicates a general low level in the ability or merely that a particular question is unusually difficult.

5. Oral and Written Recall of Reading

Questions of the objective type do not measure a mental activity closely related to reading; namely, unaided recall. Since recall is an important classroom activity, the differences among pupils in this ability should be revealed. Tests of the ' essay ' type can be used for this purpose and should constitute an important item in a program that provides for individual differences.

a. Written Recall. This ability may be tested by presenting the pupil with a short article of between one and two hundred words. After the pupil has read the material, he is asked to write as much of it as he can remember. A scoring sheet is prepared by listing all the important details in order. The pupil's score is the number of these ideas written. The scoring should be in number of ideas rather than in number of words. Several other features of the written recall may be noted, such as organization, inaccuracies, facility in written expression, use of new words, and language-grammar skills.

b. Oral Recall. A test of oral recall must be given individually, since only one oral response can be recorded at a time. In one such test the child is asked to tell orally all of the story that he can remember, and his response is checked against the list of ideas included in the selection. A check list of other characteristics of the response — organization, accuracy, fluency, use of new words — may be useful in noting attainments.

c. Written Summaries of Longer Units. A test of this sort is to ask the pupil to summarize the main points of the chapter he has just read. It is sometimes found desirable to indicate the length of the summary desired by suggesting that it be one or two paragraphs or pages in length. The summary may be checked against a list of the main points that the teacher has prepared.

6. Abilities in the Mechanics of Reading.

Many methods are available for measuring the differences in abilities in oral and silent reading that appear among children of the same age.

a. Word Analysis. Present the pupil with a list of ten or more words new to him, but for which he should have an adequate background for word analysis. For primary grades, the teacher's manuals of basal reading systems often indicate the word elements with which the child should be familiar. In the upper grades, the words should contain fairly common syllables. The pupil's score is the number of words pronounced correctly. The scoring should be lenient, since accent and certain vowel and consonant sounds are often impossible to determine from the spelling of the word.[1]

b. Word and Phrase Recognition. Skill in this phase of reading may be fairly accurately determined by the use of a tachistoscope or other device for the quick exposure of words. Lists of words or phrases graded in difficulty are exposed for approximately one-fifth of a second. Other simple methods of observing these differences are: noticing phrasing in oral reading; observing the number, rhythm, and regularity of eye movements; and testing the eye-voice span. Eye movements may be counted by unobtrusively observing them over the top of the book as the child reads. The eye-voice span may be measured by having the child read orally materials relatively easy for him. As the child reads, a card is suddenly slid over the place where he is reading. The

---

[1] If a checklist of habits in word analysis is desired, a very complete one may be found in Chapter XII.

number of words that he can read from memory beyond this point indicates his eye-voice span. Usually it is well to cover the material at the beginning of a phrase approximately one-third through the line.[1]

c. Voice, Enunciation, and Expression in Oral Reading. These may be rated on the qualities discussed in Chapter X.

d. Habits in Silent Reading. Several habits and abilities in silent reading should be observed. Head movements, lip movements, and whispering are easily detected. Speed of silent reading may be measured through standard or informal tests. In informal testing, it is desirable to test comprehension after every speed test so that the reading will not become superficial. The following directions are used: " Read as rapidly as you can, but be sure that you read carefully so that you will know everything that it says." The tests should not be more than two or three minutes in length. The pupil marks the place where he is reading when time is called. His score is the number of words or lines read per minute.

It is also well to discover the pupil's attention to new or difficult words. The pupil is asked to list the words he does not know on a page or in a chapter. He is then given a word-meaning test such as that suggested above. The pupil's score is the number of words not listed by the pupil that appeared in the vocabulary test. A high score indicates low attention to unknown words. If the pupil is to increase his meaning vocabulary through extensive silent reading, he should form desirable habits of attention to new words.

7. Abilities Related to Study

Various methods of measuring the many skills related to study are suggested in Chapter XII. Standard tests suggested in that chapter will be helpful to the classroom teacher. The informal tests listed in this chapter will be helpful in understanding differences among pupils in their study skills. In addition, three more informal tests are suggested.

a. Speed and Accuracy in Locating Information. Prepare six or eight questions to which the answers may be found in a chapter not previously read. Record the time required to find the answers. Such questions may vary in difficulty from the location of certain proper names, an easy skill, to the more difficult problems of finding relevant facts or ideas.

b. Speed and Accuracy in Finding Words in a Dictionary. Prepare

---

[1] More precise methods of measuring phrase reading through the use of laboratory equipment are described in references listed in Chapter XIII.

a list of ten words for the child to find in the dictionary. Have him write beside each word the page number or the guide word at the top of the column in which the word is located. Note the time required for the assignment.

c. *Use of Reference Materials.* If the pupils are to use reference materials, it is well to test their ability to locate references by means of the index, the card catalog, *The Reader's Guide,* and similar aids. Give a pupil a topic and ask him to find as many references as he can in the library or in the reference sources available.

8. Recording and Evaluating Data Concerning the Individual

The results of the tests used should be tabulated on a class record sheet, so that the needs of the pupils may be studied. The following sample record is from a low section of a fifth grade:

	Jean	Charles	Frank	8 others
Interest rating (1 — excellent, 4 — very poor)	1	2	4	
Oral-reading errors (fourth-grade selection)	6	14	22	
Word-meaning difficulties (30 words — history)	10	10	26	
Comprehension (history — 10 items)	8	4	0	
Written recall (24 ideas)	12	9	1	
Speed of silent reading (fourth-grade material)	176	124	83	
Dictionary (time for ten words)	8'	14'	27'	
Reading grade (standardized test)	4.2	3.1	2.7	

The following sample chart is from a second grade:

	Walter	Mary	Robert
Voluntary outside reading	no	yes	yes
Errors in oral reading (second-grade selection)	25	4	0
Comprehension, oral reading (ten questions)	8	10	10
Word analysis (oral — 20 words)	2	17	20
Phrasing in oral reading	no	yes	yes
Speed of silent reading (words per ¾ minute)	24	70	145
Comprehension, silent reading (ten questions)	1	8	10
Lip movements or whispering	yes	no	no

By consulting such tables it is possible to group pupils for instruction on the basis of their outstanding needs. As stated previously, teachers of the primary grades usually prefer to group on the basis of the number of errors in oral reading, while teachers of the intermediate grades prefer to use comprehension scores, word-meaning difficulties, or results of speed tests as bases for grouping. Whatever the basis chosen for grouping, it should be determined mainly by the reading abilities given most emphasis in the local situation. After the group adjustments are made, additional tables may be máde that reveal other instructional needs of the various members of the group. The tables may show that the entire class needs help in certain items, such as dictionary skills or speed of silent reading.

Records should be made of the progress of the child in various abilities so that lack of progress may be detected early in the year. If certain tests are repeated, using materials of similar difficulty, the amount of gain may be estimated. If no gain is evident, further effort should be made to determine more suitable methods and materials of instruction. Whenever the teacher is undecided about the proper procedure for the child, or when the rough classroom analysis appears inadequate, the child should be given the more elaborate analysis of reading difficulties outlined in Chapter XIII.

III. Administrative Provisions for Individual Differences in the Classroom

The previous section has suggested several ways in which a teacher may discover some of the more important differences in the achievement and needs of pupils in reading. This section suggests what the teacher may do about such differences after they have been discovered. The suggestions are drawn mainly from the practices of skilled classroom teachers. The first part of the section deals with methods of administering an individualized classroom; the second part suggests various methods of providing for the specific differences revealed by the classroom measurement.

1. Providing Suitable Reading Materials

Textbooks and supplementary materials for reading instruction, as well as for the other subjects involving reading, should be chosen so as to provide adequately for the range of reading abilities within the classroom. The range of reading interests should also be considered in selecting the books for individualized instruction.

The assumption is too often made that a teacher of a particular grade need teach only a certain set of reading skills that have been assigned by the course of study to that grade. If the needs of the children are to be served, the teacher must be prepared to provide instruction suited to the observed differences among the pupils in abilities, habits, and interests. This means that if certain pupils who have been admitted to the grade require training in the skills of the earlier grades, the needed instruction should be provided. If others have achievement levels beyond that required by the particular grade, materials should be available to widen their interests and provide for growth. With the results of the testing in hand, the teacher should examine the books and other teaching materials to see that there is available for every child a sufficient supply on his level. In choosing such books and materials, the interests of the children and the rights of the teachers of grades above and below should be kept in mind. Books used by the pupils in lower grades will seldom be welcomed by the child. Books that are to be used for basal instruction in upper grades probably should not be used. Although an adequate plan for supplying appropriate books should be developed by the supervisor or principal, the initiative in securing books of appropriate reading difficulty and interest rests with the teacher.

The teacher should see that materials of suitable levels of difficulty are available for each unit in the content subjects. If materials are well chosen, each child, no matter what his reading level, may contribute items of interest to the central topic. Individualized assignments in the content subjects enhance the socialization of the classroom, since each child is able to enrich the experiences of the others, whereas in the uniform assignment each child competes for the opportunity of parroting information already known to the other members of the class.

The problem of providing books of the proper level is not easy. Accurate methods of grading books have not yet been developed. Formulas for grading books by word counts and other mechanical means fail to take into account that a high degree of interest obtained through illustration or well-planned composition may make a book readable in spite of a rather heavy vocabulary burden, while a low degree of interest may make the book difficult to read in spite of an easy vocabulary.[1] The method suggested in the section on " Determining the Suitability of Materials," above, will assist the teacher in this regard. There is a dearth of books written simply enough for the poorer readers. Publishers are taking some steps to supply this need. Fortunately, many books are now being produced for classroom use that do not carry the grade designation conspicuously on the cover.

---

[1] See Chapter VII for an extended treatment of this topic. — *Editor.*

2. Individual Guidance and Instruction

Individual conferences with pupils may be helpful in many ways. If the child knows the specific skills he is trying to master or the possibilities for useful information or interests that lie ahead, he will understand the purposes of the assignments and will assist in furthering them. Ordinarily the child should be told of his needs as revealed by the tests and observations. Children with high achievement need to be challenged with the possibilities of wider interests available to them. Some teachers see that each child is provided with a notebook in which he records his own new learnings.

Extensive individual silent reading appears to bring about gains in reading achievement commensurate with those obtained in class instruction. One investigator [1] found that in the second grade extensive individual reading with short comprehension exercises was superior to class instruction for children who were reading more than sixty words per minute, but that class instruction was better for children reading below this rate. Needless to say, the results of such comparisons will vary with the character of the class instruction. Another investigator [2] found no significant differences in achievement resulting from extensive reading and from class instruction in Grades II to IV. In individual silent reading, materials suited to the reading level and interests of the child may be provided and, if suitable assignments and work sheets are furnished, certain skills and habits may be taught as well.

Long-range assignments in which the pupil follows an interest over an extended period of time are often found useful in providing for individual differences. This sort of specialization may be purely personal or it may be planned to contribute to the increased experiences of the group. Many teachers now utilize individual or small-group, specialized reading assignments as the main method of study in such subjects as history and geography. Several weeks in advance the child is assigned a problem to be reported on during the study of a certain unit. The report on the independent study may take the form of an illustrated talk, an illustrated booklet, an article in a class journal, or some other

---

[1] L. Zirbes. *Practice Exercises and Checks on Silent Reading in the Primary Grades.* (Bureau of Publications, Teachers College, Columbia University: New York, 1925)

[2] H. A. Field. Extensive individual reading versus class reading. Contributions to Education, No. 394. (Teachers College, Columbia University: New York, 1930)

form. A small group of pupils may be assigned to carry the entire responsibility of presenting certain units in history, geography, or science.
The enrichment that the group gains when reports from reading various
sources are presented to the class makes that a more meaningful and interesting exercise than a class discussion of materials from a single
source. That the long-range specialized assignment may serve a variety of purposes is illustrated by the sixth-grade boy whose behavior
in the classroom was very poor until he was made a specialist in the
hunting and fishing possibilities of each region studied in geography.

In connection with individual extensive reading and with the specialized assignments, a close coöperation between teacher and librarian is
desirable. Suggestions for achieving such coöperation are given in
Chapter VIII.

Workbooks, standard test lessons, and other self-administering materials will be helpful in providing for individual differences. The possibilities of workbooks for increasing various reading abilities are just
beginning to be realized. Undoubtedly, such materials will be developed to provide more abundantly for practice in many phases of
reading.

3. Small Groups within the Classroom

In this method of providing for individual differences, the class is
divided into several groups of four to six pupils each. The grouping is
made on the basis of the most significant needs as revealed by testing
and observation. Occasionally the groups may be larger than six or
smaller than four, depending upon the degree of similarity of instructional needs. Although the division of a class of thirty-five children
into two or three groups aids greatly in adapting instruction to individual needs, the results of tests usually reveal the need for smaller
divisions. The merit of instruction for small groups lies in the opportunity provided for making the lessons more nearly fit the level, rate of
progress, and interests of the individual pupils. Such instruction has
the added merit of giving the child a feeling of greater individual responsibility. Especially in oral reading and in the research type of
assignment, the child in the small group carries a much larger share of
the load and profits accordingly. Since instruction for a small group
requires very careful planning, appropriate procedures will be discussed
at some length.

a. Organizing Small Groups. The basis for grouping depends upon
what needs are revealed by the tests of the pupils. The usual basis for

grouping in the primary grades is the difficulty of the material the child can read fluently. Suggestions for effecting this sort of grouping were given above under " Suitability of Level of Materials." Children having approximately the same number of errors in word recognition in materials of given difficulty are grouped together. This plan enables the teacher to select materials in which the vocabulary burden is not too great, and to provide introductory exercises in word recognition that overcome most of the difficulties the members of the group will encounter in oral or silent reading. Sometimes teachers organize groups of children for special help in word analysis, in oral recall of materials read, in overcoming inattention and lip movements in silent reading, and in various phases of oral reading, such as enunciation, pitch of voice, phrasing, and expression. Some children may need temporary help in the use of workbooks.

Pupils who have the same level of word recognition or understanding of word meaning will often have different learning rates. A more sensitive adjustment to learning needs will take these differences into account by measuring the amount and permanence of the child's daily mastery of new words. A child who can learn and retain easily often makes the most satisfactory progress in a group that is working at a level somewhat higher than the level to which he would ordinarily be assigned. A simple way of estimating learning rate is to teach a group of children ten or fifteen new words — either for recognition or for meaning — and then test their retention immediately or on the following day.

b. *Administration of Group Instruction.* The transition from large-group to small-group instruction must be gradual; otherwise pupils may be distracted from their special tasks by the activities of other groups. It is advisable to begin with one or two independent groups that work by themselves while the teacher directs the work of the remainder of the class. The independent groups should be made up of superior readers, since they are more capable in self-direction. The fact that they are allowed to do independent work will make the privilege seem more desirable to the others. After these groups are working smoothly, others may be added.

The success of small-group work depends primarily on the suitability of the assignments for the groups. Such assignments need to be very specific at first, so that the pupils will know exactly what is expected. Pupil teachers are often trained to direct the group in oral reading and in other exercises that require a leader. Assignments should usually include some form of written record for each pupil. Short objective tests, questions on the blackboard, or other plans of report will require the attention of each pupil.

Small-group instruction should be flexible. Children should be shifted from one group to another when it is apparent that they will profit by the shift. Two or three groups may combine for one piece of work and then divide again when the work is complete. Pupils who are reading on different levels may have similar needs in specific phases of reading, such as word analysis, expression or enunciation in oral reading or oral recall, ability to organize material, use of the dictionary, or speed of reading. These pupils may occasionally be grouped for an exercise suitable for them all. Small groups may be taught on two or three days each week and larger sections on other days. Certain exercises may be profitable for the entire class.

c. Assignments in Small-Group Work. Probably the most successful method of handling small-group assignments is to have a single center of interest for the entire class, around which are built the different levels and types of assignments. This program permits unified activities for enrichment and encourages exchange of ideas gained from reading. If Mexican life is the center of interest, the discussions, pictures, collections, music, and dramatization will be suitable for all groups regardless of the difficulty levels of the books they are reading. Groups and individuals with superior reading ability may be investigating special topics related to Mexican life, while those who have difficulties in basic reading abilities may work at more uniform and easier materials related to the same topic, and designed to overcome their difficulties. Pupils of low reading achievement should also read and report on special topics if materials are found suited to their reading levels. As more attention is paid to individualized instruction, lesson plans and reading materials will undoubtedly be published that will make it easier for the teacher to provide for different levels of instruction around various centers of interest.

When the range of abilities is small and it seems desirable for the majority of the pupils to read the same book at the same time, the assignments are often made on the basis of two weeks' work, or on a specific unit of the book. The pupils start each unit together so that the enrichment provided will serve to motivate all pupils and so that correlated activities can be organized. The work is divided into larger sections for pupils who comprehend well and who have few difficulties in word mastery or vocabulary. The unit is divided into much smaller

sections for slower pupils.   Each group is allowed to work through the
assignment as rapidly as mastery is achieved.   Supplementary stories
and activities are provided for the groups finishing ahead of the
scheduled time.   All pupils then start the next unit together.   Extra
materials, special instructional assistance, additional practice, and
careful review are often necessary to make the gains secure for the
slower learners.

A typical day's work in small-group instruction is presented below.
The children in each group are assumed to have similar levels of
reading ability and learning rates.   The plans often center around a
similar topic for all groups.   If space permitted a display of plans for
several successive days, it would be seen that the teacher provides a
variety of different exercises for each step in the lesson.

SAMPLE LESSON PLAN FOR SMALL-GROUP WORK [1]

Group 1.   (Laura — pupil teacher)
1. Return yesterday's papers.
2. Present new vocabulary on " The Giants' New Year."
3. Phrase card drill.
4. Silent reading to find answers to specific questions.
5. Discuss and correct papers.
6. Review of flash cards from past two lessons.

Group 2.   (Janet — pupil teacher)
1. Return yesterday's comprehension checks on " Elizabeth Eliza."
2. Audience reading lesson today on " The Kettle That Would Not Walk "
   preceded by 3–6.
3. Auditory test on new vocabulary.
4. Visual memory test on new vocabulary.
5. Audience reading preceded by silent study.
6. Comprehension check and discussion.

Group 3.   (David — pupil teacher)
1. Review yesterday's flash cards.
2. Silent reading lesson, based on paragraphs adapted from geography test.
3. Present new words.   Motor visual method.
4. Phrases from story on individual charts.
5. Read story for speed, by units, discussing answers to preliminary questions.
6. Read the difficult parts orally.

---

[1] The materials quoted are taken at random from the plan book of Helen
E. Donnelly, fourth-grade teacher at Reading, Massachusetts.

Group 4. (Nelson — pupil teacher)
1. Flash card review of old words.
2. Silent reading lesson today on " Begging Deer," preceded by 3–6.
3. Vocabulary presentation.
4. Individual phrase cards from story.
5. Silent study of phrases, then oral reading of same.
6. Silent reading of sections 1–3.

Group 5. (Miss Donnelly)
1. Review yesterday's words on the tachistoscope.
2. Discuss story that is to be read.
3. Auditory test, finding new words.
4. Visual test on new words.
5. Phrase work from blackboard.
6. Oral reading of second section.
7. Comprehension test.

IV. Adjustment to Specific Needs of Pupils

The topics in this section parallel those in Section II, " Discovery of Individual Differences in the Classroom." Measurement of individual differences is of little value unless specific provision is made to adjust instruction to the needs of the children as revealed by the results of measurement.

1. Providing for Differences in Attitudes and Interests in Reading

Both the intensity and the range of reading interests must be taken into account in evaluating the needs of any child. Children who have excellent attitudes toward reading may often be narrow in their range of interests, or may be content with a succession of shallow dips into various fields. Such children may leave school with the aimless reading habits found among many adults — reading to fill dull moments or reading the current socially approved book. Children who have poor attitudes toward reading require a specific program of motivation. The teacher will find in Chapter VI help in providing suitable interests and attitudes. Only a few suggestions will be presented here.

Children with excellent attitudes toward reading should be encouraged to do self-directed reading for social or personal purposes. These children may learn to prepare and follow long-range reading plans in connection with topics to be discussed in the history, geography, science, or literature classes. They may learn to enjoy the pleasure that comes from reading and working at a hobby over a period of several years. They may be taught to follow current happenings in a variety of fields. They may learn to select items that will be useful in their social relations with others, such as stories, jokes, interesting descriptions of people or places, and other items that will widen the range of their conversation. They may master the writings of a single author or may specialize in certain vocational or avocational fields — bird study, paintings, sonnets, rug-weaving, mining, drama, geological formations and areas, metallurgy, landscape design, or any of the host of other interests now available. They may serve as group leaders. They may also learn to use reading as a means of controlling their emotions or of gaining stimulation to various activities.

A child is occasionally found who uses reading as an escape from reality or as a means of avoiding social contacts or disagreeable work. Such children are best handled by suggesting various forms of expression and activity based on reading. They may be encouraged to make illustrations, posters, maps, or folders to be used by other children. Later, they may make oral reports, prepare and take part in dramatized selections, assist in group planning, and gradually increase their expressive activities.

The suggestions for pupils with excellent attitudes may also help in assisting those with poor attitudes, particularly those in intermediate and upper grades. Poor attitudes are often due to the fact that the child finds the assigned reading very difficult or feels that he is making no progress in the abilities being taught. This condition will be helped by providing materials of the right level and by showing improvement made in test performance.[1]

2. Providing for Differences in Reading Levels and Rates of Learning

Methods used in solving this problem are found in Section III on " Administrative Provisions for Individual Differences in the Classroom." Chapters VI, VII, and VIII contain suggestions for obtaining suitable reading materials.

3. Providing for Differences in Abilities in Comprehension and Interpretation

Effective help in overcoming differences in these abilities will be found in Chapter IV. If the difficulty arises from lack of understanding of word meanings or inability to recognize words, Chapter IX offers

---

[1] Other suggestions for helping these pupils will be found in Chapters VI and VII.

many practical suggestions. A recent article [1] presents a variety of graded lesson plans for teaching children to organize what they read. A summary of suggestions follows:

The following list of reading exercises attempts to outline a series of training lessons for developing the ability to organize in reading, first in analyzing what is read, and second in synthesizing, or formulating, the selected elements of what is read into a useable result.

I. ANALYZING WHAT IS READ

A. *Finding the principal ideas*

Lesson Type 1. Matching questions with answering paragraphs.
" " 2. Asking key questions. Stating the key questions which each paragraph answers.
" " 3. Matching titles or paragraph headings with paragraphs.
" " 4. Naming paragraphs.
" " 5. Improving paragraph headings.
" " 6. Finding a keynote sentence in a paragraph.
" " 7. Recognizing the climax in a story.
" " 8. Taking running notes.

B. *Recognizing the relation of ideas to each other*

Lesson Type 9. Anticipating the content of a chapter.
" " 10. Arranging ideas in order.
" " 11. Classifying or grouping ideas.
" " 12. Grouping paragraphs around main points.
" " 13. Locating subordinate or supporting points.
" " 14. Completing a skeleton outline.
" " 15. Making an outline.

II. SYNTHESIZING THE IMPORTANT IDEAS FOR USE

Lesson Type 16. Reproducing from an outline or from notes.
" " 17. Securing material in answer to a problem.
" " 18. Summarizing.

Chronic inattention in silent reading, often a source of difficulty, may be overcome by added enrichment and motivation, by giving the child an interesting project, or by making the reading assignments more specific. Several studies indicate that reading guided by questions gives better results than reading without such guidance. If diffi-

---

[1] Bess Goodykoontz. "Teaching pupils to organize what they read." *Elementary English Review,* 7: April, 1930, 87–90.

culties in attention are severe, the child may be helped by following a list of prepared questions, one for each paragraph.

4. Providing for Differences in Oral and Written Recall of Reading

One of the most effective means of overcoming difficulties in oral and written recall is to allow the child to speak or write from notes. Since experienced speakers and writers may be expected to use outlines, there is no justification for forbidding pupils to use them in school. Such outlines may consist of a series of key words or phrases, placed under a few general headings. For example, if the child is reporting on "The Age of Fishes" from Craig and Johnson's *Our Earth and Its Story*, pages 123–126, such a simple outline as the following may serve to prompt his memory:

(1) Age of fishes.
    Early forms simple.
    Many fish-like fossils.
(2) Fish with backbones.
    "Vertebrates."
(3) First vertebrate.
    Two inches long.
    Like an eel.
    Sucked its food.

(4) Shark.
    One of oldest.
    Five feet long.
    Scales and fins to protect.
(5) Large seaweeds.
    Tall — different shapes.
    Food for sea animals.
    Hid small animals.
    Etc.

If the pupil is to build his own outlines, he needs to be taught the ability through graded steps such as those summarized in the preceding topic. The use of outlines will help the child to overcome timidity in oral recall and to retain his ideas in written composition despite difficulties in writing or spelling.

5. Providing for Differences in Ability in the Mechanics of Reading

If the child has difficulties in the basic habits of reading, special attention must be given to them. Some children acquire excellent progress in all phases of reading without special instruction, while others exhibit many confusions and make slow progress in spite of excellent motivation. Particularly in the primary grades, the habits involved in word analysis, word recognition, phrase recognition, various oral reading skills, and certain silent reading skills require direct instruction.

a. Word Analysis. Every basal reading system makes some provision for instruction in word analysis. If the pupil is unable to pronounce new words by himself, an inventory should be made of the more common word elements that he is able to employ. This inventory should provide the basis for word study and analysis and the related instructional program. The type of instruction will vary with individual needs. If the child laboriously sounds words with little success or does word-by-word reading, he may need help in developing ability to use context or meaning clues. If the child does random guessing of words without regard to sound or form, he usually requires specific guidance in word analysis.[1]

There is a tendency to assign phonics entirely to the primary grades. An analysis of the word study difficulties found above this level shows that many pupils even on the secondary-school level profit by exercises that require close attention to the structure of words, such as the study of common word roots, syllables, and suffixes.

b. Word and Phrase Recognition. Many pupils need help in increasing their facility in word and phrase recognition. Several types of lessons appear to aid in developing this ability, some of which are the following:

(1) Enrichment of words through use and illustration.
(2) Flash card drills, with provision for transfer.
(3) Extensive easy reading.
(4) The use of the tachistoscope or the Metron-O-Scope.
(5) Lantern-slide exercises, used as flash cards.
(6) Tracing, writing, or typewriting new words.
(7) Use of masks over the page, revealing only the difficult words or phrases.
(8) Games for word and phrase comparison.
(9) Use of prepared materials in which phrases are emphasized by spacing or vertical marks between phrases.
(10) Extensive reading in easy material.

Additional information in regard to word analysis and word recognition may be found in Chapter IX.

c. Voice, Enunciation, and Expression in Oral Reading. Many practical suggestions for improving these abilities may be found in Chapter X.

---

[1] Detailed treatments of various approaches to word analysis appear in various professional texts, for example:

A. I. Gates. *The Improvement of Reading.* (The Macmillan Company: New York, 1935)

A. D. Cordts. *Word Method of Teaching Phonics.* (Ginn and Company: Boston, 1929)

d. Habits in Silent Reading. Head movements and lip movements may often be eliminated by calling the child's attention to their presence and cautioning him against them. Exercises that call for rapid silent reading in easy material are also helpful. The speed of silent reading may be improved rapidly by frequent use of timed tests on easy material. Methods of overcoming habits of inattention in silent reading have been discussed already. The child's attention to new or difficult words is often improved by frequent repetition of the tests that involve the recognition of unfamiliar words.

V. Administrative Problems in Providing for Individual Differences

While the Committee recognizes that the major problems of handling individual differences must be met by the classroom teacher, administrative officers may assist in many ways in the solution of the problem.

1. Grouping for Instruction

The burden of the classroom teacher will be considerably lessened if the classes are relatively homogeneous. The *Thirty-Fifth Yearbook* of this Society outlines various methods for grouping and offers evidence in regard to their merits. Since policies of promotion and opportunities for grouping vary in accordance with local conditions, no single method of grouping is applicable to all situations. Certain problems of grouping that relate particularly to reading are worth mentioning here.

a. Classes for Children with Sensory Handicaps. While much may be done for the child with low vision or poor hearing by arranging favorable conditions in the ordinary classroom, the equipment and methods of instruction for children with severe handicaps of this nature usually require the formation of special classes. The educational problems of the hard-of-hearing child and methods of teaching the visually handicapped child have been ably discussed by various authorities.[1]

b. Remedial-Reading Groups. When only one or two children in a

---

[1] See, for example, on the deaf, J. L. Waldman, F. A. Wade, and C. W. Aretz. *Hearing and the School Child.* (Volta Bureau: Washington, D. C., 1931)

On the blind and partially blind, see: K. E. Maxfield. *The Blind Child and His Reading.* (American Foundation for the Blind, Inc.: New York, 1928); also R. V. Merry. *Problems in the Education of Visually Handicapped Children.* (Harvard University Press: Cambridge, 1933)

classroom are so severely retarded that they cannot be taught successfully with the plans used for other groups, or when a child fails to progress in spite of individualized instruction, remedial-reading classes should be made available for them.

Two types of remedial classes have been found effective, the remedial-reading homeroom and the remedial-reading laboratory. In the first type, children with reading difficulty are placed under the guidance of a trained remedial teacher for all their subjects. Instruction is in small groups. The advantage of this organization is that it can be started in the larger schools without additional salary cost. By shifting pupils between rooms, a room and a teacher can be assigned to this work for at least part of the day.

In the remedial-reading laboratory, a remedial teacher takes small groups separately for reading instruction. Since each group receives one period of instruction daily, the teacher may work with about forty children daily by taking six or seven groups of about seven children each. Children should be assigned to suitable groups on the basis of diagnostic testing. In order to serve the most effectively, remedial classes should provide first for the children with the greatest reading retardation in relation to their Stanford-Binet mental ages.

c. Classes for Dull Children. Several studies have shown that dull children can acquire reading abilities equal to or above their mental ages. Provision must be made for the slower development of reading skills in such cases. This includes extra practice, greater enrichment, and more careful correlation of language skills than is usually required for the average child.

d. Instruction of Children with Physical Handicaps. Children with physical handicaps that interfere with the turning of pages, the speaking or writing of words, or with the attention or effort demanded in reading, require individual reading programs adjusted to the defect. In making appropriate adjustments competent medical advice should always be sought.

e. Other Special Groups. Whether or not special classes or groups should be made for children with marked handicaps due to foreign-language influences, speech defects, or emotional difficulties depends upon the severity of the difficulty and the possibilities for satisfactory adjustment in the regular classroom.

The educational problems of special groups with various types of handicaps are so complex that no adequate treatment of them can be given in a single chapter.

2. Other Administrative Problems and Activities

a. Textbooks. The selection of textbooks commensurate with the range of reading abilities will need to be supervised by administrative or supervisory officers. Since textbooks and supplementary materials on several levels will be required for each grade, definite planning will be necessary in order to avoid undesirable duplication. This problem is discussed more fully in the chapter on " The Materials of Reading."

b. Supplementary Materials. Accessory materials that are relatively self-administering should be provided when teachers are asked to instruct in a classroom in which there is a wide range of abilities.

c. Securing Individualized Units. Committees of teachers should be guided in working out individualized units that may be duplicated for use, thus saving individual teachers many hours of unnecessary effort in lesson planning. An alert supervisor may discover many individualized lesson plans and instructional devices from classroom teachers or from publishers and may make them available in the various classrooms.

d. Miscellaneous Activities. Teachers' meetings, professional literature, demonstrations, and visiting days should be used as methods for showing teachers various approaches to individualized instruction. Administrative officers should encourage publishers to produce more materials that aid in providing for individual differences.

SUB–COMMITTEE ON CHAPTER XII

Chairman

ARTHUR I. GATES, Professor of Education, Teachers College, Columbia University, New York City

Associates

HARRY A. GREENE, Associate Professor of Education, State University of Iowa, Iowa City, Iowa

MELVIN E. HAGGERTY, Dean, College of Education and Professor of Educational Psychology, University of Minnesota, Minneapolis, Minnesota

GERTRUDE H. HILDRETH, Psychologist, The Lincoln School of Teachers College, Columbia University, New York City

E. F. LINDQUIST, Associate Professor of Education and Director of Iowa Every-Pupil Testing Program, State University of Iowa, Iowa City, Iowa

PAUL V. SANGREN, President, Western State Teachers College, Kalamazoo, Michigan

ARTHUR E. TRAXLER, Research Worker, Educational Records Bureau, New York City

CHAPTER XII

THE MEASUREMENT AND EVALUATION OF ACHIEVEMENT IN READING

ARTHUR I. GATES
Professor of Education, Teachers College, Columbia University
New York City

I. GENERAL RECOMMENDATIONS CONCERNING PROGRAMS FOR EVALUATING ACHIEVEMENT IN READING

The *Twenty-Fourth Yearbook* on reading recommended the occasional use of standardized tests and the frequent use of informal tests as part of the normal teaching program. That the use of standardized and informal tests and examinations is now regarded as a vital phase of classroom work is implied by the fact that most of the preceding chapters in this *Yearbook*, which deal with teaching some phase of the subject, include numerous suggestions on measurement and evaluation of attainments. This special chapter on the topic has been included for two purposes; first, to supplement the discussions of other chapters, and, second, to suggest certain newer practices that, although employed in some schools, have not as yet come into general use. More specifically, the purposes of this chapter are as follows:

1. To reaffirm the soundness of the policy of making systematic use of standardized tests at intervals during the year and of employing informal appraisals regularly as part of the normal classroom work.

2. To recommend wider use of the systematic inventories of specific reading skills and techniques that provide a very detailed analysis of an individual pupil's abilities, interests, and difficulties.

3. To recommend wider use of other devices, such as certain observational methods, ratings, questionnaires, combination teach-and-test materials, subjective appraisals of study habits, and other less widely used techniques.

4. To recommend a comprehensive study by various means of the pupil's readiness to undertake each of the several steps or stages in the reading program described in Chapter IV.

5. To recommend the adoption of a well-planned program of measurement and evaluation to cover effectively the entire school period, including high school and college, and

359

6. To recommend the adoption of a plan of keeping full, permanent records, not only of the results of measurements and appraisal of reading ability and of examinations of intelligence, vision, hearing, and so forth, but also of information concerning the pupil's home background, interests, personal characteristics, difficulties and successes in school, methods of teaching or correction, voluntary and required reading, and other data of value in arranging the most fruitful reading program for a pupil at any particular time.

A sufficient justification for these recommendations is found in the fact that the needs of school children can be successfully met only when information about individual pupils, classes, schools, and the school system as a whole can be made available quickly and economically to various school officers. For example, in a progressive school system such requirements as the following arise:

1. The superintendent needs to know the reading status of the pupils, variously grouped, in order to determine the relative emphasis being placed on different phases of the curriculum, to see the effects of the promotion system, to evaluate the needs of various schools, to determine the effects of new materials or methods, or to solve other major problems.

2. The principal needs to know the reading achievements of the classes in his school to evaluate his plans of promotion and placement, methods of instruction, provision of books and equipment, within-class organizations, and any new procedures being tried out.

3. The curriculum department needs to know the level and character of reading ability in the various grades to plan wisely for the choice of materials, activities, and methods in other phases of the curriculum.

4. The Book Committee needs to know the types of reading interests and activities as well as the levels of reading ability in order to recommend the most useful books and other reading matter for the year.

5. The supervisor needs to know many details about the interests, abilities, attitudes, and difficulties of the pupils in order to help the teachers make the most needed improvements in classroom work.

6. The teacher — as emphasized in most previous chapters, especially in Chapter XI — needs to know all she possibly can about the manifold aspects of the reading interests and ability of every pupil in her class.

To be somewhat more specific, there should be available at all times and in form intelligible and useful to all these officers, such information as the following:

1. The age, intelligence, language abilities (including abilities in foreign languages and lack of familiarity with English), previous reading experiences and interests, and other characteristics of children entering school and at later periods.

2. Vocabulary and range of information of the pupils.

3. Basal silent-reading skills, including levels of comprehension, speed, and accuracy, in reading various types of material and for various purposes.

4. Word mastery skills, including types of attack in studying new words, directional orientation and methods of analyzing unfamiliar words, and types of perception of single words and groups of words.

5. Basal oral-reading skills, including level, speed, and accuracy, and characteristics of expression.

6. General reading habits, including types of head movements, posture, position of books, use of finger or pointer, lip movements, inner speech, signs of tension and fatigue.

7. Reading interests in different materials and voluntary activities in various situations.

8. Advanced reading and study skills, including skill in using books, including texts, dictionaries, and reference books; ability to summarize, outline, and organize material; ability to take notes, use maps and graphs; ability to make effective use of the library.

These topics represent merely certain areas in which many specific interests and abilities, as well as distastes and difficulties, may be identified and appraised or measured sufficiently well to be serviceable in teaching by one or more methods. The weakness of much current practice lies in the disregard of many of these factors, appraisal by unnecessarily inadequate methods, failure to record results in forms both permanent and intelligible to all who may need them, or failure to make full use of valuable data in hand. In recommending the program briefly indicated above, the Committee has attempted to present a plan that will provide more adequately the obviously important needs of schools today.

II. Characteristics and Purposes of Comprehensive Diagnostic Inventory Examinations

The preceding chapters, especially Chapter XI, have emphasized the importance of thoroughness and continuity in measuring and otherwise appraising the pupils' interests, abilities, and difficulties in reading. The difficulty in most classes is that the teacher is only vaguely aware of the pupils' status most of the time and rarely if ever achieves a really thorough familiarity with the numerous specific skills and techniques upon which ability to read depends. Consequently, confusions, omissions, and inappropriate procedures are permitted to appear and persist until they hamper or completely block further development. It is the primary purpose of this section to outline a plan of appraisal that will enable the teacher to achieve fuller insight and to determine when intensive study by herself or others is advisable.

The most effective way to appraise a pupil's reading ability thoroughly is to employ the outline and the materials and methods necessary for conducting a diagnostic inventory examination. The diagnostic inventory embodies a systematic program for investigating all the phases of reading ability considered by its author to have diagnostic and remedial significance. It usually consists of a sheet or booklet in which the entire series of appraisals are listed with spaces for recording scores of tests, notes concerning facts observed, significant pupil responses, and summaries of the diagnosis and recommendations for instruction or remedial work. These records should be filed as part of the permanent record of the pupil. In such an examination various devices are employed, such as standardized tests, informal tests, observations of performance, error analyses, questionnaires, ratings, records of activities. The manuals accompanying the program give instructions concerning the devices to use for studying each item, how to use them, and how to interpret the results. Most inventories include a number of tests and examinations designed especially for diagnostic purposes. In brief, the inventory includes in most usable form the data needed for a thorough diagnosis.

To give a general idea of the range of abilities, techniques, and difficulties that teachers can and do appraise by employing the diagnostic inventory, the following outline has been drawn up. Accompanying the items are notes indicating various methods used in securing the desired information. It will be noted that many abilities and difficulties can be appraised by several methods, some of which have been discussed earlier and some of which will be dealt with later. This outline gives a composite of several programs now in use. If the classification seems extensive and formidable, the reader should realize that the lists include items applicable to pupils from the initial stages in reading to the upper-grade and high-school levels. The list really represents an outline of the abilities and skills that should be investigated during the school career of a pupil from kindergarten to college. At any one time only a portion would be given to a particular child in accordance with his needs.

OUTLINE OF ITEMS CONSIDERED IN AN APPRAISAL OF READING ABILITY

1. Background Skills
    a. Understanding of words (using oral vocabulary tests, such as Stanford-Binet or group reading-vocabulary tests).

    b. Understanding of sentences, paragraphs, and shorter units (using standardized or informal oral tests).

    c. Ability to understand class discussions (using observations and ratings).

    d. Ability to coöperate in class discussions (using observations and ratings).

    e. Voice and speech habits (using observations and ratings).

    f. Ability to handle books, pencils, materials (using records, informal tests, and questionnaires).

2. Word-Mastery Skills

    a. General status, represented by age or grade or other standard scores (obtained from standardized tests), in such abilities as:

        Level and accuracy of silent word recognition.

        Level and accuracy of pronunciation of isolated words.

        Level and accuracy of recognizing and pronouncing words in oral reading of sense material.

    b. Methods employed in word mastery (discovered by observation and by analysis of errors, using such tests as above) to determine:

        Use of context clues.

        Attention to visual form of words as wholes.

        Attention to syllables and phonograms.

        Attention to letters.

        Attention to miscellaneous details.

        Parts mainly noted — beginning, middle, end, whole word.

        Attention to sound characteristics of words; detects and sounds mainly syllables, phonetic elements, such as *tr. th,* individual letters, various elements.

    c. Characteristics of the pupil's word analysis (discovered by observation and by standardized or informal diagnostic tests) to reveal whether pupil uses quick and superficial or slow and laborious procedures.

        Tries persistently or gives up quickly.

        Tries different units, or sounds, or devices, or varies little from first response.

        Sounds elements too independently or readily fuses them.

        Easily satisfied with any result or critical of results and willing to try again.

        Forgets to use context clues when studying word forms or combines use of context and word-form clues.

        Shows evidence of faulty directional orientations, resulting in reversal errors, confused order of parts.

        Shows zest in word analysis or appears tense, or bored, or annoyed.

    d. Types of separate elements and devices used in word study (using standardized or informal short diagnostic tests) to reveal ability to:

        Recognize familiar parts in such combinations as *roing, dopar.*

        Recognize (immediately) familiar syllables and phonograms, such as *ing, ter, st, in, ea, la.*

Recognize or name letters.

Give sounds of individual letters.

Give letters corresponding to letter sounds.

Blend or fuse letter sounds or combinations of letter sounds, phonograms, and syllables.

Give rhyming words, words beginning with stated sound.

e. Methods of studying new words (determined by observation of ordinary words or use of more or less standardized lessons of learning lists of words) to reveal:

Number of repetitions required.

Speed and accuracy of recognition and pronunciation immediately after tests.

Fullness of recall or recognition after twenty-four hours.

Methods of studying (see 2*b* and 2*c* above).

Methods of attacking words poorly remembered.

Types of words poorly remembered.

f. Directional orientation in studying new words and working out recognition of unfamiliar words (using special standardized or informal arrangement of words with tabulation and analysis of errors; observation of eye movements) to reveal:

Tendencies to reverse words (*was* for *saw*), or get parts in incorrect order (*ten* for *net, swan* for *answer*) in oral reading of selections, lists of words, or recognitory exercises.

Tendencies to see only first, middle, end, or miscellaneously only one part of a word clearly.

Irregular, unsystematic roving of eyes over word.

3. Silent Reading

a. General levels of comprehension.

Level of sentence understanding (using primary-grade standardized or informal tests).

Level of paragraph comprehension (using primary or advanced standardized tests composed of paragraphs of varied complexity and difficulty, or informal tests).

Appraisal of longer selections (using standardized or informal tests).

b. Rate of reading.

Tests of rate of reading with specified accuracy of comprehension composed of varied materials, or of each of several types of reading, such as reading to get the main idea, to note significant details, to execute precise directions (using standardized or informal tests).

c. Accuracy of comprehension and interpretation, usually obtained by computing percentage of responses correct in tests used in 3*a* or 3*b* above.

d. Recall and use of material read. Use standardized tests for age or grade status and informal tests for qualitative analysis in determining:

General amount and accuracy of recall of given facts.

Unaided recall full, medium, scanty.

Response well organized or poorly organized.

Response free and full, or labored and slow.

Response accurate or inaccurate.

Response liberal or imaginative.

Response contains few or many new words and expressions.

Responses to specific questions good, medium, or poor.

Recall after interval good or poor; literal or imaginative.

Shows great, medium, or little zest in reading and recall.

Ability to outline.

Ability to summarize.

Ability to apply to special problems.

Ability to associate ideas with other information.

Ability to organize for special purposes.

4. Oral Reading

   a. General status (standardized tests).

   b. Characteristics of oral reading. Use observation of performance in standardized or informal tests to reveal such characteristics as the following:

Hurried, strained reading.

Slow labored reading.

Reading word-by-word rather than by thought units.

Ignoring of punctuation marks.

Habitual repetition of words.

Habitual omission of words.

Habitual addition of words.

Habitual errors in pronunciations.

Habits of 'making up' nonsense to keep going.

Evidence of strain, embarrassment or insecurity.

Pleasing, well-modulated, expressive reading.

Strained, high-pitched voice.

Monotonous tone.

Volume too loud or too low.

Slurred, and otherwise faulty, enunciation.

   c. Recall. (Observation and informal questioning after reading a standardized or informal selection.) (See silent reading, Item 3*d*, above.)

5. Advanced Reading and Study Skills

   a. Amount of independent reading (determined from library records, book notes, records of time spent in reading, familiarity with content of books shown in class, use of free periods, results of questionnaires, and so forth).

   b. Types of independent reading (determined from free reports of pupil, analysis of questionnaires, reviews, newspapers and periodicals read regularly, and so forth).

   c. Appraisal of skills in using books (determined by standardized and in-

formal tests, questionnaires, observations of classroom and library work)
with reference to such techniques as the following:

Tendency and ability to use table of contents, index, footnotes, references, and various types of headings.

Tendency and ability to use the dictionary and glossaries and their
various features.

Ability to locate, read, and recall information of various types.

Ability to summarize, outline, and organize material.

Ability and tendency to use encyclopedias and other reference books.

Ability to develop bibliographies and to organize materials from various sources.

Ability in various types of study reading, such as skimming, scanning,
reviewing.

Ability to read and use specific directions, maps, graphs, formulas, outlines, headlines, posters, cartoons, figures, and legends.

Ability to think, evaluate, and decide during the process of reading.

Ability to take notes of various types during reading.

Ability to review, recall, amplify, speak from, and variously use the
notes.

Ability to read orally ' at sight.'

Ability to memorize poetry, prose, and formulas.

Ability to become quickly familiar with printed, typewritten, or hand-
written material sufficiently to permit effective oral reading or combined recall-and-reading before an audience.

Ability to use local library facilities.

6. General Reading Habits

Observe performance in silent and oral reading of standardized or informal test materials or in routine of classroom activities to reveal such
habits as the following:

Type of head movements.

Posture.

Position of book, hands, head.

Use of finger or pointer.

Lip movements, inner speech.

Squinting, moving near and away from book, frowning, rubbing eyes.

Signs of tension, such as gritting teeth, wrinkling brow, clenching fists,
squirming, jerking.

Signs of low interest, such as stopping, gazing about, fumbling with
book.

Signs of zestful, eager interest.

Most inventories are designed to carry forward an exhaustive
analysis of the most extreme reading disabilities, and include instructions for giving tests and examinations of intelligence, vision, hearing,

and perception, none of which was included in the above outline because their administration demands considerable technical skill. Use of inventories for this purpose is discussed in Chapter XIII. The important thing for the teacher to realize is that, although such diagnostic inventories are set up for use with extreme cases, most of the sub-tests for reading skills and techniques (as distinguished from tests for perception, audition, vision, and intelligence) can and should be used by the teacher as part of her classroom routine. She should, and readily can, achieve, moreover, a good understanding of the more technical parts of such a program in order to know when one of her pupils may need more intensive study and to understand the results of such an analysis. It should be realized, further, that pupils within a given class are functioning at different levels and require special observation of quite different abilities and difficulties. It is strongly recommended, therefore, that the teacher become familiar with as wide a range of the items as may be needed in her class and learn to use as many of the sub-tests as may be necessary.

Some of the inventory examinations, even those going into great detail, are organized in sufficiently brief form to permit a teacher to make a fairly comprehensive survey of the pupil's abilities and difficulties in an hour or less. The manuals accompanying such inventories indicate the signs that point to occasional need of further diagnosis by specialists and supply suggestions for instructions and remedial work.

The diagnostic inventory is not to be thought of as merely providing for a special, extensive diagnosis on rare occasions or for especially troublesome cases. It provides also, and primarily, a systematic and effective program for studying any reading ability or difficulty at any time. For example, if the teacher wishes to satisfy herself concerning the ability of certain pupils to deal with unfamiliar words encountered in reading, the inventory provides a simple, graded series of brief examinations. In a short time the teacher may discover that Pupil A simply spells out the words and is unable to use other attacks, which he should be promptly helped to utilize. Pupil B uses several useful devices but looks over the word in various directions instead of consistently rightward. He needs a quite different type of instruction. Pupil C's trouble lies in too much attention to the word forms and too little to the context clues and, consequently, needs help in reading primarily to understand and in using the sense of the passage to suggest the word. Other pupils in the same grade are observed chiefly for an explanation of slow, labored silent reading, or hasty, breathless, high-pitched oral reading, or inability to recall today what was apparently understood yesterday, or for other possible limitations. The diagnostic inventory furnishes what is needed to study briefly but systematically at any convenient time any one or more of the better-known skills and difficulties and to suggest desirable types of instructional or remedial work indicated by the results. In general, such inventory diagnoses are designed to assist the teacher in her direct observational contacts with the pupil by giving examples of activities to study and by providing reasonably clear-cut indications of the significance of different degrees of superiority and backwardness. Experience in using the more systematic analyses, with the accompanying norms and other aids for determining the significance of what is found, is the most effective way of increasing one's sagacity in learning about the pupil in any and all contacts with him in regular classroom work.[1]

III. Merits and Limitations of Various Special Methods of Measurement and Appraisal

As stated above, the typical diagnostic inventory includes materials and directions for employing various types of standardized and informal tests, observations, error analyses, and other devices. Effective classroom instruction, as suggested in the preceding chapter, demands a familiarity with these devices whether they are employed occasionally and irregularly as needs arise or more systematically in surveys of classes or intensive studies of individuals. For this reason, some comments on the characteristics of the more commonly used devices will be offered.

1. Standardized Tests

The objective, standardized tests should, in general, give more uniform, more valid, more meaningful, and more objective results than unstandardized tests. The norms accompanying the tests provide a definite standard by means of which one may compare the exact ability of one child or group of children measured in one time or place with that shown by another child or group of children measured at another time or place. The use of norms, morever, makes it possible to compare a child's competence in one phase of reading with his competence in another, and thus to secure a diagnosis of relative strengths and weaknesses in the different aspects of reading ability on an objective

---

[1] References to several diagnostic inventory plans are given at the end of this chapter.

basis. These data are invaluable for permanent records. Since their meaning is permanent, they may be used by various persons, in dealing with the pupil at any given time, in estimating his needs and prospects over a long period of time, and in analyzing results of the work in a school system as a whole, such as setting up experiments and arriving at decisions concerning the time allotments, grouping plans, choice of materials, and methods of instruction.

Standardized tests are sometimes misused. One of the most common misuses is to employ norms as if they were ideals of attainment instead of statistical statements of average achievements. An infrequent but serious misuse of tests is to consider them as if they were an abbreviated course of study, or to use several forms of a test as practice materials. Inasmuch as tests are not organized for instructional purposes, such practices are never justified. Another error results from failure to understand exactly what a particular test actually measures, as when a teacher assumes that a single test measures general reading ability, or that different reading tests measure the same types or phases of reading. No single test, however long or complicated, can provide a measurement of the totality of abilities involved in reading; each test measures only one aspect or type. For this reason, the recent tendency has been to develop groups or batteries of reading tests [1] that permit an analysis of several important phases of reading ability and thus yield results that suggest definite types of follow-up instruction. To secure a full diagnosis of every component of reading

---

[1] For example, the Sangren-Woody Reading Tests measure word meaning, rate of reading, comprehension of factual material, comprehension of total meaning of paragraph, understanding of simple thought, following of directions, and organization of the materials. The Gates Tests for Grades III–VIII measure independently rate and accuracy of each of four types of reading: (1) reading to get the general significance of a passage; (2) reading to anticipate outcomes of a passage; (3) reading of precise directions; and (4) reading to note significant details. The tests are frequently given with a test for level of comprehension, thus providing separate measures of speed, accuracy, and level of reading comprehension. The Iowa Silent Reading Tests for the upper grades and high school provide measurements in comparable form of the following: (1) paragraph comprehension of material from (a) social science, (b) literature, and (c) science; (2) word meaning or subject-matter vocabulary in (a) social science, (b) science, (c) mathematics, and (d) English; (3) comprehension of single sentences, of various contexts; (4) ability to organize or rearrange (a) phrases into sentences, (b) central ideas of paragraphs, and (c) sentences from paragraphs; (5) ability to use sample index material, select key words, and alphabetize lists of words, and (6) rate and comprehension in reading a passage of 648 words.

ability, however, it is necessary to supplement standardized tests by other types of tests observations, and examinations.

2. Informal Tests

Since informal tests have been discussed and illustrated in detail in preceding chapters, especially Chapter XI, only a few general matters will be considered in this chapter.

Informal tests may take a great variety of forms and purposes, many of which are similar to those employed in standardized tests. For example, one teacher or several teachers in a school system may give the tests to different classes or to individual children in exactly the same way and score them by the same key. The significance of the score is increased, furthermore, by noting the position of each child in a group. This group may be a teacher's own class or a larger population of other classes of the same grade status or of higher and lower positions in the same school. When handled in this way, the informal test is essentially the same as a standardized test, differing only in the degree to which the desirable features of standardization are realized. For purposes of diagnosing the characteristics of the children within a particular group, the use of such informal measurements is extremely valuable.

Informal tests may be more nicely adjusted to specific needs of an individual pupil or class. For example, the teacher may select lists of words or textual materials that the pupils have read or studied, or which are composed of the elements of materials previously perused. In this way the test measures definitely the outcome of specific instruction. The informal test may be designed to reveal the extent to which different children have achieved a technique the teacher has been attempting to develop. For example, if the teacher has been recently giving instruction in methods of maintaining a left-to-right orientation in the study of words and in the avoidance of reversal tendencies, she may organize a test to reveal the pupil's competence in this specific skill. Skillfully used, informal tests may be employed to measure gains over a short period of time; indeed, even the outcome of a single lesson may be determined. One of the effective features of certain types of teaching consists in the organization of informal tests in such form as to comprise essentially a review exercise. If certain children reveal deficiencies or errors, the amount and kind of additional instruction may be clearly indicated.

3. Appraisals by Observational Methods

Some of the most important features of reading ability consist in the *activities* engaged in by the pupil that can be appraised by observation. For example, although one may ask a pupil to work out the recognition and pronunciation of a series of words graded from very easy to rather difficult and obtain a record of the number of words handled successfully, several children obtaining the same score may use quite different methods of attack. The development of skill in diagnosing a pupil's needs by observing his performances is one of the most important requirements of the superior teacher and reading specialist.

Most of the manuals for conducting diagnostic inventories contain directions for conducting observations of the techniques revealed in word study and recognition, oral and silent reading, methods of study and other phases of the reading process. Suggestions concerning what to look for, how to look, and what to do about the conditions observed are given. Various devices are now available for guiding and standardizing the records of observations. The Oral Reading Check Tests [1] and The Chicago Sustained Application Profile Sheet [2] for observing study habits of pupils in the upper grades and high school are examples.

4. Analysis of Errors

The nature of the techniques employed by a child may often be discerned by a study of errors made during an exercise. Methods of analyzing errors in word recognition, word meanings, study procedures, and the like, as well as in many types of oral and silent reading, are outlined in most manuals devoted to reading diagnosis. Chapter XI gives a number of suggestions for analyzing the significance of errors.

In the earlier tests and in much informal observation of errors, the examiner was largely dependent upon his own judgment concerning the implications of the types and frequency of errors made. An examiner's judgment would improve, like a physician's diagnosis, with experience. Recently, efforts have been made to make the analysis of errors more significant and accurate by standardizing materials and methods and developing norms. For example, various investigators [3] have improved

---

[1] Published by the Public School Publishing Company, Bloomington, Illinois.

[2] Published and sold by the University of Chicago Book Store, Chicago, Illinois.

[3] See references at the end of the chapter.

upon the original type of oral reading test by perfecting the content, defining the procedure more exactly, studying the meaning of errors in relation to instruction, and developing tables of frequencies of different types of errors, to assist in determining the significance of the number and types of errors shown.

5. Questionnaires and Self-Inventories

Questionnaires and self-inventories have been developed to provide information concerning many phases of reading interest, attitudes, achievements, and previous experiences. For example, one diagnostician [1] has made extensive use of such types as the following:

1. Pupil's Report on Interests and Activities.
2. Pupil's Report of Books Read.
3. Pupil's Report of Handedness and Laterality.
4. Interviewer's Impression of the Child.

The first of these consists of five pages of questions, of which the following are samples:

What do you usually do:
    (a) Directly after school? _____
    (b) In the evening? _____
    (c) On Saturdays? _____
    (d) On Sundays? _____
Underline the kinds of pictures you like best:
    comedy   western   sad   news   love   serial   mystery
    gangster   educational   society   cartoons
Who is your favorite actor? _____ actress? _____
If you were going into the movies, what kind of parts would you like to play? _____

Questionnaires to pupils and self-inventories of study habits comprise a type of instrument that is being used in a considerable number of schools. In the case of most questionnaires or self-inventories, the evaluation of the replies depends on the judgment of the investigator, but a few of these instruments have an objective scoring device. One of the few published self-inventories is the *Wrenn Study-Habits Inventory.*[2] It is designed for college use, but most of the items are

---

[1] Samples may be secured by addressing Paul A. Witty, Northwestern University, Evanston, Illinois.

[2] C. Gilbert Wrenn. *Study-Habits Inventory.* (Stanford University Press, 1934)

applicable to the high school as well. It deals with note-taking and reading tendencies, habits of concentration, school interests, and general habits of work. A scoring key is provided that shows the value of each response made by the student.

The better questionnaires embody the result of extensive experience in interviewing and observing the pupil's interests, activities, abilities, and other characteristics. They are likely to be more comprehensive than lists drawn up extemporaneously. When accompanied by distributions of the number of responses made by average children and by other types of children, such as the pupils retarded in reading or low in intelligence, they assist the teacher to interpret results and to become better acquainted with the pupil's special interests, distastes, handicaps, and special needs. Questionnaires may be developed by teachers to meet local needs more exactly and a helpful way to learn to make good questionnaires is to use samples of published forms. Suggestions for using questionnaires in the classroom situations are given in Chapter XI.

6. Ratings

Certain aspects of a pupil's reading ability depend primarily upon the impression the pupil makes upon other people. This is notably true, for example, of oral reading. In such cases, the final basis of judgment is the opinion of the auditors. In order to secure a meaningful expression of the observer's judgment, rating scales and other devices may be used. Ratings of such traits as quality of voice and oral expression, ability to coöperate with the teacher and other pupils, interest in books, desire to read, and the like are recommended later in this chapter for determining a pupil's ' readiness ' to begin reading. By utilizing a simple rating scheme, opinions may be more effectively combined and given more meaning in the child's cumulative record.

7. Records of Activities

It is frequently said that some of the most important phases of a pupil's ability and interest cannot be measured. This, strictly speaking, is true. The statement does not mean, however, that such characteristics must be disregarded, nor that they cannot be given permanent and meaningful expression. Interest or attitudes tend to express themselves in action. For example, other things being equal, such as opportunities and time, the pupil who reads the greatest amount is the pupil with the highest interest in reading. Information concerning books drawn from libraries, the kind and parts of newspapers and magazines read, the proportion of the pupil's time spent in reading are samples of data of great value in diagnosing a pupil's general intellectual interests. Sometimes such data point quite clearly to means of improving the pupil's instruction in school. For example, if it is found that a pupil left to his own resources chooses to read materials several grades higher in level than those supplied him in the schoolroom, needed modifications of his program are indicated.[1]

8. Workbooks, Preparatory Books, Practice Books, and Other Printed Booklets of Teach-and-Test Materials

Within recent years various types of organizations of materials similar to published standardized and teacher-made informal tests have appeared. They usually come in printed form, comprising pads or booklets or loose-leaf collections, and are given such titles as Workbooks, Preparatory Books, Practice Exercises, Companion Books, or Self-Help Books. Some are developed to accompany a particular series of readers and others are designed for general use with any series of reading books.

The better types represent an effort to develop a comprehensive series of exercises that include in well-printed and illustrated form the best informal devices and tests that the teacher would otherwise have to prepare herself. They are organized systematically to provide self-manageable learning of the basal words, word recognition, comprehension, appreciation, and study techniques and simultaneously to test and diagnose ability and difficulty. Their purpose is to provide the nearest possible approach to the policy of daily diagnosis with the least expenditure of the time of the pupils and teacher. They have the advantage over teacher-made informal materials of being more carefully developed, more attractive in material, form, and illustration, more convenient to use and, when all things are taken into account, more economical. The manuals accompanying many of the booklets give suggestions for observing performances, interpreting errors, keeping records of interests and activities, using ratings and questionnaires, and conducting needed follow-up or remedial work.

Such booklets may include all the types of materials and test exercises that teachers prepare for their own use. They are extremely valu-

---

[1] Suggestions for observing and recording pertinent data concerning reading abilities in the content subjects are given in Chapter V, reading interests and tastes in Chapter VI, and oral reading in Chapter X.

able in enabling a teacher to make better adjustments to individual needs. Being in a form that pupils can use with a minimal of teacher assistance, they are of unique value in assisting the pupil who has been absent from school or who has otherwise fallen behind, and in saving the abler pupils from wasting time in unnecessary study and review. Where proper care has been exercised in developing a program of such material, many of the elements of the inventory diagnosis are also included, so that a teacher is provided with an opportunity to supplement her other methods of gaining insight into the pupil's progress. The fact that they provide the pupils with opportunity to work by themselves (as well as in coöperative enterprises) with little or no teacher direction frees the teacher more frequently and fully to supervise and study individual children. When these materials are developed in technically sound form and embody attractive and worthwhile content, they produce one of the most effective ways of enabling the teacher to keep an almost daily contact with each individual's progress and difficulties and of increasing efficiency by teaching and testing at the same time.

IV. Suggested Programs for the Various Grades

The determination of a satisfactory program of measurement and appraisal for a particular school depends upon its financial resources, the equipment of teaching materials, the size of classes, the skill of teachers, the type of available professional services of physicians, psychologists, specialists in reading diagnosis, departments of measurement and research, and other factors. Little more can be done in this chapter than briefly to suggest desirable materials and activities for a typical school.

1. Appraisal on Entering Grade I

If the devastating effects of failure or serious frustration in reading in the first year's work are to be avoided, an extensive examination of the pupils on entering school is necessary. The justification of this statement is given in Chapter XIII. If possible, the following data should be secured:

1. Reliable measure of intelligence.
2. Careful examination of vision and hearing.
3. Careful medical examination, including detection of various physical and physiological handicaps.
4. Appraisal of speech and motor coördination.

5. Appraisal of visual and auditory habits of perception.

6. Appraisal of ability to understand and use English in class activities and in conversation.

7. Appraisal of meaning vocabulary and range of information.

8. Appraisal of background or prerequisite reading abilities, such as interest in books; ability to handle books; ability to recognize or distinguish works and to read simple material.

9. Appraisal of ability to function in a schoolroom situation, including effectiveness of adjusting to teachers and other pupils, ability to attend to what the teacher or other pupils say, to work by oneself, to use pencils, chalk, pictures, scissors, paper.

' Reading readiness' depends upon these factors, and perhaps on other factors, and, inasmuch as they are discussed in other chapters, especially IV and XI, the discussion here will be confined chiefly to the tests used for appraisal, excepting the medical and psychological examinations, which are treated in Chapter XIII.

Using informal methods of the types mentioned earlier in this chapter, rough appraisals of speech, motor coördination, ability to understand and use English, and the various reading and scholastic interests enumerated under Items 8 and 9 may be secured. Several reports outline fairly detailed plans for making such appraisals.[1]

A number of ' reading-readiness' or ' first-grade-readiness' tests are now available. Most of these are pencil-and-paper tests that provide objective appraisals of some of the abilities included in the above list. For example, the Metropolitan Readiness Test includes six subtests: (1) comparing like and unlike pictures, letters, numbers, and words; (2) copying geometrical forms; (3) word meanings; (4) sentence meanings; (5) number knowledge, and (6) range of general information.[2]

Two more extensive reading readiness examinations have appeared lately. The Monroe Reading Aptitude Test [3] includes seventeen subtests, mostly group tests requiring no apparatus except pencil and paper. In addition to measuring word and sentence meanings and

---

[1] For example, M. Lucile Harrison. *Reading Readiness.* (Houghton Mifflin Company: Boston, 1936, 166 pp.)

[2] Other reading readiness tests are the Van Wagenen, the Lee-Clark, and the Stone and Grover. See M. Lucile Harrison. *Op. cit.*, and other references at the end of the chapter.

[3] Marion Monroe. *Reading Aptitude Tests and Manual.* (Houghton Mifflin Company: Boston, 1935)

word-form discrimination, this series includes tests of eye-motor control, speech coördination, hand, eye, and foot dominance, motor speed and steadiness, auditory discrimination of words and other sounds, auditory memory, ability to blend sounds, and other abilities. The Betts Ready-to-Read Tests [1] include, in addition to certain tests of 'auditory readiness,' such as auditory span, auditory fusion, acuity and perception, a series of tests of visual sensation and perception and of discrimination of letters and words in which a special instrument, the Keystone Opthalmic Telebinocular, is used. The tests of visual sensation and perception are designed to appraise sharpness of the image, visual efficiency, vertical and lateral imbalance, coördination level, and fusion in far or near (book-distance) vision.

Where facilities permit, other characteristics believed to be related to reading difficulties should be explored when the pupil enters school.[2]

In evaluating the results of testing for reading readiness the following cautions should be observed. Children on entering school are usually more difficult to test reliably than more experienced pupils are. They are more subject to unsteadiness in application, distractions, and misunderstanding of directions. It should be realized, moreover, that a pupil's readiness must be considered in relation to the program he is to undertake. Some programs are much harder and less fully adapted to individual differences than others. A pupil may be 'ready' to undertake one program some time before he is ready to deal successfully with another. This means that considerable investigation of readiness must be made in each school before the attainments essential for its program can be definitely determined. Secondly, as pointed out in Chapter IV, readiness is not best achieved merely by waiting. It is something to be developed. Many of the factors appraised by examinations of reading readiness are subject to marked improvement by well-chosen experiences. Third, readiness involves many different factors in which a typical pupil is unevenly advanced. Unfortunately, we still lack information concerning the weight to be given to each and every characteristic. This makes it inadvisable to adopt a highly rigid set of standards of readiness, all of which must be met. In general the Committee recommends careful study of as many factors as possible with a teaching program that permits flexibility in adjusting to indi-

---

[1] E. A. Betts. *Betts Ready-to-Read Tests and Manual.* (Keystone View Company: Meadville, Pennsylvania, 1934)

[2] In Chapter XIII several of these are outlined and references are made to diagnostic programs that include appropriate tests and examinations.

vidual differences in the initial stages. The 'reading readiness' or 'pre-reading' program should not be sharply separated from the initial reading program but, rather, should be skillfully coördinated and merged with it.

2. Appraisal during Grade I

Appraising ability, interests, techniques, and difficulties in reading during the first school year is of maximal importance, since it is during this period that the major catastrophes occur. Unfortunately, it is particularly difficult to develop standardized tests suitable to all pupils during the first three quarters of a typical first year's progress. This is due primarily to the fact that, since children's reading is limited largely to the specific words they have learned, their showing depends greatly on the number of such words included in the test. For this period frequent appraisal by informal materials, workbook exercises, error analysis, and other examinations based on the materials the pupils have studied, coupled with observations of performance, is a vital need. The teacher should make systematic analyses by the diagnostic-inventory technique at intervals, especially of the children who do not progress satisfactorily.

Pupils will require different amounts of time to reach a stage at which they may safely — that is, without too much danger of misunderstanding, becoming discouraged, or practicing erroneous techniques — be permitted to read various books by themselves with little or no supervision. The characteristics of this stage are described in Chapter IV. To determine when a pupil has reached this stage, informal tests, observations of performance, analysis of errors, and standardized tests may be used. Suggestions concerning informal methods, observations of performance, and study of errors are given in Chapter XI. In general, the procedure consists merely in observing the pupil's oral and silent reading, determining his comprehension of the thought, and noting the number and kinds of errors and difficulties encountered in reading the easiest of the available books or informal-test selections. For pupils at this stage, the easier standardized tests are more suitable, since some of the harder ones are too difficult for pupils who can safely read very simple primers.

It should be realized that there is rarely a sharp division between the initial stage and the stage of independent reading ability. The purpose of testing is not so much to determine when the pupil needs no supervision and help as *how much* he should receive at any particular time. Consequently the program of instruction should include frequent, almost daily, checks by observation of oral and silent reading performances and analysis of results of informal tests and study exercises so that the teacher is always aware of the amount and kind of help each child needs.

Near the end of the year — but not so near as to leave insufficient time to make full use of the results — standardized tests of both oral and silent reading and a careful survey of reading interests, difficulties, and needs should be made. At this time the teacher should summarize the results of the year's experience in form suitable for a permanent record to be transmitted to the pupil's next teacher. This summary should include a clear statement of the methods employed during the year, the pupil's interests and special difficulties, the type and amount of reading done, and various suggestions for the next teacher.

Many standardized tests are available for use in the latter part of the first grade. A survey [1] of silent-reading tests shows sixteen different tests of word recognition, thirteen of sentence comprehension, and twelve of paragraph comprehension. Accuracy or difficulty-level, or both, rather than speed of word recognition and comprehension, is measured by practically all these tests. Several consist of series that include tests of two or all three of these phases of reading ability.[2] Either the Oral Reading Check Tests or the Standardized Reading Paragraphs are very useful for examining oral-reading ability and analyzing reading techniques.[3]

3. Appraisal in Grades II and III

During this period, the typical pupil shifts from relatively slow, labored reading to a smoother, faster, and more diversified reading. This transition makes testing difficult. At the beginning stage, the primary tests that measure the level and accuracy or fullness of comprehension are more suitable, but somewhere in this period, tests of speed and accuracy of reading, both of distinctly primary material and

---

[1] This survey was made with the assistance of Dr. Gertrude Hildreth, Mr. Elden Bond, and Mrs. Mercedes Lorch. It is probably not exhaustive. The list of tests for the various grades has become so extensive that space was not available in this *Yearbook* to enumerate them all. Readers are referred to references at the end of the chapter for further details.

[2] For example, the Brueckner-Heylum, the Cutright, the De Vault, the Garvey, the Gates Primary, the Lee-Clark, and Ingraham's Los Angeles Primary.

[3] Developed by William S. Gray.

of more advanced content, should be introduced.[1] Usually the latter should be used when the pupil gets a grade score of 2.9 or better on the primary types of tests.

During the latter part of the second grade it is difficult to test properly all the pupils in a class either with a primary, or a third-grade, or an advanced series test. If one test is used, it is usually necessary to follow up by testing some of the pupils with the other. Sometimes teachers are disturbed to find that a pupil gets quite a different age or grade score on tests of the two types. Thus a pupil may get a grade score of 3.4 on a primary test and only 2.9 on an advanced. Usually this is due to the fact that the tests measure different abilities. The pupil may read primary vocabulary material with accuracy and understanding but score lower when tested on speed of reading typical third-grade material.

The program of testing for these grades should include batteries or series of standardized tests two or three times a year, at the beginning, middle, and a month or six weeks before the end, or else near the beginning and some time between the middle and the end of the year.

During Grades II and III, standardized tests should be abundantly supplemented with informal and workbook tests. These must be diversified to provide appraisal of new types and aspects of the growing skills. Oral reading should be carefully appraised not only for its technical reading features but also for qualities of expression. The pupil's outside reading interests and activities should be studied. Skills in working out the recognition, pronunciation, and meaning of words, in using context clues, in reading by ' thought units ' instead of words, in achieving fair speed, in skimming and using simpler reading aids, such as the table of contents, chapter subheadings, and the like, now deserve attention. In the third grade, the various types of study habits, as well as specialized reading types (such as reading precise directions and using simple glossaries) should be investigated.

During these two grades, the teacher must be alert to detect difficulties, which though not severe enough to disrupt reading entirely, will lead to serious limitations. She should satisfy herself continually

---

[1] Among the series of tests of the primary type covering word recognition, sentence comprehension, and paragraph comprehension, or at least two of these three, are the De Vault, the Garvey, the Gates, the Manwiller, the Metropolitan, the New Stanford, Haggerty Sigma I, the Ingraham, and the Williams. Samples of batteries of several tests suitable for Grade III or above are listed in the footnote that closes the discussion of appraisal in Grades IV to VIII (4, below).

concerning the development of every pupil. She should be prepared to make or secure a systematic diagnostic inventory of the essential techniques of every child concerning whose progress any doubt exists. The pupils showing marked difficulty should, if possible, be given a thorough reading diagnosis (see Chapter XIII).

As pointed out in Chapter IV, the child during Grade III must be getting ready to meet the 'fourth-grade hurdle' — a grade score of 4.0 in reading by the beginning of that grade. This is a problem for Grade III; it is a problem for a considerable proportion of the children who are backward but not seriously retarded. Since any handicap is serious, careful appraisal, diagnosis, and instruction in the second half of Grade III will be richly repaid.[1]

4. Appraisal in Grades IV to VIII

Appraisals in these grades, except for greatly retarded pupils, should provide explorations of reading skills of increasing subtlety and complexity and the techniques of study. As the grade becomes higher, pupils in increasing number should be studied in connection with the acquisition of skills mentioned in the next section devoted to the junior and senior high school. Typical fourth grades, however, include pupils who have not as yet sufficiently mastered the fundamental techniques of reading to enable them to use their intellect to the full in regular classroom work. For these, the tests and diagnoses suggested for earlier grades should be employed.

Pupils comprising the middle 60 percent of the enrollment in Grades IV to VIII should be tested for speed, accuracy, and level of comprehension in silent reading and for general competence and special limitations in oral reading to insure continued development. Tests of skill in using the dictionary, reference books, and the like should be employed. Skill in summarizing, outlining, organizing, and variously using typical texts should be occasionally diagnosed. Special attention should be given to the discovery of the quantity and quality of reading of books, magazines, and other materials, and the cultivating of good tastes. Indeed, appraisals should be made of practically all types and phases of

---

[1] The justification for this recommendation is given in general terms in Chapter IV and in detail in D. M. Lee. *The Importance of Reading for Achieving in Grades Four, Five, and Six.* Contributions to Education, No. 556. (Teachers College, Columbia University: New York, 1933) In this monograph are listed several batteries of tests (usually four in number) that were used to determine critical scores.

reading suggested in earlier chapters as objectives of teaching in these grades.

The program of appraisal need be less definitely prearranged in these grades. Standardized tests may be given to some or all the pupils at the time when results may be most readily used. Since most tests, standardized or informal, can be taken by a pupil with relatively little assistance, individuals may be examined singly at convenient times without using much of the teacher's time. Systematic practices, such as recording and making graphs of the speed of reading shown by tests given at intervals of, say, once a month form a useful part of the permanent record for each pupil. In general, breadth and frequency of appraisal are the requirements for testing in this period.

A final suggestion is concerned with the fact mentioned earlier; namely, that reading abilities in these grades show an enormous range, from skill far exceeding that of average adults down to that typical of the primary grades. A too frequent defect of teaching is the failure to realize that some pupils in these grades are essentially beginners in competence and that they should be analyzed and treated for difficulties in the most elementary reading techniques, such as those involved in word mastery. Teachers in these grades, therefore, should be familiar with the diagnostic inventories and tests used in the primary grades. They should also employ regularly informal methods of determining the most suitable materials for independent reading suggested in Chapter XI.

As the pupils approach the upper grades, the likelihood of their being able to leap the ' high-school reading hurdle ' should be considered. While this hurdle is less reliably defined than the intermediate grade minimum, it is probable that pupils falling below a reading grade score of 7.0 will be handicapped in the typical junior- and senior-high-school curriculums.[1] Failure to reach this minimum should be anticipated in the lower grades, in Grade VI at the latest, and proper provisions made to achieve this level when, all things (such as intelligence) considered, this course seems possible and advisable.

A survey of published standardized tests for Grades IV to VIII shows a large number and a great variety. Among the tests located, twenty-seven measure *speed* of reading materials of uniform difficulty and five of these measure both *speed* and *accuracy;* and twenty-three measure *level* or *power* of comprehension. Fourteen tests of vocabulary or word knowledge were found. It is apparent, moreover, that there is

---

[1] See Chapter IV for a fuller discussion.

an increased tendency to produce series, or batteries, of tests, which include measures of several phases or types of reading, each of which is standardized on the same population.[1]

5. Evaluation of Reading Achievement in High School and College

Many students in both high school and college have not yet mastered the mechanics of reading. Such students, in reality still on the elementary-school level with respect to reading, must be regarded as remedial or corrective cases. As suggested in the preceding section, students whose reading falls below the seventh-grade norms should be given special diagnostic and remedial treatment.[2] For other students the main reading problem is the development of reading interests and skills by which their experience will be enriched. The problem of the measurement of reading at these higher levels, therefore, becomes much more complex. Methods of measurement are needed to evaluate changes taking place in a variety of directions, among which the following are important:

1. A genuine and spontaneous interest in books independent of class requirements.
2. Ability to read material for a variety of different purposes, such as:
   Locate facts.
   Find the central thought.
   Select details that support the main idea.
   Understand directions.
   Answer specific questions.
   Make a summary.
   See the writer's plan or organization.
   Locate proof.
   Interpret total meaning.

---

[1] This survey was made with the assistance of Gertrude Hildreth, Elden Bond, and Mercedes Lorch. Samples of the batteries of tests for the intermediate grades are: Gates Silent Reading Tests (Grades 3–8); Ingraham-Clark Diagnostic Tests (Grades 4–8); Iowa Every-Pupil Test of Basic Skills (3–8); Iowa Silent Reading Tests, Elementary and Advanced (9–13); Metropolitan Achievement Tests, Intermediate Battery (4–8) and Advanced Battery (7–8); Modern School Achievement Tests (3–8); Nelson Silent Reading Tests (3–8); Philadelphia Reading Tests (3, 4–6, 7–11); Pressey Diagnostic Reading Tests (3–9); Sangren-Woody Reading Tests (4–8); New Stanford Achievement Tests (2–3, 4–9); Traxler Silent Reading Tests (7–12).

[2] See Chapter IV.

3. Ability to read material in different fields — particularly literature, social science, and natural science.

4. Ability to read material presented in forms different from continuous discourse, such as tables, graphs, maps, and charts.

5. Skill in the finding of appropriate material in libraries and books, including the use of the card catalog, the reference aids in books, the dictionary, magazine indexes, and encyclopedias.

6. Adequate vocabulary, both general and technical.

7. Ability to relate what is read to past experience, to utilize it in constructive activities, and to apply it to new situations, rather than merely to remember the words.

8. Maximal rate of reading each type of material that is consistent with understanding.

Of thirty-one standardized reading tests for the high-school and college levels, fourteen yield but a single score. Of these, two measure speed of reading,[1] seven measure comprehension,[2] either in general or in some special phase, and five measure vocabulary.[3] It is possible to combine a number of such tests into a battery and thus to secure a fairly broad evaluation of reading achievement. Eight tests for the upper levels of the school are designed to measure two aspects of reading ability.[4] Nine tests usable in high school or college measure three or more phases of reading ability.[5]

Fairly adequate tests, such as the Iowa Silent Reading Test, are available that measure ability to locate facts, to find the central thought, to select details supporting the main idea, and to answer specific questions. There are a few tests of ability to understand directions, to make a summary, and to see the writer's plan. No satisfactory standardized reading tests are available for ability to locate proof or to interpret the total meaning of passages.

[1] Michigan Speed of Reading and Minnesota Speed of Reading.

[2] Chapman Unspeeded, Chapman-Holzinger Unspeeded, Shank Comprehension, Van Wagenen Unit Scales, Whipple, Poley Précis, and Woodworth-Wells Directions.

[3] Helley Sentence Vocabulary, Inglis Vocabulary, O'Rourke Vocabulary, Southington-Plymouth Vocabulary, Markham Vocabulary.

[4] Buffalo Speed and Comprehension, Monroe Silent Reading, Pressey Speed and Comprehension, Nelson-Denny Reading, Minnesota Reading, O'Rourke Vocabulary and Reading Power, O'Rourke Survey, and Witham's Silent Reading.

[5] Haggerty Reading, Sigma III, Mount Holyoke College Reading, Booker Silent Reading (unpublished), Traxler Silent Reading, Pressey General Reading, Pressey Special Reading, Iowa Silent Reading, Progressive Achievement, and Van Wagenen.

The ability to read materials in different fields, particularly in literature, social science, and natural science, can be measured with several standardized tests and also with informal tests taken from textbooks in these fields. The Van Wagenen reading scales probably cover the special fields of literature, history, and natural science more adequately than other reading tests at the high-school level.[1]

Few tests are available at the high-school and college levels for ability to read material presented in forms different from continuous discourse, such as tables, graphs, maps, and charts. One of the most promising tests of ability to read graphs and maps is contained in the last part of Pressey's *Special Reading Test*. A test that has implications for the measurement of ability to read tables and graphs, although it is not called a reading test, is Part I of the *Coöperative Test of Social Studies Abilities*, Form 1936, by J. W. Wrightstone. The results of standardized tests of ability to do these special kinds of reading can be checked readily with selections from textbooks.

A few reading tests attempt to measure certain aspects of skill in finding appropriate materials in libraries and books. One part of the Iowa Silent Reading Test deals with the use of the index in books. The Pressey Special Reading Test contains a test on the use of the dictionary. Two new reading books for the high school have tests on the use of reference aids and the finding of reading materials in books and libraries.[2] Tests by Barker[3] and by Boyington[4] are especially suggestive for teachers interested in making informal tests for these purposes. There are several valid and reliable tests of word meaning, of which the Inglis Test of English Vocabulary is one of the longer and more dependable. Some of the newer vocabulary tests are designed to measure knowledge of the vocabulary of special fields, such as social science, science, mathematics, and literature. Where instruction in reading is carried on in regular English classes, frequent appraisal with informal reading test materials is desirable. If the teacher does not

---

[1] Other suggestions for appraising study techniques are given in Chapter V.

[2] See especially: Carol Hovious. *Following Printed Trails*. (D. C. Heath and Company: Boston, 1936); and Angela M. Broening, Frederick H. Law, Mary S. Wilkinson, and Caroline L. Ziegler. *Reading for Skill*. (Noble and Noble, Inc.: New York, 1936)

[3] Vilda Barker. "Informal testing of the use of books and libraries." *Elementary English Review*, 143, 174, 205.

[4] Gladys Boyington. "Experiments with diagnostic tests to determine knowledge of study tools and techniques in the social studies." *Second Yearbook, National Council for Social Studies*. 1931–1932, pp. 132–163.

have time to construct these herself, she may find tests of this kind in some of the newer reading books [1] and workbooks for high-school use.[2]

Ability to relate what is read to past experience, to utilize it in constructive activities, and to apply it to new situations must be chiefly appraised by observation and informal tests. Some materials for measuring ability to apply what is read to new situations may be found in a few of the recent tests in social science and natural science, but nearly all these materials are still in the experimental stage.

The several tests of rate of reading for high-school and college students are fairly satisfactory and easy to administer. More comprehensive informal tests can be based on classroom materials. Ordinarily, students should read material adapted to their grade level in high school and college at a rate of 3.5 to 4 words per second. A rate that is consistently less than 3 words per second usually calls for corrective instruction.

A complete and detailed evaluation of reading ability calls for such a variety of procedures that few high schools and colleges have undertaken it. Seven reading evaluations to be recommended as most important are listed herewith:

1. Administer a standardized reading test, involving rate, vocabulary, and several aspects of comprehension, annually at the beginning of the year, and use the results in educational guidance.

2. Keep a record of the independent reading done by the students and evaluate the record periodically in the high school.

3. Test the ability of the students to find material in libraries and books.

4. Check the study habits of the students by observation, individual conference, and self-inventory.

5. Measure the ability of the students to read in the various subject-matter fields by informal tests in connection with their class work.

6. Where instruction in reading is given as a regular part of the program of the school, measure progress at the end of the year with an alternate form of the test given at the beginning of the year.

7. Provide expert diagnosis and remedial treatment for students whose reading ability falls below the norm for Grade VII.

---

[1] Hovious. *Op. cit.*, and Broening, Law, Wilkinson, and Ziegler. *Op. cit.*

[2] One series of this kind is William A. McCall, Luella B. Cook, and George W. Norvell. *Experiments in Reading.* (Harcourt, Brace and Company: New York, 1934) A discussion of means of appraising students' interests and tastes in voluntary reading is contained in Chapter VI.

References

A carefully compiled list of tests employed in measuring reading attainments and diagnosing difficulties will be found in G. H. Hildreth. *A Bibliography of Mental Tests and Rating Scales.* (The Psychological Corporation: New York, 1933, 242 pp.)

An excellent review of literature dealing with upper-grade, high-school, and college levels will be found in M. N. Woodring and C. W. Flemming. *Directing Study of High School Pupils.* (Bureau of Publications, Teachers College, Columbia University: New York, 1935, 253 pp.)

Following are representative general references; see also references at the end of Chapter XIII.

Betts, Emmett A. *The Prevention and Correction of Reading Difficulties.* (Row, Peterson and Company: Evanston, Illinois, 1936, 402 pp.)

Broening, A. M., Law, F. H., Wilkinson, M. S., and Ziegler, C. L. *Reading for Skill.* (Noble and Noble, Inc.: New York, 399 pp.)

Brueckner, L. J., and Melby, E. O. *Diagnostic and Remedial Teaching.* (Houghton Mifflin Company: Boston, 1931. Pp. 1–159, 247–332)

Dolch, Edward William. *The Psychology and Teaching of Reading.* (Ginn and Company: Boston, 1931. Pp. 210–253)

Educational Diagnosis. Thirty-Fourth Yearbook of this Society. (Public School Publishing Company: Bloomington, Illinois, 1936. 563 pp.)

Gates, A. I. *The Improvement of Reading.* Revised edition. (The Macmillan Company: New York, 1935. 668 pp.)

Gray, William S. *Improving Instruction in Reading: An Experimental Study* (with assistance of Gertrude Whipple). (The University of Chicago Press: Chicago. 226 pp.)

Gray, William S. *Provision for the Individual in College Education.* (University of Chicago Press: Chicago, 1932. Pp. 144–148)

Greene, Harry A., and Jorgensen, Albert N. *The Use and Interpretation of Elementary School Tests.* (Longmans, Green and Company: New York, 1936) Especially Chapter XIII.

Harrison, M. Lucile. *Reading Readiness.* (Houghton Mifflin Company: Boston, 1936. 166 pp.)

Lincoln, E. A., and Workman, L. L. *Testing and the Uses of Test Results.* (The Macmillan Company: New York, 1935. 317 pp.)

McCallister, J. M. *Remedial and Corrective Instruction in Reading.* (D. Appleton-Century Company: New York, 1936. 300 pp.)

McKee, Paul. *Reading and Literature in the Elementary School.* (Houghton Mifflin Company: Boston, 1934. 589 pp.)

Report of the National Committee on Reading. Twenty-Fourth Yearbook of this Society, Part I. Pp. 227–289. (Public School Publishing Company: Bloomington, Illinois, 1925)

Smith, H. L., and Wright, W. W. *Tests and Measurements.* (Silver Burdett Company: Newark, 1928)

Traxler, Arthur E. *The Measurement and Improvement of Silent Reading at the Junior-High-School Level.* (University of Chicago Libraries: Chicago, 1932)

Tyler, R. W. *Constructing Achievement Tests.* (University of Ohio: Columbus, Ohio, 1934. 102 pp.)

Woody, C., and Sangren, Paul V. *Administration of the Testing Program.* (World Book Company: Yonkers, N. Y., 1932. 397 pp.)

390

CHAPTER XIII

DIAGNOSIS AND TREATMENT OF EXTREME CASES OF READING DISABILITY

Arthur I. Gates
Professor of Education, Teachers College, Columbia University
New York City

The preceding chapters in this *Yearbook* are devoted primarily to developmental and preventive rather than to remedial measures. In Chapter XII, for example, is sketched a plan for making such comprehensive studies of pupils on entering schools and such careful appraisals of progress thereafter as to enable teachers promptly to detect limitations and difficulties. Other chapters deal with the materials and methods needed to make prompt adjustments to individual needs and limitations so as to correct difficulties before they have become fixed habits and thus to forestall serious disabilities. Up to the present time, however, few schools have employed programs of appraisal and instruction sufficiently effective entirely to avoid serious reading difficulties among pupils. In fact, in most schools will be found many reading defects that cry for diagnosis and correction. This is the justification of a chapter on extreme reading difficulties.

I. Characteristics and Definitions of Extreme Cases of Reading Difficulties

This chapter is written in the conviction that, although certain cases may present problems too complex and subtle for most classroom teachers to solve at present, the information and practices employed by specialists should be illuminating to every teacher for her own work. Extreme disabilities are similar in kind to less serious difficulties that teachers should understand. The factors that cause extreme disability are mainly also those that produce milder defects. The diagnoses of extreme cases follow the same general patterns outlined in the preceding two chapters and, in general, differ only in being more exhaustive and extensive. Effective remedial instruction for extreme cases, although it may sometimes take unusual form for a time, is based upon principles of good teaching. The instruction designed to remove many less-serious reading defects by the teacher may be more fruitful by assistance from the reading specialist, and the treatment of the extreme cases may likewise be benefited by the teacher's coöperation. The better the teacher understands the extreme disability, moreover, the more competent she will be in her daily work with all pupils.

Another justification of this chapter is to be found in the uncertainties and misconceptions in the minds of many school officers concerning the theories and practices in the treatment of extreme cases. Indeed, the main purpose of the chapter is not to give detailed information to guide the work of specialists or to enable anyone to become a specialist, but rather to explain to the teacher the nature of the work done by experts in diagnosing and correcting serious reading defects.

It is impossible for several reasons to give a definite percentage of pupils who should be classed as subject to ' extreme reading difficulty.' One is the fact that those suffering the most extreme difficulty grade by almost imperceptible degrees into the less extreme, who in turn merge with normal pupils. The distribution is continuous; no wide gaps exist between ' most severe,' and ' less severe ' defects. Hence, any effort to define the percentage of ' extreme cases ' is arbitrary. Not only is the dividing line an arbitrary one; it also varies from one community to another, depending upon the general environment, the degree to which foreign languages are spoken in the homes, the adequacy with which physical and psychological examinations are provided, the skill of the teachers, the equipment of the classroom, the size of the classes, and other factors. A conservative estimate is that three or four children of each hundred that enter the first grade encounter difficulties so severe as to make expert diagnosis and remedial treatment advisable, if not absolutely necessary, and that a larger number would unquestionably benefit from individual diagnosis by a well-trained reading specialist.[1]

---

[1] See discussion in Chapter XI. Larger percentages are usually recognized as requiring special diagnosis and small-group or individual help. Thus Durrell (Donald D. Durrell. "Influence of reading on intelligence measures," *Journal of Educational Psychology,* 24:1933, 412–416) suggests 15 percent and Monroe (Marion Monroe. *Children Who Cannot Read.* University of Chicago Press: Chicago, 1932. P. 15) suggests 12 percent. New York City teachers and principals reported approximately 8 percent of the population of Grades II, III, and IV, exclusive of the ' special classes ' for pupils of less than 75 I.Q., as seriously in need of special help when the city-wide remedial reading project was organized in January, 1934. Although most of these deficient pupils made normal or better gains under individual instruction conducted by teachers after a brief period of preparation in diagnostic and remedial methods, at least one-tenth of

Extreme reading difficulty, according to the information now in hand, may be the result of one or more of various causes to be considered in some detail in the next section. It is possible to find a child suffering the most extreme degree of difficulty, for which no explanation can be offered except failure to acquire any type of technique essential for word recognition. While this general type of explanation probably applies to a considerable number of cases, the most extreme and persistent disabilities typically reveal more than one handicap. For example, a pupil of low I.Q. may have started to learn to read with children whose mental ages were higher than his; he reveals one or more difficulties in vision, or his physical condition is a little below par; he shows slight tendencies toward emotional instability or his home background is not satisfactory. Had this pupil been subject to only one of these difficulties, or had he been gifted with unusual compensatory factors, such as more than average interest in school work and determination to learn to read, he might have learned to read fairly well. Such combinations of handicaps, numerous and different, make diagnosis exceedingly difficult.

Effective diagnosis and remedial treatment depend upon the discovery of the special types of handicaps operating at the time of diagnosis and the development of a program designed to remove them or somehow to take them into account. The choice of the detailed type of remedial instruction in reading often depends upon knowledge of the specific interfering factors and it always should be developed in the light of the pupil's failures, confusions, defects, and tendencies in reading itself. The typical case of reading disability, moreover, shows more than mere retardation in reading. Not only is the pupil likely to be older than his classmates, but he also suffers from the effects of a long period of frustration and unhappy comparison with other children in his group. Emotional tensions and personal and social maladjustments of various sorts are likely to arise sooner or later, even in those children whose original equipment was no less stable than that of pupils who were successful in learning to read. Properly to reinstate the pupil as a normal member of his group, capable of taking a happy and constructive attitude toward the life of the school, requires effective management of his whole personality as well as of his specific difficulties in reading.

---

them represented problems so complicated as to require more expert diagnosis and remedial treatment to insure reasonably satisfactory progress.

Several different terms have been applied to extreme cases of difficulty in reading. Some decades ago, when attention was first directed to these children, such terms as ' word-blindness,' and ' congenital alexis,' were commonly used. These terms are now rarely employed, since they imply that the cases of extreme difficulty in reading are the result of specific organic defects and that the prognosis is far from hopeful. Certain other technical terms, originally suggested to describe specific types of extreme cases, have become very widely used. The Committee recommends, however, the adoption at the present time of the descriptive terms, ' extreme reading difficulty,' and ' extreme reading disability.' They will be used interchangeably in the following pages.

II. The Causes of Extreme Disability in Reading

Several difficulties are encountered in an attempt to outline the main causes of extreme disability in reading. Intensive scientific work in the discovery of the causes of extreme difficulty in reading has been mainly confined to the past two decades. When one realizes that studies thus far conducted have brought to light a large number of possible sources of difficulty, one need not be surprised that there should be both uncertainty and considerable disagreement among various workers. Different persons have specialized in different areas and on different sources of difficulty. One, for example, has been devoting many years to a study of various types of visual defects in relation to reading difficulty; another to hand-and-eye dominance; another to the rôle of motives that are brought into play in the reading lessons; and another to the tendencies of given types of classroom materials and methods to produce specific difficulties. The possible causes are so diverse that no one has been able as yet to conduct elaborate investigations of all of them. Indeed, unquestionably many vital influences have scarcely been touched by thoroughly scientific attacks. The suggestions in the following pages concerning causes and treatment should, therefore, be considered as falling short of a complete or ideal treatment.

Many studies tend to overemphasize one or another source of difficulty in reading. This is due to the fact that few investigators have been able to explore expertly and in full detail every possible source of difficulty in the cases they have studied. The result is that some, but not all, of the contributing factors have been located. The investigator then reports the handicaps he has discovered. In many cases these handicaps may possibly seem more potent than they are, because they are linked with other undiscovered limitations. If these undetected deficiencies did not exist, the child might not have suffered so serious a deficiency. In general, then, it appears that, even in cases where some handicap is definitely located, it must not always be assumed that this handicap alone was responsible for the difficulty. A combination of factors working together may often be at the base of the trouble. This possibility should be kept in mind in reading the following sections, in which, for purposes of exposition, each factor is necessarily treated relatively independently.

The reciprocal relation between certain types of causal factors often leads to apparent disagreements. For example, a pupil who has an appreciable hearing deficiency might fail to learn to read if he should be seated in the rear of the room in which oral instruction and phonetic work play a large rôle. Looked at from one point of view, inadequate teaching; from another, the defective hearing, appears to have been the cause of the failure. Both factors are, in a sense, causes. Nearer the truth is the general statement that reading difficulties result from failure to recognize and make effective instructional adaptations to individual needs — both deficiencies and special abilities. This statement should be kept in mind in reading the following discussion of specific causes of reading difficulties.

1. Low Intelligence

Scores of studies show a fairly high correlation between reading ability and general intelligence. It is well known that children with I.Q.'s of 75 or lower usually find learning to read more difficult than children of higher I.Q.'s. At the present time, however, an I.Q. cannot be set, below which children may not, as a rule, be expected to learn to read. The outcome depends upon the methods of teaching and other factors. The relation of intelligence to reading, however, points to the necessity of obtaining a good measure of general intelligence in diagnosing reading difficulty and prognosing reading ability. Although intelligence is by no means the only factor determining reading ability, it is nevertheless still customary to assume that reading age should, and usually could, reach approximately the level of mental age and that the need of diagnostic study is indicated when it falls appreciably lower.

Most of the extreme reading difficulties, with which this chapter is concerned, result from detrimental factors at work during the first year of instruction in reading. Undoubtedly an important source of difficulty results from mass teaching by a program suited to an appreciably higher intellectual level (mental age) than that possessed by many of the pupils in the class. For example, if the program is, in fact, suited only to a mental age of 6 years and 6 months, or higher, it will be very difficult for a pupil entering the class at 6 years and 2 months of age with an I.Q. of 80 or a mental age of approximately 4.9 years. Unless special preparatory work and effective adjustments to this pupil's limitations and needs are made, he is likely to encounter serious difficulty in learning to read. With a more suitable program of instruction, this pupil might have learned successfully. Indeed, the policy of teaching the class as a whole rather than each individual according to his needs, is responsible for many difficulties in reading. Needless to say, moreover, as pointed out in Chapters XI and XII, a teacher cannot adjust her work to the highly varied needs and limitations of her pupils unless she has exact information concerning their nature and is supplied with abundant resources of time and materials for instruction.

2. Constitutional and Educational Immaturity

Some authorities hold that reading difficulty may also result from starting instruction in reading before a pupil is sufficiently mature in respects other than those indicated by the intelligence test. Possibly the child's sensory, especially his visual, apparatus is insufficiently developed to function effectively in reading, or his general motor adaptability is still low in the scale of development, or he is immature with respect to scholastic status involved in reading. It is assumed that by starting such a pupil prematurely, the task of learning to read offers mechanical difficulties and is not supported by a fully ripened interest and well-matured effort.

If a pupil is required to begin before he has had certain preliminary experiences and interests and certain prerequisite skills, he may be deficient both in attitude and technique and consequently encounter difficulties of increasing severity. In general, a pupil may suffer from attempting to begin before he is constitutionally and educationally 'ready.' 'Readiness' in general may be mainly due to constitutional or environmental factors or to both in various respects and degrees.

Although this theory has not as yet been fully confirmed by scientific study, it is reasonable. A thorough-going exploration of the different phases of maturity and readiness in relation to success in the initial stages of reading represents a varied and complicated project that has barely been begun. If adopted, the recommendation of the preceding chapter to the effect that the equipment of pupils be carefully examined on entering school would provide an exceedingly fruitful approach to the solution of the problems involved. The provision of various degrees and types of preparatory training, as recommended in Chapter IV, would safeguard children in the future and help to solve the basal problems. As noted in the preceding chapter, however, more than the degree of maturity the pupil brings to the first grade must be ascertained. It is necessary also to study more effective ways of adjusting materials and methods to the various needs of beginners. Where the pupil's maturity and competence in its various aspects are better understood and met, serious disabilities may possibly result infrequently, if at all, except in children who have other limitations or suffer misfortunes in the learning process.[1]

3. Special Mental Defects

In some of the older theories it was customary to assume that a child of moderate intelligence might fail to learn to read satisfactorily because of some specialized intellectual defect, such as a weakness in imagery, memory, perception, or reasoning. Studies within the last two decades have tended to show that extreme cases of disability can rarely, if ever, be ascribed to any single highly specialized deficiency in the intellectual processes. These specialized defects are, furthermore, difficult to diagnose independently of other factors. Many specialists in

---

[1] For further discussions see Chapters IV and XII, also the following references:

E. C. Deputy. *Predicting First Grade Reading Achievement.* (Teachers College, Columbia University, Contributions to Education, No. 426, 1930)

M. L. Harrison. *Reading Readiness,* pp. 6–9. (Houghton Mifflin Company: Boston, 1936)

M. V. Morphett and Carleton Washburne. "When should children begin to read?" *Elementary School Journal,* 31:1931, 496–503.

Grace Arthur. "A quantitative study of the results of grouping first-grade classes according to mental age." *Journal of Educational Research,* 12:1931, 135–143.

H. P. Davidson. *An Experimental Study of Bright, Average, and Dull Children at the Four-Year Mental Level.* (Genetic Psychological Monographs, Nos. 3 and 4: 1931)

A. I. Gates and G. L. Bond. "Reading readiness: A study of factors determining success and failure in beginning reading." *Teachers College Record,* 37:1936, 679–685.

reading disability at the present time, however, explore certain mental processes in order to secure particular clues for use in remedial instruction. For example, one might ascertain the pupil's immediate memory for letter sounds in order to see whether the pupil can note and keep in his mind for a few seconds as many sounds as he attempts to isolate in a word during phonetic analysis. If the pupil has a short span for sounds, say, for only three sounds, and tries to analyze a word phonetically into five sounds, he probably would have difficulty fusing five sounds because he could not keep them clearly in mind. Some examiners look for sluggishness in visual perception of various kinds of items that children who reveal no visual defects sometimes appear to show. Such diagnoses are of value in the hands of persons thoroughly familiar with the underlying psychology. In general it should be said, however, that there is much less tendency today than formerly to assume that serious disability in reading is the result of a specialized disability in memory, visual imagery, auditory imagery, imagination, associative capacity, or other such processes.

4. Physical Deficiencies

Learning to read is a difficult and subtle task requiring keen insight and attention and well-integrated, active, organic responses to the learning and teaching situation. The child whose physical stamina is low, or who is suffering pain or distress from malnutrition, fatigue, lack of sleep, infections, defective glandular activities, and other physical difficulties, is certain to be handicapped in learning to read. Serious physical impairment may, indeed, be a primary factor in some instances. In this respect, of course, difficulty in learning to read is only one of the many limitations suffered by the pupil. When serious difficulty in reading does appear, search should be made for physical impairments, which should be remedied as part of a constructive remedial program.[1]

5. Bodily Injuries and Defects

Quite apart from general constitutional factors, such as were discussed earlier, children at the time of beginning to read may be suffering from motor clumsiness or incoördination resulting from infantile paralysis or other diseases, from the results of injuries of the eyes, from congenital or acquired defects of the speech mechanism, or

---

[1] For further reading, see Marion Monroe, *Children Who Cannot Read.* (University of Chicago Press: Chicago, 1932, 205 pp.)

other physical handicaps. Our knowledge of the extent to which any one of these possible defects contributes to difficulty in reading is still limited, but there is evidence to indicate that, both directly and indirectly, some of these deficiencies may be contributing factors. For example, the child who has special difficulties in articulation or pronunciation is handicapped in oral reading. Not only is more of his attention and effort required to read aloud, but his mistakes or peculiarities may be the source of embarrassment to him. This embarrassment may lead to emotional tensions or antipathies to the work that operate as added handicaps. Where other weaknesses or defects exist, these additional ones may be sufficient to make the difference between a moderate and a rather severe difficulty in learning to read.[1]

6. Defects of Sensory Apparatus

a. Visual Defects. There is substantial evidence that defects of the sensory apparatus, especially limitations of vision and hearing, are important and relatively frequent contributing causes of reading difficulties. Various requirements of the visual apparatus and functions must be fulfilled to achieve satisfactory vision in reading. Farsightedness, nearsightedness, astigmatism, lack of uniform clearness and sharpness of the images in the two eyes, difficulties in visual fusion or the blending or unifying of the images from the two eyes, resulting from the foregoing defects or from over-convergence, failure of convergence, or other difficulties, are samples of visual defects that have been explored in relation to reading disabilities.[2] Since a number of deficiencies comprise contributary causes of difficulty, a skilled examination of the eyes, including muscular control and conditions of the tissues as well as vision, should form a part of the diagnosis. Indeed, it is obvious that the eyes of every child should be examined carefully before he begins his first lesson in reading.

b. Auditory Defects. There is evidence that several types of defects

---

[1] For further reading, see references listed at the end of the chapter.

[2] Reports of the literature will be found in most of the references at the end of the chapter. See especially P. Fendrick, *A Study of the Visual Characteristics of Poor Readers.* (Teachers College, Columbia University, Contributions to Education, No. 656, 1935); T. H. Eames, "A comparison of the ocular characteristics of unselected and reading disability groups." *Journal of Educational Research,* June, 25: 1932; J. J. Regan, "Routine vision testing of school children: A plea for standardization." *N. E. Journal of Medicine,* 213: 1935, 519-520; P. A. Witty, and D. Kopel, "Causation and diagnosis of reading disability." *Journal of Psychology,* 2:1936, 161-191.

of hearing may be a major contributing cause of reading difficulties. Several studies [1] have shown that teachers are often unaware of hearing deficiencies so serious that the pupils cannot clearly understand what is being said or read to them. Children suffering from such defects are often thought merely to be inattentive, indifferent, or lazy. There is some evidence, furthermore, that some children have deficiencies for tones within a certain range only and other specialized types of defects that may make it especially difficult for them to follow phonetic exercises. Since adjustment may usually be made to most of the types of hearing defects now known, a survey of such limitations is a necessary part of a thorough-going diagnosis in reading.

7. Hand, Eye, and Brain Dominance and Other Organic Characteristics

Within the last decade much research has been attempted to discover the facts concerning lateral dominance; that is, the superiority of one side over the other in visual, motor, or brain functions in general. Some investigators,[2] for example, have developed theories that reasonably explain the special difficulties that the left-handed or left-eyed pupil may have in learning to read. If it is assumed that the sighting eye is generally the dominant eye in looking things over, and also that the left eye operates more effectively leftward than rightward, the explanation for certain difficulties, including reversal tendencies in reading, may be found. Other theories concern difficulties that result from a lack of dominance of one side over the other or from mixed dominance; as for example, left-handedness combined with right-eyedness. In this case, to illustrate, the eye tends in one direction and the hand activities in the other, which may result in conflict or confusion or alteration. Some studies have dealt with dominance in terms of the comparative visual acuity, and have found that the eye possessing the best vision is not always the eye dominant in sighting activities and that either of these factors can be variously related to hand dominance.

---

[1] For example, that of G. L. Bond. *The Auditory and Speech Characteristics of Poor Readers.* (Teachers College, Columbia University, Contributions to Education, No. 657, 1935)

[2] W. F. Dearborn, L. Carmichael, and E. E. Lord, *Special Disabilities in Learning to Read and Write.* (Harvard University Press: Cambridge, Massachusetts, 1925. 76 pp.) A recent bibliography of studies in this field will be found in P. A. Witty and D. Kopel, "Sinistral and mixed manual-ocular behavior in reading disability." *Journal of Educational Psychology,* 27:1936, 132–134.

At present there is considerable uncertainty concerning the importance of these factors. The prevailing opinion is that they are of less significance than most of the factors considered in this chapter. The Committee, however, advocates further investigation until the exact rôle of the characteristics named can be determined. Meanwhile, caution should be exercised in attributing an important rôle in reading to them.

8. Differences in Temperament and Personality

There is some evidence that pupils handicapped by reading disability rate somewhat lower than the average in nervous stability, general control, ambitiousness, alertness and stability of attention, general drive, and in other such temperamental or personality factors.[1] It is often advisable to probe by reliable methods the temperamental and personality make-up of cases of serious disabilities in reading, not only to throw light on causes, but also to make possible a choice of treatment suited to different personalities. For example, the pupil who is badly discouraged and disposed to give up easily may profit by skillful management designed to increase his confidence and effort; the highly tense and excitable child may be helped by management that tends to improve his poise; the child whose attention readily fags may be assisted by using a variety of materials and content and in other ways. This topic leads naturally, then, to the allied problem of motivation and management.

9. Unfortunate Management of the Child, Misleading Motivation, and Lack of Motivation

Nearly every experienced reading diagnostician has encountered cases in which it appears that, although reading may have been technically reasonably well taught, the child seems to have failed because he was not well managed as a person. It must be realized, of course, that it is the *child* who learns to read and that learning to read is an achievement that can be accomplished only when the pupil possesses some interest in learning and an urge to learn and is comfortably enough adjusted to the teaching situation to integrate his efforts and to maintain his attention. There are instances in which the child is so dis-

---

[1] M. R. Ladd. *The Relation of Social, Economic and Personal Characteristics to Reading Disabilities.* (Teachers College, Columbia University, Contributions to Education, No. 582:1933). Also E. M. Hincks, *Disability in Reading and its Relation to Personality.* (Harvard Monographs in Education, No. 7, 1926)

tracted by the teacher's methods or the classroom activity as to be unable to keep his mind effectively on the work. There are other instances in which the child feels that the teacher or the class is indifferent or hostile to him. In some cases the child has been so embarrassed by the treatment of his difficulties in oral reading that he becomes subject to emotional tensions that disrupt his mental integration in all classroom activities. Such children are more likely to have difficulties in reading, and effective remedial treatment must embody a more satisfactory type of general management to restore the pupil's confidence and mental and emotional equilibrium.

10. Inadequate Guidance and Teaching

Many difficulties in reading, perhaps the majority, may be considered outcomes of inadequate teaching materials, methods, and techniques. This seems to be implied by the fact that many children who have made no progress in reading in regular classroom work are successfully taught to read by a more expert teacher or by a reading specialist who devotes himself more directly to their individual needs.

Aside from failures to recognize defects in vision, hearing, motor control, low intelligence, and other limitations and to make effective adjustments to them, several other inadequacies in instruction are known that, singly or in combination, may be serious enough to permit rather extreme cases of difficulty to develop. For example, there is now evidence that many pupils, especially those who learn slowly, require a much larger quantity of easy material — that is, material largely or wholly free of new vocabulary difficulties — to enable them to learn to read intelligently. Classrooms may be found in which the available material embodies such a large vocabulary burden as practically never to provide the pupil with an opportunity really to read. Before he has learned the new words in one lesson sufficiently to enable him to recognize them quickly and accurately, he moves on to a new assignment that includes more new words. In the course of time the child is overwhelmed and confused in his efforts to make sense out of the material. In other cases, lack of sufficient quantity of suitable materials may be responsible for failure of the reading situation to challenge the pupil's interest. The lack of vitality of the content may lead to a listless type of approach in which limitations and inappropriate techniques develop.

When the teacher teaches a class rather than individual children, difficulties in reading may be expected for reasons presented in previous chapters, especially Chapter XI. Failure to understand directions or to learn a particular assignment, a few days' absence from school, or a few days of distraction caused by physical disability may place the pupil behind the class or permit the development of inappropriate techniques. Unless the failures and difficulties of such children are later detected and corrected, matters may gradually go from bad to worse until the pupil is completely out of step with the class program. Later instruction may, therefore, be wasted upon him and the chagrin of failure may result in stagnation or retrogression.

In general, it is significant that most authorities in reading disabilities believe that failures to detect a pupil's mistakes, misunderstandings, blockings, gaps in his development, and the like may lead to more or less serious trouble, in some cases to very serious disability. This, of course, is particularly true of children who face the normal difficulties of learning, in a program poorly adapted to individual needs, handicapped by one or more types of constitutional defects.

The list of causal factors just discussed is not exhaustive; many specific factors not mentioned in the outline may be potent. It is difficult to arrange the probable causes in an order of importance. Some factors, such as certain defects of the sensory apparatus, are more numerous than others and in this sense are more important. Certain influences, although rarely found, are very important when they do occur.

III. DIAGNOSIS OF EXTREME CASES OF READING DIFFICULTY

Current diagnoses of extreme cases of disability employ methods and devices that vary from simple, well-known procedures, such as those outlined in Chapter XII, to complex, technical procedures requiring specialized training and experience. Usually, the diagnosis of the extreme case is similar to the study of the less severe case, except that it is more extensive and thorough and, frequently, more technical. Following are the main types of techniques and procedures employed by specialists.

1. Inventories of the Techniques Involved in Reading

In Chapter XII is given an illustration of an inventory of the abilities and the difficulties — and thus in general of the techniques — involved in reading that would be used in the diagnosis of the extreme case. Most specialists agree that a systematic study of the abilities and difficulties included in such an inventory is an indispensable part of the examination. Most inventories are arranged systematically in a progressive series in such a way that the examiner can judge how far it is advisable to pursue the diagnosis of a particular case. A diagnosis of the most extreme disability should be sufficient to give the examiner a clear understanding of which abilities and techniques the pupil has acquired, which he has failed to achieve, and which appear in inappropriate and distorted form. Whatever the more fundamental causes of the pupil's difficulty may be, the remedial work must begin with the pupil's present equipment and move forward from it. Information about other factors, such as vision, hearing, intelligence, emotional instability, and the like, is mainly valuable in so far as it produces clues of value in the choice of material, the selection of techniques, and, in general, the organization of the remedial program.

Several organized inventories of reading techniques used by experienced diagnosticians are described in the references listed at the end of this chapter. They differ in many minor, and to some extent in major, respects. Experience will disclose their relative merits.

2. Observation of Reading Techniques

Diagnosticians of extreme reading disability depend considerably upon their observation of the pupil as he attempts to recognize, pronounce, and understand words, to identify new words, to read connected material, to phrase properly in oral reading, and to do other tasks assigned in a diagnostic inventory examination. Expertness in this type of observation depends primarily upon understanding what processes and techniques are useful or necessary in the learning of words and in the other activities involved in reading. There are no easy and simple formulas, no apparatus or batteries of tests that will supply a substitute for this expertness. In addition to knowing the fundamental characteristics of reading, the examiner must have skill in discerning the processes involved in the pupil's responses. This skill, in fact, is one of the major requirements of a successful diagnostician, to which reference will be made again in the next section.

3. Psychological Tests

The diagnostician of extreme cases of disability makes use of a number of psychological and educational tests. Most diagnostic inventories include tests of achievement, of intelligence, and of other mental operations, as mentioned in Chapter XII. Some examiners make considerable use of inventories, examinations, and tests of personality and temperament. Although most of these examinations were not developed primarily for use with reading disabilities, they may be helpfully employed by persons who are expert enough to know their special values and limitations. Ability to secure valid results by the use of intelligence and similar tests is a necessary part of the examiner's equipment.

4. Analysis of Motivation, Interests, Mental Adjustment

Emotional tensions, antipathies, and various misleading motives may be in part the cause, or wholly the result, of reading disability. Believing that the disturbance and tension, whether the cause or the effect of the reading difficulty, are likely to be present when the diagnostician assumes responsibility for the case, and that successful remedial treatment depends upon knowing what the disturbances are in order to learn how to deal with them, some examiners make a point of investigating these factors with care. The diagnosis of emotional, temperamental, and volitional adjustment is not yet standardized; on the contrary, there is in use a variety of types of approach. The opinion of the Committee is that the training provided by modern programs of instruction in child development and mental adjustment may be made of very high service in assisting an examiner to investigate the aspects of reading disability here being discussed. Knowledge of abnormal psychology and psychiatry is of value in certain cases, but naturally not all those who specialize in these fields are thereby well equipped to diagnose reading disabilities. While the physician's opinion concerning certain nervous disorders, especially disorders which have a general organic basis, is of value in setting up a proper hygienic program of the pupil, few physicians are equipped to understand the more subtle mental and emotional aberrations involved in a reading disability.

An analysis of a pupil's dominant purposes and special interests is often attempted to get a basis for effective motivation in the relearning process. An inventory of the pupil's activities and talents may yield information that may be capitalized in formulating a remedial program.

5. Tests of Sensory Apparatus and Perception

There is practically unanimous agreement that the diagnosis of an extreme case of disability should include a thorough-going analysis of vision and audition, for reasons given in the preceding section. The expert diagnostician will be familiar with some of the newer, as well as the conventional, instruments used in such examinations. The *Keystone Ophthalmic Telebinocular* [1] for detecting a variety of visual de-

---

[1] This instrument forms a part of the *Betts' Ready-to-Read Tests*, mentioned in Chapter XII. See E. A. Betts. *The Prevention and Correction of Reading Difficulties*. Pp. 162–163. (Row, Peterson and Company: Evanston, 1936)

fects, especially pertinent to the functions of reading, and the *Ophthalm-O-Graph,* a device for analyzing visual characteristics by securing photographs of the eye movements in reading, are examples of some of the newer technical developments.[1]   Other procedures requiring much less expensive apparatus have been developed by oculists for the study of vision of reading defects.[2]

A general idea of the acuteness of a pupil's hearing may be obtained by simple tests in which whispered or softly spoken words, or a controlled sound are employed while the pupil faces away from the examiner at definite distances in a standardized room.   Such tests, however, will not give as exact or qualitatively diversified data as such an instrument as an audiometer.   Audiometers are available either for roughly measuring the hearing acuity of pupils in small groups or for more exact measurements of hearing of an individual alone in a room of standardized sound characteristics.[3]

6. Detailed Case History

In studying an extreme case, most examiners attempt to secure a case history.   A case history often includes information concerning the child's general health, his prevailing activities and interests, relations with other members of the family, special opportunities or lack of them, and significant successes and failures in school and out of school.   Information concerning birth injuries, delayed speech or motor development, unhappy associations with adults, dominance of, or by, parents or other members of the family, histories of enuresis, of emotional or nervous difficulties, brutal methods of forcing the child to use the non-preferred hand, efforts to teach reading or to learn to read before school, and other similar data, properly interpreted, are sought by some examiners.   The attitude of the parents and teachers and of other persons toward the child's difficulty is often significant.   The sort of explanation of his difficulty offered by his parents and his teachers may be revealing.   If the child has attended school for several years, a full report, giving good and poor subjects, teachers' marks, failures to earn

---

[1] See Betts. *Op. cit.*

[2] For example, the *Eames Eye Test for School Children,* distributed by Herbert L. Hammond, 16 Chapel Street, West Somerville, Massachusetts.

[3] Fuller discussions will be found in books by Betts, Gates, and Monroe, or in books dealing specifically with tests, such as G. M. Whipple. *Manual of Mental and Physical Tests* — Test 14, Visual Acuity; Test 18, Auditory Acuity. (Warwick and York: Baltimore, Md.)   See also references at end of this chapter.

promotion, disciplinary methods adopted, and opinions of previous teachers, is usually secured.

7. Using the Six Approaches

The six types of study just described are the ones customarily made in dealing with extreme, especially prolonged, cases of reading difficulty. Although the complete diagnostic program will differ in accord with the pupil being studied, or the preferences of the examiner, some portions of these six approaches will be found in most expert analyses. Some examiners, for example, place more emphasis on studies of motivation, home influences, play interests, personality, temperament, and health than do others; some are content with nothing less than a comprehensive clinical study of the child's development and present status, including the neurological, psychiatric, physiological, and social, as well as the educational, aspects; yet others confine themselves mainly or wholly to a study of the pattern of immediate reading difficulties and needs. Most examiners feel that any inflexible procedure is inadvisable because reading cases differ so widely. The skillful diagnostician can proceed from simple to complex, from near to remote, causes, going as far as the particular case requires and no farther. In reading diagnosis as in medical diagnosis, this happy faculty is partly a result of broad and balanced training and experience, and partly a result of great capacity to profit by them. If one possesses the latter, the former can be secured. Some suggestions in this connection will be made in the final section of this chapter.

IV. Types of Remedial Materials and Methods

Recommendations for remedial instruction for reading disabilities seem to range between two extremes. At the one extreme is a specialized and rather definitely prescribed program of remedial materials and methods. Certain systems may begin with a study of the details, such as letters, and proceed until the pupil is able to recognize each without error. The next step might be the learning of the sound equivalent of these letters; still a later step the fusion of two or more letter sounds into units, and so on until words are developed from a synthesis of elements. Other systems may include little or no phonetic work, but place great emphasis upon the kinesthetic factor as it functions in tracing and later in copying letters and words.

At the other extreme are procedures carrying the implication that the reading disability case needs nothing more than a good program of the type used for normal pupils. If this view seems to conflict with the fact that pupils having the most extreme disabilities have failed to learn despite regular attendance at school, sometimes at a very good school, the explanation proffered is that the method was poorly adjusted to these pupils in some way or other.

While remedial instruction for extreme cases should embody the general principles that have been recommended in the preceding chapters of this volume for use with normal children, it should be noted that an outstanding general principle is the necessity of making many and varied adjustments to meet individual needs. It should be noted, furthermore, that reading disability often points to certain handicaps, perhaps resulting from periods of frustration and faulty techniques, that do not handicap the normal beginning child. For these reasons, any rigid formula, whether applied to a narrow, formal remedial system at the one extreme, or applied to general classroom methods at the other, is likely to fall short of a satisfactory program for serious cases. Although persons defending either extreme view could argue that many or most cases of disability have been greatly benefited by the plan advocated, they would offer an unsatisfactory defense. Although few authorities take either of these extreme views, less experienced persons not infrequently do pursue one or the other of them.

Certain characteristics of ideal teaching are, however, desirable features of remedial instruction for cases of extreme disability.

First, most important is the requirement that the teacher be able with keen insight to observe the pupil's progress, his successes, difficulties, misconceptions, omissions, his reaction to the materials, demonstrations, and instruction given from day to day. She must know when the assignment has been too difficult and the pupil has failed to learn, or has partly learned, or has mislearned. She must be able on the next occasion to start at a point that will enable him to secure the stimulating effect of knowledge of actual progress. She must be able to carry him forward at a pace that will mean progress without going so rapidly as to produce confusion or breakdown.

Second, in instructing the extreme cases of disability, it is necessary to have an abundance of well-organized and interesting materials, skillfully adjusted to keep pace with the pupil's progress. The more this material appeals to the pupil's interest, the more effective it will be. Consequently, some remedial teachers place great emphasis upon finding and utilizing the special interests of the pupil. Every remedial instructor, however, has observed pupils who continued to flounder in difficulty despite unquestioned interest in the content. The continuation of failure is often due to other defects, such as the difficulty of material, or lack of effective progression from one step to another, or some other unsuitable characteristics of the material. Careful selection and arrangement of material for remedial work comprise an important and difficult task for the teacher.

A third requirement of successful remedial instruction is skill on the part of the teacher in demonstrating and explaining the techniques, detecting and correcting difficulties, initiating and following up successful steps, developing confidence, avoiding fatigue, and sustaining alert effort. To the child who has long suffered serious difficulty, reading is not only an annoying, but also a very perplexing and confusing, activity. Such children need to be shown — and they have special difficulty in seeing — what is to be done and how it is to be done. Hence, a primary requisite of the remedial teacher is skill in explaining and demonstrating, and in managing the child, so that he does make progress along the most serviceable lines.

The fourth requirement of effective remedial instruction of extreme cases is skill in adapting materials, methods, and the program in general so as to utilize to the full the pupil's special abilities and interests and to avoid or reduce dependence upon techniques for which he has the least aptitude — unless, for good reasons, it is decided to attempt to correct or improve a deficiency before or during the remedial work. For example, if the pupil has defective vision, large type, such as that used in sight-saving classes, may be essential in some cases. This may require the preparation of special material to meet the needs of a particular pupil, quite apart from what may be required in the way of remedial treatment for the visual difficulty as such. For the pupil who has difficulty with speech and is sensitive and nervous during any kind of oral work, the teacher may for some time require relatively little oral response and use oral reading only on occasions that guarantee successful and satisfying activity. For the pupil whose handwriting and whose general motor coördination are very poor, the teacher should probably avoid a ' kinesthetic ' approach or the exaction of much early work in written form, whereas, if the child has a special interest and deftness in manual control, the use of manuscript or script writing, typewriting, or typesetting may comprise a valuable supplement to the program. These are but rough illustrations of the fact that the remedial instruction of the extreme cases needs to be carefully conceived in the light of the pupil's interests, abilities, and limitations.

The fifth requirement is insight in deciding what to do, if anything, about the pupil's special deficiency. As implied in the preceding paragraph, one plan is to substitute a stronger field for a weak one. Thus, if the pupil has poor hearing or phonetic aptitude, oral, especially phonetic, approaches would be used but little. There are, however, instances in which direct therapy in the field of weakness might be advisable. For example, the pupil low in phonetic skill might be given ear training and simple phonetic experiences when there is promise that he might respond. The child poor in visual control might be given training to improve his eye-motor habits. Certain clumsy pupils might be helped most, in the long run, to regain their ability and confidence, by kinesthetic training. Such an approach usually demands exceptional skill and insight and is a risky venture for the inexperienced instructor. When applied successfully, it may be more fully corrective and in general more beneficial to the child than the approach that capitalizes his strength but neglects his weakness. Decision must be based on a careful study of the individual case. Often a plan may be arranged that provides both for capitalizing strengths and for correcting weaknesses.

Thus, although it may be said that normal teaching embodies all the main principles suggested for extreme types of disability, the practical operation of the program in a given case might differ appreciably from what the average child would normally meet in the regular classroom. For this reason, it is impossible to outline definitely a program for the remedial instruction of the extreme cases of disability. It is largely an individual matter, even though the principles to be followed are the same, in general, as those that apply to ideal teaching of average pupils.

A sixth requirement is that the remedial teacher should have ample opportunity to study and follow the individual case intimately. Some of the more important principles suggested as essential for remedial instruction of extreme cases are much more effectively put into operation in individual, face-to-face instruction than in group teaching. For example, the matter of keeping a detailed mental or written record daily of the pupil's progress, his difficulties and successes, the effective adaptation of materials to his needs, the adoption of various supplementary devices for occasional or frequent use, the determination of whether a pupil has understood the demonstration, whether he is going ahead on the right track in the development of a skill, the observation of the point at which interest has flagged and the danger of practicing errors has been reached — these and many other fundamental requirements can be realized much more easily in individual instruction than in classroom teaching, even when the teacher is equally competent in both situations.

Although individual instruction is justified for the extreme cases, as more likely to be successful and more rapid in gaining its objective than is group instruction, it is not always essential to limit remedial teaching to work with one individual at a time — at least, not for the entire period of instruction. In practice, a variety of devices is used to reduce the costs of prolonged individual teaching. For example, the teacher may take the children individually until she becomes well acquainted with them and has her program of remedial work well under way. Then she may divide her time between two or three pupils, especially if their difficulties are somewhat similar. Later more pupils may be added, until a sizeable group is formed. Or the teacher may begin with a few pupils, shifting from one to another for short periods of personal supervision, making arrangements for the temporarily unsupervised pupils to busy themselves with individual work. Some teachers have sufficient skill to handle a number of pupils from the beginning, especially if they are similar in interests and in ability. On the whole, however, the extreme cases profit much more from individual instruction, at least for a time.

What is done in a particular situation must depend in considerable measure upon the total facilities of the school. The suggestions made in Chapter XI for meeting individual needs within a classroom more adequately are applicable to cases of extreme disability, with this exception: the more severe and prolonged the difficulty, the more individual attention the pupil needs, and the more difficult the problem of handling him adequately in groups.

V. The Place of the Specialist in Remedial Reading

The considerations offered in the preceding sections provide an ample justification for a diversified and intensive study of the make-up of individual children, not only to make possible a correction of reading deficiencies but also to insure the rehabilitation of the individual in his school life. Schools operating without such information are almost certainly responsible for some cases of scholastic failure. Once an extreme difficulty has developed, expert diagnosis and remedial instruction are essential to guarantee rehabilitation. The Yearbook Committee believes that, were careful study made of each pupil as he enters school, as recommended in Chapter XII, most of these educational tragedies could be avoided. Eventually schools will make intensive inventories of entering pupils, as a matter of course, to forestall failure. Both in terms of social productivity and in terms of dollars and cents, a comprehensive plan of individual study is justified. This means that the schools should, so far as possible, provide (at the present time) persons capable of making the sort of study outlined in the preceding pages, and also should look forward to the future provision of facilities for more comprehensive analyses of the needs of all children coming to them. The final purpose of this chapter is to enumerate briefly some of the characteristics of the special services required and some of the equipment useful in providing them.

Some of the major requirements of an expert in diagnostic and remedial instruction for extreme cases in reading, suggested in the preceding sections, may be briefly summarized as follows:

1. Thorough understanding of the reading process and of the steps involved in it.

2. Thorough understanding of the various reading methods, devices, books and materials, classroom practices, and apparatus now in use in normal classroom instruction and also in various reading clinics and similar organizations concerned with reading disability.

3. Keen critical ability to appraise the techniques of the teacher, either from observing her at work or from records or reports of her work.

4. Skill in teaching, demonstrating, and guiding the pupil in acquiring the techniques of reading.

5. Familiarity with child psychology and child development, and skill in handling pupils as persons, in motivating them and encouraging effort.

6. Skill in employing the tests and examinations used in analyzing reading disability.

7. Knowledge of the principles underlying the test results and other diagnostic data. For example, properly to interpret the data concerning ocular defects, the specialist should know the underlying psychology and physiology of vision.

8. Sufficient knowledge of the concepts and practices of other professional specialties, such as clinical psychology, psychiatry, endocrinology, etc., to recognize symptoms requiring the attention of specialists in these fields.

Obviously the requirements of a specialist capable of handling all phases of diagnostic and remedial work in reading are extensive and formidable. Persons properly qualified to handle certain sorts of mental and educational tests, or to make medical or psychiatric examinations, or to analyze and remedy a curriculum for normal pupils, may be seriously lacking in other qualifications of a competent specialist in this field. Indeed, the range of information and skill needed to meet the first four requirements is so great as to demand fairly prolonged training and experience. Although books are available that describe most of the functions to be assumed by the specialist in reading diagnosis and remedial treatment, few of the treatises are sufficiently comprehensive to cover all the aspects met in practice. Something more than mere familiarity with book accounts is needed. Much of the skill essential for successful work, both in diagnosis and remedial instruction, is secured only by dint of suitable practice and experience. Several universities and colleges are developing programs of instruction combined with adequately varied and supervised experience in all phases of this work.

As regards equipment, it seems inadvisable to attempt a list of essential materials for use in so new a field, in which new devices have appeared only recently and in which other devices are known to be in preliminary stages of development. Several instruments were mentioned in the section on diagnosis, and reports are expected soon on others. For example, the Metron-O-Scope, embodying the principles of the tachistoscope, has been developed for teaching and remedial work, as for correcting muscular anomalies.[1]

Complex instruments, of course, are useful only if the investigator understands them and uses them expertly. No devices or machines automatically diagnose or remedy reading defects. The specialist should be able to evaluate and appraise critically the merits of such intricate apparatus and be alive to new developments. He should be provided with an equipment of reasonably well-tried apparatus, tests, questionnaires, and remedial materials. There is special justification for an abundant supply of the accepted types of diagnostic material, such as books, workbooks, practice devices, and other instructional materials.

The success of a specialist in diagnostic and remedial work depends in no small measure upon his ability to work with, through, and for the teacher, and not independently of her. The danger is that the classroom teacher may feel that diagnosis and remedial instruction of extreme cases are matters too intricate for her to understand. In effect,

---

[1] E. A. Taylor. *Controlled Reading. A Correlation of Diagnostic, Teaching, and Corrective Techniques.* (University of Chicago Press: Chicago, 1937)

therefore, she may wash her hands of the problem if a specialist is available; or if one is not, she may say that the case is hopeless unless an expert is provided.

On the other hand, the specialist is sometimes tempted to consider that extreme cases present highly specialized problems too complicated for the teacher to understand. In some cases his technical skill exceeds his ability to learn from the teacher. The result of such a situation is unfortunate in every way. Obviously both diagnosis and remediation are most effective when the specialist and the teacher coöperate. The teacher can give the specialist illuminating accounts of the pupil's difficulties and the methods that have been employed with him. Furthermore, she can successfully conduct many of the needed tests, examinations, and observations. In this way the specialist's time is conserved. Even in interpreting the results of the more technical examinations, the teacher's comments may be of value; she may note significant facts that escape the specialist. Furthermore, remedial instruction should be organized in the light of information available both to the teacher and the specialist. Remedial instruction should not disregard earlier classroom instruction, neither should it disregard subsequent classroom instruction. Remedial instruction in the hands of a specialist, moreover, occupies only a part of the day, the remainder of which must be spent under the supervision of the teacher. In general, since the teacher must assume responsibility for most of the pupil's school time, she should be as fully informed, sympathetic, and coöperative as possible in all such specialized work.

The specialist in reading should be familiar with contributions that the local physician, psychiatrist, psychologist, and other specialists can make. A complete study of the individual, such as is sometimes required of extreme cases of extreme retardation, may lead into many lines of specialization and, just as the teacher and the specialist should work together, so the reading specialist should coöperate with other specialists to whom cases may be referred for specific help.

The facts revealed by the very active work within recent years upon extreme cases of disability in reading point more and more emphatically to the need of more expert and complete understanding of the individual child in education. Evidence to this effect is found in the fact that the serious disability in reading may spring from so many different, even superficially remote, causes. Although the successful specialist in reading must first of all know reading thoroughly, he cannot safely be merely a specialist in reading. He must be aware of the other aspects of child nature and equipment as it is revealed in all phases of school work and of life out of school. It should be noted that the data obtained in a typical diagnosis of reading disability may be used to improve the pupil's adjustment in almost every phase of his life. Failure in reading, in most instances, is one of the obvious results of failure to provide a child with as intelligent general management as it is now possible to give. The facts in large measure needed to improve instruction in reading are the same facts needed to promote the pupil's development in general.

References

Following are references to certain general treatises and bibliographies on the subject of the chapter. Most of the former contain extensive lists of references.

Betts, Emmett A. *The Prevention and Correction of Reading Difficulties.* (Row, Peterson and Company: Evanston, Illinois, 1936, 402 pp.)

Betts, Emmett A. "Reading Disabilities and Their Correction. A Critical Summary of Selective Research." *Third Annual Research Bulletin of the National Conference on Research in Elementary School English.* (Detroit, Michigan)

Betts, Emmett A. *Bibliography on Problems Related to the Analysis, Prevention, and Correction of Reading Difficulties.* (Keystone View Company: Meadville, Pennsylvania, 1935, 86 pp.)

Durrell, Donald D. *Diagnosis of Reading Disabilities.* (Boston University: Boston, 1936. A mimeographed manual and tests.)

Gates, Arthur I. *The Improvement of Reading: A Program of Diagnostic and Remedial Methods.* (The Macmillan Company: New York, revised ed., 1935, 668 pp.)

Gray, William S. "Summary of reading investigations." Annual Reports in the *Elementary School Journal,* 1926–1931, and in *Journal of Educational Research,* 1933–1936, inclusive.

Hegge, T. G., Kirk, S. A., and Kirk, W. D. *Remedial Reading Drills,* with a Manual of Directions by Kirk, S. A. (George Wahr: Ann Arbor, Michigan, 1936)

Jastak, J. "Interferences in reading." *Psychological Bulletin,* 31: 1934, 244–272. (A bibliography)

Hildreth, Gertrude. *Reading Analysis Tests and Manual.* (Lincoln School: New York, 1934)

McCallister, J. M. *Remedial and Corrective Instruction in Reading.* (D. Appleton-Century Company, 1936)

Monroe, Marion. *Children Who Cannot Read.* (University of Chicago Press: Chicago, 1932)

Monroe, Marion. "Diagnosis and Treatment of Reading Disabilities." *Thirty-Fourth Yearbook* of this Society, 1935, pp. 201–228.

Tinker, Miles A. "Diagnostic and remedial reading." *Elementary School Journal*, 33: December, 1932, and January, 1933, 293–306, 346–357. (Summaries and references)

Witty, Paul A. *Tests and Instructions for Reading Diagnosis.* (Northwestern University: Evanston, Illinois. Distributed by the author)

Witty, Paul A. "Causation and diagnosis of reading disabilities." *Journal of Psychology*, 2: 1936, 161–191.

SUB–COMMITTEE FOR CHAPTER XIV

Chairman

GERALD A. YOAKAM, Professor of Education and Director of Courses in Elementary Education, University of Pittsburgh, Pittsburgh, Pennsylvania

Associates

FRED C. AYER, Professor of Educational Administration and Chairman of the Department of Educational Administration, University of Texas, Austin, Texas

LEO J. BRUECKNER, Professor of Elementary Education, University of Minnesota, Minneapolis, Minnesota

ALICE N. CUSACK, Director of Kindergarten-Primary Education, Kansas City Public Schools, Kansas City, Missouri

PRUDENCE CUTRIGHT, Assistant Superintendent of Schools, Minneapolis, Minnesota

I. JEWELL SIMPSON, Assistant State Superintendent of Schools, Baltimore, Maryland

CHAPTER XIV

THE REORGANIZATION AND IMPROVEMENT OF INSTRUCTION IN READING THROUGH ADEQUATE SUPERVISION

GERALD A. YOAKAM
Professor of Education and Director of Courses in Elementary Education
University of Pittsburgh
Pittsburgh, Pennsylvania

The early chapters of this *Yearbook* present a summary of progress during the last decade in the development of adequate instruction in reading and a statement of the basic facts and principles that should guide teachers and school officers in the immediate steps to be taken in reorganizing and improving instruction in reading. In subsequent chapters important phases of a broad reading program are considered at length. In the present chapter an effort is made to suggest to supervisory officers how they may adequately organize and supervise instruction in harmony with the recommendations of the Yearbook Committee.

I. THE MODERN CONCEPTION OF SUPERVISION

The fact is now widely recognized that supervisory officers should assume positive, constructive leadership in the improvement of teaching. Not only must they evaluate the results of instruction, as they have done in the past, but they must also furnish inspiration and guidance that will insure the development of clearer objectives, better organization of the curriculum, more effective use of materials, and improved procedures. Of primary importance is the need for a vigorous program of activities leading to improved instructional practices. This does not mean, however, that supervision must regiment teachers; on the contrary, in progressive supervision the proposition is accepted that teachers should be given opportunity for creative activity and the exercise of individual initiative and responsibility. Supervision should organize teachers for coöperative effort in the reorganization and the improvement of instruction.

A supervisory program includes a series of carefully planned and well-organized activities, the purpose of which is to secure improvement in one or more phases of instruction. In reading, the supervisory program should be as comprehensive as possible. It should be constructive as well as remedial. It should be definite and positive. It should provide for unity and continuity in the educational experiences of pupils and for steady growth on the part of teachers. A broad supervisory program is especially necessary in reading, because of the large importance of reading in school subjects and activities. Because increasing demands are made on the child for intelligent reading at successive levels of advancement, adequate supervision and guidance should be provided from the kindergarten to college.

II. Supervisory Problems in the Improvement of Reading

1. Problems Reported by Supervisory Officers

The first chapters of this *Yearbook* make clear that recent social developments, changes in educational theory, and the results of scientific study have brought teachers and supervisors face to face with important problems relating to instruction in reading. One of the most challenging of these problems is how to reorganize instruction in reading to meet new demands. An inquiry sent recently to state, county, and city officers requested them to enumerate the most frequent and crucial problems that they have faced as supervisors and to describe the procedures employed in meeting them. The responses reveal widespread concern with respect to the following five problems:

a. *The Objectives of Reading Instruction.* Supervisors recognize the need of the adoption on the part of teachers of a more comprehensive view of the objectives of reading instruction, including a recognition of the fact that reading should be taught in connection with all subjects in the curriculum and that emphasis should be placed on the development of reading interests, abilities, and tastes among children.

b. *The Organization of a Reading Program.* The need is widely recognized for improved programs of instruction for children entering school and for slow learners at all levels of advancement, for corrective and remedial instruction at the high-school and the college levels, and for an enriched program of reading for all pupils.

c. *Improved Materials of Instruction.* How to obtain adequate supplies of materials suited to different ability levels and for remedial instruction, and how to secure more adequate use of the library are related problems with which supervisors are deeply concerned. A few supervisory groups have experimented with the development of new materials for specific purposes.

d. Improved Procedures. Supervisors find that teachers need aid also in the development of adequate teaching procedures. Many teachers still teach reading as if it were a general skill; they do not know how to develop specific abilities needed by children in the reading of different types of materials. Supervisors realize that teachers must be given an improved understanding of the techniques of diagnostic and remedial teaching, of methods of developing reading readiness, and of techniques for differentiating instruction at various levels.

e. More and Better Tests. Keen interest prevails in more progressive centers in the problem of securing adequate tests for the measurement of specific abilities. Experiments in the development of new kinds of tests have been somewhat common. Many supervisors and teachers still feel the need of knowing how to judge the adequacy of test materials.

The preceding chapters offer many helpful suggestions that will aid the supervisor of reading in meeting these five problems. In a subsequent section of this chapter successful efforts on the part of supervisors to solve these and other problems are described.

2. Problems Implied by the Recommendations of the Yearbook Committee

In the remaining paragraphs of this section, an effort will be made to point out the crucial problems of reading instruction that are implied in the recommendations of the Yearbook Committee in Chapter I, but which are not suggested in the preceding discussion.

1. Planned guidance in reading must be introduced at all levels to provide adequately for the contemporary social needs of readers.

2. Greater independence and efficiency in reading must be developed in all readers.

3. Materials suitable to the reading abilities of readers at various levels must be sought and used.

4. Desirable types of development at each level of progress must be determined and appropriate types of growth stimulated in accordance with the maturity of the learner.

5. Teachers in all curricular fields must be stimulated to accept responsibility for promoting desirable reading attitudes and habits.

6. Emphasis must be placed upon stimulating and taking advantage

of the learner's purposes in reading and upon guiding the learner to those materials that will enable him to achieve his purposes.

7. The elevation of standards and tastes in reading among pupils at all levels of advancement bids fair to be one of the most important problems of the immediate future.

In addition, then, to those problems that have occupied the attention of supervisors in the last decade, supervision in the immediate future will place a new emphasis upon enriched experiences in reading for all pupils, upon adequate guidance in reading by all teachers, and upon increased attention to the specific needs of pupils. In short, concern with the kind, the quality, and the adequacy of the reading experiences of pupils will be the distinctive characteristic of the supervision and teaching of reading.

III. Steps Involved in Organizing a Supervisory Program

In the light of the general theory of supervision now prevalent, and also with special reference to the problems peculiar to the supervision of reading, an attempt will be made to suggest the appropriate steps that should be taken by the supervisor in the reorganization and the improvement of instruction in this field.[1] Ten such steps will be described.

1. The supervisor's first step must obviously be to acquaint himself with the best of modern theory and practice concerning the teaching of reading. The relatively inexperienced supervisor may well work backward from the conclusions, recommendations, and suggested procedures included in this volume to their sources in reports of scientific investigations of reading, discussions of educational theory, and descriptions of improved practices found in educational writings. The helpful supervisor is very familiar with the information now available concerning his subject. He must, however, be able also to organize this knowledge and to impart it effectively to his teachers — or, better still, to organize them for coöperative study leading to greater understanding and skill.

2. Next (logically, if not chronologically), is the need for becoming thoroughly acquainted with the local reading situation. This step necessarily involves the gathering of data; general impressions are not sufficient. The supervisor must study not only the needs of the pupils

---

[1] Further discussion of the problem appears in the following article: G. A. Yoakam. "The supervision of instruction in reading." *Educational Method*, 15:1935, 3–10.

and of the teachers, but the needs of the community as well. Data relating to the following problems should be gathered and analyzed:

(a) The character of the pupil population in the different schools. — Group and individual differences among the pupils in the various schools in respect to their interests, abilities, habits, and attitudes must be considered. A program effective for one school may be ineffective in another.

(b) The out-of-school reading activities of pupils. — Such data are of great significance in planning appropriate instruction for pupils and in developing better reading standards, interests, and tastes.

(c) The reading facilities available in the community, school, library, and home. — Teachers and supervisors must coöperate with librarians and other social workers to improve reading facilities in school, home, and community.

(d) The specific needs of the pupils with respect to reading attitudes and habits. — These needs are revealed by tests, observations, and diagnostic studies. Instruction must more adequately meet the needs both of groups and of individuals. The pupils in many communities are seriously retarded in reading, while others are advanced. The program developed must be adjusted to the specific needs of the pupils taught.

(e) The ability and efficiency of teachers. — The supervisor must know the characteristics of his teachers in order to know how best to stimulate and guide them in improving instruction. Individual differences among teachers are often as great as those among pupils. The supervisor who ignores these differences cannot fail to be ineffective. The authors of a recent supervisory report [1] suggest that instruction in reading as observed in classrooms represents five levels of efficiency: (1) a formal type of limited teaching (teaching the textbook); (2) an enriched program of activities during the reading period; (3) wide reading in all the school subjects, in addition to Levels 2 and 3; (4) the organization of material read in terms of interesting units or problems, in addition to Levels 2 and 3; and (5) specific guidance in reading in all school subjects and activities, in addition to Levels 2, 3, and 4. A clear understanding of the teacher's level of efficiency will enable the supervisor to plan intelligently activities leading to improvement by individual members of the staff.

---

[1] William S. Gray and Gertrude Whipple. *Improving Instruction in Reading.* Supplementary Educational Monographs, No. 4. (University of Chicago: Chicago, 1933)

3. After the supervisor has secured the necessary data by means of observation, questionnaires, interviews, analyses of tests, and examination of records, he is able to begin developing with his teachers a program of improved instruction in reading suited to the needs of the community, the pupils, and the teachers. The program involves, first of all, the determination of the objectives of instruction for the community as a whole and for the different levels of the particular school. These objectives need not be derived *de novo* in each community; they may consist in an adaptation of the general objectives of modern reading instruction outlined in this *Yearbook*. The extent to which these objectives should be set up in advance is at present a debatable question. The important thing is that the teachers and the supervisor come to an agreement and understanding with respect to the purposes or objectives that are to guide them in their constructive activities. However, the agreed objectives should always be in harmony with the general objectives of reading instruction as derived from expert opinion and scientific research. Through joint consideration of the objectives, the school workers may reach an agreement on a reading program for the community and on the fundamental principles that shall guide teachers and supervisor in the selection of materials and the organization of activities and procedures. Only through a consideration of objectives may agreement be reached that will lead to unity of action and continuity in the educational experiences of the pupil.

4. As soon as general objectives of reading instruction have been determined and their adaptation to the needs of the community considered, teachers and supervisor should proceed to develop an appropriate program of instruction for the immediate future. Such a plan often involves either a complete or a partial reorganization of the existing program, the extent of the reorganization depending on the needs of the situation and on the understanding and ability of the supervisor and the teachers. Modern theory and successful practice indicate that the best approach to the problem involves coöperative thinking and action among supervisors, principals, and teachers, which will lead to agreement among them as to the next steps to be taken. This plan is far more effective in the long run than the arbitrary imposition upon teachers by the supervisor of a fully developed program of instruction. It may be well to consult laymen and pupils when efforts are made to develop an appropriate program for a given community. The program should be set up in such a way as to provide

for flexibility and for continuous reconstruction in order to provide for changes in conditions that are sure to arise.

5. The reorganization of a reading program involves the evaluation of materials of instruction, the selection of new materials, and the use of old materials in new ways. The Yearbook Committee recognizes the urgent need for new and better materials of instruction. Supervisory groups in several sections of the country are now engaged in the development of materials adapted to specific instructional needs. Research shows that progress in reading is far more rapid in those communities that are well supplied with appropriate reading materials. Supervisors and teachers in every community must recognize the need for the development of school and community libraries and for the wider use of libraries in all school activities. They may also aid in the discovery of new needs that will lead to the development of new materials by authors and publishers, as they have done in the case of corrective and remedial materials for junior high schools.

6. The adoption of new types of teaching often accompanies the discovery of new needs and the selection of new materials. New procedures are often sought, also, in response to the desire of teachers and supervisors to keep up with the times. It is doubtless more defensible to select new procedures because they meet well-defined needs than to select them merely because they are new. As new problems arise, changes in procedures are essential. Without doubt attention will be directed during the next decade to the development of new ways of guiding children in reading, new methods of adapting instruction to individual differences, new corrective and remedial measures, new ways of securing effective reading instruction in all subject fields, and new methods of appraising instruction in reading. Teachers and supervisors must constantly seek for better procedures and must adopt and use them as they are discovered. Greater variety of procedures and greater flexibility in the use of these procedures are inevitable. The constant stream of new devices and techniques suggested for use must, however, be examined by supervisors and teachers in the light of educational principles and of the known facts concerning the nature of learning and of child development. While teachers should be allowed considerable latitude in the selection and use of devices and methods, the supervisor must encourage thoughtful evaluation of the proposed procedures.

7. Once it becomes apparent that new procedures are desired, the supervisor should seek the best ways of helping his teachers to under-

stand and use them properly. Perhaps the most valuable device for this purpose is a demonstration of the new techniques, followed by evaluation and criticism. The teacher, like the physician, profits by attending clinics at which improved techniques are demonstrated by accomplished technicians. It is difficult to gain an understanding of methods merely through reading and discussion. Supervisors, outside experts, and able teachers in the system should demonstrate new techniques for the benefit of all. Intervisitation within the system and directed observation in other systems are often helpful in acquainting teachers with improved methods used in progressive centers. Study groups that seek to familiarize themselves with new and better ideas in education may well include observation and demonstration, in addition to the serious study of professional literature.

8. After a new and improved program of instruction has been adopted, a period of trial will naturally follow. During this time the supervisor should visit teachers at work, analyze the results achieved, demonstrate improved procedures, and attempt to develop among teachers increased insight, understanding, and power in the use of new materials and methods. Encouragement of the creative teacher and the strengthening of the mediocre and weak teacher can perhaps be best accomplished through constructive activities employed in visitation and conference. Authorities are agreed that supervisors should spend a considerable proportion of their time in the classroom.

9. Appraisal of the success of an improved program of instruction, while a constant problem, must be made at appropriate intervals. The use of both formal and informal methods is highly desirable. Standardized tests must be employed to measure general achievement in reading, and diagnostic tests are necessary to discover specific weaknesses. These may be supplemented by inventories, questionnaires, interviews, and other less objective devices, as suggested in Chapter XII. The supervisor should not fail to collect and to use all data that may seem significant in appraising the results of instruction. To learn whether the program is effective, the supervisor may often find it necessary to consult pupils and parents. Intelligent appraisal will reveal the need for revision of the general program for improved use of materials and for changes in procedure and will bring out other significant facts. The supervisor should look at the program as a whole and detect faults in its organization, articulation, and continuity.

10. Supervisors now realize with increasing clarity that the improvement of instruction is a continuous process and that one project

is but preliminary to another. A cycle of teaching and supervisory activities may be completed by the steps of appraisal at the end of a term or a year, but the process must be regularly repeated. Each appraisal should lead to the consideration of new problems and to improvements based upon the evidence secured. One of the functions of the supervisor is to guard against complacency either in himself or among his teachers.

Only by the use of a series of activities like those outlined in this section can the supervisor of reading organize an effective program of reading instruction and secure continuous improvement among his teachers. He must not be satisfied merely to maintain instruction at the level at which he finds it; he must be on the alert to improve it. Thorough familiarity with new developments in the field and the use of sound supervisory procedures are required if the supervisor is to attain this goal.

IV. SUCCESSFUL ACTIVITIES IN THE SUPERVISION OF READING

The discussion of procedures presented in the foregoing section can be made more concrete and helpful if successful supervisory activities are discussed more fully. The data on which the following summary is based were obtained as the result of an inquiry sent to supervisors in state, county, and city schools requesting them to describe the most successful activities in which they had engaged.

The information submitted reveals considerable originality and creativeness among the supervisors. It shows that the supervisors involved have accepted the responsibility for leadership, that they have not only endeavored to help solve the instructional problems arising in their schools but have also attacked new problems and engaged in activities leading to the development of improved reading programs. These creative activities of supervisors command great admiration.

1. Supervisory Procedures in State Departments of Education

Although the supervisory activities of state departments of education are, in general, limited to visitation, inspection, and general consultation, inquiry brought out the fact that several state departments have interested themselves in the improvement of reading. The following procedures were most frequently reported: (1) the administration of survey tests, either in the whole state or in certain districts, (2) the publication of informational bulletins on particular aspects of reading instruction, (3) the development of state courses of study in reading, (4) the holding of local and county-wide meetings to promote improved instructional practices in reading, (5) the encouragement of more adequate supervision in this field, and (6) the use of follow-up testing programs to determine the effectiveness of remedial and corrective procedures.

One particularly successful state program for the improvement of instruction in reading was begun in 1920. This program was undertaken because most of the children of the state, exclusive of those in its largest city, were found to be two or three years behind standard reading norms. As a corrective procedure state-wide tests were given twice a year for five years to 75,000 children. Each year information concerning improved procedures was made available to teachers. Supervisors in every county of the state made ' drives ' to improve reading instruction. As a result, the average reading scores of the pupils of the state have, during recent years, equalled or exceeded the norms of standardized tests.

The department of education in another state has under way plans for the improvement of work-type reading throughout the state. Tests of achievement will be given in Grades IV, V, and VI in the schools of a number of counties. These tests will determine the attainments and needs of pupils. A program of improvement in this phase of reading will be initiated through special bulletins, local and county-wide meetings, and contacts by members of the state department. At the end of the year another test will be given, and the results of the campaign will be appraised. Ground has been prepared for this work by the publication of several bulletins on reading instruction.[1] The leadership assumed by the state department of education will certainly stimulate many schools of the state to improve their teaching of work-type reading.

It is assumed by some state departments that, because of the limited number of elementary-school supervisors and the distances to be covered, their work cannot be so effective as that of supervisors of more limited areas. These descriptions of the programs of two states, however, indicate clearly that state departments of education can do much to raise the standards of reading instruction within their states and that effort exerted by them may be extremely effective.

---

[1] Clara M. Wallace. *Questions Teachers Ask about Primary Reading.* (Reading and Study Bulletin Number One. State of Iowa, Des Moines, 1931, 91 pp.); also *Questions Teachers Ask about Reading and Study in the Upper Grades.* (Reading and Study Bulletin Number Two, 1931, 48 pp.)

2. Supervisory Procedures in Cities and Counties

Inquiry among supervisors of reading instruction in cities and counties revealed numerous activities the purpose of which was to raise the level of instruction in reading. Some of these activities were somewhat routine in character, but a considerable number revealed new and stimulating forms of supervisory activity that should be suggestive to supervisors of reading in general. The fourteen procedures judged to be most effective are summarized in the following paragraphs.[1]

   a. The Periodic Administration of Standardized Tests in Reading. This very common procedure is reported by large and small cities. The purpose of administering tests is usually to discover the weaknesses in instruction, which may then be attacked by supervisors and teachers as a phase of their regular work. In some cases tests are almost the only supervisory instruments used to stimulate interest in the improvement of instruction in reading. Informal tests and observation are also used by supervisors to supplement standardized tests. The tests aid in evaluating the success of reading instruction in the district and in supplying the data on which more-or-less comprehensive remedial programs are organized and administered. This method of supervision, while far from adequate, is to be preferred to that which is more widespread; namely, supervision by means of a rather purposeless routine of individual visitations and conferences, with no effort whatever at systematic appraisal.

   b. The Development of Remedial and Preventive Teaching. In many progressive centers there is marked tendency to emphasize as an important phase of supervisory activity, the promotion of programs of remedial and preventive teaching both for groups and for individuals. Two significant projects of this kind may be cited, one at the high-school level and one in the elementary grades.

   As the result of a coöperative study in reading in the high schools

---

[1] The writer is indebted to the following persons for the data upon which this summary is based: Miss I. Jewell Simpson, Mr. A. R. Williams, Miss Delia Kibbe, Dr. Angela Broening, Miss Eva R. Gerstmeyer, Dr. Ruby Minor, Miss Mary C. Mellyn, Mrs. Lillian Lamoreaux, Mr. D. J. Beeby, Miss Evaline Waterbury, Dr. Helen K. Mackintosh, Mrs. Ethel Mabie Falk, Miss Prudence Cutright, Sister Anselma Miller, Miss Mabel Simpson, Mr. H. G. Masters, Dr. Julia Hahn, Dr. Carleton Washburne, Miss Maggie Daws, and Dr. C. C. Trillingham. Others too numerous to mention sent valuable information, much of which could not be used because of the necessity of concluding the investigation to allow for early completion of the chapter.

of one city, marked changes were made in the course of study in English. This reorganization resulted in new units of work in English,[1] including materials for fast and slow learners, and in a battery of practice exercises and tests [2] that will enable teachers and pupils to discover weaknesses in reading and to develop new power. The supervisory group exercised constructive leadership and engaged in creative activities that may well serve to stimulate supervisors in other cities to creative effort.

In the same city a program of remedial and preventive teaching of reading in the primary grades is under way. Selected first-grade and kindergarten teachers, who have the last hour of the school day free, are assigned to teach remedial reading to groups of not more than sixteen children each in Grades IA, IIA, IIB, IIIB, and IIIA. The pupils in each group are first tested to determine their weaknesses and are then given small-group and individual instruction to overcome their difficulties. Teachers are guided in this work by a bulletin on " Preventative and Remedial Work," and by conferences and demonstrations. This plan of work, representing constructive effort on the part of the director of the primary grades to meet a need, should be suggestive to supervisors of reading in other areas.

c. Organization of Coöperative Study Groups. The organization of teachers into coöperative study groups was reported rather often as a constructive type of supervisory procedure. In some cases these groups are organized for continuous study of reading problems. The teachers of one supervisory division have been organized into three coöperative study groups, with a steering committee for each group to solicit suggestions for study each year. This year two groups are studying remedial reading and the preparation of materials for the preprimer period, and the other group is studying the integration of reading and social studies in the middle grades. The supervising principal assists the groups. In another city a coöperative study of reading by the school principals was organized as a general supervisory project. These supervisory activities indicate a growing tendency on the part of supervisors to regard the stimulation of purposeful study among teachers as one of

---

[1] City of Baltimore, Department of Education. *Units of Work and Standards of Attainment: Supplement to the Course of Study in English. Grades 7 to 12.* 1934.

[2] A. M. Broening, F. H. Law, M. S. Wilkinson, and C. L. Ziegler. *Reading for Skill.* (Noble and Noble, New York, 1936)

their most effective procedures. Current supervisory theory supports this view.

d. Comprehensive Organization and Evaluation of Reading Materials. Several school systems have undertaken coöperative projects involving the evaluation of existing reading materials and their organization for particular purposes, including tentative gradation for difficulty. In one city a careful study has been made of the sequence in which available readers should be read, and a classification has been made of the readers suitable for different ability levels. These data have been made available to teachers through mimeographed bulletins. This practice is in sharp contrast to that of issuing supplementary materials with no suggestions as to use. The practice of definitely organizing the materials of instruction in reading with respect to subject matter, difficulty, and suitability for corrective and remedial work is certainly to be recommended.

e. The Establishment of Reading Clinics. The tendency to establish reading clinics for intensive study of serious cases of reading disability is one of the newer developments associated with improved supervision of reading. In one city at least three reading clinics have been established. In another city remedial classes under cadet teachers have been organized in junior high schools and senior high schools; furthermore, reading clinics for elementary schools and junior high schools have been established and provisions have been made for training teachers in remedial reading. The practices in these cities illustrate the tendency to make the best possible use of clinical methods of diagnosis in the discovery of causes of reading disabilities.

f. The Development of Specific Corrective and Preventive Materials. Several cities have promoted the development of new materials of instruction, the purpose of which is to supply a need not adequately met by existing materials. Reference has already been made to the development of materials for the measurement and the development of reading skills. In one of the smaller cities of the country the supervisory staff has developed remedial materials [1] for the development of work-type reading skills essential in the social studies. Tests had revealed that pupils in the middle grades were having difficulty in reading effectively in that field. Specific reading materials, based upon units of

---

[1] Three mimeographed bulletins, " Remedial Reading in the Content Fields," for Grades IV, V, and VI. (Burbank City Schools, Burbank, California)

instruction and providing exercises for training in work-type reading, were prepared. The use of these materials has resulted in the raising of the city norms on reading-achievement tests.

Lack of space prevents the mention of other interesting projects of this kind. Here, again, the obvious value of attacking specific problems should be suggestive to supervisors.

g. The Differentiation of Instruction for Slow Learners. Experimental work in the development of reading programs for slow learners, especially in the primary grades, has been carried on as a phase of supervisory activity in several cities. Differentiation of instruction in the first three grades to meet the needs of slow learners is well under way, and provisions are being made for the child who is too immature to learn to read at the beginning of the first year. It is likely that in those centers where ability grouping is administratively feasible, programs for slow, average, and accelerated groups will soon result in a three-way curriculum in reading. As suggested in earlier sections of this *Yearbook,* the discovery of materials suitable for the use of pupils of different abilities at each grade level is one of the crucial problems of supervisors. Likewise, methods of instruction suitable for differentiated groups must be devised. Preventive teaching demands ' first teaching ' that is better organized than much current instruction and that is adjusted to the needs and the capacities of children of different levels of ability. Suggestions pertaining to the differentiation of instruction in heterogeneous groups are given in Chapter XI.

h. Promotion of Case Studies of Backward Readers. As a phase of the remedial program in one city, teachers have been encouraged to make a study of from two to six backward readers every year. The purpose of this plan is to aid the children, to educate the teacher, and to bring about better ' first teaching ' in the ensuing year. It is probable that teachers, by studying the difficulties of backward children, learn much that will enable them to prevent the development of reading disabilities. Although the busy teacher of thirty to fifty children may often feel that she has no time for individual case study, the experience is broadening and often leads to increased efficiency in preventive class instruction.

i. The Development of Courses of Study in Reading. In several cities the development of courses of study, generally in mimeographed form, for the guidance of teachers has formed an important part of the work of supervisors. The value of such studies probably lies in the fact that it forces consideration of the reading program as a whole rather than concentration on some specific phase of instruction. Such projects are worth while as means of promoting the coöperative study of reading problems and of securing agreement among teachers on fundamental principles underlying instruction in reading. The danger in such studies is that they may result in a feeling of complacency that will block further progress for a time. Generally it is best to develop courses of study in tentative, rather than in permanent, form.

j. General and Special Informational Bulletins. Bulletins and monographs furnished for this study indicate that there is a great deal of activity on the part of reading supervisors in preparing for publication, or in encouraging others to prepare for publication, bulletins, pamphlets, and monographs on general or special phases of reading instruction. These bulletins vary widely in quality. Some of them are devoted to special problems, such as remedial instruction; some to the listing of materials available for special purposes; and some to the discussion of new problems, such as reading readiness. In large systems it is undoubtedly necessary to use such materials for educating teachers. The development of the outlines of a reading program in written form must certainly lead to more definite understanding, on the part of the teachers, of the fundamental problems involved in reading instruction. The collection of illustrative material is worth while. Better still is the training given the teacher in securing independently, and in using, the excellent published materials now available on almost every phase of reading instruction. Supervisory bulletins should guide teachers in the study of problems of reading rather than attempt to furnish them with prescribed solutions of reading problems.

k. The Development of Remedial Programs in Junior and in Senior High Schools. The leading school systems of the country have become aroused to the need for corrective and remedial instruction in reading in junior and senior high schools. Remedial classes and preventive work were reported by a number of cities. Educational books for the guidance of supervisors and teachers are already available, and textbooks for pupils at these levels have begun to appear. Diagnostic testing, case studies, individual and group remedial instruction are now being used widely. Such programs are retarded by the lack of trained personnel and the shortage of materials for remedial purposes. The need for guidance in reading throughout the junior and senior high schools and in college is emphasized repeatedly in this *Yearbook*. In many schools success has already been achieved by the organization of special remedial groups instructed by teachers who are sympathetic toward the needs of pupils and who will make preparation for directing them by special study. One of the broader outcomes of such activities is the development of a guidance program in reading in all curricular fields in both junior and senior high schools.

l. The Development of Improved Testing Materials. In some centers supervisors have turned their attention to the development of adequate testing materials. One city has developed curriculum achievement tests [1] and tests of reading abilities essential to successful work in the various curricular units. These tests have been designed to provide data upon which to base continuous promotion. The reading phases of the tests are planned to measure specific skills and should therefore be useful for diagnostic purposes. In another city a continuous program of objective testing in the social studies is in progress, and throughout the year some fifty objective tests in work-type reading are used. These tests measure comprehension and understandings of relationships, as well as skills. Under favorable conditions, supervisors of instruction in reading can undoubtedly make contributions to measurement, either by suggesting to test experts the need for new tests or, if they are adequately prepared, by devising new tests of their own.

m. Organization and Administration of Experimental Studies. In harmony with the suggestion of authorities on supervision that one of the important problems of supervision is research, supervisory staffs in some centers have set up experiments to evaluate reading materials and procedures.

In one city, for example, an extensive experiment has been undertaken in the use of preprimers in initial reading instruction. The experiment was designed to determine whether it would be advantageous for beginning pupils to read several preprimers before undertaking to read a primer rather than to pass directly from preprimers to primers. In fourteen schools used as experimental centers, five preprimers were carefully selected and used serially by the pupils in the experimental classes before a primer was introduced. The results were appraised by observation and measurement. The procedure was found to be so successful that it was rapidly extended to other schools.

Another supervisor carried on, as a supervisory project, an experiment to determine the value of extensive reading as compared with intensive study of geographical material by pupils in the seventh and the eighth grades in certain private elementary schools. The experiment, carried out with parallel groups, revealed great superiority of the intensive reading method.

---

[1] Board of Education, Rochester, New York. *Curriculum Achievement Tests.*

The use of the experimental method by supervisors in evaluating instructional materials and procedures is to be encouraged in systems where supervisors are adequately trained and the necessary time and materials are available. If reliable results are to be obtained, the experiments should be carefully administered and the results adequately measured. It is difficult to prevent bias or wrong interpretations if conditions cannot be rigidly controlled.

n. The Use of Standard Procedures. While the newer types of supervisory procedures in reading are certainly to be encouraged, the value of visitation, group and individual conferences, reading groups, study groups, and other standard supervisory procedures should not be deprecated. These procedures remain indispensable in supervisory work, but the newer procedures originating in the scientific movement in education should be used with them.

The illustrations of successful supervisory activities in reading given in this section indicate that the improvement of reading through adequate supervision is already under way in this country and that a fairly general use of progressive practices is characteristic of the work of supervisors of reading, at least in the more favored areas. In many places supervisors have already organized the teachers for continuous improvement of the reading program. The chief task before some supervisors, therefore, is to disseminate among teachers new ideas concerning reading instruction and to secure the adoption of revised objectives, improved materials, better procedures, and more effective appraisal of results. Other supervisors, because of conditions existing in their schools, will need to make a complete reorganization of the reading program somewhat after the pattern suggested earlier (Section III) in this chapter. The data reported in this section should provide many suggestions for use in effecting the needed reorganization.

V. Guiding Principles for the Supervisor

In the light of the background developed in this chapter, it seems possible to present in summarized form a series of guiding principles that may aid supervisors to organize effective supervisory programs in reading.

1. In order to be effective in the organization of improved reading programs, supervisors must engage in continuous study of the current developments in the field.

2. Not only must supervisors be familiar with the standard procedures in the supervision of instruction, but they must also exercise

considerable ingenuity in the invention of new procedures to meet new needs.

3. The best results are achieved when coöperative effort on the part of teachers is stimulated by the organization of study groups, experiments, and projects of various kinds that keep teachers working continuously with the supervisors on the improvement of instruction.

4. Educating the teacher to accept improved procedures, to use materials more adequately, to participate in curricular reorganization, to engage in diagnostic and remedial work, and to participate in creative activities constitutes the most important and successful type of supervisory activity for the improvement of instruction in reading. Changing demands of society, new theories of learning, and new data from research studies make imperative a continual readjustment of the reading program to meet new needs.

5. Only when constructive leadership is available can consistent progress in the improvement of instruction be made. In spite of the improved preparation provided for prospective teachers in higher institutions, much training in service is essential to continued progress.

6. The new and more comprehensive program of reading recommended in this *Yearbook* creates the need for immediate organization of study groups to take advantage of the rich suggestions provided for improving instruction in reading.

7. The implications of the recommendations in this *Yearbook* should be made clear to teachers through conference, demonstration, and visitation. The best results are probably achieved when instruction is reorganized as a result of coöperative study by teachers and supervisors of recent developments in this important field.

References

Anderson, C. J. *The Development of a Supervisory Program in Reading.* (Laurel Book Company: New York, 1928)

Anderson, C. J., and Merton, Elda. "Remedial work in reading." *Elementary School Journal*, 20: 1920, 685–701, 772–791.

Use of a special helper teacher in individual and small-group remedial work to improve speed and comprehension of problem cases in reading.

Anderson, C. J., and Merton, Elda. "Remedial work in silent reading." *Elementary School Journal*, 21: 1921, 336–348.

Report of a supervisory program to improve reading through demonstration and individual records of pupils' defects and attainments.

Braun, Mary S. "A supervisory program." *Journal of the National Education Association,* 18: 1929, 297.

A supervisory program in Baltimore, Grades IV to VI, for the improvement of instruction, involving testing, demonstration, remedial work, and evaluation.

Browning, Mary; Howard, Bonnie C.; and Moderow, Gertrude. "Supervisory reading program." *Educational Method,* 11: 1931, 32–38.

Report of a remedial program in reading, involving testing, reclassification, individual case studies, remedial teaching, demonstration lessons, etc.

Brueckner, L. J., and Cutright, Prudence. "A technique for measuring the efficiency of supervision." *Journal of Educational Research,* 16: 1927, 323–331.

Report of a study in Minneapolis to improve reading and supervision.

Crabbs, Lelah M. *Measuring Efficiency in Supervision and Teaching.* (Teachers College, Columbia University: New York, 1925)

Reports correlations between teachers' ability to teach reading and other subjects.

Davis, Georgia. "Procedures effective in improving pupils of poor reading ability in regular reading classes." *Elementary School Journal,* 31: 1931, 336–348.

Shows that remedial classes are effective in Grades IV, V, and VI.

Gray, William S., and Whipple, Gertrude. *Improving Instruction in Reading.* (Supplementary Educational Monographs, No. 40: Chicago, 1933)

Report of a coöperative program of improvement in reading in schools of northern Illinois.

Hahn, Julia. *A Critical Evaluation of a Supervisory Program in Kindergarten-Primary Grades.* (Teachers College, Columbia University: New York, 1931)

Reports a supervisory program in which enriched reading materials were used and emphasis placed on thoughtful reading.

Laurie, Helen. "Units of work and reading." *Elementary School Journal,* 33: 1932, 215–226.

A report of a supervisory project in which teachers were guided in the development of units of work in reading.

National Education Association. *Better Reading Instruction.* (Research Bulletin, N. E. A., Vol. 13, No. 5: Washington, D. C., 1935)

Reports of reading problems found difficult by teachers; judgments of supervisors concerning the adequacy or inadequacy of certain phases of instruction in reading.

Neal, Elma A., and Foster, Inez. "A program of silent reading." *Elementary School Journal,* 27: 1926, 275–280.

Report of a study to improve silent-reading achievement in San Antonio.

Pierce, Paul R.   " The administration of first-grade reading in a foreign industrial community."   *Elementary School Journal,* 32: 1932, 774–784.
Deals with a problem of importance to many industrial centers.

Simpson, I. Jewell, and Stern, Bessie C.   " Improving instruction in reading."   *Elementary School Journal,* 25: 1925, 594–606.
Account of a state program in the improvement of reading and its results.

Simpson, Mabel E.   " The development of standards in reading; An important function of supervision."   *Educational Method,* 12: 1933, 420–429.
Excellent suggestions for the supervisor relative to the development of standards by which to appraise results.

Yoakam, G. A.   " The supervision of instruction in reading."   *Educational Method,* 15: 1935, 3–10.
Principles involved in the development of a supervisory program in reading.

Zirbes, Laura.   *Comparative Studies of Current Practice in Reading with Techniques for the Improvement of Teaching.*   (Teachers College, Columbia University: New York, 1928)
Value of a professional course in reading in changing the results of teaching.

INFORMATION CONCERNING THE NATIONAL SOCIETY FOR THE STUDY OF EDUCATION

1. PURPOSE. The purpose of the National Society is to promote the investigation and discussion of educational questions. To this end it holds an annual meeting and publishes a series of yearbooks.

2. ELIGIBILITY TO MEMBERSHIP. Any person who is interested in receiving its publications may become a member by sending to the Secretary-Treasurer information concerning name, title, and address, and a check for $3.50 (see Item 5).

Membership is not transferable; it is limited to individuals, and may not be held by libraries, schools, or other institutions, either directly or indirectly.

3. PERIOD OF MEMBERSHIP. Applicants for membership may not date their entrance back of the current calendar year, and all memberships terminate automatically on December 31, unless the dues for the ensuing year are paid as indicated in Item 6.

4. DUTIES AND PRIVILEGES OF MEMBERS. Members pay dues of $2.50 annually, receive a cloth-bound copy of each publication, are entitled to vote, to participate in discussion, and (under certain conditions) to hold office. The names of members are printed in the yearbooks.

5. ENTRANCE FEE. New members are required the first year to pay, in addition to the dues, an entrance fee of one dollar.

6. PAYMENT OF DUES. Statements of dues are rendered in October or November for the following calendar year. Any member so notified whose dues remain unpaid on January 1, thereby loses his membership and can be reinstated only by paying a reinstatement fee of fifty cents, levied to cover the actual clerical cost involved.

School warrants and vouchers from institutions must be accompanied by definite information concerning the name and address of the person for whom membership fee is being paid. Statements of dues are rendered on our own form only. The Secretary's office cannot undertake to fill out special invoice forms of any sort or to affix notary's affidavit to statements or receipts.

Cancelled checks serve as receipts. Members desiring an additional receipt must enclose a stamped and addressed envelope therefor.

7. DISTRIBUTION OF YEARBOOKS TO MEMBERS. The yearbooks, ready prior to each February meeting, will be mailed from the office of the publishers, only to members whose dues for that year have been paid. Members who desire yearbooks prior to the current year must purchase them directly from the publishers (see Item 8).

8. COMMERCIAL SALES. The distribution of all yearbooks prior to the current year, and also of those of the current year not regularly mailed to members in exchange for their dues, is in the hands of the publishers, not of the Secretary. For such commercial sales, communicate directly with the Public School Publishing Company, Bloomington, Illinois, which will gladly send a price list covering all the publications of this Society and of its predecessor, the National Herbart Society. This list is also printed in the yearbook.

9. YEARBOOKS. The yearbooks are issued about one month before the February meeting. They comprise from 600 to 800 pages annually. Unusual effort has been made to make them, on the one hand, of immediate practical value, and on the other hand, representative of sound scholarship and scientific investigation. Many of them are the fruit of coöperative work by committees of the Society.

10. MEETINGS. The annual meeting, at which the yearbooks are discussed, is held in February at the same time and place as the meeting of the Department of Superintendence of the National Education Association.

Applications for membership will be handled promptly at any time on receipt of name and address, together with check for $3.50 (or $3.00 for reinstatement). Generally speaking, applications entitle the new member to the yearbook slated for discussion during the calendar year the application is made, but those received in December are regarded as pertaining to the next calendar year.

GUY M. WHIPPLE, Secretary-Treasurer.

Box 822, Clifton, Mass.

PUBLICATIONS OF THE NATIONAL HERBART SOCIETY

(Now the National Society for the Study of Education)

	Postpaid Price
First Yearbook, 1895	$0.79
First Supplement to First Yearbook	.28
Second Supplement to First Yearbook	.27
Second Yearbook, 1896	.85
Supplement to Second Yearbook	.27
Third Yearbook, 1897	.85
Ethical Principles Underlying Education. John Dewey. Reprinted from Third Yearbook	.27
Supplement to Third Yearbook	.27
Fourth Yearbook, 1898	.79
Supplement to Fourth Yearbook	.28
Fifth Yearbook, 1899	.79
Supplement to Fifth Yearbook	.54

PUBLICATIONS OF THE NATIONAL SOCIETY FOR THE STUDY OF EDUCATION

Postpaid Price

First Yearbook, 1902, Part I—*Some Principles in the Teaching of History.* Lucy M. Salmon $0.54

First Yearbook, 1902, Part II—*The Progress of Geography in the Schools.* W. M. Davis and H. M. Wilson .... .53

Second Yearbook, 1903, Part I—*The Course of Study in History in the Common School.* Isabel Lawrence, C. A. McMurry, Frank McMurry, E. C. Page, and E. J. Rice ...... .53

Second Yearbook, 1903, Part II—*The Relation of Theory to Practice in Education.* M. J. Holmes, J. A. Keith, and Levi Seeley .... .53

Third Yearbook, 1904, Part I—*The Relation of Theory to Practice in the Education of Teachers.* John Dewey, Sarah C. Brooks, F. M. McMurry, *et al* .... .53

Third Yearbook, 1904, Part II—*Nature Study.* W. S. Jackman .... .85

Fourth Yearbook, 1905, Part I—*The Education and Training of Secondary Teachers.* E. C. Elliott, E. C. Dexter, M. J. Holmes, *et al* .... .85

Fourth Yearbook, 1905, Part II—*The Place of Vocational Subjects in the High-School Curriculum.* J. S. Brown, G. B. Morrison, and Ellen H. Richards .... .53

Fifth Yearbook, 1906, Part I—*On the Teaching of English in Elementary and High Schools.* G. P. Brown and Emerson Davis .... .53

Fifth Yearbook, 1906, Part II—*The Certification of Teachers.* E. P. Cubberley .... .64

Sixth Yearbook, 1907, Part I—*Vocational Studies for College Entrance.* C. A. Herrick, H. W. Holmes, T. deLaguna, V. Prettyman, and W. J. S. Bryan .... .70

Sixth Yearbook, 1907, Part II—*The Kindergarten and Its Relation to Elementary Education.* Ada Van Stone Harris, E. A. Kirkpatrick, Maria Kraus-Boelté, Patty S. Hill, Harriette M. Mills, and Nina Vandewalker .... .70

Seventh Yearbook, 1908, Part I—*The Relation of Superintendents and Principals to the Training and Professional Improvement of Their Teachers.* Charles D. Lowry ...... .78

Seventh Yearbook, 1908, Part II—*The Co-ordination of the Kindergarten and the Elementary School.* B. J. Gregory, Jennie B. Merrill, Bertha Payne, and Margaret Giddings .... .78

Eighth Yearbook, 1909, Parts I and II—*Education with Reference to Sex.* C. R. Henderson and Helen C. Putnam. Both parts 1.60

Ninth Yearbook, 1910, Part I—*Health and Education.* T. D. Wood .... .85

Ninth Yearbook, 1910, Part II—*The Nurse in Education.* T. D. Wood, *et al* .... .78

Tenth Yearbook, 1911, Part I—*The City School as a Community Center.* H. C. Leipziger, Sarah E. Hyre, R. D. Warden, C. Ward Crampton, E. W. Stitt, E. J. Ward, Mrs. E. C. Grice, and C. A. Perry .... .78

Tenth Yearbook, 1911, Part II—*The Rural School as a Community Center.* B. H. Crocheron, Jessie Field, F. W. Howe, E. C. Bishop, A. B. Graham, O. J. Kern, M. T. Scudder, and B. M. Davis .... .79

Price for Yearbooks VI to X inclusive, 8 vo. cloth 5.00

Eleventh Yearbook, 1912, Part I—*Industrial Education: Typical Experiments Described and Interpreted.* J. F. Barker, M. Bloomfield, B. W. Johnson, P. Johnson, L. M. Leavitt, G. A. Mirick, M. W. Murray, C. F. Perry, A. L. Safford, and H. B. Wilson .... .85

Eleventh Yearbook, 1912, Part II—*Agricultural Education in Secondary Schools.* A. C. Monahan, R. W. Stimson, D. J. Crosby, W. H. French, H. F. Button, F. R. Crane, W. R. Hart, and G. F. Warren .... .85

PUBLIC SCHOOL PUBLISHING COMPANY, BLOOMINGTON, ILLINOIS
Agents — The Baker and Taylor Company   New York

8816055